ALTERNATE EDITION

Principles of
Business Data Processing

WITH BASIC

There are three versions of this text. Two versions include a thorough discussion of punched-card data processing and punched-card machines and systems (Chapters 4 and 5, respectively). In both those versions, Appendix A explains how to use a card punch. One of those versions also includes a thorough discussion of the BASIC language so that students can write programs to solve a variety of business problems (Appendix B).

This alternate version, unlike the other two versions, includes (in its Chapters 4 and 5) discussion of management information systems, their impact on organizations, and several illustrations that reinforce these concepts. This version also includes (in its Appendix A) an expanded discussion of the BASIC language. A new Appendix B in this version provides corresponding BASIC programming problems and representative solutions. This alternate version, then, is designed for the instructor who wants to minimize the time and attention given to punched-card data processing and punched-card systems, and to maximize the coverage of management information systems and the BASIC programming language.

To
our
parents
Virgil and Lois
Bob and Ruth
for their support and love

ALTERNATE **3**RD EDITION

Principles of Business Data Processing

WITH BASIC

V. THOMAS DOCK

University of Southern California

EDWARD ESSICK

College of Marin

SCIENCE RESEARCH ASSOCIATES, INC.
Chicago, Palo Alto, Toronto
Henley-on-Thames, Sydney, Paris, Stuttgart

A Subsidiary of IBM

Compositor	Advanced Typesetting Services
Illustrator	House of Graphics
Designer	Don Fujimoto
Acquisition Editor	Steve Mitchell
Project Editor	Ron Lewton

Special Editorial Assistance by Marilyn Bohl

Acknowledgments

The following illustrations are reproduced or adapted with permission:
6-2, courtesy of Sperry-Univac Computer Systems; A-2, courtesy of NCR Corp.;
A-13, courtesy of Western Electric Co.; A-14, courtesy of AT&T Co.; A-16, courtesy
of Tektronix, Inc.; A-17, courtesy of Texas Instruments Inc.; A-19, courtesy of
Incoterm Corp.; A-20, courtesy of Cummins-Allison Corp.; A-21, courtesy of
Mohawk Data Sciences Corp.; A-26, 11-10, courtesy of Honeywell; 11-1, 11-2,
11-3, courtesy of Intel Corp.; 11-5, courtesy of Digital Equipment Corp.; 11-6,
courtesy of Wang Laboratories, Inc.; 11-14, courtesy of International Data Corp.;
D-1, reprinted with permission from *Changing Times Magazine*, Oct., 1975,
© 1975 Kiplinger Washington Editors, Inc.; 6-1, 6-3, 6-4, 7-4, 8-5, 8-6, 8-7, 8-8, 9-5,
9-8, 10-1, 10-7, 10-10, 10-11, A-3, A-6, A-12, A-15, A-18, A-23-A, A-23-B, A-24, 11-4,
11-7, 11-9, 11-11, 11-12, 13-6, 13-7, courtesy of IBM; 4-2, courtesy of McGraw-Hill
Book Company.

Library of Congress Cataloging in Publication Data

Dock, V. Thomas
    Principles of business data processing, with BASIC.

    Includes index.
    1. Business—Data processing. 2. Basic (Computer
program language) I. Essick, Edward L., joint author.
II. Title.
HF5548.2.D582   1978b   001.6'4   78-12217
ISBN 0-574-21220-5

© 1978, 1974, 1970 Science Research Associates, Inc.
All rights reserved.

Printed in the United States of America.

10   9   8   7   6   5   4   3   2   1

Contents

Unit 4 An Overview of Systems

Unit 5 Data Processing Management and the Computer Industry

Preface

New developments in computer data processing continue to appear at a rapid pace. Technological advances are making computers faster and smaller in size. They can do more work at a lower cost. It is a challenge to keep a textbook current in such a dynamic and diverse field and yet limit the content to what is appropriate for the introductory data processing student. We feel that we have met this challenge. The purpose of this textbook is to meet the needs of students who want a basic understanding of data processing as well as of those who plan careers as business application programmers. All the features that made the second edition one of the top-selling introductory data processing texts have been retained. At the same time, we have carefully reviewed and edited each chapter to insure that both the text and the illustrations reflect the latest technology and equipment.

Many of the improvements in this new edition resulted from responses to a national survey of users and former users. The reading level and knowledge base of the students were primary considerations when making these changes. We wanted to insure that the material is appropriate for the students using the book, and is presented in a clear and concise manner. All new terms are defined as they are used and explained again in the glossary, now conveniently combined with the index. Like the second edition, the third edition is not encyclopedic; it presents an up-to-date survey of business data processing.

The major changes in the third edition are the following:

1. A module on top-down program design and structured programming is included after the discussion of the traditional approach to problem solving so that students can compare these techniques.

2. An expanded discussion of computer systems is given in Chapter 11. Emphasis is placed on small business systems, the minicomputer, and the microcomputer. The microprocessor and its applications in business data processing are discussed.

3. Newer methods of data entry and output such as optical bar codes, computer output on microfilm, intelligent terminals, and floppy disks are covered in Module A.

4. The coverage of program flowcharting is expanded. A modular approach to flowcharting is discussed.

5. A series of career profiles is included to acquaint students with the actual experiences of individuals who hold positions in data processing. In these profiles, the individuals relate the duties and responsibilities involved in their jobs and the education and training or other experiences that were most valuable to them in obtaining the positions they hold.

6. The study guide has been restructured. Discussion questions for each chapter have been included in the study guide.

7. The instructor-support materials include an extended instructor's guide, a new and expanded set of transparency masters correlated to each chapter, and a computerized test bank. The test bank includes some of the best questions submitted from second-edition users as well as questions we have developed.

There are three versions of this text. Two versions include a thorough discussion of punched-card data processing and punched-card machines and systems (Chapters 4 and 5, respectively). In both those versions, Appendix A explains how to use a card punch. One of those versions also includes a thorough discussion of the BASIC language so that students can write programs to solve a variety of business problems (Appendix B).

This alternate version, unlike the other two versions, includes (in its Chapters 4 and 5) discussion of management information systems, their impact on organizations, and several illustrations that reinforce these concepts. This version also includes (in its Appendix A) an expanded discussion of the BASIC language. A new Appendix B in this version provides corresponding BASIC programming problems and representative solutions. This alternate version, then, is designed for the instructor who wants to minimize the time and attention given to punched-card data processing and punched-card systems, and to maximize the coverage of management information systems and the BASIC programming language.

In all three versions of the text, the following key aspects of the second edition have been retained:

1. The grouping of the chapters into logical units.
2. The inclusion of modules to present specific topics. Each module is placed at a strategic point to support the presentation of material in the chapters. The modules can be skipped by the student without disrupting the continuity of learning the essential principles and functions of business data processing. The modules include: Special-Purpose Input and Output Devices, Flowcharting, Top-Down Program

Design and Structured Programming, and Social Implications of the Computer.
3. A chapter outline at the beginning of each chapter.
4. A unique approach to the discussion of high-level programming languages (Chapter 13).
5. A discussion of the typical relationship between the business organization and the data processing department and of the structure of a data processing department (Chapter 17).
6. A discussion of the computer industry (Chapter 18).

This edition has the same twofold objective as the second edition: (1) to illustrate the use of various data processing systems for business applications, and (2) to familiarize the reader with the functional and operational characteristics of data processing systems. Thus, the basic business applications of order writing, billing, accounts receivable, inventory control, and sales analysis are discussed. We note particularly how data within these systems can be machine-processed. Throughout the text, major emphasis is placed on the appropriate principles and functions of business data processing rather than on the specific details of equipment.

All the individuals who have contributed to the development of this text are too numerous to mention, but the authors acknowledge particular indebtedness to Bob Safran of SRA and Marilyn Bohl of IBM for their guidance and assistance during the revision of the manuscript. We would also like to express our appreciation to the following individuals who reviewed the final draft of the manuscript and provided us with many valuable comments and suggestions:

S. J. Birkin, *University of Southern Florida*
R. Chenoweth, *County College of Morris*
Gardner Mallonee, *Essex Community College*
B. N. Michaelson, *Palomar College*
James Payne, *Kellogg Community College*
T. A. Pollack, *Robert Morris College*

Some Fundamentals of Data Processing

Introduction to Data Processing

Every organization, whether business, government, or social requires a certain amount of paperwork. This paperwork is called data processing, and any procedures, equipment, programs, and people by which this paperwork is processed make up the data processing system. Data processing systems are essential in handling the informational needs of an organization. Through computer data processing, organizations are attempting to meet the ever-increasing needs for information in a complex and ever-changing society.

Data are unorganized facts, and *data processing*, whether manual, electromechanical, or electronic, consists of the operations needed to capture and transform data into useful information and the transmission of this information to managers or other specific individuals or groups. Thus, data processing is a means to an end and not an end in itself. When the results from the capture and organization of data are used, they become *information*. Information, then, is the basis upon which efficient and effective decisions can be made. This is one of the major reasons why data processing is very important to the successful operation of any organization.

THE PROCESSING OF DATA

Data processing is usually divided into two major areas: business and scientific. The major function of business data processing is the establishment of files of data, the retention of this data, and the processing of it to produce meaningful information. Business data processing usually involves large volumes of data, few mathematical and/or logical operations performed on this data, and a large volume of results. For example, a public utility must maintain a record for each customer and, each month, present a bill to the customer for services used. This requires reading the customer record to determine name, address, and any past due amount. The customer bill involves a few simple calculations. Then it is printed. In this example, many thousands of records have to be read, updated, and printed; thus the majority of processing time is spent manipulating data.

Scientific data processing usually involves a small volume of data. Many logical and/or mathematical operations are performed on the data, producing typically a small volume of results. For example, a weather satellite collects data for a period of time, then the data is analyzed by a computer to produce a weather forecast. Scientific data may be retained in files for future analysis, but the emphasis is on data analysis rather than on extensive file processing.

Whether the processing of data is business-oriented or scientific-oriented, it involves five basic functions—origination, input, manipulation, output, and storage.

Origination

The first function involved in the processing of data is the origination of the data to be processed. Specifically, the nature, type, and origin of the source documents must be determined. The *source documents* are those documents produced in the process of communicating within an organization, such as sales orders, purchase orders, or employee time cards, that contain the data to be processed.

Input

The second function involved in the processing of data is the input of data stored on these source documents into the data processing system. The input of data into a data processing system occurs when the data stored on the source documents is recorded in some manner acceptable for entry into the data processing system.

Manipulation

The third function involved in the processing of data is the manipulation of the data. This function centers around the performance of certain necessary operations on the data. The operations may include classifying, sorting, calculating, recording, and summarizing the data.

Classifying.   The classifying of data involves the identification of like data according to one or more characteristics. For example, employee time cards may be grouped by department; each employee time card belongs in the group for the department in which the employee works.

Sorting.   After data is classified, it is usually necessary to arrange or rearrange the data into some logical order to facilitate processing. This arranging or rearranging procedure is called sorting. For example, employee time cards classified by department may be sorted within each department by employee last name. This insures that the time cards in each department group are arranged alphabetically.

Calculating.   The arithmetical manipulation of data to create meaningful results is known as calculating. This process is usually the most significant part of the manipulation operation because the results are generally provided as part of the output. For instance, after employee time cards have been classified and sorted, the net pay for each employee may be calculated.

Recording.   Generally, the processing of data involves the obtaining of intermediate results. These intermediate results must be recorded until further processing of them occurs. For instance, in the calculation of each employee's net pay, intermediate results such as the gross pay, retirement, and taxes of the employee must be retained temporarily for later use.

Summarizing.   Finally, to be of value, data must often be reduced to a meaningful, concise form. This process is called summarizing. Generally, the data is summarized into a form desired for output. For example, each employee's gross pay, retirement, and taxes accumulated since the beginning of the year may be summarized (totaled) and printed.

Output

After the various operations on the data have been completed, the results (information) must be communicated in an intelligible form (to appropriate individuals or groups). For example, a printed report of an employee's gross pay and the amounts subtracted for retirement and taxes may be handed to each employee who receives a pay check. As another example, a total of the retirement and taxes withheld for all employees may be reported to the payroll department for record-keeping purposes.

Storage

Finally, the results of the processing of data must be retained for future use or reference. This function is called storage. A storage function in payroll processing, for example, may be the storage of the output reports and the canceled checks of employees.

HOW DATA PROCESSING AFFECTS
THE OPERATIONS OF A BUSINESS

The processing of data takes place in many parts of an organization. For instance, a manufacturing company requires data processing in its research, manufacturing, and financial departments. The research scientist records the data from experiments, makes calculations on the data, and then summarizes the data in various recommendations and reports. The manufacturing department requires summarized data to control the production of the company. The financial department processes data to keep track of profit and loss and the total worth of the business. Data processing takes place in many other departments of the company as well.

Any of several methods can be used to process data. An organization does not have to use punched cards or computers. While more and more organizations are using computer data processing systems, the simplest systems require only pencil and paper. Between pencil and paper and the computer is a range of equipment—adding machines, typewriters, bookkeeping machines, electronic accounting machines, and punched-card processing machines, to name a few.

Whatever the method used, data processing directly affects the success of the organization. Whether or not a company's data processing system is efficient and effective can, in part, determine whether or not the operations of the company are efficient and effective. A data processing system can greatly influence whether or not a company makes a profit.

Although it is easy to say that data processing is important to an organization, it is not so easy to say exactly how it is important. For example, can you explain how data processing affects the operations of a company? Or can you understand why an executive may complain that the data processing system of a company has made it impossible to make a profit? One may well ask, "How can paper juggling be that important?"

If you analyze a business such as a manufacturing company, you can see that data processing, or paperwork, affects the business in several important ways. Among these are the following:

1. Data processing affects the cost of running the business.
2. Data processing affects customer service.
3. Data processing affects the management of the company.

How Data Processing Affects the Cost of Running a Business

Data processing affects the cost of running a business because it is one of the costs of running a business. In fact, it may be one of the major costs. As such, it must be controlled. Think, for example, of an insurance company. Its product is represented by a paper policy, and all phases of its operations involve paperwork. If the cost of its data processing operations can be reduced, an overall cost reduction for the company is likely.

Why be concerned about cost reduction? If the cost of doing something in a business is reduced without lowering the quality of the end result, this reduction has a direct effect on the profits of the company. To show a profit, a company tries to make the most sales at the least cost. At the end of the year, a company determines its total profits by subtracting total costs from total sales. Thus, if the cost of data processing can be decreased without decreasing its value, the profits of the company can be increased by the same amount. In this respect, then, one can say that data processing affects not only the cost of running a company but also the profits of the company.

How Data Processing Affects Customer Service

When a customer places an order with a company, he wants the order to be delivered to the right place at the right time. He wants the correct items delivered in the correct quantities. Later, when he is billed for the shipment, he wants to be billed for the correct items in the correct amounts. The quality of a company's service depends upon how well the company meets these and other customer requirements.

Data processing affects customer service because it is involved in fulfilling customer requirements. Consider, for example, whether or not a company delivers its orders promptly. One might think that the company's ability to do so is determined by how efficient its shipping department is in packaging goods for shipment. However, between the time an order is received and the time it reaches the shipping department, many data processing steps take place. The steps vary from company to company, but most, if not all, of the following processes may occur:

1. The order is received in the sales department. It is either mailed or phoned in by the customer, or taken in person by a salesclerk. In the sales department, the order is checked for accuracy. The customer's address, the item numbers, and the item descriptions are checked to make sure that the order has been taken correctly.
2. The original order is sent from the sales department to the credit department where a credit check is performed to make sure that the customer is able to pay for the items ordered.
3. The customer's order is typed so that it can be read accurately. (The original is often handwritten.) Several copies are made.
4. The typed order (now called the shipping order) is checked to make sure that it has been typed correctly. Then one or more copies are sent to the shipping department where the order is filled.

From this example of what may happen to an order, one can see how data processing can affect whether or not a company delivers its orders promptly. Before an order reaches the shipping department, much data processing must take place. If several days are required to complete this paperwork, shipments tend to arrive that much later.

Accuracy in processing data is also important for customer service. If mistakes are made in preparing a shipping order, the shipment may contain wrong items or wrong quantities, or it may be shipped to the wrong address. If mistakes are made in preparing a customer's bill, the customer may be charged too much or too little. Clearly, data processing affects many aspects of customer service.

Inventory control is another area in which data processing can affect customer service. One of the functions of inventory control is to insure that items are on hand when needed. To do this, inventory-control personnel rely on records and reports that are prepared by processing data. If the reports and records are accurate and up-to-date, inventory-control personnel can identify and reorder items that are running low. When a customer orders an item, it is in stock and can be shipped promptly. On the other hand, if the inventory records are not accurate and up-to-date, it is difficult to determine which items are running low. The shipping department may discover a stockout when a customer orders an item. If this happens, the customer does not get what was ordered (at least not when it is wanted); the lack of inventory control will have affected customer service unfavorably.

How Data Processing Affects
the Management of a Company

So far, shipping orders and inventory records produced by a data processing system have been mentioned. Other routine outputs include payroll checks, monthly statements to customers, checks to suppliers, and purchase orders. Now consider the effect of data processing output on the management of a company.

There are one or more levels of management in a company. A large company, for example, is led by a board of directors and top-level management, followed by several levels of middle management and front-line management. Regardless of the level, however, the basic functions of management are the same: to plan, organize, staff, direct, and control the operations that take place in the company. To carry out these basic functions, management relies on data processing for necessary information.

Take, for example, a sales manager. The major part of this job is to plan and control the efforts and expenses of the sales department. Suppose that one of the information reports the manager gets is the *Comparative Income Statement* shown in Illustration 1-1. The report shows sales and selling expenses for the current month and totals for the year-to-date.

In the "Increase or Decrease" column, the report compares the totals for the current year with the totals for the same period in the preceding year. How might the information in this report help the sales manager to control the expenses of the department?

By comparing expense items for the current year with those for the preceding year, the sales manager can identify expenses that have increased beyond reasonable limits. The manager can then try to find and eliminate the causes of the increases.

But, does the Comparative Income Statement give information that helps the sales manager to increase the company's sales?

From the report, one can tell that sales are decreasing, but one cannot tell the cause of the decrease. Has a salesman stopped calling on certain customers with the result that they have given their business to someone else? Have salesmen failed to give enough attention to selling the more profitable items in the product line? These are the kinds of questions that a sales manager has to answer. The Comparative Income Statement will not help; the manager needs more information. The reports in Illustration 1-2 may give this information.

ROUTING ☐ PRESIDENT'S OFFICE ☐ TREASURER ☐ COMPTROLLER ☐ ACCOUNTING ☑ SALES MANAGER ☐ PLANT SUPERINTENDENT	COMPARATIVE INCOME STATEMENT	PERIOD ENDING 05/31/78 PAGE 1

ACCT. NUMBER	DESCRIPTION	CURRENT MONTH		YEAR-TO-DATE		INCREASE* OR DECREASE —	%* —
		THIS YEAR	LAST YEAR	THIS YEAR	LAST YEAR		
411	SALES	$1,223,195.85	$1,283,474.02	$4,739,999.14	$4,915,174.67	$175,175.53 –	3.6 –
411-100	GROSS SALES	1,726.40	1,912.71	3,245.97	3,464.22	218.25 –	6.3 –
411-200	LESS RETURNS & ALLOW- ANCES	$1,221,469.45	$1,281,561.31	$4,736,753.17	$4,911,710.45	$174,957.28 –	3.6 –
	NET SALES	581,786.15	611,950.16	2,352,146.73	2,408,762.23	56,615.50 –	2.4 –
412-100	LESS COST OF GOODS SOLD	$639,683.30	$669,611.15	$2,384,606.44	$2,502,948.22	$118,341.78 –	4.7 –
	GROSS PROFIT						
421	SELLING EXPENSES						
421-100	SALARIES & COMMISSION	$184,373.27	$189,264.48	$705,623.06	$725,579.46	$19,956.40 –	2.8 –
421-200	TRAVELING	14,425.15	13,790.80	53,726.92	48,968.21	4,758.71 ∷	9.7 ∷
421-300	DELIVERY	6,140.20	6,256.00	28,364.15	29,428.19	1,064.04 –	3.6 –
421-400	ADVERTISING	1,582.00	1,450.25	18,250.00	15,225.75	3,024.25 ∷	19.9 ∷
421-500	OFFICE SALARIES	27,684.35	25,829.15	94,342.18	85,415.14	8,927.04 ∷	10.5 ∷
421-600	STATIONERY & SUPPLIES	1,380.60	1,295.00	4,982.76	4,576.82	405.94 ∷	8.9 ∷
421-700	TELEPHONE	1,315.85	1,305.62	4,148.15	3,381.26	766.89 ∷	22.7 ∷
421-800	BUILDING	4,725.00	4,215.10	21,175.00	18,634.55	2,540.45 ∷	13.6 ∷
421-900	MISCELLANEOUS	1,460.38	1,460.38	4,965.48	3,519.47	1,446.01 ∷	41.1 ∷
	TOTAL SELLING EXPENSE	$243,086.80	$244,866.78	$935,577.70	$934,728.85	$848.85 ∷	0.1 ∷

Illustration 1-1. Comparative Income Statement.

The first report in Illustration 1-2 is a *Sales-by-Customer Report.* It indicates which customers are buying less of the company's products than they did in the preceding year. This decrease may be the result of competition, or poor salesmanship, or a combination of causes. In any case, the report points out where sales have been lost. The same thing is true of the second report, the *Sales-by-Item Report.* This report indicates which products have increased or decreased in demand. The items that have dropped in sales may have been replaced by another product in the company's product line, or they may have been affected by an item in a competitor's product line. Once again, the sales manager is alerted to trouble spots. The last report in the illustration, a *Sales-by-Salesman Report,* shows the gross profit made by each salesman. By studying this report, a sales manager can determine which of the salesmen has sold the most and which one has made the most profit for the company. This report may indicate that some changes in the bonus plan for salesmen should be made—changes that will encourage the men to sell the high-profit items in the product line.

One can see how information provided by a company's data processing system affects how well a company's management can manage. Without reliable information, managers do not know which operations are not going as planned. With dependable information, they know what the trouble areas are and can act accordingly.

Take a different example—a manager in charge of credit or collections. This manager's job is to keep the amount of money owed to the company as low as possible without offending customers. In other words, the credit manager tries to get customers to pay their bills on time without exerting undue pressure. Suppose that the amount of money owed to the company has been increasing. The credit manager must try to reduce the amount. Can information provided by a data processing system help?

Illustration 1-3 is a report that may help the credit manager collect outstanding debts. It is called an *Aged Trial Balance*. It tells which customers owe money and how long they have owed it. The collection department, by using this report, can first contact customers who have owed money for more than ninety days, then customers who have owed money for more than sixty days, and so on. This reasonable approach to collecting is impossible without the information given in this report.

From these two examples, one can see that information intended to indicate problem areas or exceptional conditions must be provided in sufficient detail. Another characteristic of good information is that it must be up-to-date, or current.

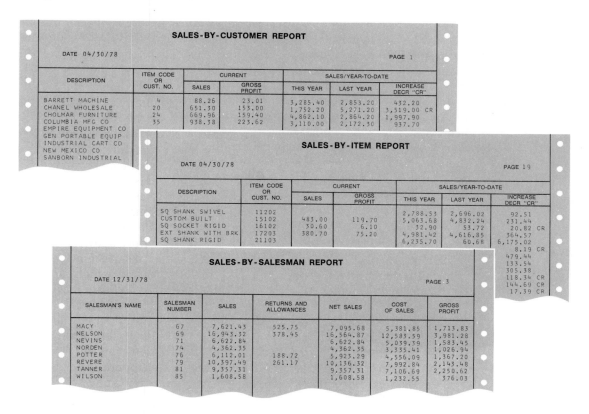

Illustration 1-2. Three sales reports.

CUSTOMER	ACCOUNT NUMBER	BR	SALESMAN	BALANCE	CURRENT	OVER 30 DAYS	OVER 60 DAYS	OVER 90 DAYS
CRANDAL & COMMINS	46346	1	44	503.42	503.42			
CULVER CONSTRUCTION CO	58607	1	19	1,696.34	1,315.67	380.67		
CUMBERLAND DAIRY	32264	3	72	379.05	379.05			
CUTTERBILL INC	88211	1	68	2,791.22	1,136.00	1,256.20	321.12	77.90
CUYENSTAHL DIE WORKS	10910	1	43	4,537.29	4,131.29	406.00		
DADAROLA CONTRACTING	19777	1	11	55.80			55.80	
DADE & FORSTERMAN INC	20791	2	30	747.65	737.65			10.00
DAHL DAHL & YONKO	49382	2	19	2,492.10	2,492.10			
DARCHESTER PLATING CO	11071	1	84	146.43	146.43			
DEAN HARDWARE CO	52086	1	26	1,087.50	1,087.50			
DEULEVIN SUPPLY CO	14125	1	44	727.77	727.77			
DEVENY AND SONS	22767	1	11	54.83		54.83		

AGED TRIAL BALANCE

DATE 04/30/78 PAGE 2

Illustration 1-3. Aged Trial Balance.

The Aged Trial Balance in Illustration 1-3 gives the status of accounts as of April 30. Between April 30 and the date the report was available, some of the debts listed on the report may have been paid. If the report was prepared quickly—say, in one day—and the credit manager had access to it by May 2, chances are that all debts listed on the report were still owed. Such a report is up-to-date. On the other hand, if it takes three weeks to prepare such a report, many of the debts listed on the report will have been paid before the report is received. In this case, unless new records are checked, some customers who have paid their bills will receive notices that their payments are ninety days overdue. This leads to confusion and ill will and is one of the reasons why it is important to the credit manager that the Aged Trial Balance be up-to-date.

In the same way, all management information is most valuable when it is current. If information does not reflect the most recent conditions, it runs the risk of indicating trouble spots that have been corrected or that have corrected themselves. Similarly, if information that is delivered to management reflects conditions as they were a month ago, management may not find out about a problem until long after anything can be done about it.

When a computer data processing system is installed, managers may find that the computer produces more information than they can analyze for decision-making purposes. In order to provide only the information needed for decision making, selected items requiring management attention can be listed on *exception reports*. Only items requiring attention are indicated. Exception reports are the basis for a management technique called *management-by-exception*.

Another type of data processing system that is gaining popularity with management is called a *management information system* (MIS). The objective of an MIS is to provide appropriate information to all levels of management when it is needed. This information may include exception reports, specialized reports required by managers, and reports that forecast possible outcomes of management decisions. (Management information systems are discussed in detail in Chapters 4 and 5.)

Summary

1. Data processing is collecting, processing, and distributing facts and figures. It may be automated, but it need not be.

2. Data processing is divided into two basic types: scientific data processing, which deals with small amounts of data requiring extensive calculations, and business data processing, which involves large volumes of data but few calculations.

3. Data processing systems originate, input, manipulate, output, and store data. The series of steps involved in manipulating data include classifying, sorting, calculating, recording, and summarizing.

4. Data processing is important to business because it affects the success of a business in several ways. It represents one of the costs of running a business and can be a major cost. It can help or hinder the customer service that a company provides. It can affect how well the managers of a company are able to manage.

5. The cost of processing data is one of the costs of running a company. If the cost of the data processing system can be decreased without decreasing its value, the profits of the company can be increased by the same amount.

6. Data processing can affect customer service in many ways. It can affect whether or not orders are shipped promptly, the accuracy of shipments, the accuracy of bills sent to customers, and whether items are available for shipment.

7. The management information provided by a data processing system should have two qualities: it should give enough detail to call attention to operations that are not going as planned, and it should be up-to-date enough to permit something to be done about them.

Data Processing Applications

To understand data processing, there are four things one needs to know:

1. What a data processing system is used for
2. How a data processing system is designed
3. What types of equipment are available for processing data
4. How the pieces of equipment are set up to do specific jobs

THE PURPOSE OF A DATA PROCESSING SYSTEM

Data processing systems are used to collect, manipulate, and store data for reporting and analyzing business activities and events. Data is organized into *files* to achieve these purposes.

A file can be defined as an organized group of associated *records* that relate to a particular area of a business. Each record generally contains data about a single unit in the file such as an inventory item, a customer, or an employee. Illustration 2-1 is an example of a payroll file. It contains a record for each employee, and each record contains *fields*. A field is a specified area reserved for data of a specific nature such as the employee's number, name, pay rate, or address. It is the smallest element of a file that is processed.

A *character* is actually the smallest subdivision of a file. It consists of a single alphabetic, numeric, or special character. Generally, a single character within a field is not dealt with as an entity; rather, the entire field is manipulated when processing a record.

Files are usually divided into two classifications: master and detail. *Master files* contain permanent data, as does the payroll file. *Detail* (or *transaction*) *files* contain data of a temporary nature; an example is a file of weekly employee time cards.

Most data processing involves file manipulation. When it is determined that there is a need for information concerning some area of a business, a file may be *created* to provide that information. Once a file has been created, it often is necessary to *add* records to it. For example, when an employee is hired, a new record must be added to the payroll file. When a record is no longer useful, say, when an employee leaves a company, it is usually *deleted* from the file. It is sometimes necessary to change fields of a record, such as when an employee's pay rate or job classification is changed. In this case, a record is *updated*.

In most files, records are arranged in some sequence or order. At times, if the purpose or nature of a file is altered, it is necessary to change this sequence. For example, if employee records in a payroll file are organized by department, but at a later date it is necessary to organize them by division, it is necessary to resequence the file. The data field on which the *sequencing* is based is called the *control field* of the records in the file.

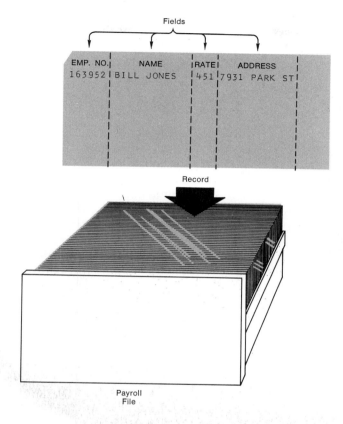

Illustration 2-1. A payroll file.

The process of updating, adding, and deleting records in a file to reflect changes is referred to as *file maintenance*. When a file is updated on a periodic basis or reports are created, the action is *file processing*.

DATA-RECORDING MEDIUM
FOR A DATA PROCESSING SYSTEM

For many years, business organizations used a wide variety of manual systems to process data. More recently, data processing systems involving various types of machines have been used to process data. Before the introduction of the computer, *punched-card data processing systems* were prevalent. These systems consisted of a series of electrically operated machines that processed data recorded on punched cards.

The punched card shown in Illustration 2-2 was introduced in the late 1800s when Herman Hollerith was hired by the Census Bureau to develop a punched-card processing system for use in the 1890 census. In 1896, Hollerith resigned his job with the Census Bureau and started the Tabulating Machine Company, which specialized in the manufacture and sale of punched-card equipment for commercial use. After merging with two other firms, this company formed the Computing-Tabulating-Recording Company. Its name was changed to the International Business Machines (IBM) Corporation in 1924.

When Hollerith left the Census Bureau, he was replaced by James Powers. Powers furthered the use of punched cards by the Census Bureau by developing a number of electromechanical machines to process cards. These machines were used to calculate the 1910 census. In 1911, Powers left the Census Bureau to produce commercial equipment; he formed the Powers Accounting Machine Company. In 1927, this company merged with others to form the Remington Rand Corporation. In 1955, the Remington Rand Corporation merged with the Sperry Rand Corporation. Today the company is known as Sperry-Univac.

The basic idea underlying punched-card data processing was to record source data as holes punched into cards, and then to process the data with the use of machines. Once data had been recorded on a machine-readable document, it could be processed repeatedly at machine speeds and with machine accuracy to prepare documents for a number of different departments and for a number of different business applications.

The punched card has been a very popular medium for recording source data to be entered into a data processing system. Although the punched card is still used to record source data for entry into a computer data processing system, other methods are becoming more popular. These methods of recording source data are examined in more detail in Module A.

Currently, two types of punched cards are used to record data for use in computer data processing systems. They are discussed below.

The 80-Column Punched Card

The punched card designed by Hollerith consists of 80 vertical *columns* and 12 horizontal *rows*. The columns are numbered from 1 to 80, starting from the left side of the card. The names of the rows from the top to the bottom of the card are the 12-row, the 11-row, the 0-row (zero row), and the 1-, 2-, 3-, 4-, 5-, 6-, 7-, 8-, and 9-rows.

Holes can be punched into any rows or columns of the card. In Illustration 2–2, there is a 1-punch in column 63, a 9-punch in column 72, and a 4-punch in column 77. The 12 punching positions are illustrated in columns 21 through 32.

When data is recorded in a punched card using the most common punched-card coding system, each letter, number, or special character

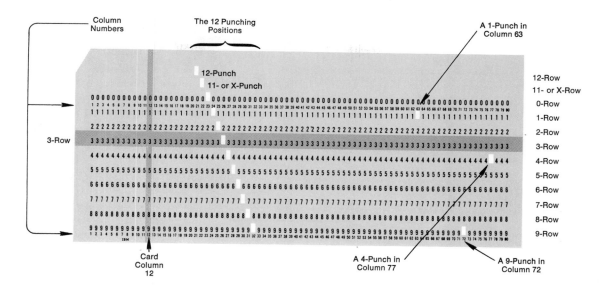

Illustration 2-2. 80-column punched card.

occupies a separate column of the card. One punched card can contain up to 80 characters of data. These characters are represented by combinations of punches in the columns of the cards. For example, the combination of a 12-punch and a 1-punch stands for the letter A; the combination of a 0-punch and a 2-punch stands for the letter S. The punched-card coding system is called *Hollerith code.*

Illustration 2-3 shows all the combinations of punches in Hollerith code. It also introduces the two punching areas of the card: the *zone-punching area* and the *digit-punching area.* The zone punches are in the 12-, 11-, and 0-rows. The digit punches are in the 0- through 9-rows. (The 0-punch is therefore both a zone punch and a digit punch.)

In Illustration 2-3, the digits 0 through 9 (*numeric characters*) are punched in columns 15 through 24. Each number consists of a single digit punch. A letter (*alphabetic character*) consists of two punches in a column: a zone punch and a digit punch. The letters are recorded in columns 31 through 56. The letters A through I consist of the 12-punch and the digit punches from 1 through 9; letters J through R consist of the 11-punch and the digit punches from 1 through 9; letters S through Z consist of the 0-punch and the digit punches 2 through 9. The remaining characters (*special characters*) are represented by one, two, or three punches. They are punched in columns 63 through 73 in the illustration. As one can see, the ampersand (&) is represented by a 12-punch, the at sign (@) by a 4- and an 8-punch, and the asterisk (*) by an 11-, a 4-, and an 8-punch.

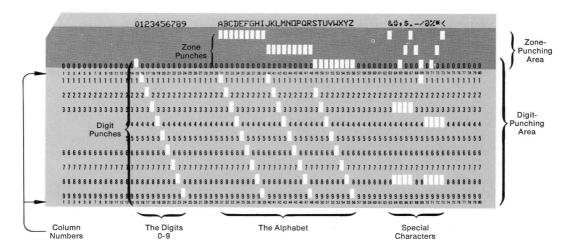

Illustration 2-3. Hollerith code.

The chart in Illustration 2-4 shows the zone and digit punches for every Hollerith-code alphabetic character in a convenient tabular form. The letter A consists of a 12-punch and a 1-punch; the letter B consists of a 12-punch and a 2-punch; and so on.

Before data is punched into a card, a specific number of consecutive columns is assigned to each item of data the card will contain. Each group of columns is called a *field* of the card. The card in Illustration 2-5 is separated into many fields. Columns 2-6 are the order-number field, columns 13-14 the salesman-number field, columns 15-19 the customer-number field, and so on. Since the salesman-number field is two columns wide, the salesman number may have a value in the range from 00 through 99. Similarly, the customer number may have a value from 00000 through 99999. The item description may be up to 18 characters long.

		Digit Punches								
		1	2	3	4	5	6	7	8	9
Zone Punches	12	A	B	C	D	E	F	G	H	I
	11	J	K	L	M	N	O	P	Q	R
	0		S	T	U	V	W	X	Y	Z

Illustration 2-4. Hollerith-code alphabetic characters.

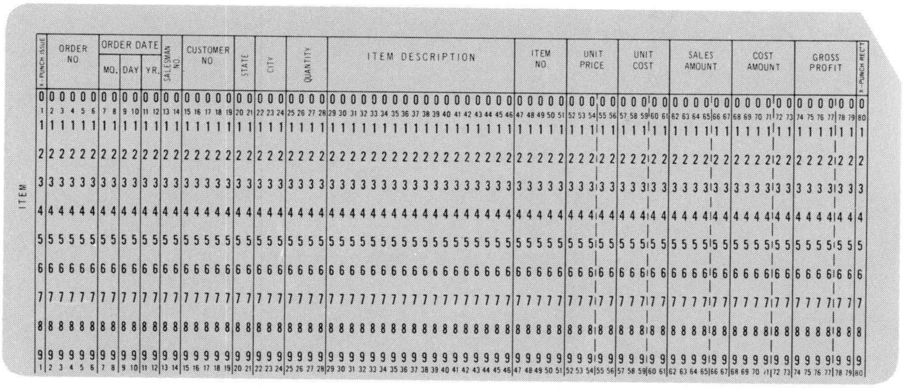

Illustration 2-5. Data fields of a punched card.

Note also that when data containing a decimal point is punched into a card, the decimal point may not be punched. It may be omitted for two reasons: (1) to reduce the characters in a field, thus shortening the key-punching operation, and (2) to minimize the number of card columns assigned to the field. Look, for example, at the unit-price field in the illustration. A dotted line represents the position of the decimal point. In some systems, the dotted line is not printed on the card, but the position of the decimal point is understood. The printing on a card is, after all, only for the convenience of the people handling the card. When cards are processed by a computer the positions of decimal points are determined by instructions given to the computer.

The 96-Column Punched Card

A new punched card, designed for use with small computer systems, was announced in 1969. Known as the 96-column card, it is smaller in size than the 80-column punched card and uses a different coding system for data representation.

As shown in Illustration 2-6, the 96-column card is divided into two areas: the *print area* and the *punch area*. The 96-column card is considerably smaller than the 80-column card, but it can store almost 20 percent more data.

Because of the size of the 96-column card, the Hollerith code is not used, but the concepts of zones and digits and columns and rows are applied. Data is punched into the card as round holes rather than as rectangular ones (compare Illustrations 2-3 and 2-7).

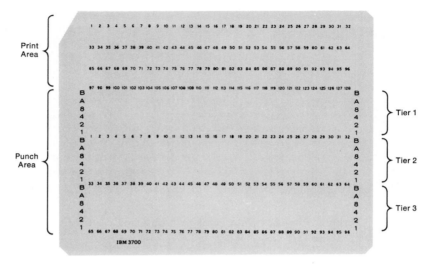

Illustration 2-6. 96-column punched card.

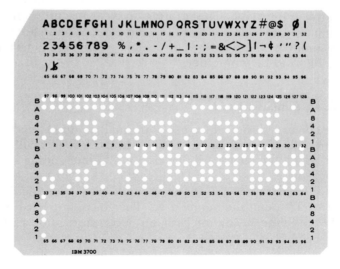

Illustration 2-7. 96-column card code.

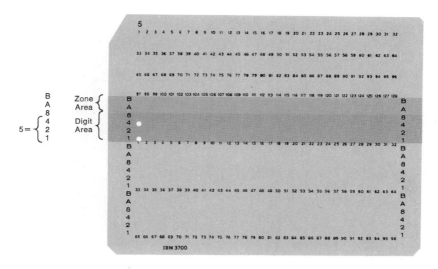

Illustration 2-8. Recording a digit on a 96-column card.

As the term *96-column card* indicates, there are 96 columns in the punch area of a 96-column card. The columns are separated into three 32-column *tiers* rather than placed on one continuous horizontal line. There are six rows in each column, and each column can hold one alphabetic, numeric, or special character. Thus, each of the characters shown in Illustration 2-7 is represented in the six rows in one column of the card.

As Illustration 2-8 shows, a single column contains both a digit area and a zone area. To record a numeric character in a column, only the digit area of the column is needed. Any number from 0 through 9 can be represented by one or more punches in the digit rows 8, 4, 2, and 1. In Illustration 2-8, the number 5 is represented by punches in rows 4 and 1 in column 1.

The two top rows in a column are used to represent the zone portion of a character; they are called the B and A zones. The alphabetic character B is represented by the zone punches B and A and the digit punch 2 as shown in column 1 in Illustration 2-9.

The print area of a 96-column card is divided into four rows to provide print interpretation of characters punched in any of the 96 columns. There are 32 positions in each row, or a total of 128 print positions. The extra print positions are provided so that spacing can be inserted between the printed characters to allow the card to be read easily by persons who use it. Numerous characters have been punched in the card in Illustration

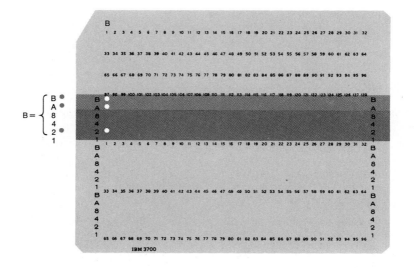

Illustration 2-9. Recording an alphabetic character on a 96-column card.

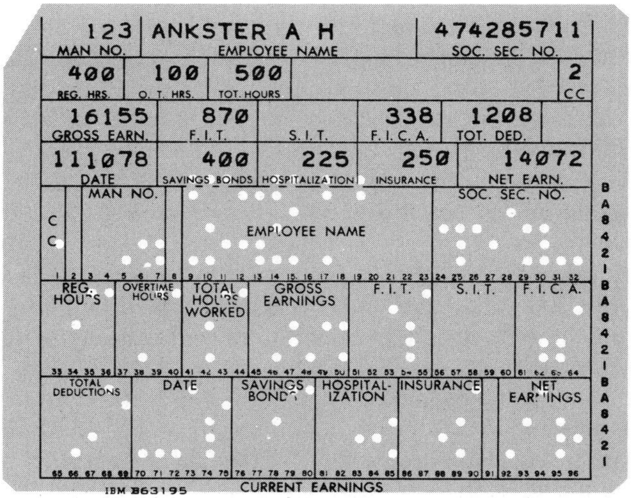

Illustration 2-10. Use of spacing between printed characters on a 96-column card.

2-10 just as in Illustration 2-7. However, spacing has been inserted between the printed characters on this card to improve readability.

THE USES OF A DATA PROCESSING SYSTEM

Data processing systems are used in a variety of business operations. These operations are called *data processing applications*. Billing is one data processing application. The operation of billing is accomplished by the data processing system applied to the billing of customers. Another example of a data processing application is inventory control. The objective of the inventory-control application is to keep track of inventory items so that they can be reordered or reproduced when necessary. The data processing system applied to inventory control prepares records and reports to help inventory-control personnel do their jobs.

In any business, there are many data processing applications. In fact, any operation of a business that requires information or paperwork is a data processing application. The applications vary from business to business just as the operations vary. Nevertheless, certain basic operations and data processing applications are common to most businesses.

THE BASIC BUSINESS OPERATIONS

A manufacturing company is a typical business. It carries out several basic operations in order to make its products, sell them, and realize a profit. These basic operations are (1) *producing* the items in the product line, (2) *storing* these items, (3) *selling* the products, (4) *shipping* the products, (5) *billing* customers for purchases, (6) *collecting* payments from customers, (7) *purchasing* goods when needed, (8) *receiving* the purchased goods, (9) *paying* for the purchased goods, and (10) *paying* the employees of the company.

A manufacturing company also carries out other important operations. Accounting, for example, takes place in one form or another, as in all companies. In the accounting department, financial records are kept to indicate whether the company is making a profit and whether the total value of the company is increasing. Since accounting is not directly connected with making and selling a product, it is not considered a basic operation. Similarly, the research and development department, the legal department, and the personnel department may carry out operations that are not included in the list of basic operations of manufacturing.

Of course, not all companies manufacture products; some companies are distributors. A distributor buys products and then sells the products to customers. A wholesale toy distributor, for example, buys toys from toy manufacturers and sells them to department stores and other retail outlets. A distributor does not need a production operation. However, the other basic operations are the same as those of a manufacturing company.

Other organizations, banks and insurance companies, for example, sell services rather than products. For this reason, their basic operations are somewhat different from those of a manufacturing company. A service company may not store material to be sold, but it does store material that it uses. Similarly, a service company bills its customers, collects from them, purchases goods and services from other companies, and so on.

Another variation of basic operations is seen in nonprofit organizations, such as the government. Many of the basic operations of a manufacturing company may not occur in a government agency. For example, many government agencies do not bill customers or collect payments. They do, however, purchase material and pay employees.

Since the basic operations of a manufacturing company also take place in most other businesses, these operations are a useful background for studying the common data processing applications.

THE COMMON APPLICATIONS

Data processing can be applied to any operation of a company. The most common applications are: (1) *order writing,* associated with shipping; (2) *billing,* associated with customer billing; (3) *accounts receivable,* associated with collection; (4) *inventory control,* associated with stores (or stock-keeping); (5) *sales analysis,* associated with selling; (6) *accounts payable,* associated with paying for material; (7) *payroll,* associated with paying employees; and (8) *production control,* associated with producing manufactured goods.

This text deals primarily with five of these: order writing, billing, accounts receivable, inventory control, and sales analysis. The reader should learn the objective of each application and its basic forms and reports.

Order Writing

In the language of data processing, any report or form used by a company is called a *document.* The objective of a data processing application is to prepare output documents from source (input) documents. In the order-writing application, the objective is to prepare a document called the *shipping order* from the original *sales order.* The input to the order-writing system is the sales order; the output is the shipping order.

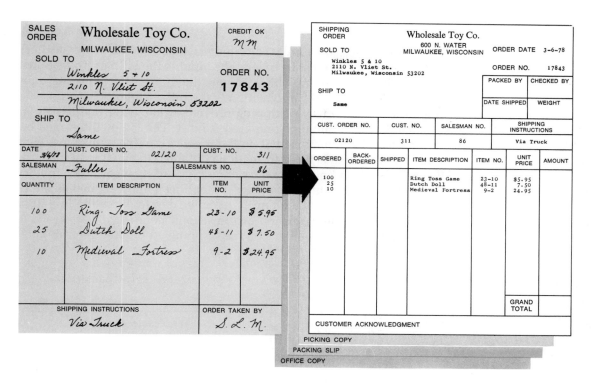

Illustration 2-11. Sales order and shipping order.

Both a sales order and a shipping order are shown in Illustration 2-11. The sales order is filled out by the salesman, the customer, or a clerk. It is often prepared as a single copy. The shipping order is then prepared in several copies, using the sales order as a source document. One copy of the shipping order is sent to the customer as an acknowledgment that the order has been received. One copy is used to tell the person who picks the order in the warehouse (the order picker) what items should be shipped. And one copy is packed with the shipment to tell the customer what items have been included in the shipment.

In some companies, order writing (or order entry, as it is sometimes called) is the most important application. This is often true of distributors. The sales of a distributor may depend on whether orders can be shipped faster than sales can be made. On the other hand, in companies where speed in shipping an order is not critical, order writing is a less important data processing application.

Billing

Billing is an application similar to order writing. Once an order has been shipped, the customer must be billed. The input to the billing application is often the shipping order, which shows the items that were actually shipped. The output of the application is the bill, or *invoice*.

Illustration 2-12 shows a shipping order that has been marked by an order picker and the invoice prepared from it. The major difference between the two documents is that on the invoice the *line items* have been *extended*. A line item is the information contained in one line in the body of the invoice. Each line item refers to one type of item sold. The invoice in Illustration 2-3 has three line items. Extending a line item means multiplying the unit price by the quantity to arrive at a total for the line item. In the illustration, the extension of the second item is $187.50.

Notice that not all of the items on the shipping order have been shipped.

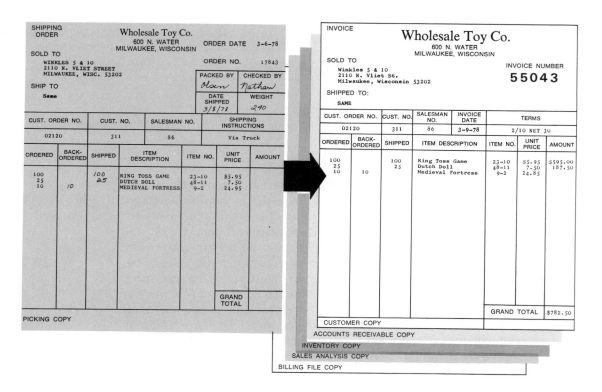

Illustration 2-12. Shipping order and invoice.

	Average Daily Billing	Time Delay for Billing	When Paid	Total Days	Total Dollars
Company A	$10,000	2 days	14 days	16	$160,000
Company B	10,000	7 days	14 days	21	210,000
	Difference			5	$ 50,000

The items that were not shipped (because they were not in stock) have been indicated in the "Back-Ordered" column on the shipping order and on the invoice. As soon as these items are available, they will be shipped to the customer. In some systems, inventory records are checked and the items that must be back-ordered are detected before the shipping order is prepared. Then only the items that are available are extended on the shipping order, and the invoice can be a copy of the shipping order.

Speed and accuracy are important in billing just as they are in order writing. Accuracy is important for obvious reasons: overbilling a customer is unsatisfactory customer service; underbilling a customer can mean lost income. Speed in billing is important because it affects the amount of money owed to the company. To appreciate this, consider the following: Each of two companies has an average daily billing of $10,000 (see the table above). One company sends its bills out two days after shipment, and the other sends its bills out seven days after shipment. The customers of both companies pay their bills an average of fourteen days after the bills have been sent. How will the difference in billing speed affect the total amount owed to each company? To ask this another way, what is the average amount of money owed to each company at any given time?

Since customers pay their bills fourteen days after they are sent, a total of 14 times $10,000 or $140,000, is owed to each company before it starts receiving payments from customers. Since two days pass before the bills are prepared, an additional 2 times $10,000, or $20,000, is owed to the first company at any given time. The total amount of money owed to the first company, then, is $140,000 plus $20,000, or $160,000. Using this same reasoning, the total owed to the second company at any given time is $140,000 plus $70,000, or $210,000. The difference between the total amounts of money outstanding is $50,000, and it results from the difference in the billing speeds of the two billing systems.

Why is the amount of money owed to a company important? Available cash or capital determines to what extent the company can develop new products, purchase new machinery, or build additions to buildings. If a company's capital tends to be tied up because of a slow billing system, improvement of the billing application may be advisable.

	CUSTOMER NAME		CUSTOMER NO.	CREDIT LIMIT
	ALBERT AND SONS		23891	$5,000.00
	2911 SOUTH LANE			
	PITTSBURGH, PA. 15219			

DATE	REFERENCE NO.	CHARGES	CREDITS	BALANCE
			BALANCE FORWARD ▶	200.00
07/02/78	12368	187.72		387.72
07/21/78	12566	13.91		401.63
07/30/78	12671	304.11		705.74
08/07/78	56739		187.72	518.02
08/20/78	12802	156.12		674.14
09/04/78	13094	73.17		747.31
09/14/78	13308	75.00		822.31
10/04/78	73333		195.00	627.31
10/09/78	01299		20.00	607.31
10/16/78	15103	46.98		654.29
10/25/78	15487	141.71		796.00
10/29/78	15782	88.06		884.06

Illustration 2-13. Accounts receivable ledger card.

Accounts Receivable

The objective of an accounts receivable application is twofold: (1) to keep records of the amounts of money that are owed to the company, and (2) to provide information that helps collection personnel to collect outstanding debts. The inputs to a system for accounts receivable are usually invoices and documents indicating cash payments. The outputs of the system are accounts receivable records that indicate charges and payments to a customer's account, monthly statements to customers indicating what is owed, and management reports such as the Aged Trial Balance shown in Illustration 1-3 (see Chapter 1).

Illustration 2-13 shows a common accounts receivable record called a *ledger card*. It contains a record of all charges and payments to a customer's account. In a system that uses ledger cards as the basic accounts receivable record, one card is kept for each customer. The sum of the balances on all ledger cards is the total amount of money owed to the company. The difference between the ledger card and the monthly statement sent to the customer is that the card shows all charges and credits that have occurred since the card was originated. The statement shows only recent credits and outstanding charges.

Management information is a valuable output of an accounts receivable system. Some accounts receivable systems prepare management reports like the Aged Trial Balance. In other accounts receivable systems, preparing the Aged Trial Balance may require so many person hours of work that a company has to decide whether the report is worth the cost of preparing it. The result of this decision varies from industry to industry. For example, a retail distributor (such as a large department store) is likely to have thousands of customers with charge accounts. Keeping track of overdue accounts is an important and sizable job. For such a distributor, aged credit information is often valuable. On the other hand, some manufacturers have no need for such information because they have a relatively small number of customers, few of whom let their accounts become delinquent.

Speed is important in the accounts receivable application. Accounts receivable records are more valuable when they are up-to-date. When a customer asks how much he owes, a company should be able to check his accounts receivable record and give him an answer immediately. But if the charges and payments for the last week have not been recorded on the accounts receivable record, it cannot be used for this purpose. Similarly, the monthly statement should represent the actual amount of money owed by the customer at the end of the billing period. Thus, the speed of the accounts receivable system is important in preparing customer records and monthly statements.

Inventory Control

Inventory control is often the data processing application that provides the greatest potential benefit to a company. In some cases, the needs of this application cause a company to install an automated data processing system. The objective of inventory control is to meet two basic goals. One of the goals is always to have on hand those items that are needed—in other words, to avoid *stockouts*. The other goal is to keep the value of inventory as low as possible. A complication is that these goals tend to work against each other.

A stockout occurs when a customer orders an item that is not available in inventory. The item is then back-ordered. Since the customer demand for an item varies, avoiding stockouts is not an easy job. If a large demand for an item occurs unexpectedly and exceeds the supply on hand, a stockout occurs. Of course, one way of avoiding stockouts is to keep large inventories of all items in the product line. If an item averages fifty units sold per month, and a thousand units are kept on hand, one can assume the company will not run out of the item. However, if this is done, the second inventory goal—keeping the inventory value low—is not achieved.

Inventory should be kept as low as possible because it costs money to store (or carry) inventory. First, warehouse space has to be provided, and handling, insurance, and tax costs must be paid. Second, action must be taken to prevent deterioration of the items in inventory; rust must be inhibited, handling abuses eliminated, and so on. Meanwhile, the money tied up in inventory cannot be used for other purposes. Finally, a certain percentage of items in inventory becomes obsolete each year. When this happens, the obsolete items must be discarded or sold at a lower price. The costs of carrying inventory vary from industry to industry. However, one common estimate is that carrying costs are 25 percent of the average inventory value. Therefore, if a company's average inventory value is $100,000, the yearly cost of carrying the inventory is $25,000.

To reach a balance between the conflicting goals of inventory management, an inventory-control department must have certain information. The information provided by the inventory-control department must have certain characteristics. This information, provided by the inventory-control system, should be detailed enough to answer the following questions:

1. What items need to be reordered?
2. How much of each item should be reordered?
3. What items have had an unusual increase or decrease in sales?
4. What items account for the major part of the inventory investment?
5. What items have become obsolete?

By installing an inventory-control system that gives this kind of information, some companies have been able to make striking advancements toward both inventory goals. By improving inventory information, they have been able to control inventory levels and, at the same time, reduce stockouts.

The source data in an inventory-control system is the recorded transactions of items sold, issued, destroyed, received, or returned. This data appears on input documents such as invoices, scrap notices, packing slips from shipments received, and return slips. When this data is processed, it is converted into inventory records and inventory management reports.

One of the common documents of inventory control is a ledger card, such as the one shown in Illustration 2-14. There is one ledger card for each item in inventory. In addition to the transactions (receipts and issues) and balance on hand, each ledger card shows the item reorder point,

ITEM NUMBER			ITEM DESCRIPTION		
4561237			TRANSFORMERS		
REORDER POINT					
200					
UNIT PRICE					
$7.50					
UNIT COST					
$3.75					

DATE	REFERENCE NO.	RECEIPTS	ISSUES	BALANCE ON HAND	ON ORDER
03/02/78			BALANCE FORWARD	560	
03/11/78	12379		125	435	
03/18/78	12402		50	385	
03/26/78	12509		135	250	
04/02/78	12697		100	150	
04/03/78	5894			150	
04/13/78	12774		15	135	500
04/13/78	13007		25	110	
04/16/78	13277		75	35	
04/16/78	13308		10	25	
04/17/78	5894	500		525	
04/28/78	15003		75	450	
05/05/78	15233		80	370	
05/15/78	15324		175	195	
05/20/78	5999			195	500
05/21/78	15987		50	145	
05/26/78	16001		15	130	
06/01/78	16043		92	38	
06/03/78	5999	500		538	
06/11/78	16319		125	413	
06/18/78	16403		75	338	
07/01/78	16522		15	323	
07/02/78	16539		25	298	

Illustration 2-14. Inventory ledger card.

the price of one item (unit price), and the cost of one item (unit cost). By looking at a ledger card, inventory-control personnel can tell whether the balance on hand for an item has fallen below the reorder point and whether the item should be reordered. One can also determine what the sales of the item have been for any given period. However, this information is not in a form that points out the items needing attention. To discover unusual sales patterns, one may have to study many cards. Moreover, all of the cards must be examined if one wishes to determine all items that should be reordered. Since many of the ledger cards will not have changed since they were last reviewed, many of the items will not require attention.

One alternative to ledger-card examination is to provide a report indicating items that require attention and items whose sales have changed significantly since the immediately preceding report was provided. As indicated in Chapter 1, this kind of reporting is called management-by-exception. The idea behind it is to have management concern itself only with exceptional items (those that require attention) rather than with all items.

Illustration 2-15 shows three kinds of exception reports. The first report is called an *Inventory Action Report.* It lists items that have fallen below their reorder points and shows the transactions that have taken place since the last report, the current balances, and the amounts on order. Using this report, inventory-control personnel can verify (before passing the list on to the purchasing department) that the listed items should be reordered. The second report is a *Slow-Moving Items Report.* It is a list of items that have had little activity over the last twelve months. The report gives the date the item was last sold and shows how many months supply of stock is on hand, based on the sales for the last twelve months. According to the report, the seventh item on the list has a balance on hand that will last 135 months, or more than eleven years! The third report, a *Cumulative Percent of Sales Report,* is another kind of activity report. It lists the items of inventory in order of total dollar sales for the year. In addition, in the "Cumulative $ Sales" column, is a total for all items listed thus far. The cumulative percentage is developed on the same basis. This report helps inventory-control personnel identify the items that account for the greatest percentage of sales. One of the interesting things that often shows up in this kind of report is that about 20 percent of a company's items account for 80 percent of its sales. When this is the case, the inventory-control department usually directs most attention to those items.

One can see how information can be valuable in managing inventory. Effective inventory control can benefit a company in several ways. By reducing the average inventory, carrying costs are decreased. By reducing the number of stockouts, sales are increased.

Sales Analysis

The objective of the sales analysis application is to provide information that helps sales management increase sales. The inputs to the system are the invoices showing items sold and the return slips showing items returned by customers. The outputs of the system are management reports that show sales by salesman, customer, item class, geographical area, branch, and any number of other classifications. Three sales reports are illustrated in Chapter 1 (Illustration 1-2).

Unlike some application systems, the value of a sales analysis system is difficult to measure. The manager has to estimate how much sales will increase as a result of using the information provided by the system. This increase must be balanced against the cost of the system. Apparently many companies find that the value of sales analysis information does not offset

INVENTORY ACTION REPORT

DATE 11/30/78   PAGE 7

PRODUCT NUMBER	OPENING BALANCE	+ RECEIPTS	— ISSUES	ᴸALANCE = ON HAND	ON ORDER	REORDER POINT
7310921	150		150			100
3871123	1100		600	500		1000
4061397	200		200		500	400
4561237		300	200	100		200
0120125	50		25	25		25

SLOW-MOVING ITEMS REPORT

DATE 07/01/78   PAGE 37

STOCK LOCATION	STOCK NUMBER	DESCRIPTION	UNIT	DATE OF LAST ACTIVITY	NET ISSUES FOR PERIOD			BALANCE ON HAND		
					NUMBER OF TRANSACTIONS	QTY.	AVERAGE PER MONTH	QTY.	MONTHS SUPPLY	VALUE
2715-237	127205	LIGHT RECEPTACLE	EA	07/72	2	4	.3	16	53.3	$4.32
2715-420	247389	SOLENOID, HEATER	EA	07/72	1	1	.1	7	70.0	4.43
2715-267	111462	SWITCH, STARTER	EA	08/72	1	4	.3	4	13.3	8.64
2715-601	896124	PINION STUD	EA	09/72	4	16	1.3	84	64.6	9.24
2716-234	59827	GASKET, MANIFOLD	EA	11/72	2	12	1.0	16	16.0	7.52
2716-320	614	WASHER, RUBBER	DZ	12/72	1	3	.2	14	70.0	2.52
2717-086	6213	BOLT, CARRIAGE	DZ	12/72	1	2	.2	27	135.0	32.40
2717-742	1032	BEARING,								
2717-748	148722	AXLE								
2719-147	2642	BRUSH, GE								
2719-382	222649	REGULATOR								
2720-416	421	VALVE								

CUMULATIVE PERCENT OF SALES REPORT

DATE 09/78   PAGE 1

ITEM COUNT	ITEM NUMBER	ANNUAL UNITS	UNIT PRICE	ANNUAL $ SALES	CUMULATIVE $ SALES	CUMULATIVE % OF SALES
01	T7061	51,553	3.077	158,629	158,629	25.5
02	S6832	243,224	.317	77,102	235,731	37.9
03	S7036	98,406	.470	46,251	281,982	45.4
04	G9655	6,768	4.876	33,001	314,983	50.7
05	T3320	4,250	7.369	31,318	346,301	55.7
06	K8946	44,560	.675	30,078	376,379	60.6
07	K5322	8,680	3.286	28,522	404,901	65.2
08	K2026	27,581	.930	25,650	430,551	69.3
09	I6267	3,428	5.901	20,228	450,779	72.6
10	H1981	52,765	.379	19,998	470,777	75.8
11	G9282	1,105	14.676	16,217	486,994	78.4
12	N8565	23,908	.640	15,301	502,295	80.8
40	S6219	15,360	.050	768	618,897	99.6
41	K2068	3,494	.176	615	619,512	99.7
42	G7413	1,904	.282	537	620,049	99.8
43	H3772	2,842	.120	341	620,390	99.86
44	N9773	2,439	.123	300	620,690	99.91
45	T6613	2,670	.103	275	620,965	99.95
46	M2613	3,750	.048	180	621,145	99.98
47	G2605	198	.505	100	621,245	99.995
48	T6562	210	.143	30	621,275	100.0
49	S6132	0	.062	0	621,275	100.0
50	M3742	0	.073	0	621,275	100.0

Illustration 2-15. Three inventory reports.

its cost, because many companies do only a limited amount of sales reporting. On the other hand, a company with many products and customers, a large sales force, and a number of branch offices often finds sales analysis information well worth the cost of its preparation.

THE OTHER COMMON APPLICATIONS

Although the other common applications are not discussed in detail in this book, one should be familiar with their objectives. In accounts payable, the objective is to pay suppliers (vendors) for items and services. The output of the system is the payment check. The discounts that vendors offer for prompt payment of bills are an important source of savings in the accounts payable application. A common discount is 2 percent if bills are paid within 10 days of the time they are received. One of the goals of an accounts payable system is to take advantage of all such discounts, but pay each bill on the last day of its discount period.

Payment of employee salaries and wages is the objective of the payroll application. Payroll checks and payroll reports are the outputs of this application. The input is employee time cards. Because payroll expenses are usually one of the major costs of running a business, payroll information can be an important aid to the management of a company.

For a manufacturing company, the production-control application may offer great potential saving. A company has to control several resources—personnel, machines, and materials. The objectives of production control are to keep machines and people working efficiently at all times, and to keep the investment in production materials as low as possible without running out of them. To work effectively toward these goals, production-control personnel need current information that points out critical situations. Such information is the output of the production-control system.

In addition to these common applications, there are others less common, but similarly related to basic operations. Vendor analysis, for example, is an application associated with the purchasing operation. In this application, reports are prepared to indicate which vendors have the lowest prices, the highest percentage of on-time deliveries, the lowest percentage of defective shipments, and so on.

There are still other applications peculiar to particular types of organizations. For example, grade reporting is associated with educational institutions, mortgage loan accounting is unique to financial institutions, and policy rating is done in the insurance industry. The point is that there are many applications besides those commonly associated with the basic operations. Any operation that takes place in a company can be the basis for a data processing application.

HOW THE APPLICATIONS ARE RELATED

To introduce the common applications one at a time may be misleading. It may imply that the applications are not related. Actually, the applications in a business are closely related, one to another. In fact, a group of related applications is often referred to as a *family of applications*. Order writing, billing, accounts receivable, inventory control, and sales analysis are members of a family that is sometimes called the *distribution family of applications*. Within this family, the output of one application is the input to the next. The shipping order returned from the shipping department is the input to the billing system; the bill produced by the billing system is the input to the accounts receivable, inventory-control, and sales analysis systems.

Looking at it another way, the data on the original sales order is source data for the entire distribution family of applications. When data from customer and item files is added to this source data, and certain calculations are performed, the various outputs of this family are derived. As discussed above, the sales order is the source document for the shipping order. The invoice is the result of extending the line items on the shipping order, adding the extensions, and subtracting the customer discounts. Inventory records are the result of summarizing the line items by item number and, for each item, subtracting the total number sold from the previous on-hand balance. Sales analysis reports are the result of grouping the line items by salesman, customer, or item and then summarizing them. In short, the applications in a family are related, not only through input and output, but also through use of the same source data.

One should keep in mind that a company's files, like source data, are often used by an entire family of applications rather than by just one. For example, a customer file usually contains permanent data such as each customer's name and address, number, credit limit, discounts, special terms, and shipping instructions. Such a file is used in the order-writing, billing, and accounts receivable applications. Similarly, an item file containing information such as unit price, unit cost, item number, reorder point, and reorder quantities is used in the order-writing, billing, inventory-control, and sales analysis applications.

Some companies organize all of the data needed by the various applications into a structured set of related files, known as a *data base*. This eliminates the need for duplicate information and permits additions, updates, and deletions of records to be made to one file. A key to the success of the data base concept is that files are not duplicated in several applications. All applications use the same files, and changes made to the files are available to all applications. When a data base system is not used, updating of multiple files may not occur at the same time. This can cause some instances of data that is common to several files not to be current when needed by a family of applications. The basis for a management information system is a comprehensive data base or several well-planned data bases. Companies are developing management information systems using data bases to insure that data is current for all applications. (See Chapters 4 and 5.)

In evaluating the system for a given application, it is important to keep in mind how that application relates to others. It is a mistake, for example, to consider a billing system without considering the order-writing system. If the relationships between applications are not considered, the data processing system for one application may be improved at the expense of the system for a related application.

Summary

1. The purpose of a data processing system is the collection, manipulation, and storage of data for reporting and analysis. To achieve this purpose, data is organized into files. Files consist of groups of associated records that pertain to one aspect of a business. Records are further subdivided into fields. Files of a permanent nature are called master files, while those of a temporary nature are referred to as detail files. File manipulation includes file creation, and adding, deleting, and updating records in the file.

2. The most common punched card has 12 rows and 80 columns. The zone rows are the 12-, 11-, and 0-rows; the digit rows are the 0- through 9-rows. When data is represented on a punched card, a specific field (group of card columns) is assigned to each item of data. In Hollerith code, a digit is represented by a single digit punch, a letter by the combination of a zone punch and a digit punch, and a special character by either one, two, or three punches in a column.

3. The 96-column punched card has 96 card columns. These columns are broken into three tiers, each having 32 columns. Each tier has six rows. The zone rows are the B- and A-rows; the digit rows are the 8-, 4-, 2-, and 1-rows. In the 96-column card code, a digit is represented by one or more holes in the digit rows, and a letter by a combination of holes in the zone and digit rows. A special character is represented by a combination of holes in the zone and digit rows (with one exception—a blank is represented by no punches in a column).

4. The common data processing applications are order writing (order entry), billing, accounts receivable, inventory control, sales analysis, accounts payable, payroll, and production control. These applications are closely associated with some of the basic operations of a company.

5. In the order-writing application, a document is prepared that can be used by the shipping department for picking and shipping the customer's order. This document is usually called the shipping order. In many industries, the speed of this application is very important because it determines in part how fast an order can be shipped.

6. Billing prepares the customer's bill (invoice) after the order has been shipped. Speed in billing is important because it affects the amount of money that is owed to the company.

7. In accounts receivable, monthly statements are prepared, records of customers' accounts are kept, and management information is pre-

pared. One common form of accounts receivable record is the ledger card. A common form of accounts receivable management information is a report called an Aged Trial Balance.

8. The goals in inventory control are to avoid stockouts and at the same time to keep down the amount of money invested in inventory. To meet both of these goals, an inventory-control system keeps inventory records and prepares management information. One useful type of inventory reporting is exception reporting.

9. The function of a sales analysis system is to prepare reports containing sales information. The importance of this application varies, depending on the size of the sales force, the number of products, and the number of sales offices within the company.

10. Although they are often talked about separately, the applications of a business are closely related—the source data and files for one are often used in others. Data base systems are being developed by companies because of this relationship.

System Analysis and Design

A *system* is an assembly of methods, procedures, and techniques united by regulated interaction to form an organized whole. In effect, it is an organized collection of people, machines, and methods required to accomplish a set of specified objectives. At any time and for any number of reasons, a company may decide that all or part of its data processing system must be improved. It is the responsibility of the *systems analyst* to produce a detailed description of what the present system does and then to complete an analysis of the procedures, techniques, and methods employed in the part of the data processing system under review. This work is commonly referred to as a *system study*.

If the company is large, a systems analyst (or systems department) within the company may conduct the system study to decide what changes to make. A smaller company may hire a consultant or a consulting firm to perform the function. In either case, the objective is to develop a plan for a system that will provide maximum speed, accuracy, and useful management information at minimum cost.

THE STEPS IN SYSTEM ANALYSIS AND DESIGN

Several steps must be taken to revise or design a system once it has been recognized that there is a need to do so. These generalized steps include: (1) analysis of the present system; (2) analysis of the various data processing methods available; (3) design of a new data processing system, including its forms, records, reports, files, and processing methods; and finally, (4) determination of implementation procedures for the system.

The first task of the systems analyst is to analyze what is taking place in the existing system. This is not as easy as it may sound. A data processing system can involve many people in several departments, working with dozens of documents and a variety of machines, ranging from typewriters to computers. Furthermore, written descriptions of what takes place are often incomplete or nonexistent. In this case, the systems analyst must obtain information by interviewing the people who actually do the processing in each application being analyzed.

Interviews do not always yield the information that the systems analyst needs. People who are interviewed may forget to mention important steps or be too concerned about minor details. They sometimes include long descriptions about irrelevant matters. In some cases, even managers of departments are not in a position to explain how particular operations relate to the data processing system as a whole.

In addition to conducting interviews, the systems analyst studies all of the documents used in the present system. These may be manually or machine-produced. The analyst studies the steps used to create the documents, noting the interrelationship of data processing equipment, personnel, and documents.

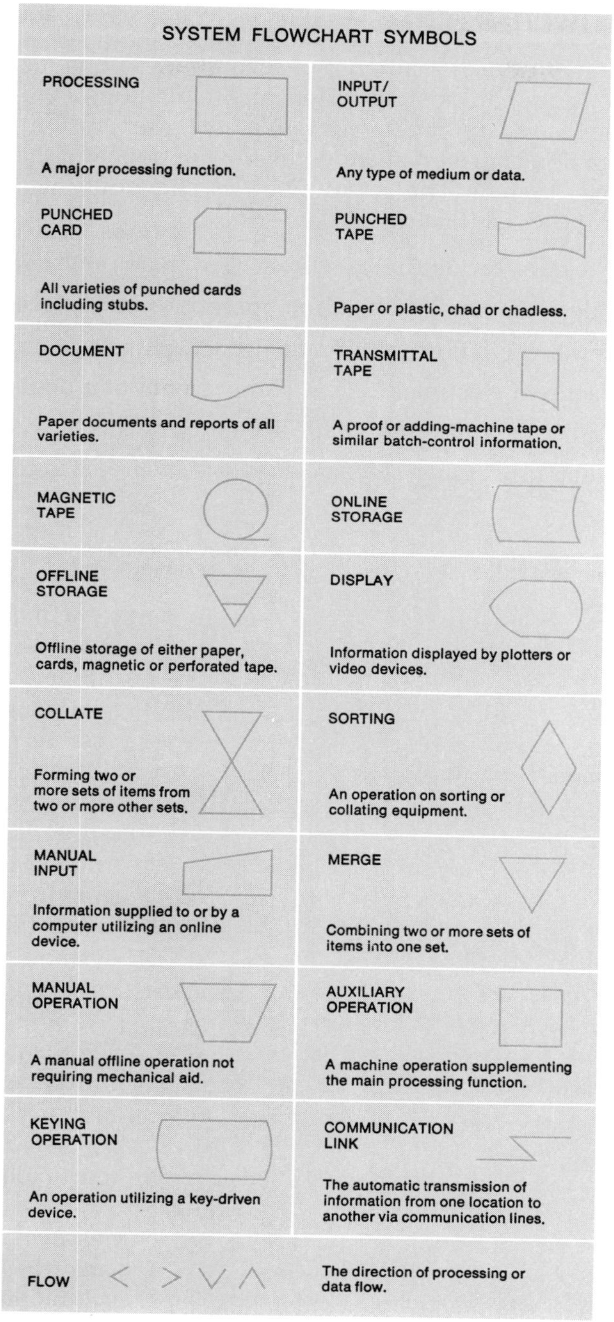

SYSTEM FLOWCHART SYMBOLS

PROCESSING	**INPUT/ OUTPUT**
A major processing function.	Any type of medium or data.
PUNCHED CARD	**PUNCHED TAPE**
All varieties of punched cards including stubs.	Paper or plastic, chad or chadless.
DOCUMENT	**TRANSMITTAL TAPE**
Paper documents and reports of all varieties.	A proof or adding-machine tape or similar batch-control information.
MAGNETIC TAPE	**ONLINE STORAGE**
OFFLINE STORAGE	**DISPLAY**
Offline storage of either paper, cards, magnetic or perforated tape.	Information displayed by plotters or video devices.
COLLATE	**SORTING**
Forming two or more sets of items from two or more other sets.	An operation on sorting or collating equipment.
MANUAL INPUT	**MERGE**
Information supplied to or by a computer utilizing an online device.	Combining two or more sets of items into one set.
MANUAL OPERATION	**AUXILIARY OPERATION**
A manual offline operation not requiring mechanical aid.	A machine operation supplementing the main processing function.
KEYING OPERATION	**COMMUNICATION LINK**
An operation utilizing a key-driven device.	The automatic transmission of information from one location to another via communication lines.
FLOW	The direction of processing or data flow.

Illustration 3-1. System flowchart symbols.

SYSTEM FLOWCHARTING

The systems analyst uses a number of techniques in organizing the mass of information about an existing system and in planning a new one. One of these techniques is system flowcharting, the preparation of diagrams (called *system flowcharts*) that show the flow of data and the sequence of operations in a system. The set of symbols commonly used on system flowcharts is shown in Illustration 3-1.

There are several forms that a system flowchart may take. One form specifies the departments in which the operations take place. Illustration 3-2 is an example. It is a flowchart for an order-writing system. The symbol ⬚ represents a document; ☐ represents a processing step (or operation); and ▽ represents a file. By studying this flowchart, one can determine what processing steps take place in preparing the shipping

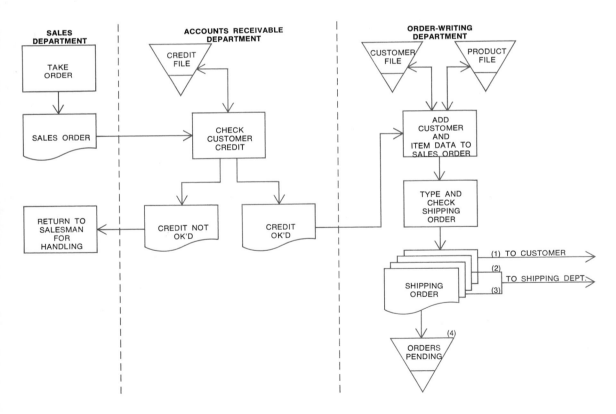

Illustration 3-2. System flowchart for order writing.

order, in what department each step takes place, where each document is sent, and what files are used.

Illustration 3-3 is an example of another form of system flowchart, showing the operations performed to produce a monthly sales report; it represents a system that uses a computer. The input is a deck of punched cards ⬛ that contains both customer cards and product cards. This deck is fed into the computer which then prepares the output document ⬛ in a processing step ⬛ . After the processing step (*run*) is completed, the deck of input cards is separated △ . The customer cards and product cards are returned to their respective card files ▽

One basic rule of flowcharting concerns direction. The sequence of data processing steps should proceed from top to bottom and from left to right. Arrowheads should be used on the lines connecting the symbols to indicate

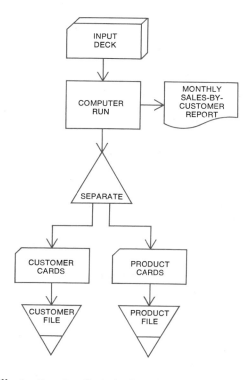

Illustration 3-3. System flowchart for sales analysis.

direction otherwise. In other words, one can assume that processing starts at the top (or left-hand corner) and goes down and to the right unless there are arrows that point up or to the left. This rule is especially important when designing or reading complex flowcharts.

The value of a flowchart is that it represents, by use of symbols, relationships that are difficult to present in words. For example, it is easy enough to understand what a single clerical worker does in preparing a shipping order, but it is not always easy to visualize where that single clerical step fits into an entire order-writing application. By preparing a flowchart like the one in Illustration 3-2, a systems analyst can show clearly that the application involves three departments, five separate clerical operations (the rectangles), and four different files (the triangles).

When the flowchart for a system is completed, the analyst can use it to analyze the relationships between the illustrated steps. The analyst can decide where errors might be taking place, whether or not some steps can be combined for greater efficiency, how interdepartment mailing can be reduced, and so on.

ALTERNATIVE WAYS OF PROCESSING DATA

Now the systems analyst is ready to tackle the problem of what equipment and procedures should be used in the new system. There are many different kinds of equipment that can be used in any application, and there are many different ways in which operations can be carried out. The analyst, therefore, has a large number of alternatives to choose from. Of course, many kinds of equipment can be immediately eliminated because of high cost or low capacity. A company that has gross monthly sales of $100,000 cannot afford a computer that rents for $5000 a month. A company that bills 10,000 items a day is not interested in a billing machine with a maximum capacity of 500 line items a day.

Even after satisfactory equipment is chosen, many alternative procedures must be considered. Can a checking step be eliminated without affecting the accuracy of the system? Can a procedure be improved by changing the sequence of steps? Can a processing step be simplified? Can the efficiency of a procedure be improved by combining steps? Because there are so many possible solutions to the problem of equipment and procedures, the systems analyst's job is a complex and continually challenging one.

THE RELATIONSHIPS BETWEEN APPLICATIONS

Another matter that concerns the systems analyst is the fact that applications in a business system are related. Because this is so, questions come up: Which applications in a family of applications should be analyzed? Should the systems analyst, in trying to improve the accuracy of a billing system, also consider the order-writing system? Should one also analyze the systems for accounts receivable and sales analysis? In fact, when considering any application, should one perhaps consider all related applications?

To analyze all applications every time one aspect of an application needs improvement is impractical. On the other hand, thinking in terms of only one specific improvement to only one specific application may be unjustifiably expensive.

Suppose the system flowchart in Illustration 3-4 represents a billing system that allows too many errors. The input to the system is the shipping order, after it has been used to pick the order and marked to show backorders and quantities shipped. The flowchart shows three processing steps: (1) the extensions and invoice totals are calculated and written on the shipping orders; (2) the arithmetic is checked; and (3) the invoices are typed. To pinpoint where errors are occurring, a number of shipping orders and corresponding invoices are studied. The study reveals that, although the calculations on the shipping orders are correct, errors frequently appear on the invoices. How can the accuracy of the system be improved?

By looking at the flowchart, the systems analyst can see that no checking is done to verify that the data on the invoice is typed correctly. This may indicate that one way to improve the system would be to add a comparison step after the typing of invoices. With this additional step, the data

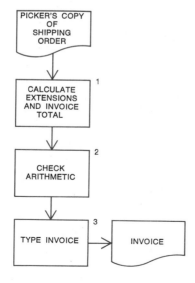

Illustration 3-4. System flowchart for billing.

on the invoice could be compared with the shipping order, and any data that was not the same on both forms could be corrected. This solution is reasonable and probably would reduce the number of inaccurate invoices.

A better solution could perhaps be designed by thinking not only of the billing system but also of the order-writing system. For example, when the shipping order was prepared, one copy of it could be filed for later use as the invoice. By using a copy of the shipping order as the invoice, such data as customer name and address, quantities ordered, and item description would not have to be retyped when the invoice was prepared. Then, when the order picker's copies of shipping orders were returned from the shipping department, the billing procedures could take place as flowcharted in Illustration 3-5.

In steps 1 and 2, the extensions and invoice totals are calculated, written on the shipping orders, and checked. In step 3, the invoice copies of the shipping orders are pulled from the file. Since these copies already contain much information, only the quantities shipped and back-ordered, the extensions, and the invoice totals are typed from the shipping orders (step 4). This procedure reduces typing time and decreases the chance of error in the billing system. Then in step 5, only this typed information need be checked, again saving clerical time and reducing the chance of error.

This example is not intended to indicate that a systems analyst should always think in terms of more than one application. It simply illustrates one of the problems of system design. When starting a job, an analyst has to determine how much time can be allotted for system analysis and take as broad a view as possible within that limitation.

EVALUATING ALTERNATIVES

After analyzing a business system by (1) using techniques such as flowcharting, (2) considering all varieties of equipment and procedures that could be used, and (3) taking into account the relationships between members of a family of applications, the systems analyst must evaluate the various alternative systems that could be used. All of them satisfy the objectives of the application; all vary in cost, speed, accuracy, and the amount of information they provide. The systems analyst's last job, then, is to decide which system is best for the company. This decision is influenced by two final considerations.

First, no single system will be the best in all respects. The most accurate one may not be the fastest. A system that is both fast and accurate may not provide sufficient management information. The one that provides the most usable information probably costs the most. A simple example is a manual system for sales analysis. For each additional report that management wants, additional procedures have to be designed. The result is that

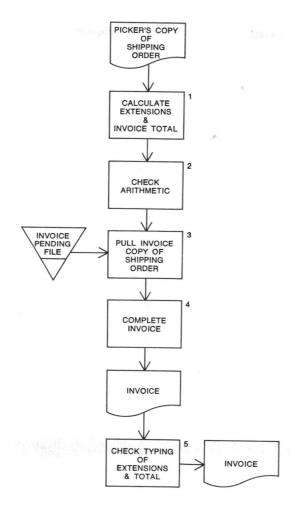

Illustration 3-5. Flowchart for alternative billing system.

each report increases the total cost of the sales analysis system. This trade-off between the qualities of a system holds true whether the system is manual or computerized.

Second, it is hard to measure the value of speed, accuracy, and information. The cost of a system is expressed in dollars, but the speed, accuracy, and information of a system can be converted to dollars only indirectly. A dollar value can be placed on the speed of a billing system by estimating how much will be saved by reducing the amount of money owed to the company. The accuracy of an order-writing system can be converted to dollars by estimating the effect of accuracy on customer service and therefore on sales. (That is, by answering such questions as: How many dollars in sales will be lost by inaccurate shipments? How many customers will be lost?) The information of a sales analysis system can be converted to dollars by estimating the effect of information on sales and therefore on profits.

After considering cost, and placing dollar values on the speed, accuracy, and information of each of the alternative systems, the systems analyst must decide which one is best. Remember, however, that the dollar values placed on speed, accuracy, and information are only estimates, and that they are arrived at indirectly. The merit of the analyst's decision depends to a large extent on how accurate these estimates are.

Summary

1. One of the first steps in system design is to analyze the system that is to be improved. This is often difficult because the system can consist of many people, many separate procedures, and many different kinds of equipment.

2. Flowcharting is a technique commonly used in system design and analysis. A system flowchart consists of symbols that represent the data flow and the operations performed. Flowcharts vary in form, depending on the purposes for which they are used, but all should be designed to be read from the top down and from left to right.

3. Many different kinds of equipment and procedures can be used in a business system. As a result, in designing a business system, the systems analyst has many alternatives from which to choose.

4. One of the major problems in designing a system is to determine how much of a family of applications should be analyzed. Since applications are related, it is often advantageous to look at the largest group of applications that can be analyzed in the time allotted to the project.

5. In choosing the best system from among a number of alternatives, a systems analyst assigns dollar values to the speed, accuracy, information, and cost of each alternative. This is difficult. It can be done by estimating the effect of each quality on operating costs and sales.

Management Information Systems

It has been shown in preceding chapters that the managers of an organization need accurate and timely information at a reasonable cost; only then can they insure that their organization operates profitably. It is essential that managers be provided this information. They need it to make effective and efficient decisions regarding the operation of their organizations. The function of management is to use available resources to accomplish the objectives of the organization. This requires that managers guide and direct the efforts of others. One of the key resources they need in doing so is information.

Computers have had a tremendous impact on both the methods of processing data and the analysis of it to provide information for decision making. As organizations first began to use computers to process data, they were likely to transfer many of the business applications discussed in Chapter 2 onto the computers. The way in which the application was processed was changed, but in many instances the information provided was not changed. Although the application was processed faster, more accurately, and at a lower cost, little, if any, additional management information was provided for decision making.

Managers who used the information provided by computer data processing systems began to make requests for additional information and for analysis of it for decision making. As these new demands were placed on the data processing systems, the characteristics of the systems began to change. More attention was placed on the analysis of data for decision making; less emphasis was placed on the collection of data and its organization solely for reporting purposes.

It is the objective of this chapter to examine the information needs of management and how management information systems can meet these needs.

THE NEED FOR MANAGEMENT INFORMATION

The computer has instigated significant changes in the techniques used by management to plan and control the activities of an organization. Managers who possess relevant information are better equipped to make decisions regarding the activities of the organization.

One of the most important processes in managing the activities of an organization is making decisions about alternatives. When the information available is not sufficient to make a decision, the manager needs to gather more information about the alternatives, compare them, and then choose an alternative. Decisions made without sufficient information are at best only estimates and typically lead to poor management performance. As shown in Illustration 4-1, quality information in the hands of those who can make good use of it supports appropriate management decision mak-

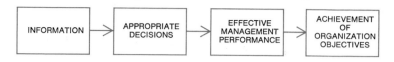

Illustration 4-1. The role of information.

ing. The resulting management performance should then lead to the successful achievement of the organizational objectives.

Thus, information is the common element that holds an organization together. The relationship of the information systems of an organization to the decision making within that organization is shown in Illustration 4-2.

What Information Is Needed?

What information is needed by the manager to manage effectively and efficiently? A basic need common to all managers is an understanding of the objectives of the organization. Individual managers differ in the manner in which they view information, in their analytical approaches in using it, and in their conceptual organization of the relevant facts. For this reason, the question of what information is needed by managers (be-

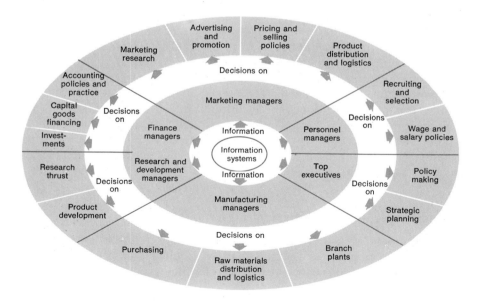

Illustration 4-2. The relationship of information to decision maki·

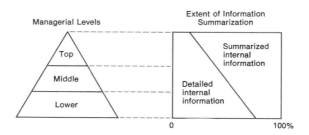

Illustration 4-3. Summarization of information by management level.

yond the basic informational requirements of every manager) can only be answered in broad, general terms.

The level of the manager in the organization is also a key factor in determining the kind of information that is needed in a specific managerial position. Lower-level management needs information with which to make daily decisions about the operations of the organization, since their activities are mainly control functions. At higher levels of management, concerns are more long-range and require summarization of information from a variety of sources within the information system of the organization. This relationship is shown in Illustration 4-3.

Top management needs information that summarizes trends and identifies whether the objectives of the organization are being met. The higher a person is in the management structure, the more likely he or she is to need and use information obtained from external sources (see Illustration 4-4). For example, a plant manager needs information to control operational activities such as production schedules and plant maintenance; the president of the company needs information to make decisions about the introduction of new products, the location of new plants, and the sources of new capital for expansion. The plant manager can obtain the information he or she needs from within the organization. The president needs to consider information from a number of external sources to make the decisions for which he or she is responsible.

Desired Properties of Management Information

Every organization is dependent upon information for its survival. In order for managers to take action that will yield effective results, they need information that is accurate, timely, complete, concise, and relevant. There is no assurance that the manager will use this type of information effectively; however, it must be available to be used. In most cases, the availability of information to a manager will have a strong influence on the rationale applied in decision making.

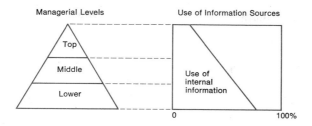

Illustration 4-4. Sources of information by management level.

Managers are often required to make decisions with information that lacks one or more of the properties above. This can have an undesirable impact on the effectiveness and efficiency of their decisions.

The *accuracy* of information is the ratio of correct information to total amount of information produced over a period of time. For example, if the monthly sales forecasts provided to a plant manager are not consistently accurate, it is difficult for the manager to make effective decisions concerning production schedules.

Timeliness of information is a reflection of whether or not the information arrives in time to be used by a manager in making a decision. The plant manager must receive the monthly sales forecast in time to make a decision about the monthly production schedule.

Completeness of information requires that a manager be provided with all of the information needed to make a decision. If sales forecasts cover only two-week periods, it is difficult to make decisions about monthly production schedules.

Conciseness of information is obtained through the summarization of relevant data. Such data may point out exceptions to normal or planned activities. A manager who receives concise information is saved a great deal of time otherwise spent in analysis of information for decision making. One type of summarization of information is provided in exception reports, as discussed in Chapter 1.

For information to be *relevant,* it must provide to each involved manager what he or she "needs to know." Information should not be given to a manager who does not have the authority to make the decision(s) which should be based on the information.

DISTINCTION BETWEEN A DATA PROCESSING SYSTEM AND A MANAGEMENT INFORMATION SYSTEM

In Chapter 1, the data processing functions of data collection, manipulation, and storage as used to report and analyze business activities were discussed. The data processing system is oriented primarily to processing transactions for day-to-day operations. The transactions include sales orders, shipping orders, inventory orders, and payroll data. For most of these transactions, routine procedures can be established and carried out repetitively to do the processing required. The procedures become part of the data processing system.

A management information system (MIS) performs substantial functions beyond those of a data processing system. The MIS involves a man/machine system that provides information for managers to use as they perform their managerial functions of planning, organizing, staffing, directing, and controlling. Such a system supports basic transaction processing as does a data processing system. It also provides information about the past, present, and future (forecasts) as each relates to the operations within the organization and within its environment.

A data processing system is not necessarily an MIS. Two major distinctions between these types of systems are: (1) the characteristics of the information they require, and (2) the decisions that are made, based on this information. Illustration 4-5 summarizes these differences.

THE INFORMATION THAT AN MIS PROVIDES

An MIS that functions properly processes and analyzes data to provide, in particular, *planning* and *control* information that supports the decision-making role of management.

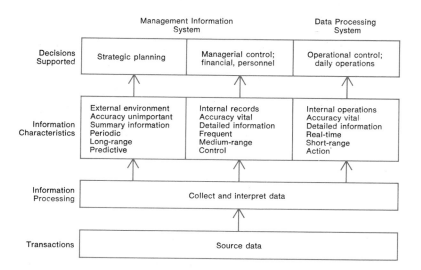

Illustration 4-5. A comparison of data processing and management information systems.

Information for Planning

Information for planning is needed at the strategic, tactical, and operational levels. The long-range or strategic planning in an organization involves making decisions about long-range objectives, and setting policies to meet them. Tactical planning involves securing resources and using them in an effective manner to reach these objectives. Operational planning involves determining the actual short-range tasks that must be performed. Lower-level managers are primarily concerned with operational planning. The types of information they need are more limited than those of managers at higher levels who are doing tactical or strategic planning.

The basic types of information needed for planning are environmental, competitive, and internal. Therefore, planning information comes from three basic sources: (1) within the organization, (2) the competition, and (3) other environmental sources.

Organizational information is obtained internally from both the formal information system and informal sources. This internal information must describe the organization in enough detail so that the planner is aware of both the strengths and the weaknesses of the organization as it relates to the competition and to the environment.

Competitive information should indicate the nature of competing organizations—their past, present, and expected future activities. Such information about the competition can be obtained from a number of sources that are available to the general public. These include annual reports, product announcements, statements accompanying additional stock and bond issues, and public statements by company officials.

Environmental information should take into account the factors in the economy, the government, and the society which may impact the organization. Governmental regulations, such as health and safety standards for new plants, minimum wage legislation, and tax rates, are factors that often need to be considered in planning. Economic trends and forecasts, and changes in societal trends in education, age, and mobility, may also be essential information for planning.

All three of these types of information should be available through a management information system intended to support planning at the strategic, tactical, and operational levels.

Management Control Information

In order for a management control system to be effective, it must be based on a plan that can be used as a standard. Then, any variances from the plan can be identified and corrected. The system that provides information for management must be able to measure and report the performance of the organization compared to the plan. Periodic performance reports are typically provided by a data processing system for this purpose. In addition to periodic reporting, exception reports should be provided on an as-needed basis, whenever immediate action is required.

THE CONCEPT OF AN MIS

There is no universal agreement as to what constitutes an MIS; however, it is generally agreed that an MIS can only be supported with a modern computer system that has ample storage capacity. The concept of an MIS is not new, but MIS has been successfully implemented in business organizations only in the past several years. Generally, these are organizations whose size allows them to acquire the medium-size or large computer system needed to support an MIS.

An MIS, then, is a computer-based system that provides both routine data processing of transactions and the information required for management control of the organization in an integrated manner. There have been attempts to create *total* management information systems. Because of the complexity of and resources required for such a task, few, if any, organizations have achieved this objective.

No system is static. As time passes, the usage of and requirements imposed on an MIS necessarily change. Thus, a total MIS is difficult, if not impossible, to achieve.

No system planners can anticipate all future management information needs, either next year or five years from now. The ways in which managers provide and use information also change over time and as the individuals change. This human element is another reason why the concept of a total MIS will probably remain primarily a concept.

An organization is more likely to install an MIS that falls short of a total MIS, yet meets most of the needs of management for planning, controlling, and decision making. Such a system should provide for a data base, comprehensive data, analysis capabilities, and models. Operationally, it would provide for file definition, file maintenance, transaction and inquiry processing, periodic and exception reporting, and maintenance of accurate and secure files.

As indicated in Chapter 1, a data base is a structured set of related files. Generally, groups of files within the data base are linked by some common characteristic such as a social security number. When an MIS is implemented, several related data bases are often linked into one organizational data base (Illustration 4-6). An organization may have only one data base that includes all of its files. However, it is more common to find several data bases within an organization that has established a computer-based MIS.

Illustration 4-6. An MIS data base.

Within an MIS, a single transaction can cause the updating of all related data base files at one time. For example, the recording of a credit sale may also automatically update the accounts receivable file, the inventory stock file, the shipping order file, and the product sales file. An MIS data base should reduce the amount of data kept repetitively—that is, duplicated in two or more of these files. It should also insure that the data is current since all related files are updated whenever a transaction affecting them occurs.

To access an MIS data base effectively, a *data base management system* is used. The data base management system is a series of computer programs that handle the complex tasks associated with creating, accessing, and maintaining the data base. These computer programs must provide the instructions necessary for the computer to handle the manipulation of the data. (Computer programs will be discussed in greater detail in a later chapter.)

Comprehensive data is required as input, to make it possible for the MIS to provide the planning, control, and decision-making information needed by management as output. The characteristics and sources of this data were noted previously. In addition to being able to extract data from the data base, the MIS should be able to perform statistical and related analyses as required by managers. Management often has a need to evaluate alternative plans of action or strategies. *Modeling* allows the imitation of an event, a process, or an object that must be studied prior to the making of a management decision. Models can help reduce the uncertainty in decision making. A large number of alternatives can be tried using a computer-based model to simulate the results that could occur for each alternative. A model simulates an event, a process, or an object that would otherwise be too costly or time-consuming to create. For instance, if an organization is considering a change in employee retirement plans, it can simulate the operation of a number of plans over a number of years to determine the costs of each plan. Management considering a new plant can simulate its operation in a number of different locations in the country. This simulation may represent the operation of the plant over a number of years considering such factors as availability and cost of labor, utility rates, shipping facilities, tax rates, and climate. Computer modeling is often referred to as *simulation*.

MIS AS SEEN BY THE USER

The primary users of a computer-based MIS are identified in Illustration 4-7. The routine processing accomplished by clerical personnel is least affected by the installation of an MIS. They will collect and record essentially the same transaction data. Some additional data collection will be necessary to support the expanded functions of the MIS. Much of the data is likely to be collected, using procedures for data editing and validation to increase accuracy.

Most levels of personnel in the organization will be required to provide more data for use in the MIS. In return, they should be able to obtain more information, including support for special reports. The information should be obtainable in a more accurate and timely manner. The data provided by each of the departments in the organization will no longer be considered the possession of that department. The user will have to recognize that the data belongs to the entire organization. The user should also understand that the data will be used at many levels in the organization.

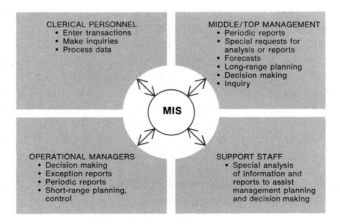

Illustration 4-7. Primary uses of an MIS by organizational staff.

Organizational Function Subsystems

The MIS of an organization is generally viewed as a federation of information systems. This view has been accepted for several reasons.

First, management information systems are developed around the functions to be managed. A distinct function is often the basis for the creation of an information system (subsystem) to meet the information needs of the managers of the function. The managers of the function have the responsibility for defining and collecting the information necessary in the subsystem and for insuring its accuracy as it is entered into the organizational data base.

Second, many of the information systems in use prior to the introduction of a computer-based MIS were developed primarily for the functional areas that had to be managed. Thus, in many instances, the structures of these systems (now, in effect, subsystems) are incorporated into the MIS as it is developed.

The relationship between the functional subsystems of an organization and the organizational data base is shown in Illustration 4-8. Depending on the size and complexity of the organization, the subsystems may be divided further into component subsystems. For any of the subsystems, the data base management system is the link between the user and the information the user needs from the data base.

DESIGN OF THE MIS

Much of what was discussed in Chapter 3 concerning systems analysis and design of data processing systems can be applied in designing an MIS. Although the subject is quite complex and is often the topic of an entire book, two approaches to MIS design are identified here. There is

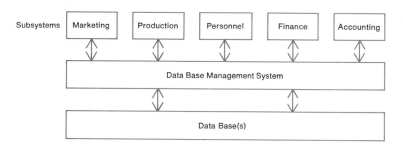

Illustration 4-8. Functional subsystems of an MIS.

no single, agreed-upon method or procedure for designing an MIS; however, both top-down design and bottom-up design have been used extensively.

Top-Down Design

The key to this method of designing an MIS is top management involvement. The objectives of the organization are the basis for planning and designing the subsystems needed within the organization. Top management is deeply involved in this approach to MIS design to insure that all of the information needed to meet organizational objectives is identified and provided. Thus, the overall system information needs are considered first. Then the design of the various subsystems and data bases proceeds, to meet these needs. Subsystems are further subdivided as necessary until each individual data processing application is identified and designed. The necessary files are also designed at this time.

Bottom-Up Design

In designing an MIS using this approach, the common business applications are identified and developed first. These include the applications discussed in Chapter 2, which are required for the daily operation of the organization. Identification and design of the subsystems can be started after the applications are designed. Then the interrelationship of the subsystems is established, through the data base. This design process is continued until the highest-level planning and control applications are designed. A bottom-up approach allows for the orderly development and implementation of the MIS, with the first emphasis placed on basic applications that can provide the most immediate benefit to the organization.

INSTALLATION OF THE MIS

The actual installation of the computer system to support the MIS will extend over a long period of time. Progressing from the initial planning stages of the MIS through the actual installation of the computer to support the system may take from one to two years. In most organizations, the changes in processing methods and the need for data base capability necessitate replacing an existing computer with one capable of supporting the MIS. The computer that is selected should not only be capable of supporting the MIS that is being designed but also allow for future expansion of it.

The normal procedure that is followed in selecting a computer system is to develop specifications for the processing capabilities needed by the system and some minimum equipment specifications to meet those needs. Computer vendors are then invited to submit proposals for computer systems that will meet the specifications. Often the proposed systems are tested prior to a selection being made. These tests are called *benchmarks*. They usually include performance testing, to insure that the computer system proposed by the vendor is capable of meeting all performance requirements stated in the specifications.

After a computer has been selected, it must be installed and personnel trained to operate it. At this point, the process of computer system conversion and implementation begin. Often, processing on the old computer system is continued as usual until the new computer system has been tested thoroughly. Both computers are run in parallel, and their processing results are compared. For example, the monthly payroll may be run on both computers and the processing results checked to see if they are the same.

OPERATION AND CONTROL OF THE MIS

It has been shown above that an MIS should be designed to provide for all of the activities needed to establish and maintain files, for transaction and inquiry processing, and for periodic and exception reporting.

Files must be defined, established, and maintained so that the MIS can provide the proper data and information in an organized and controlled manner. When defining a file, its use and the source of the data within it should be considered. What other files, if any, will be associated with the file? Will these files be linked together by some common characteristic? The organization of the file should make the data within it easily obtainable for its expected use. The data should be retrievable in a meaningful manner.

After files have been defined and established, the processing of transactions or management requests results in data's being entered into or retrieved from the files. It is important that this data be accurate. Further, access to the data should be restricted to those who have the need and the authority to use it. It has already been established that accurate data entry is an extremely important step in any data processing system. Once data has been recorded and verified for its accuracy, it may be used many times within an MIS. Proper control procedures should be included in an MIS to insure the accuracy of all data entered into any files and to prevent unauthorized use of the files.

It is likely that a variety of persons within the organization will access the MIS at some level. Clerks will be responsible for entering data; managers will make inquiries for decision making; and data processing personnel will maintain and operate the system. Many of these users will communicate directly with the computer through *terminals* located throughout the organization. A typical terminal is a device with a keyboard similar to that of a typewriter. It usually has some type of display capability, either a screen similar to a television screen or printer type of output. (See Module A for further discussion of terminals.)

Because terminals make it easy for users to access the MIS, internal controls within the MIS must limit this access to the appropriate levels. For example, an inventory clerk should not be able to access the payroll file or the personnel file from a terminal.

Transaction and inquiry processing are generally associated with clerical personnel. An airline reservation clerk may make an inquiry to determine the availability of an airline seat. If a seat is available, the clerk may record the reservation (enter a transaction). A telephone sales clerk may record sales transactions phoned in by customers.

Management is likely to use the inquiry capability of the MIS to obtain information that is needed immediately. A sales manager interested in determining whether or not any salesperson has reached the weekly sales quota may use a terminal to request this information. Thus, it is possible for management to obtain information through inquiry processing that would otherwise require the preparation and subsequent analysis of a report. Often, a complete report is not needed by management. Rather, the answer to some specific questions is wanted. The MIS should be able to provide this type of inquiry information in a usable form and within a short time period.

Periodic reporting provides management with information that is needed on a regular basis for decision-making purposes. It is the responsibility of managers to identify the reports they need and the information required on the reports. These reports must be supplied on a timely basis so that they can be used to full advantage in the decision-making process.

Exception reports have been discussed previously, so they need not be discussed again here. However, it should be noted that the MIS should be designed to provide these reports automatically—that is, whenever an exception condition needing management attention is sensed by the system.

THE BEHAVIORAL SIDE OF THE MIS

One of the major problems encountered in the design and implementation of an MIS is the acceptance and cooperation of the personnel who will interact with the system. An MIS is not installed without top management support. This may not be the case with lower levels of management and other operating personnel. Each level of personnel within the organization participates in the design and operation of the MIS and is affected in a different way by it. How each of these groups perceives its relationship to the MIS influences its success or failure. People resist change, especially if they suspect that they will be adversely affected by it. Change is necessary when an MIS is implemented. Changes usually occur in the structure of the organization and in the functions of the personnel. How disruptive these changes seem to personnel affects the degree of acceptance and support they give the MIS.

Personnel who believe their jobs may be threatened are likely to offer the most resistance to the implementation of the MIS. Clerical workers are least likely to feel threatened, while middle managers are most likely to feel that their jobs are threatened.

A positive program of educating personnel about the MIS and how it will affect them can have a tremendous impact on the support they give it. Personnel who have any direct contact with the MIS should clearly understand the purpose and characteristics of the system as it affects them. Those who are influenced by the MIS are more likely to support it if they feel that they have participated in its design.

How will personnel react if they do not support the implementation of the MIS? Few will attempt sabotage, but some cases have been reported. Clerical personnel responsible for entering data into the MIS may not do so accurately. Middle management may resist using the information provided by the MIS and rely on other sources instead. In some cases personnel will resist supporting the MIS regardless of the steps taken to encourage them to do so. These personnel should be identified and removed from positions where they can impact the performance of the MIS.

EVALUATION OF THE MIS

Formal evaluation of the installed MIS should continue as an ongoing project. The evaluation of the MIS can be performed in a variety of ways and at several levels within the organization. The evaluation should assess: (1) the technical performance of the hardware and software; (2) the utilization of the MIS by the management in the organization; (3) the effectiveness of the various subsystems in achieving the stated MIS design objectives; and (4) the cost/benefit provided. The evaluation of the MIS should be conducted either by a committee of middle and top management, or by a group of information systems personnel and management. Management representing the major MIS subsystems or functions must be involved in the evaluation. They are best able to assess whether or not the MIS is meeting their information needs. In any case, the group needs the technical support of information systems personnel. In some instances outside consultants may be used in the evaluation process.

The hardware and software supporting the MIS should be reviewed to determine whether or not they are meeting the objectives of the MIS in the most effective manner. Included in this evaluation should be an examination of the utilization levels of the hardware and software and of their reliability.

The extent that managers are using the current MIS can be determined by: the number of reports they request, the number of terminal inquiries that are made, the ratings they place on the value of information supplied, and the frequency of its use. Managers should be asked to determine whether the MIS meets the design objectives specified for their subsystems or functions. Suggestions and recommendations for system improvements should also be requested. Interviews with clerical and other support personnel should be conducted to uncover problems if it is determined that the MIS does not meet the specified design objectives. These problems may include faulty systems design and personnel problems related to both systems design and implementation.

The cost/benefit analysis of the proposed MIS considered expected costs of the system and anticipated savings in relation to the benefits provided by it. This same cost/benefit proposal can now be used for a comparison with the actual costs and benefits being experienced.

Summary

1. Management needs accurate, timely, complete, concise, and relevant information. It helps them to make decisions—to be effective in achieving the objectives of the organization. Lower-level managers typically need short-range control information to make decisions about the daily functions of the organization. Higher-level management needs summary information that indicates whether or not objectives of the organization are being met. The sources of information for low-level management are primarily within the organization. Higher-level management requires information from external sources also.

2. A management information system differs from a data processing system in that the former emphasizes the information needed for decision making, while the latter emphasizes the processing of daily transactions. An organization functions through transactions, which it must process to carry out its day-to-day activities. The payroll must be prepared; sales must be recorded; and payments on account must be recorded. These data processing activities are clerical in nature. They follow rather standard procedures. The computer is useful for these clerical data processing tasks. An MIS includes this transaction processing. It also provides information about the past, present, and future (forecasts) as each relates to the decision-making environment of the organization.

3. An MIS should provide planning and control information to support management decision making. Planning information is needed at the strategic, tactical, and operational levels. Planning information can be identified as environmental, competitive, and internal.

4. An MIS is a computer-based system that supports managerial decision making through a data base, comprehensive data, analysis capabilities, and models. In its operation, it must provide for the definition of files that are accurate, secure, and maintainable; transaction and inquiry processing; and periodic and exception reports.

5. A data base is a series of integrated files containing the data needed by an organization for its operation. An organization may have one data base containing all of its files. It is more likely to have several data bases for this purpose. Often, some common characteristics of the files in the data base are used to link the files together for access purposes.

6. A data base is created, accessed, and maintained through a series of computer programs called a data base management system.

7. The MIS of an organization is often viewed as a federation of information systems. Each of these can be considered a subsystem that is a part of the MIS.

8. Many approaches have been taken in designing an MIS. The top-down and bottom-up approaches are often used. The former places emphasis on top management involvement in the planning process to insure the MIS reflects the objectives of the organization. The latter approach emphasizes the development of the lowest-level processing applications first; it leaves the building of the higher levels of the system until later.

9. Prior to installation of an MIS, an organization should consider the effect the MIS will have on personnel, such as creating new jobs and eliminating others, and requirements for training. The installation of the computer system to support the MIS will occur several years after the MIS is first planned. Computer selection tasks include the development of specifications, evaluation of computer vendors' responses to specifications, and computer capability testing.

10. Terminals are likely to provide a major part of the access to the MIS, both to process transactions that occur and to make inquiries for management information. The MIS should provide the periodic reports needed by management and exception reports to identify problems that need management attention.

11. The success of an MIS in an organization is directly related to the support that the personnel are willing to give it. Personnel will generally support the implementation of an MIS to the extent that they feel: (1) they have participated in its design as it affects them; (2) they have been clearly and honestly informed about its implementation; and (3) their jobs are not threatened by it.

12. The evaluation of an installed MIS should be a continuous process. A formal evaluation committee or group should be established, and it should include representation from top management. The evaluation process should assess the technical performance of the hardware and software, the management utilization of the MIS, whether the MIS meets design objectives, and the cost/benefit provided.

CHAPTER 5

Management Information Systems Applications

I n the preceding chapter, the information needs of management were discussed. The use of a management information system to meet these needs was proposed. There are several hundred thousand business computer systems in operation today. The processing capabilities of these computer systems vary. Some provide only the basic transaction processing needed in day-to-day business activities (data processing). Others encompass an integrated MIS that provides both transaction processing and management information.

The objective of this chapter is twofold: (1) to present a timely journal article that summarizes and reinforces the material of Chapter 4, and (2) to discuss three management information systems.

The article discusses research findings and practical business experiences related to management information systems. The characteristics of management information systems are discussed first. This discussion is followed by an examination of data management, data independence, and the structure of MIS. Finally, behavioral and organizational principles involving employee resistance to the development of MIS, user and management involvement in MIS development activities, and the integration of MIS into the organization are discussed. Thus, this article provides a reinforcement of the material discussed in Chapter 4 and a framework for discussing the three examples presented in this chapter.

The first two MIS examples are relatively brief. Each serves primarily as an indicator of how MIS can be used in a representative, current business environment. The third example is a case study. It looks in depth at the design, development, and implementation of an MIS by a large state university system.

ESSENTIAL PRINCIPLES OF INFORMATION SYSTEMS DEVELOPMENT*

By James A. Senn

The use of computer-based management information systems (MIS) to support managerial decision making has increased significantly since computers were introduced into the business community during the 1950's. The realization of a number of distinguishing characteristics of MIS has come with this increase in use and investigation of computer-based systems. These characterisitcs form the basis for an emerging set of very fundamental and basic principles of systems development for management information systems.

*This section is reprinted by permission from James A. Senn, "Essential Principles of Information Systems Development," *MIS Quarterly*, Volume 2, Number 2 (June, 1978), pp. 17–26.

This discussion presents and examines some MIS development principles and characteristics as we know them today. Many are drawn from experiences that organizations have had developing and using these systems while others are based on research findings through both field studies and laboratory experiments. While this report draws together knowledge about MIS principles, it is hoped that the basic set will be expanded substantially as the field continues to grow and mature.

Background

One of the problems in dealing with the subject of management information systems is that in the past there has been no agreement on exactly what the term means. The Society for Management Information Systems has examined this problem in depth and has developed an extensive list of the various ways the term has been defined [16, 38].

The primary emphasis of MIS is that of providing decision support to management as contrasted with mere transaction processing to replicate clerical functions. Throughout this discussion the term MIS will be used when referring to decision-oriented activities and data processing or transaction processing systems will imply clerical activities. The important point to remember is that MIS is aimed at more than replication of clerical processing of data.

An information system is organized, it condenses and filters data until it becomes information for use in decision making at various levels of the organization. Ideally an MIS should provide outputs that are reliable, timely, and accurate to support making decisions. Today this frequently involves the use of computer systems. However, an information system does *not* presume computer processing. Instead, it requires a system that can deliver the necessary information for management in a timely fashion at a reasonable cost. In many instances, information may be transmitted as either an oral or written report. Some manual systems may produce information on a routine basis at fixed time intervals, perhaps monthly or quarterly, and sometimes the information may be produced on request as study results based on a special analysis.

The important point to recognize is that systems for clerical processing have quite different purposes from systems for providing information for management decision making, and that systems of either type need not involve computer processing. Despite the fact that important differences exist between the two, there is definitely a relationship. Efficient clerical systems are vital to the operation of large, highly complex organizations. Frequently these systems form the basis for organizational information systems [23]. An organization may have many clerical systems, parts of which provide inputs to a management information system.

Based on these fundamental realizations, it is logical to conceive of a management information system as

> " . . . an organized method of providing past, present and projection information relating to internal operations and external intelligence. It supports the planning, control and operational functions of an organization by providing uniform information in the proper time-frame to assist the decision making process."[25]

We can begin to assemble technical and developmental, and behavioral factors from this common definition that should be guidelines for development and use of computer-based management information systems.

Technical and Developmental Factors

The technical and developmental factors associated with information systems focus on the structure of the components comprising the system. They also deal with the role of data and how it is managed within the system framework.

A federation of information systems   The views of the MIS model in the literature and among practitioners in industry and government have generally taken one of two forms. The early view was one of MIS as a total, global system carefully integrated into all parts of the firm. The system was monolithic in form under this philosophy, where formal information networks were interrelated by conscious design *before* implementation. The underlying assumptions were that managers' information needs could be identified and/or anticipated, as could the ways in which such information might be used. As a result, the total systems approach is based on the thought that it is appropriate to define explicitly the proper information flows to management and then to design a system that would assume the continual support of these flows.

One of the most disconcerting factors underlying the global concept was the fact that system expectations, requirements, and use change as the MIS exists over time. Hence what might be considered a total system today most likely will be only a partial system tomorrow. Similarly, it is somewhat naive to assume that it is possible for one person or one group of managers and experts to design a total or global MIS, to develop effective boundaries and interfaces with the various organizational systems, and to integrate *the* system into the management stream.

Out of dissatisfaction with the global view came a more workable framework for MIS development. This view distinguishes an MIS as being dependent on lower level activities in the firm because it draws upon and integrates information from the several functional area information systems, such as the marketing information system and the production information system, to provide a uniform body of details and knowledge for uncertainty reduction in decision making.

Speaking directly to this issue, Terrance Hanold, Past Chairman of the Executive Committee of The Pillsbury Company and an Honorary Founder of SMIS, indicates that:

> "As distinguished from an information system, I conceive of a management information system to consist of a cluster of business information systems ... MIS is a symbol rather than a descriptive name, which designates an integrated complex of information systems of such variety and sophistication and interrelationship as experience qualified by rational assessment determines to be essential or useful to the general or excutive management of the business enterprise."[22]

Herbert Schwartz, while at the U.S. Atomic Energy Commission, used essentially the same framework and context for development of the MIS:

> "The management information system for an entire organization must be visualized as a supersystem of systems, as a federation of management information systems. Only the most monolithic of organizations can build and gain strength from a single total system ... The federation should be structured as a set of systems, each system tightly integrated internally, but only loosely integrated when taken together."[34]

The same view is repeatedly expressed in the literature of the field.

This approach enables specialists to collect the information that they are best trained to gather. The accountant should be concerned with the collection of accounting information, the financial specialist should focus on the collection of financial knowledge, and so forth. Each has the training in a particular area of knowledge and should be more proficient in these activities than one with background in another area of the firm. Interchange of the information can then be accomplished to ensure that each functional area receives the information that it requires from other areas. We will focus on this aspect more in the following sections on management of data. But, the principle of these systems is that *a management information system is a federation of functional area information systems.*

Data as the center of MIS   The central resource in a management information system is data. Initial reaction to such a statement is often that it is an obvious fact that does not merit comment. However, past and present activities of some organizations involved with MIS seems to indicate that this principle is not always operationalized.

Data should be the central resources in an MIS since they provide the base from which processing takes place to develop the information needed for managerial decision making. Emphasis should be placed on data as opposed to hardware and software. We saw an era in which the attention of systems developers and users was focused on hardware and software during the early days of computer-based systems. The focus in many instances was on acquiring more and more computer power and larger machines. Much attention was also devoted to the development of a diversity of unique languages and software systems [32]. This was the day of the super-salesman, the glass-enclosed computer palace, and the aura of "gee whiz" systems [39]. Data almost seemed to play a secondary role as everything revolved around the hardware and software.

As applications grew in sophistication, so too did a large portion of the users. Many persons came to realize that the data that these machines processed is the key to success. The data for business applications was recognized as a resouce of the firm and thus came to be controlled and managed. As more and more users came into the information systems arena, they too placed their emphasis on data rather than on hardware or software. Data became the resource and hardware and software the tools— almost a complete reversal from the early days. Requirements for an improved level of technology came with the increased emphasis on data that allowed the users to gain the support they wanted without the need for large scale purchases of equipment or development of applications software. Thus the new view of data's place in the organization led to developements such as terminals and database management systems. These developments in effect de-emphasize hardware and software, even while they advanced the state of the art, and reinforce the central nature and importance of data. Manufacturers and vendors, however, do not always want us to view the world through these eyes; therefore, there are many camps that still do not pay proper respect to the role of data in computer-based information systems. We will see this more in the next section on databases. However, these is little question for the majority of persons involved with MIS that *data is the central resource in effective management information systems.*

The database in MIS   The database is at the foundation of an MIS. It is the primary factor in a collection of information systems that enables integration of the various business information systems, thereby providing uniform knowledge to managers and decision makers throughout the organization. Since the basic underlying purpose of an MIS requires that the information be drawn from throughout the enterprise, it follows that the database should cut across organizational lines. A database, in other words, can be viewed as *more than* the ordinary collection of all data stored for one or more related computer-based application programs. It is visualized as a generalized, common, integrated collection which fulfills the data requirements of all application programs which must access it. Additionally, the data within this entity must be structured to model the natural data relationships that exist in an organization [33].

It should be pointed out, however, that the database does not contain all the data used in an organization. Various functional areas maintain files of data that are not needed by other parts of the enterprise. A record, however, should be maintained along with the database indicating where these "outside" files exist.

A high volume of data enters the database from throughout the organization. Each department or division provides data and information for storage and use by other parts of the company. A large number of forms for the data typically are found in the input stream, because of the diversity of data sources. Yet if the database truly is intended to serve to integrate and interface the various functional areas as well as to provide support to corporate-level management, a certain amount of control needs to be placed over entering data. Haphazard recording of facts will result in service to no one and to eventual degradation of the database to the extent that it is used by few persons. Incoming data should conform to a predetermined definition of form and should be stored according to precise rules. Data that does not match the definition should not be allowed to enter the database.

The issue of data exchange or data use is an important one in that it should be feasible through the database to provide uniform information across functional area lines. That is, two managers requesting information on sales volume, for example, should receive the *same picture* of the state of sales, regardless of the area of the organization in which they are located. Further, although the form of the information may vary, e.g., sales in dollars versus sales in product units, the picture portrayed through the data should remain constant.

Control of the database is an important aspect of MIS activities. An equally important factor, however, is the assurance that the data will be available when it is needed. It must be remembered that the database will change over time due to the nature of incoming facts and because of demands which users make on it. As this resource is in existence, users' reliance will increase assuming that it is properly designed, and they will expect more extensive support from it. Consequently, the database itself must be adaptable to the demands made on it. This capability is referred to as *evolvability* [20].

In general, the database plays a central role in management information systems. This is to say that *the database is at the foundation of an MIS and makes possible integration of the business information systems. It must be controlled and used as a management resource to ensure reliability, integrity, and evolvability.*

Data independence   There needs to be a certain amount of independence between the way data is stored and the way different users intend to deal with it in a certain application. Conflicts frequently can arise between storage structures (the way the data is physically stored on devices and media) and data structures (the way each user views the data he or she needs). What may be the most efficient organization of data in stored form may not be best in terms of the data structures of the individual users. Yet the system should be able to accommodate user requirements while still physically dealing with the data in the most efficient manner. In addition, one user should be able to adjust his or her requirements without causing a change in the way data is stored. In turn, it should be possible to restructure the database when it is necessary because of new organization-wide requirements or because of improvements in computer-related technology. The restructuring efforts should not affect the users or their applications.

We do not yet have the means to accomplish all facets of this objective, but it is clear that *independence between the stored versions of the data and the requirements of each individual user should be sought whenever possible.*

Lifestream systems First, attention in MIS development needs to be given to the basic underlying system activities in the firm, i.e., the "business of the firm." Establishment of systems to support these functions, such as sales order processing, accounting, and purchasing, is important because of the sheer volume of activities in each of these areas, implying that potential cost savings can be realized if automation leads to more effective performance levels. In addition, the high level of understanding of the tasks performed in these areas usually means minimal difficulty in including them within the overall MIS framework.

Ease of conversion is not the only reason for giving priority to development of lifestream systems. Organizations may experience cost savings and higher levels of profits or revenue by decreasing the time devoted to basic transaction-oriented systems, and coupling this with improved accuracy and increased volume [13]. However, it is also essential that transaction data from these activities be captured for inclusion in the database. The combination of cost savings, increased volume of processing, and improved data capture lead to the conclusion that *first attention in the development of management information systems should be given to the firm's basic lifestream systems.*

Information system structure Information system analysts and users typically have been concerned with *what information* should be provided to the user or decision maker and into which report it should be incorporated. It is, however, also necessary to focus on being able to provide information that is appropriate to the characteristics of both the decision maker and the decision task. Information system structure consists of characteristics of the person, the decision environment, and the information system, each of which has an impact on various measures of decision effectiveness [17]. Mason and Mitroff developed a similar framework which indicated a need to focus on the individual decision maker, the problem being examined, the organizational context, and a mode of presentation for the necessary information [28]. The information structure in both frameworks is believed to have an impact on various measures of performance and decision effectiveness.

A series of experiments, The Minnesota Experiments, was conducted to determine whether or not the above beliefs appear valid [9, 17, 35]. Each of the nine experiments in the series examined various aspects of the decision support problem. The evidence from these efforts strongly suggests that a relationship exists between information system structure and decision effectiveness. It appears that information requirements and related requirements may vary with changes in form or media of information, but performance levels may not necessarily be affected. The studies also appear to confirm Ackoff's previously published beliefs that more information need not lead to improved performance and that the manager may not need the information he or she wants [1, 31].

Consequently, system designers and users alike should pay close attention to the structure they adopt for management information system efforts. It appears that it is possible to improve information system efficiency without decreasing decision effectiveness: *the structure of a management information system significantly impacts managerial decision effectiveness.*

Behavior and Organization Development Factors

Too often in developing systems *the people* in the system are overlooked and an inordinate amount of attention is given to the technical factors. It is essential that systems people consider possible resistance to the system and the need for top management and user support.

Resistance to MIS   Introduction of MIS projects necessitates consideration of some of the behavioral aspects of change. A change may be ideal in both a technical and an economic sense, but this is no guarantee of its success. Unless persons want a change or the introduction of new techniques, it cannot significantly improve operating effectiveness or efficiency.

Management information systems frequently result in changes to the formal structure of an organization (e.g., adjustments in department boundaries, individual responsibilities, and communication channels), or to the informal structure (e.g., work relations, work group norms, or status). Such changes potentially affect many persons. However, the method by which they are introduced may be an overwhelming factor in determining its acceptance and its success. Also, resistance to the introduction should be anticipated and steps taken to prevent its occurrence.

When the information system specialist is faced with the problem of gaining system acceptance from operating managers and personnel, he or she is inclined to offer as evidence the same issues that were responsible for top management approval. The logic is relatively straightforward. If the project will result in reduced operating costs or increased profits, decreased decision time, job streamlining, or more accurate information on activities, it is often expected that managers will welcome such a system. The fallacy in this reasoning centers around the use of logic to change managers' attitudes about the job and the way it is performed. Attitudes may not be formed in a logical manner, as indicated repeatedly in the psychology literature, nor are they changed through the use of logic. Emotion and not logic is a key factor in attitude change [40]. The systems person is most illogical in attempting to use logic to affect attitude change. The result of improper handling of change is a form of resistance, which falls into the categories of:

Agression. Physical or nonphysical attack on the information system in an attempt to make it either inoperative or ineffective.
Projection. A means by which persons can "energize" their resistance to the introduction of an information system (blame the system).
Avoidance. Withdrawing from or avoiding interaction with the information system, often as a result of frustration [18].

Problems such as these can easily develop if systems are not considered as major changes in various aspects of organizations. Acceptance of MIS activities cannot be based solely on the use of logic or measures of efficiency: *improved performance in organizations will not necessarily prevent resistance to the introduction of management information systems applications.*

Top management support   Successful development, implementation, and operation of an MIS require continued support of and interaction with top corporate management. The importance of top management support for such systems has been noted often in the literature [3, 4, 14, 15, 19, 24], but in many instances the importance of involvement has been overlooked in application settings. The proper organizational philosophy and attitude as seen in managerial climate, for example, are necessary to assure that a change of the magnitude of an MIS project will not be viewed unfavorably. If top management would, for example, indicate that it feels change is generally disruptive and an imposition on managers, then it is logical that MIS developments will not be favorably regarded by employees. Since change is a common phenomenon in business and government today, particularly in the area of new procedures and managerial tools, management needs to communicate this to its people.

Top management support of MIS means more than just allocation of funds, although this is certainly an important factor. It also means assistance in establishing the chain of support needed in the various parts of the enterprise. Formal and informal structures may be altered because of MIS development. If top managers are involved in such developments through the establishment of systems goals and objectives along with operating procedures, support from operating and middle management levels should be more easily obtained. After all, if top management feels that an activity is important enough to devote valuable time and effort to it, perhaps the change is an important, significant, and necessary one which all persons should support. Although the mere involvement and support of top management is not sufficient to insure system success, it is necessary. Thus, we can state that a fundamental principle of computer-based information systems is that *top management involvement, interaction, and support is a necessary but not sufficient factor for successful development and introduction of systems.*

User interaction—the project team   It is necessary also, in addition to top management involvement in the MIS, to have user interaction. The logic here is that since an individual manager or employee will be using outputs from a system to do his or her work, he should be involved in the effort to develop the supporting system. The inputs of these individuals need to be heard directly.

It has been widely held in the past that establishment of clear objectives· was a significant factor in achieving success with MIS project activities. Research indicates, however, that this is not quite accurate. Powers and Dickson [29] examined this factor in a field study on correlates of success with MIS projects. The results of this study, which involved firms in manufacturing, finance, marketing, transportation, and utilities, indicate that clarity of MIS project objectives is *not* related to user satisfaction, nor to any other criterion of success. There were some projects in those studied where the initial objectives were reportedly vague. However, through a gradual process of evolution where the users worked quite closely with the information systems staff, the users defined their objectives and information/decision-making environments. As a consequence, these projects resulted in products with which the users were highly pleased.

An additional aspect to user participation is that a *lack of correlation* was found between a successful project and utilization of a project team comprised of MIS staff and user personnel. The managers who eventually used the outputs created by the MIS project activities in several cases in the study, did not themselves participate on the teams. Rather, they delegated the team membership to staff personnel in their departments. Consequently, while there was user participation, the manager who later used the system and its outputs and rated it in terms of his own information requirements *did not* participate. Even though the assignment of user area staff personnel to project teams may be reasonable and effective for data processing or information systems developments where the primary requirement is for procedural expertise, this delegation by managers in an MIS environment appears detrimental in terms of the manager's satisfaction with the results of the project. Consequently, *successful management information systems efforts require the* direct involvement *and* participation *of the managers who will use the system outputs.*

Integration upon implementation   It follows that management information systems should be integrated into the decision system such that they are a *natural* part of daily activities, since they are designed to support managerial activities. These systems too often are somewhat extraneous to the managers when they are designed, and do not fit his or her normal way of operating. In other words, the systems are designed with the apparent underlying assumption that the manager will change to fit the system. Consequently, the systems are often perceived as "being in the way" and seem almost like an extra task for the manager rather than being of assistance.

When systems are developed and implemented, they should be integrated into the managerial process. However, the only way this can successfully come about is when the MIS project fills a real need or a hole in the information network. It does this either by providing information previously not readily available or by providing information already available with *less difficulty* and/or *greater reliability* than before. In either case, *an MIS project should be integrated into the organization upon its implementation. This is done by insuring that the system is designed to fill a real information need.*

Conclusions

The field of computer-based management information systems has developed dramatically since the first introduction of computers into business decision making. We can now begin statement of principles to guide others who are becoming involved with these systems. Much more research and development, however, is needed to answer the many questions being raised by theorists and practitioners alike.

MARKETING INFORMATION SYSTEM

A major apparel manufacturer had used computers for several years to perform data processing activities. Yet the management in merchandising planning did not have access to the information needed to accurately plan and monitor fashion trends in order to react quickly in product production. A marketing information system was installed to provide this capability. The system provides sales history information from previous seasons to support merchandise planning. Included is information on product lines: sales volume, inventory classification, price, type of fabric, and so forth. Information for the current season, including sales, forecasts, production runs, and a computerized projection of sales data, is also provided. The information system allows management to identify trends. Management is better equipped to define marketing objectives and to determine whether or not the objectives are being met.

Many businesses need product planning information. They usually rely on reports that are produced on a monthly or quarterly basis to aid in planning. The unique feature of this marketing information system is that it is inquiry-based. Managers without data processing experience can use terminals connected to a central computer to make inquiries about the various phases of preseason product planning (Illustration 5-1). Because

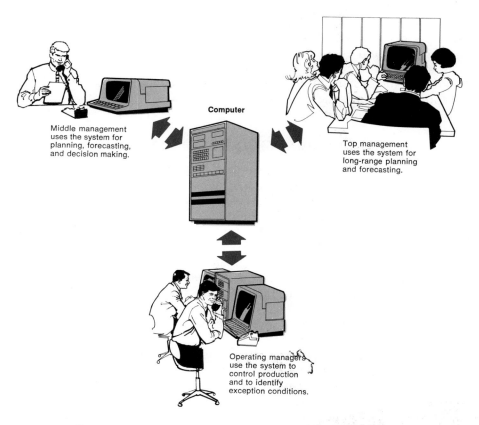

Computer

Middle management uses the system for planning, forecasting, and decision making.

Top management uses the system for long-range planning and forecasting.

Operating managers use the system to control production and to identify exception conditions.

Illustration 5-1. Inquiry system for marketing information.

the managers are communicating directly with the computer, it is called an online inquiry. The advantage of online inquiry is that the manager does not have to wait for a report to be prepared to get an answer to a question. Inquiry usage in this system includes: (1) interpreting sales history to define marketing classifications of products, (2) the study of trends of individual product sales to assist in determining which product styles to develop, and (3) the forecasting of costs by apparel fashion groups.

Personnel in purchasing also use the system to make long-term commitments on fabric purchases. A visual-display terminal can display company-wide requirements for fabric for the entire season.

Manufacturing personnel use the system to determine production requirements for various apparel styles. After the production season has started, the system is used to compare planning production by apparel groups and determine whether or not any problems exist because of under- or over-forecasting. This usage continues throughout the season. It is augmented with exception reports as needed.

Thus, this marketing information system is a direct aid to both middle management and operating managers. Middle management uses the system for planning, forecasting, and decision making. The operating managers use the system to control production and to identify conditions needing immediate management attention.

AN INTEGRATED MERCHANDISING INFORMATION SYSTEM

One of the nation's largest retailers had used a computerized data processing system for over 10 years. However, in the 1960s, as business expanded and more stores were opened, top management recognized that it must make some changes in its information system in order to maintain its competitive position. As the structure of the organization expanded, it became more difficult for the existing data processing system to provide the kind of information that management needed for decision making. It was recognized by management that poor decisions due to a lack of accurate, timely, and complete information can have a major impact on profitability. The nature of the retailing business requires quick response to consumer trends and to economic conditions affecting these trends. Because of the physical separation of the territorial management from those in the corporate headquarters, it was difficult to provide the needed information in a timely manner for decision-making purposes.

A new information system was developed and installed in two phases. First, a series of regional computer centers was established. Each one served a group of retail stores to provide merchandising and inventory information, processing of customer credit accounts, and general store accounting. Next, each store was equipped with cash-register terminals connected to a computer located within the store. (Such cash-register terminals are commonly referred to as point-of-sale terminals. They are discussed in more detail in Module A.) Thus, the second phase was the development of a merchandising information system that collected sales activity data through terminals.

Illustration 5-2 is a generalized system flowchart showing the point-of-sale portion of the merchandising information system. The sales clerk enters a sale by pressing the appropriate keys on the point-of-sale terminal. For each transaction, the following data is collected: employee identification number, merchandise division, item identification number, quantity, unit price, type of transaction, and (for credit sales) customer credit card number. The point-of-sale terminal calculates the total sale, adds any sales tax to determine a final total, and prints a customer receipt. The sales data from each terminal transaction is recorded in the store computer system as it occurs.

At the end of each day, every regional computer system communicates with the computers in all stores in its region to obtain the sales activity data for that day. In this way, the sales activity data is entered into the merchandising information system for the company.

Each store computer is also used for some local processing and reporting. This allows each store manager to obtain certain reports needed for

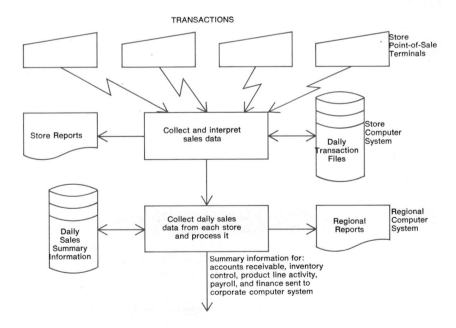

Illustration 5-2. Point-of-sale portion of merchandising information system.

store decisions without waiting for their preparation and distribution from a regional computer center.

At each regional center, the sales activity data from all of the stores in the region is processed to create a series of files for accounts receivable, inventory control, product-line activity, payroll, and finance. These files become part of the merchandising information system. In addition to serving the specific functions indicated, they provide information for management reports.

The merchandising information system can provide a great deal of information for management decision making. It does so in a very timely manner. Summarization of information takes place at each level in this information system to provide the reports needed by management at the store, region, and corporate level. The information that is collected and processed by each of the regional centers is summarized and forwarded to the corporate headquarters. A computer system at the corporate headquarters utilizes the summary information provided by each of the regional computer centers to provide top management information.

AN MIS IN HIGHER EDUCATION*

Objectives for Design

Currently, efforts are underway to develop management information systems at a wide spectrum of colleges and universities, both public and private, as well as within groups of institutions at local and state levels. Obviously, the objectives for system design vary from one organization to another, as do the objectives of the organizations themselves. Nevertheless, there is sufficient commonality to warrant discussing the objectives of a particular state-wide public system, used here for purposes of illustration.

In the state in which this system was established, careful consideration was given to what the objectives of a project to develop a higher-education management information system should be. The objectives finally selected included:

> The system must provide meaningful management information to the board of regents and to university administrators. This probably will necessitate the development of common but somewhat different systems at individual institutions to meet common but somewhat different needs.

---

*From Roger W. Comstock, "MIS in Higher Education," *Management Controls* (Sept. 1970), published by Peat, Marwick, Mitchell & Company and adapted with their permission.

Common definitions must be developed and applied at all universities in order that data supplied by the system may be comparable.

The system taken as a whole must not be oriented to any particular institution or application area.

The plan and resulting systems must be as flexible as possible to permit modification to meet changing objectives and to accommodate new educational methods and procedures. The plan must be devised to provide a firm foundation on which to base new systems development over the next several years. This will not decrease the need to identify as many of the future needs as possible early in the project.

The program for development must be structured so that it can be accomplished in distinct steps. Milestones must be charted at which project progress may be reviewed and new directions taken, if warranted. Provision must be made to review and fund discrete tasks associated with the project, and to pass on their applicability and urgency in the future. The project must also be planned so that some results are achieved at an early date. Confidence and interest tend to lag in direct proportion to the length and cost of the project.

The results of a project of this nature are only as good as the depth of commitment of key administrators and the amount of effort each is willing to devote to its development. The system incorporates many of the tools that administrators will use in seeking to satisfy institutional objectives. Hence, the reports to be provided must be fitted closely to the characteristics and requirements of the offices that will use them. For example, the methods by which faculty time utilization is classified can be critical when making decisions with regard to staffing levels, academic personnel policy, and individual advancement.

The personnel responsible for setting up this MIS project recognized that unless serious attention were paid to the project plan by key administrators, the resulting systems would fall short of the utility expected of them. University officials had to recognize this and be ready to commit a considerable portion of their time and energy to the project, despite other pressing demands on their time. A broad policy framework within which development of the system could proceed had to be established. Procedures as to how information would be controlled and disseminated had to be developed. Checks and balances had to be built into the administrative structure to insure against improper issuance or use of data. The integrity and the identity of the individual and of the institution had to be preserved.

Conceptual Design

The first step in the actual development of an MIS should be the creation of a conceptual design. Many managers do not like to bear the cost of developing such a plan (which has no immediate operational results), but it is absolutely essential to develop an overall understanding of the inter-relationships of such operating functions as registration, financial aids, space allocation, staffing and course scheduling, and unit costs.

The primary elements of the conceptual plan are definitions of the management-level system outputs, the information flow, the system software and programming languages to be used, the key data elements needed, a data classification scheme, a list of required subsystems, constraints of a planning model, and a plan for implementation.

System Outputs; Key Data Elements

The system output generally consists of a set of reports designed to serve management needs at various points in the management process. These reports may be oriented to such diverse elements of university administration as program planning and budgeting, faculty evaluation, and control of the auxiliary enterprises. They should be clearly and specifically designed. Each design should include a definition of each field contained in the report, and statements of the purpose of the report, how it will be used, and the frequency and manner of distribution.

If the MIS is to provide for inquiry via terminal or specifically written program for such jobs as student accounts and registration, the nature of the inquiries allowed and the constraints to be applied to this method of using the system must be defined.

Once the required reporting structure has been defined, data elements needed to produce the reports must be identified. These elements can then be grouped into logical file structures—a first step in the definition of the various information system master files.

Information Flow

The information flow description will consist of a set of system flowcharts and a brief narrative. Each flowchart should depict the manner in which key data elements will be handled from the time that they are originated in machine form to the point where they are incorporated into the various system outputs. To do this, it is necessary to define the major related master file update runs and the related master file structures. Once these have been defined, it will be possible to display: the manner in which data is captured by each of these systems and in which it flows from one system to the next; the basic master file structure; and the techniques by which the management reporting system of the MIS can extract the data it needs most efficiently.

The system flowchart constructed for the student records system (subsystem) is shown as an example in Illustration 5-3. It depicts clearly the inputs and outputs of the subsystem and the requirement for a student master file.

System Software

After the system outputs and system flowcharts have been designed, it should be possible for the system designer to prepare gross specifications for the operating software required in the MIS. This includes the executive system, the type of file management software to be used, the requirements for inquiry, and the basic programming language (or languages). It is advisable to include these specifications in the conceptual design.

Data Classification Scheme

A data classification scheme is needed to permit input transactions to be coded so that the individual data elements will be routed properly along the information flow path to be summarized in management reports. This scheme may include the chart of accounts, the space classification system, course designations, time utilization codes, departmental numbers, and the like. While it is impractical to completely define the scheme during the conceptual stage, a basic structure for classification should be provided.

Information Systems

The conceptual plan should include a list of the subsystems needed to support the management reporting system of the MIS. This list should provide the facts below for each of the systems:

- Name and basic functions
- Frequency of operation
- Gross estimate of time and effort required to make it operational, if applicable
- Priority for implementation in the light of institutional needs and available resources

If the systems are not in operation currently, many of these facts will be rough estimates. However, such estimates are essential to the making of an informed evaluation of the time and resources required to implement the MIS.

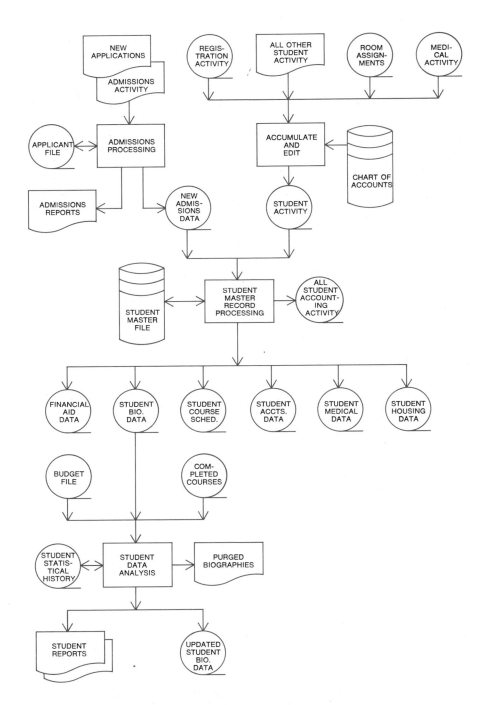

Illustration 5-3. Student records subsystem.

Planning Model

An additional element to be considered in creating the conceptual plan is the use of a university planning model. If implemented, such a model provides an analytical description of meaningful relationships among program activity levels and resources under varying circumstances. With the aid of currently available computers, demands on each resource can be computed rapidly for a specified program of activities and policy constraints. The model functions with initial planning data to provide the administration of a college or university with projections of future enrollments, staffing and faculty requirements, facilities requirements, and the like.

A pictorial description of the basic modules or computational steps of a representative planning model is shown in Illustration 5-4. This model is perhaps most applicable to a small college or group of small colleges. Such a model can be developed in stages, consistent with the available data.

Some basic estimating relationships that can be developed from the initial planning data for use in the planning model are:

- Fixed and variable costs as a function of grade levels and programs
- Student and staff attrition
- Instructional hour demand by grade level and major program
- Student/course/classroom-lab space utilization
- Construction cost estimating

Implementation Plan

Finally, using the data set forth above, together with similar estimates for the management reporting system and other software required, an implementation plan should be prepared for management approval. The plan should address the following items.

1. Overall time frame for implementation of the MIS, as well as completion dates for subsidiary elements.
2. Checkpoints for management review and approval. These should be designed in such a way that the project can be redirected or even temporarily halted without undue disruption at each checkpoint, depending upon overall conditions at that time.
3. Priority schedule for implementation of individual subsystems. Is it more important, for example, to start work now on payroll or on a library system?
4. Estimates of resources required for completion by all parties to the project. These resources include personnel, management participation, vendor assistance, and computer time for program testing.

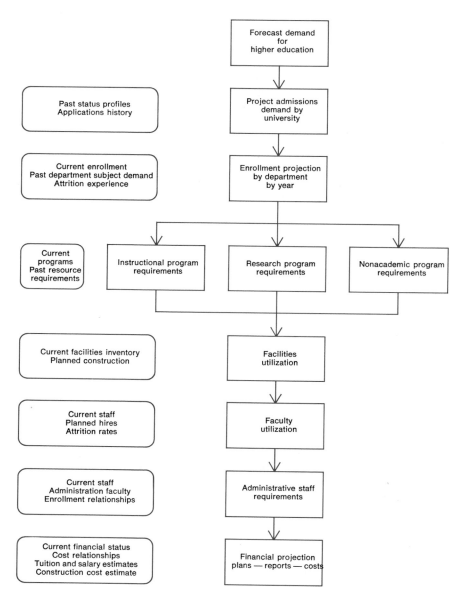

Illustration 5-4. Planning model.

Once the conceptual plan has been established, it is possible to proceed with the design and implementation of individual subsystems with reasonable confidence that they will fit into the MIS framework.

MIS implementation considerations. Though an MIS obviously can produce tangible and exciting benefits, developing it is a large undertaking. Substantial amounts of person power, money, and time are required. Problems, pitfalls, and consequences should therefore be anticipated if possible. Here are some areas that call for such special inquiry:

- *User motivation.* This is perhaps the single greatest potential pitfall for an information system. If the user of the system and the individuals responsible for supplying data to the system are not disposed to work for the success of the system, it will fail—no matter how well designed. It is a simple matter for a disgruntled employee to "permit" erroneous data to enter the system, or not to submit data at all. It is equally easy for an unhappy administrator to not use the information the system provides. Every employee involved with the system must be motivated to use it properly; conversely, the system must be designed to aid in that motivation.

- *Early results.* When senior management and funding agencies are asked to support multiple-year projects with thousands or millions of dollars, they become anxious to see results. The system development should be organized in such a way that tangible system outputs are produced early, preferably within the first year.

- *The simple approach.* An information system is a complex undertaking. The expectations of the intended user tend to reinforce the inventiveness and enthusiasm of the system designer. Too often, this leads to a sophisticated design that is neither desirable nor attainable the first time around. As the system is being developed, managers should favor consistently the simple approach. To the extent that simplicity can be achieved, the chances of realizing a successful system increase.

- *Maximum system flexibility.* It is in the nature of management to change; else, it would not be management. As management needs change, so do management's requirements of the information system. For this reason, a flexible design is imperative. An organization should not expect to achieve the optimum system on the first go-around. The system design should be an iterative process, in which the results of experiences are built upon to improve the capabilities and responsiveness of the system.

- *Data purification.* Early in the project, it is necessary to develop standard data definitions and promulgate them to all potential sources of data for the information system. Also vital is the review of historical data to determine how it may be incorporated into the information system data base without distortion. An information system that provides reports based on nonstandard data is less than useful; it can have a negative impact on the functioning of an institution.

Conclusion

An MIS must deal with quantified data. Because of this, many administrators, particularly those dealing with academic programs, have become concerned that the system will eliminate the quality factor from consideration. Their argument is that decisions more often will be made on the basis of quantitative data selected by the system designer for presentation to the administration. They fear that quality of education will be bypassed as a factor in educational decisions. Several potential solutions exist.

The information system designer should be aware of this danger and attempt to avoid it. Management, too, must learn to use information system outputs interpretively. Rather than expect the system to provide answers, management must recognize that certain constraints exist with regard to the aggregated data supplied. For example, a summary of laboratory hours may include hours spent in chem labs, music practice sessions, and physical education courses. Each of these, in fact, may require separate treatment.

Finally, management must also learn to question the "facts" neatly presented on a computer printout; to evaluate them for reasonableness in relation to other known information; and to consider both quantitative and qualitative aspects of a question before reaching a decision.

Summary

1. One example of an MIS is a marketing information system established by a major apparel manufacturer. Managers can enter online inquiries to obtain product information for planning, forecasting, and decision making. Operating managers also use the system to control production and to identify conditions needing immediate management attention.

2. A large, geographically distributed retailer obtains information for decision-making purposes by means of a three-level marketing information system:
   a. Individual retail stores collect sales activity data through point-of-sale terminals.
   b. Regional computer centers collect store data for accounts receivable, inventory control, product-line activity, payroll, and finance purposes.
   c. A computer system at corporate headquarters processes regional summary data to provide top management information.

3. The development of a higher-education MIS is a major undertaking. The conceptual design of the system must define the management-level system outputs, information flow, system software, data classification scheme and key data elements needed, information systems, subsystems, and an implementation plan. A planning model may be useful. After all of these system characteristics have been defined, the design and implementation of the individual information sybsystems can proceed.

References

[1] Ackoff, R. L. "Management Misinformation Systems," *Management Science,* Vol. 14, No. 4, December 1967.

[2] Anthony, R. N. *Planning and Control Systems: A Framework for Analysis,* Division of Research, Graduate School of Business Administration, Harvard University, Boston, 1965.

[3] Argyris, C. "Management Information Systems: The Challenge to Reality and Emotionality," *Management Science,* Vol. 17, No. 6, February 1971.

[4] Argyris, C. "Resistance to Rational Management Systems," *Innovation,* Issue 10, 1969.

[5] Bedford, N., and Onsi, M. "Measuring the Value of Information—An Information Theory Approach," *Management Service,* Vol. 13, No. 4, January-February 1966.

[6] Bennis, W. G. *Organization Development: Its Nature, Origin and Prospects,* Addison-Wesley Publishing, Reading, Mass., 1969.

[7] Blumenthal, S. *Management Information Systems: A Framework for Planning and Development,* Prentice-Hall, Inc., Englewood Cliffs, N.J., 1969.

[8] Boyd, D., and Krasnow, H. "Economic Evaluation of Management Information Systems," *IBM Systems Journal,* Vol. 2, March 1968.

[9] Chervany, N. L., and Dickson, G. W. "An Experimental Evaluation of Information in a Production Environment," *Management Science,* Vol. 20, No. 10, June 1974.

[10] Chervany, N. L., and Dickson, G. W. "Economic Evaluation of Management Information Systems: An Analytical Framework," *Decision Sciences,* June-October, 1970.

[11] Churchill, N. C., Kempster, J. H., and Uretsky, M. *Computer-Based Information Systems for Management: A Survey,* National Association for Accountants, New York, 1969.

[12] Cougar, J. D., and Knapp, R. W. *Systems Analysis Techniques,* John Wiley and Sons, New York, 1974.

[13] Cougar, J. D., and Wergin, L. W. "Small Company MIS," *Infosystems,* Vol. 21, No. 10, October 1974.

[14] Dean, N. J. "The Computer Comes of Age," *Harvard Business Review,* Vol. 46, No. 1, January-February 1968.

[15] Dearden, J. "MIS Is a Mirage," *Harvard Business Review,* Vol. 50, No. 1, January-February 1972.

[16] Dickson, G. W. "Management Information Systems: Definitions, Problems, and Research," *Society for Management Information Systems Newsletter,* July 1970.

[17] Dickson, G. W., Senn, J. A., and Chervany, N. L. "Research in MIS: The Minnesota Experiments," *Management Science,* Vol. 23, No. 9, May 1977.

[18] Dickson, G. W., and Simmons, J. K. "The Behavioral Side of MIS," *Business Horizons,* Vol. 13, August 1970.

[19] Diebold, J. "Bad Decisions on Computer Use," *Harvard Business Review,* Vol. 47. No. 1, January-February 1969.

[20] Everest, G. C. "Objectives of Database Management," *Information Systems: Proceedings of the Fourth International Symposium on Computers and Information Sciences* (COINS-72), December 1972, Plenum Press, New York, 1974.

[21] Gorry, G. A., and Scott Morton, M. S. "A Framework for Management Information Systems," *Sloan Management Review,* Vol. 13, No. 1, January 1971.

[22] Hanold, T. "The Executive View of Management Information Systems," SMIS *Special Report,* The Society for Management Information Systems, Chicago, September 1972.

[23] Head, R. V. "Management Information Systems: A Critical Appraisal," *Datamation,* Vol. 13, No. 5, May 1967.

[24] Hertz, D. B. "Unlocking the Computer's Profit Potential," McKinsey and Company, New York, 1968.

[25] Kennevan, W. "MIS Universe," *Data Management,* September 1970.

[26] Lucas, H. C., Jr. "An Empirical Study of a Framework for Information Systems," *Decision Sciences,* Vol. 5, No. 1, January 1974.

[27] Lucas, H. C., Jr. *Toward Creative Systems Design,* Columbia University Press, New York, 1974.

[28] Mason, R. O., and Mitroff, I. I. "A Program for Research on Management Information Systems," *Management Science,* Vol. 19, No. 5, January 1973.

[29] Powers, R. F., and Dickson, G. W. "MIS Project Management: Myths, Opinions, and Reality," *California Management Review,* Vol. 15, Spring 1973.

[30] Pratt, J. W., Raiffa, H., and Schlaifer, R. *Introduction to Statistical Decision Theory,* John Wiley and Sons, New York, 1966.

[31] Rappaport, A. "Management Misinformation Systems—Another Perspecitve," *Management Science,* December 1968.

[32] Schubert, P. F. "Directions in Data Base Management Technology," *Datamation,* Vol. 20, No. 9, September 1974.

[33] Schwartz, M. H. "MIS Planning," *Datamation,* Vol. 16, No. 17, September 1, 1970.

[34] Senn, J. A., and Dickson, G. W. "Information System Structure and Purchasing Decision Effectiveness," *Journal of Purchasing and Materials Management,* Vol. 10, No. 3, August 1974.

[35] Simon, H. A. *The New Science of Decision,* Harper Brothers Publishers, New York, 1960.

[36] Tiechrow, D., and Hershey, E. A., III. "A Computer-Aided Technique for Structured Documentation," *Data Base,* Vol. 8, No. 1, Summer 1976. pp. 7-9.

[37] *What Is a Management Information System?* Research Report Number 1. The Society for Management Information Systems, Chicago, 1970.

[38] Williams, L. K. "The Human Side of Systems Change," *Systems and Procedure Journal,* July 1964.

[29] Withington, F. G. "Five Generations of Computers," *Harvard Business Review,* Vol. 52, No. 4, July-August 1974.

[40] Wolk, S. "Resistance to EDP: An Employee—Management Dilemma," *Data Management,* Vol. 6, No. 9, September 1968.

Computer Systems

Introduction to Computer Systems

As discussed in the last several chapters, the processing of data is not a recent development. Rather, man has processed data, in an attempt to obtain timely and relevant information, for hundreds of years. What has changed is the means by which data is processed into information. Specifically, man has steadily continued to develop means by which data can be processed into information much faster with greater reliability and accuracy.

THE EVOLUTION OF THE COMPUTER

Charles Babbage's Analytical Engine

The first major step in the evolution of the computer was taken by Charles Babbage, a professor of mathematics at Cambridge University in England. In 1830, Babbage began to design and build what was to be the first completely automatic, general-purpose, *digital* computer (a machine with characteristics explained more fully in the next chapter). He named this computer the "analytical engine" to reflect the fact that it was to be able to perform mathematical calculations on numbers in a storage unit within it. The arithmetic and storage units of the machine were to be governed by a control unit which coordinated and supervised the sequence of operations.

Babbage continued to work on the analytical engine until his death in 1871. Because his idea was beyond the technical capabilities at that time, he was not able to complete the engine; nevertheless, he must be given credit for having the foresight to design and attempt to build a machine that was approximately 100 years ahead of its time. Babbage is considered one of the great pioneers in the field of computation.

The Mark I Computer

After Babbage's death, no significant progress was made in the development of automatic computation until 1937 when Professor Howard Aiken of Harvard University began to build an automatic calculating machine that would combine the technical capabilities of that time with the punched-card concepts developed by Hollerith and Powers (see Chapter 2). During the next several years, Aiken, with the assistance of graduate students and IBM engineers, worked on building the machine. In 1944 the project was completed, and a machine known as the Mark I was formally presented to Harvard University.

The Mark I is considered to be the first successful general-purpose, digital computer. The machine was based on the concepts of accepting data from punched cards as input, making calculations by means of auto-

Illustration 6-1. The Mark I computer.

matically controlled electromagnetic relays and mechanical arithmetic counters, and punching the results into cards. Thus, the Mark I was an *electromechanical computer.*

The Mark I was the first machine capable of solving various types of scientific-oriented problems and performing long series of arithmetic and logical operations. Each sequence of calculations was controlled by a punched paper tape. In many respects, the Mark I was the realization of Babbage's dream. Compared with modern computers, it operated quite slowly. It is still operational and is on display at Harvard University.

The ENIAC

The first *electronic digital computer* was designed and built in the early 1940s at the University of Pennsylvania's Moore School of Electrical Engineering. The project to design and build the computer was the result of a contract between the University of Pennsylvania and the United States government.

The team of John W. Mauchly and J. Presper Eckert, Jr. was responsible for the construction of the computer. They named it the Electronic Numerical Integrator and Calculator (ENIAC). The ENIAC was completely electronic in that none of its parts moved during the processing of data.

The ENIAC cost several million dollars to build, weighed approximately 30 tons, took up approximately 1500 square feet of floor space, and used 18,000 vacuum tubes instead of electromagnetic relays as were used in the Mark I. The fastest electromechanical machine of the time could perform only one multiplication per second. With the replacement of the slow electromagnetic relays by vacuum tubes, the ENIAC could perform 300 multiplications per second. It could do in one day what would have taken 300 days to do manually. When completed, the ENIAC was installed at the Aberdeen Proving Grounds in Maryland. In 1956, it was placed in the Smithsonian Institution because of its historical significance.

In 1946, John von Neumann, a well-known mathematician from the Institute for Advanced Study at Princeton University, became acquainted with the work of Mauchly and Eckert at the Moore School of Electrical Engineering. He wrote a paper in which he described the basic philosophy of computer design for the group of people connected with the ENIAC project at the Moore School of Electrical Engineering. Almost everything concerning computer design that von Neumann discussed in his paper has been incorporated in modern computers. Thus, it is often stated that the basis for the design of computers is the "von Neumann concept."

The EDVAC

The computer design considerations presented by von Neumann in his paper came too late to be incorporated in the ENIAC. However, with these design considerations as a basis, Mauchly, Eckert, and others at the Moore School of Electrical Engineering began to build the Electronic Discrete Variable Automatic Computer (EDVAC). Although the design of the EDVAC actually began prior to completion of the ENIAC, EDVAC was not completed until 1952.

EDVAC was smaller than either the Mark I or the ENIAC, but it had greater capability. Two design features that distinguished the EDVAC from the ENIAC were the use of binary numbers and the internal storage of instructions in digital form. (These design features are discussed in the next chapter.)

Up to this time, primary emphasis was placed on building computers for use on projects of a *scientific* nature. In 1946, Eckert and Mauchly founded the Eckert-Mauchly Computer Corporation to build computers for *commercial* use. The computers were to be *business-oriented*—designed primarily to process business data. The diversion of their attention to this company was one of the reasons why EDVAC was not completed until 1952. During these years, the Electronic Delayed Storage Automatic Computer (EDSAC) was built at Cambridge University in England. Completed in 1949, the EDSAC was the first *stored-program electronic digital computer*. (As above, this design feature is discussed in the next chapter.)

COMPUTER GENERATIONS

Generally, computer systems have been classified as belonging to specific "generations." The implication of the term *generation* is that a significant change in the design of a computer distinguishes it from computers classified as members of a preceding generation. The *first generation* of computers extended from 1951 to 1959. The computers of this generation were large, bulky machines characterized by the use of vacuum tubes.

The UNIVersal Automatic Computer (UNIVAC) I was the first commercially available computer (see Illustration 6-2). That is, the UNIVAC I was the first computer built with the assumption that several computers of the same type would be built and sold. Until the development of the UNIVAC I, computers were one of a kind.

The UNIVAC I was built by the company founded in 1946 by Eckert and Mauchly. The company became a subsidiary of Remington Rand in 1949. This subsidiary later became the Sperry-Univac division of Sperry Rand Corporation.

Illustration 6-2. The UNIVAC I computer.

The first UNIVAC I computer was installed at the United States Bureau of Census in 1951. The computer was used by the Bureau of Census until 1963, when it was classified as obsolete and placed in the Smithsonian Institution because of its historical significance.

In 1954, the first UNIVAC I acquired for business data processing was installed at General Electric's Appliance Park in Louisville, Kentucky. The introduction of the computer to business opened a new field and is the major factor behind the growth of the computer industry.

In 1953, IBM, which had not been particularly active in the development of computers, entered the computer field with the business-oriented IBM 701 computer. This computer was followed in late 1954 by the IBM 650 computer (see Illustration 6-3). The IBM 650, like the 701, was business-oriented. It was the most popular computer between 1954 and 1959. As a result of the popularity of the computer, IBM obtained a dominant position in the computer field. Since that time, the company has retained its position.

The *second generation* of computers extended from 1959 to 1964. The computers of this generation were characterized by the use of transistors instead of vacuum tubes. The basis for changing from vacuum tubes to transistors was that transistors are smaller, less expensive, generate almost no heat, and require little power. Thus, second-generation computers were substantially smaller, required less power to operate, and were more reliable than first-generation computers. As in the first generation, a particular computer of the second generation was designed to process either scientific-oriented or business-oriented problems. For example, the most

Illustration 6-3. The IBM 650 computer.

popular business-oriented computer was the IBM 1401; the most popular scientific-oriented computers were the IBM 1620 and the IBM 7090-7094 series.

The *third (present) generation* of computers began in 1965, when IBM first delivered its System/360 computers. The computers of this generation are characterized by (1) miniaturized circuits, which further reduced the physical size of computers and increased their processing speed, reliability, and accuracy, (2) the integration of hardware with software (these terms are explained in the next chapter), (3) data communication capability (this term is discussed in Chapter 16), and (4) the capability to perform several operations simultaneously. Also, the prices of third-generation equipment are generally lower than those of comparable second-generation equipment. (The price of computers relative to performance has decreased an average of 20 percent per year since the UNIVAC I. For example, in 1952 it cost $1.26 to do 100,000 multiplications. By 1958 the cost had dropped to 26 cents, and by 1964 the cost was down to 12 cents. By 1970 the cost had dropped to 5 cents, and today those same 100,000 multiplications can be executed for a penny.) Another distinguishing feature of third-generation computers is that while first- and second-generation computers were designed to process either scientific or business problems, most third-generation computers are general-purpose computers. They are designed to process both scientific-oriented and business-oriented problems.

AN OVERVIEW OF COMPUTER SYSTEMS

In one sense, a computer system is like any other data processing system. It takes input, processes it, and provides output. In other ways, a computer system is quite different from other data processing systems. For example, data is processed electronically, rather than manually, mechanically, or electromechanically. Computer systems are often called *electronic data processing (EDP) systems.*

The machines usually included in a basic computer system are a card reader, a computer, and a printer. A card reader reads data stored on punched cards; a computer processes the data; and a printer prints the results. A larger system may also include magnetic tape units and magnetic disk units, which are used to store data. (A computer system with all of these machines is shown in Illustration 6-4.) In addition to these machines, a variety of other machines can be used. The basic factor determining which machines are appropriate is the data processing that is required.

Although the machines in a computer system are developed as separate units, they are connected prior to operation of the system. Each of the input and output machines is attached to the computer by means of electric cables. When a card reader reads a punched card, the data is transferred to the computer. Similarly, after the computer has processed the data, the

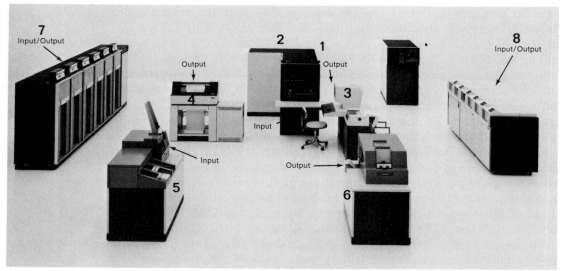

1. Console
2. Computer (CPU)
3. Console printer-keyboard
4. Printer
5. Card reader
6. Card punch
7. Magnetic tape units
8. Magnetic disk units

Illustration 6-4. Typical computer system.

results are transferred from the computer to the printer to be printed out. Thus, the components of a computer system work together.

A COMPARISON OF HUMAN AND COMPUTER CAPABILITIES

Although humans have the ability to do anything a computer can do, the reverse is not true—a computer cannot do everything a human can do. A computer has two basic capabilities. First, it is extremely fast. Its speed is reflected in its capability to execute instructions in *nanoseconds,* or billionths of a second. Second, it is almost perfect in reliability and accuracy. Studies of error rates indicate that, on an average, a computer makes one error per 1.25 million characters in processing data. A human is at a disadvantage when compared with the computer as a data processor. The human is slow and not completely accurate. Studies of error rates indicate that, on the average, a typist or clerk makes one error per 1000 characters in processing data.

Humans have two advantages over a computer. First, they can innovate or adapt during the process of solving a problem. Thus, they do not require a set of instructions that anticipates beforehand, everything that may happen during the problem-solving process. They have the ability to relate the current situation to preceding ones and act accordingly.

Second, humans can reason heuristically. That is, they can learn by trial and error. Rather than solving a problem in a step-by-step manner, humans often make decisions based on incomplete information and the effect of past experiences. Humans are aware of their environment, and learning from past experiences is available to them. A computer has only the information that a stored program has made available to it.

A human is best suited to think, reason, and discover; a computer is best adapted to calculate, manipulate, and compare. Thus, the computer can extend the power of the human being.

Summary

1. The first major steps toward the development of an automatic, general-purpose, digital computer can be traced back to the work of Charles Babbage in 1830.

2. The first working model of a general-purpose, digital computer (the Mark I) was completed by Howard Aiken in 1937. It utilized the punched-card concepts of Hollerith and Powers, and it functioned by a series of electromagnetic relays and mechanical arithmetic counters. It was a scientific-oriented machine capable of performing long series of arithmetic and logical operations.

3. The ENIAC was the first electronic digital computer. Developed by John W. Mauchly and J. Presper Eckert, Jr. in the early 1940s, it used vacuum tubes and was able to do 300 multiplications per second.

4. The EDVAC, also developed by Mauchly and Eckert, employed the basic design philosophy described by John von Neumann in 1946. Known later as the "von Neumann concept," it proposed the use of binary numbers and the internal storage of instructions in digital form.

5. The UNIVAC I was the first commercially available computer. Its introduction was followed by the entrance of IBM into the computer field with the IBM 701 computer.

6. Computers can be classified by generations—each generation separated from the previous one by significant changes in the design of the computer. The first generation was characterized by the use of vacuum tubes; the second by the use of transistors; and the third by miniaturized circuits and significantly enhanced functional capabilities.

7. The computer has two advantages over humans—it is extremely fast and almost perfect in reliability and accuracy. Humans have one disadvantage and two advantages over the computer—they are slow and not completely accurate as data processors, but they can innovate or adapt and they can reason heuristically.

Computer Concepts

The evolution and general nature of the modern computer system were discussed in the preceding chapter. In fact, the term *computer* has been used several times in this book, but it has not been defined. Before the details of the computer are discussed, the key implications of this term should be pointed out.

The term *computer,* while applicable to any machine capable of arithmetic calculation, generally implies a machine with certain characteristics:

- *Electronic.* Achieves its results through the movement of electronic impulses rather than the physical movement of internal parts.
- *Internal storage.* Has the ability to simultaneously store program statements and data. This ability enables the computer to consecutively execute program statements at a high rate of speed.
- *Stored program.* Follows a series of *statements* (also called *instructions*) in its internal storage. These instruct it in detail as to both the specific operations to perform and the order in which to perform them.
- *Program-execution modification.* Can change the course of the execution of program statements (*branch*) because of a decision based on data in its internal storage and/or the results of one or more arithmetic or logical operations.

In summary, a computer is an electronic machine possessing internal storage capabilities, a stored program of instructions, and the capability of modifying the course of execution of the instructions during processing.

THE CLASSIFICATION OF COMPUTERS

There are many useful ways in which computers can be classified. Among these are: (1) by the type of data they are capable of manipulating (digital or analog), (2) as a mixture of data-handling types (hybrid), and (3) by the purpose for which they were designed (special-purpose or general-purpose).

Analog and Digital Computers

There are two main types of computers: digital and analog. A *digital computer* operates directly on decimal digits that represent either discrete data or symbols. It takes input and gives output in the form of numbers, letters, and special characters represented by holes in punched cards, magnetized areas on tapes, printing on paper, and so on. This is the type of computer most commonly thought of and referred to when the word *computer* is used either by itself or in context.

Digital computers are generally used for business and scientific data processing. Depending upon the particular characteristics of the digital computer and the precision of the data it is processing, the digital computer is capable of achieving varying degrees of accuracy in both intermediate and final results. Digital computers are the most widely used type of computers in business. Thus, unless stated otherwise, the discussion of computers in this book concerns digital computers.

An *analog computer,* in contrast to a digital computer, measures continuous electrical or physical magnitudes; it does not operate on digits. If digits are involved at all, they are obtained indirectly. Factors such as current, length, pressure, temperature, shaft rotations, and voltage are directly measured. The output of an analog computer is often an adjustment to the control of a machine. For instance, an analog computer may adjust a valve to control the flow of fluid through a pipe, or it may adjust a temperature setting to control the temperature in an oven. For these reasons, analog computers are often used for controlling processes such as oil refining and baking. Digital computers can also be used for controlling processes. To do so, they must convert analog data to digital form, process it, and then convert the digital results to analog form. A digital computer possesses greater accuracy than an analog computer, but the analog computer can process data faster than a digital computer.

Hybrid Computers

While digital and analog computers are the most extensively used types of computers in business, in certain situations (e.g., to simulate a guided missile system or a new aircraft design), a computer that combines the most desirable features of both is employed. A computer of this nature is referred to as a *hybrid computer.* Two major features incorporated into a hybrid computer that make it especially suitable for certain types of business problems are the ability to solve problems faster than digital computers with greater accuracy than analog computers.

Special-Purpose and General-Purpose Computers

Digital computers may be designed for either special or general uses. A *special-purpose computer,* as the name implies, is designed for a specific operation. It usually satisfies the needs of a particular type of problem. While a special-purpose computer may incorporate many of the features of a general-purpose machine, its applicability to a particular problem is a function of its design rather than of a stored program; the instructions that control it are built into the machine. This "specializing" of the machine leads to efficient, effective performance of a specific operation. One consequence of this specialization, however, is that the machine lacks versatility. That is, it cannot be used to perform other operations. For example, the special-purpose computers designed for the sole purpose of controlling a petroleum refinery cannot be used for other purposes without making major changes to the computers.

A *general-purpose computer,* as the name implies, is designed to perform a variety of operations. This capability is a result of its ability to store different programs of instructions in its internal storage. Unfortunately, the ability to perform a variety of operations is often achieved at the expense of certain aspects of speed and efficiency of performance. In most situations, the computer's flexibility, with respect to its being able to perform a variety of operations, makes this compromise an acceptable one.

THE COMPONENTS OF A COMPUTER SYSTEM

A computer system is composed of (1) machines, which are referred to as *hardware,* (2) programs and operating aids, referred to as *software,* (3) user programs, (4) procedures, and (5) data processing personnel.

Thus, the term *computer system* refers to the machines; programs and operating aids, and user programs that cause these machines to function; the procedures required to prepare and process the data and distribute the results of the processing; and the people who keep the hardware, software, user programs, and procedures efficiently and effectively functioning. Each of these components is discussed below. The remainder of the chapter centers around (1) how program statements and data are represented in the storage unit of a computer and (2) the execution of program statements.

Hardware

The hardware of a computer system can be classified according to the five basic functions that the equipment performs. These functions are preparation, input, manipulation, storage, and output of data. Their typical relationships are shown in Illustration 7-1. (All of the input and output devices mentioned in the following paragraphs are discussed in Chapters 8, 9, and 10 and Module A.)

Data-preparation devices. Before data is transferred to a computer, it is usually transferred from source documents to an *input medium* that an input device can read. The most common input medium is the punched card. Consequently, the most common data-preparation device is the *card punch* (or *keypunch*). Because data preparation is time-consuming and costly, there is a trend toward elimination of this function by either encoding the data on the source document for direct input to the computer or creating device-readable input as a by-product during the process of creating the source document. For example, the bills mailed to customers by many utility companies are punched cards. The amount of a customer's bill and the information needed to process the account are punched into a card. Thus, the source document serves both as a bill and as a direct input medium to the computer. The direct input of data to the computer from an input device such as a console printer-keyboard used as a terminal also eliminates the data-preparation function.

The broken arrow connecting the data-preparation function and the input function in Illustration 7-1 reflects the fact that all machines used during the data-preparation function are *offline* to the computer. Machines that are offline to the computer are not in direct communication with it; therefore, the computer cannot receive data directly from these machines. In contrast, the input devices and output devices are *online* to the computer, that is, in direct communication with it. Therefore, the computer can receive data directly from these machines. (The concepts "online" and "offline" are discussed more fully in Chapter 16.)

Input devices.   A computer must receive both program statements and data to solve problems. The entry of program statements and data into a computer occurs by means of an input device, such as a card reader. A card reader reads the holes punched in cards, and the characters represented by the holes are transferred to the computer. In addition to the card reader, which is the most common input device, such machines as magnetic tape, magnetic disk, and magnetic drum units; console printer-keyboards; and cathode-ray-tube (CRT) devices are used as input devices. There are many other devices, some of which are discussed in Module A.

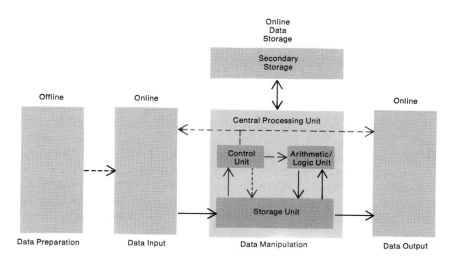

Illustration 7-1. The five equipment functions in a computer system.

Most input devices read data from an input medium (say, punched cards, magnetic tape, or magnetic disk). Other input devices, such as a console printer-keyboard used as a terminal, allow data to be transferred to a computer without recording it on an input medium. In all instances, the input devices provide the means through which humans can communicate with the computer.

Central processing unit.   The heart of a computer system is the central processing unit (CPU). Or, stating this another way, the central processing unit is the computer. Sometimes referred to as the "main frame," this unit processes the data transferred to it by an input device and, in turn, transfers the results of the processing to an output device.

CPU speeds make input/output speeds seem slow by comparison. The speed of a computer depends on the speed at which its components operate plus the length of the interconnections between them. As noted earlier, third-generation internal processing speeds are measured in nanoseconds. How fast is a nanosecond? Well, the speed of electricity is 186,000 miles per second, which is approximately 8 inches per nanosecond. For example, on one large computer, 5 million additions can be executed in one second; this means that it can do one addition every 200 nanoseconds.

As shown in Illustration 7-1, the computer is composed of three units: (1) the control unit, (2) the arithmetic/logic unit, and (3) the storage unit. The storage unit can be in the same cabinet as the control and arithmetic/logic units or in a separate cabinet. As indicated by the dark solid arrows in Illustration 7-1, data is transferred from an input device to the storage unit, and from the storage unit to an output device.

Each of these units serves a specific function and has a particular relationship to the other units of the CPU. The *control unit,* as the name implies and as indicated by the colored solid arrow, selects one program statement at a time from the storage unit. It interprets the statement and, as indicated by the colored broken arrows, sends the appropriate electronic impulses to the arithmetic/logic and storage units to cause these units to carry out the operations required. Thus, the control unit does not perform the actual processing operations on the data. Rather, its function is to maintain order and direct the flow of operations and data within the computer. The control unit also instructs the input device when to start and stop transferring data to the storage unit, and it tells the storage unit when to start and stop transferring data to an output device.

All arithmetic calculations and logical comparisons are performed in the *arithmetic/logic unit.* As indicated by the dark solid arrows in Illustration 7-1, data flows between this unit and the storage unit during processing. Specifically, data is transferred as needed from the storage unit to the arithmetic/logic unit, manipulated, and returned to the storage unit. No processing is performed in the storage unit. Data may be transferred back and forth between the two units several times before manipulation is completed. When the manipulation of the data is completed, the resultant information is transferred from the storage unit to the output device, as indicated by the dark solid arrow extending from the storage unit to the output device.

The *storage unit* (sometimes called *primary storage,* or *memory,* because of its similarity to the human memory with respect to function) is the unit in which the program statements and data transferred from the input device are stored.

The storage unit is used for four purposes, three of which relate to the retention of data during processing. First, as indicated by the dark solid arrow in Figure 7-1, data is transferred from an input device to the storage unit. It remains there until the computer is ready to process it. Second, a *working-storage area* within the storage unit is used to hold both the data being processed and the intermediate results of the arithmetic/logic operations. This is reflected by the dark solid arrows connecting the storage unit and the arithmetic/logic unit. Because of the nature of its use, the working-storage area is sometimes referred to as a *"scratch-pad" memory.* Third, the storage unit retains the result of the processing until it can be transferred to an output device. Fourth, in addition to these three data-related purposes just discussed, the storage unit retains the program statements transferred from an input device or a secondary storage medium (see below) to process the data. These statements are stored in the *program-storage area* and, as indicated by the colored solid arrow, upon request of the control unit are transferred one at a time to that area of the storage unit. They instruct the computer in detail as to the specific operations it is to perform and the order in which it is to perform them.

The storage unit of the computer can hold three types of characters— alphabetic, numeric, and special characters (as a group, these three types of characters are sometimes referred to as *alphameric characters*). The computer can be classified as either *fixed-word-length, variable-word-length,* or *byte-addressable.* This reflects the fact that the organization of the storage unit is either word-oriented, character-oriented, or both word-oriented and character-oriented, respectively.

A *word-oriented* computer storage unit is divided into sections called *words.* Each word is designed to hold several characters (the maximum number of characters that a word is designed to hold varies among computer manufacturers). So that the computer can locate a particular word, each word is assigned an *address.* Thus, a reference to a particular address is a reference to a fixed number of character storage locations, whether or not all of them are needed to hold the data being retrieved or stored. Since the word-oriented computer can manipulate a word containing a large number in the same amount of time as a word containing a small number, it is especially suited to execute scientific and mathematical problems. Such problems generally involve the processing of numeric characters rather than alphabetic characters, and word-oriented computers are well designed with respect to processing this type of data.

Generally speaking, however, a business-oriented problem is processed inefficiently with respect to the use of the storage unit when a fixed-word-length computer is employed. This type of problem usually involves the processing of alphameric characters and fields of data composed of fewer characters than can be stored at an address. For this reason, business-oriented computers having *character-oriented* storage units have been developed. In contrast to the word addressing of a word-oriented storage unit, each storage location in a character-oriented storage unit is assigned an address. Each storage location can contain one character. Therefore, a data field can be from one to several characters in size. All of the data fields composing a record, whether of a uniform size or differing in size, can be stored and processed efficiently.

An addressable section of storage (a word or a character storage location) may be compared to a mail box in a post office. Each box has a unique number (address) assigned to it. A person gets mail at each box. Similar to the fact that the contents of a mail box have nothing to do with the number of the box, the contents of storage have nothing to do with an assigned address.

Several manufacturers of computer systems have developed storage units with the characteristics of both word-oriented and character-oriented storage. In these computers, a byte-addressable organization of storage is used. Basically, the programmer can cause the computer to consider its storage unit as being either word-oriented or character-oriented. This is the primary reason why computers with a byte-addressable organization are called general-purpose computers; a computer with this type of storage unit can efficiently process both scientific and mathematical problems and business-oriented problems.

Most computer storage units in common use are *nonvolatile*. This means that once a character(s) is stored at an address, it remains at that address until another character replaces it. The term *destructive read-in* is used to indicate that any characters read (transferred) into storage locations replace any character(s) previously stored in those locations.

The storage unit of a computer can hold a specified number of characters. The capacity of a storage unit is indicated by a reference to its size. For example, the storage unit of the IBM System/370 Model 148 computer can be described as having a capacity of 512K. In data processing terminology, the letter K as used here represents 1024; thus, the exact size of the Model 148 storage unit is 524,288 storage locations.

Secondary storage media.   Secondary storage media, often referred to as *auxiliary storage,* are used to store programs and data not currently being used by the computer. Secondary storage media thus extend the storage capabilities of the computer system. The two most commonly used secondary storage media are magnetic tape and magnetic disk.

Secondary storage devices (*auxiliary storage devices*) are online to the computer. However, secondary storage media may be online or offline. For example, programs and data stored on magnetic tape and magnetic disk are online if the magnetic tape and magnetic disk are mounted on their respective units. However, if the magnetic tape and magnetic disk are stored in a cabinet, they are offline. Programs and data stored on punched cards are usually offline in that the punched cards are generally stored in punched-card file cabinets, rather than in a card reader, when not being used.

Output devices.   Just as the input of program statements and data occurs by means of an input device, the results of the processing of the data are received from the computer by means of an output device. These results are written from the storage unit onto an *output medium* such as printer forms or punched cards. The most common output device is the printer.

Software

Software is the collection of programs and operating aids associated with a computer that facilitate its programming and operation and extend its processing capabilities. For example, a program called a *utility program* (which is one of several such programs) provides the means by which data is transferred from an input medium, such as punched cards, directly to an output medium such as magnetic tape. The programs and operating aids are usually furnished by the computer manufacturer. Software can also be obtained from independent software companies.

User Programs

The processing of data occurs according to the program statements stored in the program-storage area of the storage unit. These programs are called user programs because they are written by users of the computer. The computer manufacturer usually supplies, as part of the software, several programs for common processing tasks, such as computing square root. However, the users of a computer must either write or obtain from other users most of the programs required to accomplish their specific data processing objectives.

Procedures

A primary objective of a computer system is that the processing of data be accomplished in an efficient and effective manner. For this reason, it is imperative that procedures be developed to detail the exact manner in which such activities as the collection, preparation, and processing of data, and the distribution of results to managers or other individuals or groups, are to be accomplished. Procedures are also necessary for supervisory and operational control purposes, such as to indicate the action to be taken if an error is discovered in the collection, preparation, or processing of data and/or the distribution of results; or if one of the machines in the computer system fails to function properly.

Data Processing Personnel

Generally, a data processing system is housed within a prescribed area, commonly referred to as the data processing department or the computer center. The people working within the area are classified as data processing personnel. Basically, these personnel perform numerous activities required to prepare for and execute the data processing functions. Chapter 17 contains a discussion of the various job classifications, the educational and experience background required of the personnel occupying these job positions, and the fundamental activities performed within each job.

BINARY REPRESENTATION OF DATA

The storage unit of a computer consists of electronic components that can be made to represent either of two possible states: the *off state* or the *on state*. Because one component can represent only two different states, it takes several of them to form combinations that represent letters, numbers, or special characters. The use of two-state components to represent data is known as *binary representation*.

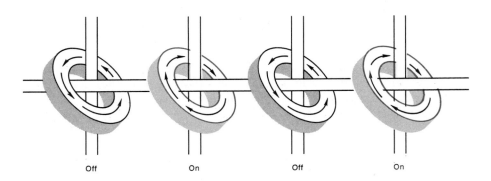

Off   On   Off   On

Illustration 7-2. Four magnetic cores.

Magnetic Cores

The two-state component commonly used to form the storage unit is the *magnetic core*. It is similar in shape to a doughnut and can be magnetized in either of two directions: clockwise or counterclockwise. When a core is magnetized in one direction, it is said to be "on"; when it is magnetized in the other direction, it is said to be "off." Illustration 7-2 shows four cores,

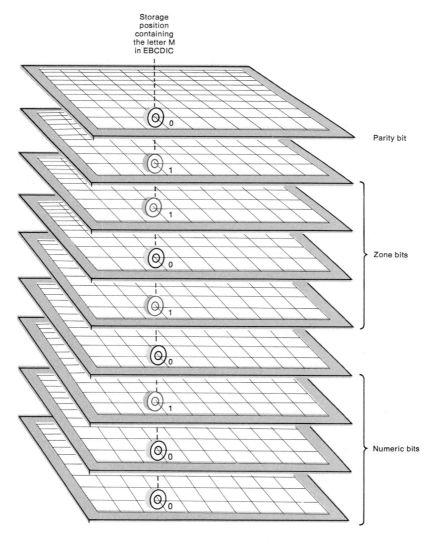

Illustration 7-3. Planes of cores.

two of which are on and two of which are off. The wires that are strung through the cores are used to set them on and off.

Computer storage that is made up of cores is called *core storage*. It consists of planes of magnetic cores. Illustration 7-3 shows nine planes of magnetic cores. Each vertical column of nine cores in the illustration constitutes one storage location. These nine planes represent 100 nine-bit storage locations (they are 10 × 10 core positions in size). The storage location that is highlighted in the illustration consists of cores that are (from top to bottom) parity bit, on-on-off-on-off-on-off-off. In one type of computer, this combination of on and off cores represents the letter M.

Semiconductors

A second type of two-state component used to form a storage unit is the *semiconductor*. The first major commercial system to use semiconductors was IBM's System/370 Model 145 computer, which was first installed in 1971. This use of semiconductor memories by IBM has since been extended to other computer models of the System/370 series. Since semiconductors can be used to form very small, compact circuitry, a semiconductor storage unit is very small. The circuitry is made up of silicon chips, each containing memory "cells" built into its surface. The on or off position of each switch (analogous to a bit) is determined by the direction of the electrical impulse running through a cell (see Illustration 7-4). A silicon chip only a little bigger than a core may hold the equivalent of thousands of bits.

In common practice, core storage circuitry are referred to as "partially integrated" (hybrid) circuits because each module is composed of several combined components. Semiconductor storage circuitry are called "monolithic" circuits because each chip is totally integrated (indivisible).

The advantages of a semiconductor storage unit over a magnetic-core storage unit are increased access speed and reduction (approximately 50 percent) in physical storage unit size. This reduction in storage unit size does not imply a reduction in storage capacity. Thus, while a large first-generation computer storage unit could retain approximately 20,000 characters, today's large computer storage unit can retain approximately 8 million characters (8 megabytes of data).

The disadvantages of semiconductor storage are higher cost and impermanence. Unlike magnetic-core storage, which retains the current settings of its bits even if the source of electrical power for the computer system terminates, a semiconductor storage unit is dependent on an *uninterrupted power supply*. If the power supply for a computer system with semiconductor storage fails, the contents of storage are lost. Thus, semiconductor storage is said to be *volatile*.

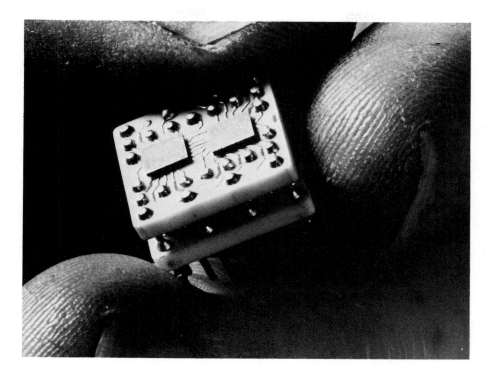

Illustration 7-4. Semiconductor storage module.

Because the costs of semiconductor storage have been reduced through the economies inherent in the mechanization of fabrication, the use of semiconductor storage units is increasing. Eventually, the use of magnetic cores, historically the basic storage unit component, will be surpassed by the use of semiconductors.

Binary Codes

Each component used in a binary representation of data is called a *binary component,* and the codes formed by these components are called *binary codes.* The states of the components can be illustrated by the use of the *binary digits* 0 and 1. If the binary digit 1 represents the on state of a component and the binary digit 0 represents the off state, then the four binary digits 0101 can be used to represent four cores that are off-on-off-on. Binary digits are also called *bits,* an *acronym* for the term *binary digits.*

Different types of computers use different binary codes for storing data. For example, one type of computer uses four bits at each storage location for representing data; its binary code is called Binary Coded Decimal (4-bit BCD). In contrast, another type of computer uses eight bits at each storage location. Its code is called Extended Binary Coded Decimal Interchange Code (EBCDIC). Among the most common binary codes are 4-bit BCD, 6-bit BCD, EBCDIC, ASCII, and true binary.

4-bit BCD.   Since one bit can represent either of two conditions (0 and 1), two bits can represent four different conditions: 00, 01, 10, and 11. Similarly, three bits can represent eight different conditions, and four bits can represent sixteen different conditions. Each time a bit is added, the total number of possible combinations is doubled.

These are the 16 combinations possible with four bits:

0000	0100	1000	1100
0001	0101	1001	1101
0010	0110	1010	1110
0011	0111	1011	1111

If a unique letter, number, or special character is assigned to each of these combinations, 16 (2^4) different characters can be represented.

In 4-bit BCD, only 10 of the 16 possible combinations of four bits are used. These combinations represent the 10 decimal digits (0 through 9). Because binary codes represent decimal digits, the code is called *Binary Coded Decimal,* or *BCD.*

To convert a 4-bit BCD code to its decimal equivalent, each of the positions in the binary number is given a place value. From left to right in the number, the place values are 8, 4, 2, and 1. Therefore, the rightmost bit can be called the 1-bit, the second from the right the 2-bit, the next the 4-bit, and the leftmost the 8-bit. When the place values of the bits that are on (on bits) in a 4-bit BCD code are added, the result is the decimal equivalent. In the binary number 0101, for example, the 1-bit and the 4-bit are on. Therefore, the decimal equivalent is 1 plus 4, or 5. Illustration 7-5 shows the place values and the decimal equivalents of the 10 binary combinations used in 4-bit BCD.

To represent a decimal number of more than one decimal digit, more than one group of four bits is needed. To illustrate, the decimal number 183 can be represented in 4-bit BCD as follows: 000110000011. If this number is broken into groups of four bits, it is: 0001 1000 0011. Then if each of the groups is converted from BCD to decimal, the result is 183.

Decimal Equivalent	4-Bit BCD Code			
	Place Values			
	8	4	2	1
0	0	0	0	0
1	0	0	0	1
2	0	0	1	0
3	0	0	1	1
4	0	1	0	0
5	0	1	0	1
6	0	1	1	0
7	0	1	1	1
8	1	0	0	0
9	1	0	0	1

Illustration 7-5. 4-bit BCD coding.

6-bit BCD.   Another type of BCD coding is 6-bit BCD. It is sometimes called *alphameric BCD* because it can be used to represent alphabetic, numeric, and 28 special characters. All 64 (2^6) possible combinations of six bits are used in this coding scheme.

From left to right, the six bits in an alphameric BCD code are called the B-bit, the A-bit, the 8-bit, the 4-bit, the 2-bit, and the 1-bit. These bits correspond to the punches in the Hollerith (punched-card) code. The rightmost four bits (the 8-, 4-, 2-, and 1-bits) correspond to the digit punches in the Hollerith code. The leftmost two bits (the B- and A-bits) correspond to the zone punches in Hollerith code. This relationship is shown in Illustration 7-6.

The numeric bits in a 6-bit BCD code are converted to their decimal equivalent in the same way that 4-bit BCD codes are converted. The place values of the on bits are added. The one exception to this rule is that the numeric bits 1010 are converted to a decimal 0 in 6-bit BCD but they have no equivalent in a 4-bit BCD. Thus, the numeric portion of the code 111010 is equivalent to a 0-punch; the numeric portion of 110010 is equivalent to a 2-punch.

To convert the zone bits in a 6-bit code, the following rules are used. If both the B- and A-bits are on, the representation is equivalent to a 12-punch. If only the B-bit is on, it is equivalent to an 11-punch. If only the A-bit is on, it is equivalent to a 0-punch. Finally, if both the B- and A-bits are off, it is equivalent to no zone punch. These rules are summarized in

Bit Positions in 6-Bit BCD					
Zone Bits		Numeric Bits			
B	A	8	4	2	1

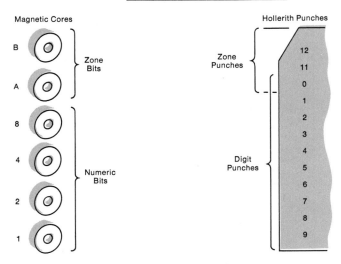

Illustration 7-6. 6-bit BCD compared with Hollerith code.

Illustration 7-7. The zone portion of the code 110001 is equivalent to a 12-punch; the zone portion of the code 010010 is equivalent to a 0-punch.

By combining zone equivalents with numeric equivalents and relating them to Hollerith codes, the 10 decimal digits and the 26 letters of the alphabet can be decoded. For example, the 6-bit BCD code 110010 has a zone equivalent of a 12-punch and a numeric equivalent of a 2-punch; it is, therefore, the code for the letter B (the Hollerith combination of a 12-punch and a 2-punch). Similarly, the code 001010 is equivalent to no zone punch and a 0-punch; it represents the decimal digit 0. The table in Illustration 7-8 gives all 64 BCD codes and their equivalent characters.

Zone Bits	Zone-Punch Equivalents
BA	
11	12
10	11
01	0
00	No punch

Illustration 7-7. Zone equivalents.

Character	Card Code	6-Bit BCD Code					
b	No punches						
.	12-3-8	B	A	8		2	1
□	12-4-8	B	A	8	4		
[	12-5-8	B	A	8	4		1
<	12-6-8	B	A	8	4	2	
‡	12-7-8	B	A	8	4	2	1
&	12	B	A				
$	11-3-8	B		8		2	1
*	11-4-8	B		8	4		
]	11-5-8	B		8	4		1
;	11-6-8	B		8	4	2	
△	11-7-8	B		8	4	2	1
—	11	B					
/	0-1		A				1
,	0-3-8		A	8		2	1
%	0-4-8		A	8	4		
⌢	0-5-8		A	8	4		1
\	0-6-8		A	8	4	2	
⧕	0-7-8		A	8	4	2	1
♉	2-8		A				
#	3-8			8		2	1
@	4-8			8	4		
:	5-8			8	4		1
>	6-8			8	4	2	
√	7-8			8	4	2	1
?	12-0	B	A	8		2	
A	12-1	B	A				1
B	12-2	B	A			2	
C	12-3	B	A			2	1
D	12-4	B	A		4		
E	12-5	B	A		4		1
F	12-6	B	A		4	2	
G	12-7	B	A		4	2	1
H	12-8	B	A	8			
I	12-9	B	A	8			1
!	11-0	B		8		2	
J	11-1	B					1
K	11-2	B				2	
L	11-3	B				2	1
M	11-4	B			4		
N	11-5	B			4		1
O	11-6	B			4	2	
P	11-7	B			4	2	1
Q	11-8	B		8			
R	11-9	B		8			1
‡	0-2-8		A	8		2	
S	0-2		A			2	
T	0-3		A			2	1
U	0-4		A		4		
V	0-5		A		4		1
W	0-6		A		4	2	
X	0-7		A		4	2	1
Y	0-8		A	8			
Z	0-9		A	8			1
Ø	0			8		2	
1	1						1
2	2					2	
3	3					2	1
4	4				4		
5	5				4		1
6	6				4	2	
7	7				4	2	1
8	8			8			
9	9			8			1

Illustration 7-8. Standard 6-bit BCD code.

Bit Positions in EBCDIC							
Zone Bits				Numeric Bits			
8	4	2	1	8	4	2	1

Illustration 7-9. EBCDIC coding.

To represent four characters in 6-bit BCD requires four groups of six bits, or 24 bits. For example, 110010100000000010001001 can represent four characters. Broken into groups of six bits and decoded, it represents the characters B-29.

EBCDIC. The *Extended Binary Coded Decimal Interchange Code,* or *EBCDIC* (pronounced ee-'bee-dick or ib-'si-dick), is an 8-bit code for character representation. Since there are 256 (2^8) possible combinations of the eight bits, up to 256 different characters can be coded. In addition to the alphabetic, numeric, and special characters that a 6-bit code allows, the alphabetic characters in lowercase (the 6-bit code allows only uppercase letters) and additional special characters, such as the question mark and quotation marks, can be represented. Not all of the 256 combinations of the eight bits have been assigned to characters.

A second major advantage of using an 8-bit code for character representation concerns the storage of numeric characters. Since a numeric character can be represented by only four bits, an 8-bit configuration allows the representation of two numeric characters. The representation of two numeric characters in eight bits is commonly referred to as *packing.*

As shown in Illustration 7-9, the rightmost four bits in EBCDIC coding are the 8-, 4-, 2-, and 1-bits. They often correspond to the numeric bits in 6-bit BCD coding. The leftmost four bits of EBCDIC are the zone bits, various combinations of which are used in conjunction with the rightmost bits to represent letters, numbers, and special characters.

The EBCDIC representations for uppercase alphabetic characters and the numeric characters 0 through 9 are shown in Illustration 7-10. The bit pattern 1111 is the zone combination for the numeric characters; 1100 is the zone combination for the alphabetic characters A through I; 1101 is used for characters J through R; and 1110 is used for characters S through Z. Thus, for example, the code 11111001 is equivalent to the decimal digit 9; the code 11000001 is equivalent to the letter A. Other zone combinations are used for special characters. The EBCDIC representation of B-29 is shown below.

B	—	2	9
11000010	01100000	11110010	11111001

Character	EBCDIC Bit Representation	
0	1111	0000
1	1111	0001
2	1111	0010
3	1111	0011
4	1111	0100
5	1111	0101
6	1111	0110
7	1111	0111
8	1111	1000
9	1111	1001
A	1100	0001
B	1100	0010
C	1100	0011
D	1100	0100
E	1100	0101
F	1100	0110
G	1100	0111
H	1100	1000
I	1100	1001
J	1101	0001
K	1101	0010
L	1101	0011
M	1101	0100
N	1101	0101
O	1101	0110
P	1101	0111
Q	1101	1000
R	1101	1001
S	1110	0010
T	1110	0011
U	1110	0100
V	1110	0101
W	1110	0110
X	1110	0111
Y	1110	1000
Z	1110	1001

Illustration 7-10. EBCDIC code for digits
and uppercase letters.

In EBCDIC, an unsigned digit is assumed to be positive and is represented by 1111 in the leftmost four bits. The 1111 combination was chosen to make certain that numeric characters would be the highest in the collating sequence (ordering) of characters. A plus sign is represented by 1100 and a minus sign by 1101. Usually, the sign of a number occupies the leftmost four bits of the least significant (low-order) digit of the number. The remaining digits of the number contain 1111 in the leftmost four bits. In the packed format, however, the sign occupies the rightmost four bits of the least significant digit and all other sign designations are eliminated.

ASCII. EBCDIC was developed by IBM. Another 8-bit code, known as the *American Standard Code for Information Interchange,* or *ASCII,* is sponsored as an 8-bit standard code by the *American National Standards Institute (ANSI).* This code was developed through the cooperation of several computer manufacturers. Their objective in developing the code was to standardize a binary code, and thus provide a computer user with the capability of using several machines produced by a single manufacturer or by several manufacturers. The concept and advantages of ASCII are identical to those of EBCDIC. The vital difference between the codes lies in the 8-bit combinations used to represent the various alphabetic, numeric, and special characters.

True binary representation. In some computers, numbers can be represented in true binary code. The number of bits used to form a true binary number varies. For example, some computers use 8-bit true binary numbers, others use 12-bit true binary numbers, and so on. Regardless of the number of bits, a true binary representation can represent numeric data only.

To convert a true binary number to its decimal equivalent, the place values of the on bits are added. These place values start at the rightmost bit position with a value of 1 and double for each position to the left. Thus, for an 8-bit true binary number, 128, 64, 32, 16, 8, 4, 2, and 1 are the place values. In a 36-bit true binary number, the place value of the leftmost bit position is 23,359,738,368! Illustration 7-11 shows how the 12-bit true binary number 111010111011 is decoded. Its decimal equivalent is the total of the place values of the on bits, or 3771.

True binary representation of numbers is useful because fewer bits are required to represent large numbers in true binary than in any of the BCD codes. For example, in the illustration, the decimal number 3771 requires 12 bits as a true binary number. However, it requires 16 bits in 4-bit BCD, 24 bits in 6-bit BCD, and 32 bits in EBCDIC. A computer that has 36 bits at each storage location and uses true binary representation can store the equivalent of 68,719,476,735 in one storage location. Contrast this with a 6-bit BCD computer that can store one decimal digit in each storage location. The largest number that it can store in 36 bits is 999,999.

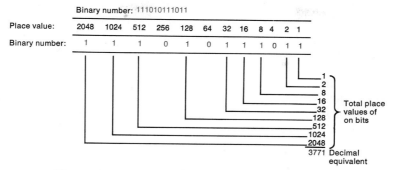

Illustration 7-11. Decoding a true binary number.

Parity Bits

In addition to the bits used to represent data, most computers have one additional bit in each storage location. This bit is used to detect errors in circuitry. It is called a *parity bit,* or *check bit.* A computer that uses 4-bit BCD has a fifth bit for parity; a computer that uses 6-bit BCD has a seventh bit for parity; a computer that uses EBCDIC or ASCII has a ninth bit for parity; and so on.

The parity bit is used to make the number of on bits in a code location either odd or even, depending on whether the computer uses *odd parity* or *even parity*. Illustration 7-12 shows the 4-bit BCD code combinations for a computer that uses odd parity. When the parity bit is taken into account, each of the combinations has an odd number of on bits. In a computer that uses even parity, the number of on bits in each code location is even.

Decimal Equivalent	4-Bit BCD Bit Positions				
	P	8	4	2	1
0	1	0	0	0	0
1	0	0	0	0	1
2	0	0	0	1	0
3	1	0	0	1	1
4	0	0	1	0	0
5	1	0	1	0	1
6	1	0	1	1	0
7	0	0	1	1	1
8	0	1	0	0	0
9	1	1	0	0	1

Illustration 7-12. 4-bit BCD with odd parity.

The parity of data is checked each time that the data is moved into or from the storage unit, or referred to while in the storage unit. To illustrate, suppose that the BCD code (and parity bit) 00011 has just been moved into the storage unit of a computer that uses odd parity. Since the number of on bits in the code is even, a bit must have been set on or off due to error. This error is caught by the checking circuitry of the computer. The computer first attempts to re-read the bit. If necessary, it continues to retry the read several times. If no retry is successful, the system informs the computer operator that an error has occurred.

Parity checking gives some assurance that the operations that take place in a CPU are accurate. If a bit is set on or off in error, the error is detected. In contrast, other types of data processing equipment—for example, accounting machines—may function improperly without giving any indication that an error has occurred.

HEXADECIMAL REPRESENTATION

In daily activities, humans generally use the decimal numbering system. In a computer storage unit, however, data is represented in binary form. It is often necessary for an individual, say a programmer trying to get a program to execute successfully, to determine the contents of particular storage locations. Suppose the programmer had to convert the data in

Binary System (place values) 8 4 2 1				Hexadecimal System	Decimal System
0	0	0	0	0	0
0	0	0	1	1	1
0	0	1	0	2	2
0	0	1	1	3	3
0	1	0	0	4	4
0	1	0	1	5	5
0	1	1	0	6	6
0	1	1	1	7	7
1	0	0	0	8	8
1	0	0	1	9	9
1	0	1	0	A	10
1	0	1	1	B	11
1	1	0	0	C	12
1	1	0	1	D	13
1	1	1	0	E	14
1	1	1	1	F	15

Illustration 7-13. Binary, hexadecimal, and decimal equivalent values.

these storage locations from binary to decimal. Doing so would be time-consuming and the chance of error would be high. Because of these two problems, most computer systems are designed to print out the contents of storage locations using a convenient and efficient representation for binary numerals: *hexadecimal (base 16) representation.*

A group of four binary digits can be represented by one digit of the hexadecimal numbering system. As the term *base 16* implies, 16 symbols are used in the hexadecimal numbering system—the digits 0 through 9 and the letters A through F. Equivalent binary, hexadecimal, and decimal numbers are shown in Illustration 7-13.

The decimal equivalent of $12F1_{16}$ can be found by (1) multiplying each symbol by the appropriate power of the base 16 and (2) adding the resultant products to get the decimal equivalent. Thus, 12F1 represents:

$$(1 \times 16^3) + (2 \times 16^2) + (F, \text{ or } 15, \times 16^1) + (1 \times 16^0), \text{ or}$$

$$4096 + 512 + 240 + 1 = 4849_{10}$$

THE EXECUTION OF PROGRAM STATEMENTS

When program statements or data items are moved into or from the storage unit, the contents of one or several storage locations are moved at a time, depending on the *access width* of the computer. The access width is the number of storage locations into or from which data is moved (or accessed) at a time. For example, if the access width of a computer is one byte (one storage location), one byte of data is moved at a time. If the access width is two bytes, two bytes of data are moved at a time.

An *access cycle* is a computer cycle during which one access width of data is moved into or from the storage unit. These cycles take place continuously as a computer operates. For instance, suppose that a computer with a one-byte access width executes a start program statement that is four bytes long. As the program statement is moved to the control unit, four access cycles take place. Similarly, suppose a computer with a one-byte access width executes an add program statement that is six bytes long and that adds two five-byte fields and places the answer in one five-byte field. This program statement takes 21 access cycles: six access cycles to move the statement into the control unit, ten to move the five-byte data fields into the arithmetic/logic unit, and five to return the answer to the storage unit.

The *access speed* of a computer is the time required for one access cycle. This speed varies among computers, but it is constant for a particular type of computer. For example, one common type of computer has an access speed of 920 nanoseconds. The access speed of a computer is one indication of the overall speed of the CPU.

To calculate the total time it takes a computer to execute a program statement, one needs to know the number of access cycles required for that execution, the access speed of the computer, and the time required to carry out the function of the statement. In the example of the four-byte start program statement with access width of one byte, four access cycles are required plus the time for carrying out the start itself. Therefore, if the access speed of the computer is 920 nanoseconds, execution of the program statement takes 3680 nanoseconds plus the time for the start. (Remember, there are approximately as many nanoseconds in a second as there are seconds in 30 years.) Similarly, if a 21-access-cycle add program statement is executed on a computer with a 920-nanosecond access speed, it takes 29,320 nanoseconds plus the time for performing the addition in the arithmetic/logic unit.

The time for carrying out the function of a program statement varies, depending on the type of statement and the computer. For instance, it may take less than the equivalent of one access cycle to carry out the start. On the other hand, the equivalent of many access cycles may be required to perform the function of a multiplication program statement. Some computers can perform this and other arithmetic functions significantly faster than other computers.

In summary, the speed of execution of a program statement depends on the time required for access cycles and the time needed for carrying out the function of the statement. Although for some program statements the time required for carrying out functions can be significant, in most cases the time required for access cycles is a good indication of the speed of the computer.

Summary

1. The term *computer* implies a machine capable of arithmetic calculation and having many other characteristics, the most notable of which are that it is electronic, has internal storage, is instructed by a stored program, and is capable of program-execution modification.

2. There are many useful ways in which computers can be categorized. Among these are classifications by the type of data they are capable of manipulating (digital and analog), by the purpose for which they were designed (special and general), and as mixtures of types (hybrid).

3. Computer systems are composed of five basic components: hardware, software, user programs, procedures, and data processing personnel. Hardware is the machines used by a data processing department, including data-preparation devices, input devices, a central processing unit, secondary storage devices, and output devices. Software consists of the collection of programs and operating aids associated with a computer that facilitate its operation and programming. User programs are programs written by the users of the computer systems. Procedures are the rules, policies, and guidelines governing the operation of the computer center. Data processing personnel are the people responsible for keeping the data processing department functioning in an effective and efficient manner.

4. The central processing unit has three parts: the control unit, the arithmetic/logic unit, and the storage unit. The control unit controls the flow of data into and out of the storage unit of the computer. It also interprets program statements that it retrieves from the storage unit. The arithmetic/logic unit provides the arithmetic calculation and logical comparison capability of the computer. The storage unit stores program statements and data until called for by some other unit. It also acts as a temporary holding point for the intermediate results of calculations.

5. Computers are designed on a two-state (binary) coding system. Storage units of most computers consist of two-state magnetic cores, each of which can be electromagnetically charged to either an on or off condition. Thus, computer storage is sometimes called core storage. To represent the two-state coding system, binary digits, or bits, are used (0 corresponds to off and 1 corresponds to on).

6. The coding schemes employing binary code are referred to as Binary Coded Decimal (BCD) representations. These include the 4-bit BCD (used to code the 10 decimal digits); 6-bit BCD (capable of representing

alphabetic, numeric, and 28 special characters); and EBCDIC and ASCII (either of which is capable of representing 256 different characters). True binary representation is used in cases where large numbers must be represented using only a few bits.

7. The BCD codes have one additional bit called the parity bit, or check bit, which is used to detect errors in circuitry so that no characters are changed inadvertently as they are transferred between units. Some computers use odd parity (an odd number of on bits per character) while others use even parity.

8. Representation of the contents of storage using the hexadecimal numbering system assists an individual in determining the contents of particular storage locations.

9. The time required for execution of a program statement depends on the access width, access speed, and type of statement being executed. The access width determines the number of bytes of data that can be transferred from one unit to another at one time. The access speed is the time required for one access cycle (a computer cycle during which one access width of data is moved into or from the storage unit).

CAREER PROFILE

Frances Mikulicich
Head Console Operator

Southern Pacific Transportation Company

Background Experience

I graduated from high school and have taken some evening courses. I was hired by Southern Pacific in 1955 as a comptometer (calculating machine) operator. I had intended to be a secretary but discovered I didn't like typing and shorthand. So, on my own, I began to experiment with the keypunch machine and found it easier than typing. My interest grew, and I started taking courses at night to find out more about computers. In 1959, I became a keypunch operator in the Data Processing Department. In order to become a console operator, I had to pass Southern Pacific's courses in Computer Fundamentals and IBM/360 and to score well on the IBM Programming Aptitude Test. I succeeded at these and, in 1970, became a console operator.

Primary Job Responsibilities

There are three computer console operators and myself on my shift. We are responsible for the operation of computer systems which provide information to all departments in Southern Pacific. Each computer operator initiates programs for processing into the computer, and mounts magnetic tapes and disk packs, as well as printer paper. Since many different programs are being processed on the computers at any given time, we make sure programs are run in the proper order and that they are run successfully. I provide to my Shift Supervisor necessary information on programs not completed.

What Has Made You Successful?

Liking my job. I find that being a computer operator is never boring. There is always something happening, changes to be made in procedures and hardware/software and keeping up with what's new. That's what makes the work interesting to me. Also, the training provided by Southern Pacific and IBM has helped me a great deal. I obtained a good working knowledge of the computer. This is required for my job. And I began to understand and appreciate the big picture of what I do—how the system works—when I took the IBM/360 course. Finally, I want to do my job well—it's very important to me. I have a strong sense of responsibility, which is something I suppose I gained from my home training.

Basic Input and Output Devices

The speed of a data processing system depends in large part on the CPU and input and output (input/output) speeds of the computer. Remember, however, that before a computer can process data, the data must be read from an input device and stored in its internal memory; and after the data is processed, results must be written on an output device. In most business applications, the reading and writing operations require more time than the processing of data. Therefore, the speeds of input and output devices have a significant effect on the overall speed and efficiency of a computer system. Generally, the speed and efficiency of a system can be increased by reducing the time required to read data and write results. For instance, a system that has a 1200-cards-per-minute card reader and a 2000-lines-per-minute printer can process more data than a system that has a 1000-cards-per-minute card reader and a 1100-lines-per-minute printer—regardless of the speeds of operations that take place inside the CPU.

This chapter deals with the basic media of input and output: punched cards and printed documents. It also deals with the input/output devices that process these forms of data: card readers, card punches, and printers. The following three chapters and module discuss magnetic tape, mass storage, and special-purpose input/output devices. These and other devices are sometimes referred to as *peripheral equipment* (see Illustration 8-1). This reference is due to the fact that while they are not physically part of the CPU, they are often located in close proximity to it.

For each type of input or output device, there are a number of physical variations. The important thing to notice is how these physical characteristics can affect the design of a data processing system and how they can help to insure the reliability and accuracy of input and output operations.

CARD INPUT AND OUTPUT

The *card reader* is one of the most basic input devices through which data enters the computer. In addition to the various models produced by different computer manufacturers, there are two distinct methods of reading a punched card and there are two separate principles on which card readers are designed. One method used in reading a punched card is called the *serial method*. This technique is characterized by reading a card column-by-column starting with the first column (and ending with the eightieth column, on a standard punched card). A card reader employing the serial method, therefore, records (or causes the computer to recognize) one character at a time.

The second method of reading a punched card is called the *parallel method*. This method is characterized by the row-by-row reading of a punched card. On a standard punched card, this operation begins with the top of the card (the 12-edge) and is completed with the reading of the last row on the card (the 9-edge). A character is recognized by the distance between the holes in the card. Therefore, a constant reading speed is required on this type of card reader. It is not until the last row is read that the computer can determine the characters on the card from the holes punched in the card. When the last row of the card has been read, all of the characters on the card (up to 80 on the standard card) are recorded.

The principle on which card readers are designed is a reflection of the physical characteristics of the reading process. Two types of card readers can be distinguished under this criterion, namely, the brush-type reader and the photoelectric reader. The *brush-type reader* employs small metal brushes to determine the positions of holes in a punched card. As the card passes through the *read station,* the metal brushes apply a slight pressure to the card. When the brushes pass over a hole, they cause an electrical

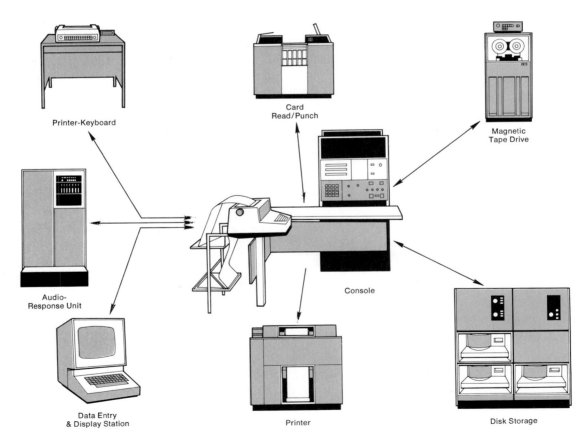

Illustration 8-1. Peripheral equipment.

circuit to be completed with the metal roller below the card. This procedure is illustrated in Illustration 8-2. As noted in the pictorial explanation of the brush-type reader, each card is read twice and·a comparison is made to avoid undetected misreading of the card. If the results of the two reading operations do not correspond, the computer refuses to process the card.

The second type of card reader is the *photoelectric, or brushless, reader.* The photoelectric reader requires the use of a *light source* and a series of *photoelectric cells.* As shown in Illustration 8-3, this type of reader is characterized by the passing of each punched card under a luminous object that projects a beam of light through the holes in the card. The light is received by photoelectric cells positioned directly behind the hole positions in the card. When a photoelectric cell is activated by the light, an electrical circuit is completed; the card reader recognizes a hole in the card. These readers operate at higher speeds and with greater reliability than brush-type readers.

The *card punch* is an output device. The function of the card punch is to record results transferred from the computer onto punched cards. While the card reader transforms punched holes into electrical impulses, the card punch converts electrical signals into card punches. As Illustration 8-4 demonstrates, the card punch takes blank cards from the input hopper of the machine and moves them one at a time to the *punch station* where the holes are punched. Then the card passes to a *read station* where the punching is checked. Finally, the card passes to the output stacker. As in

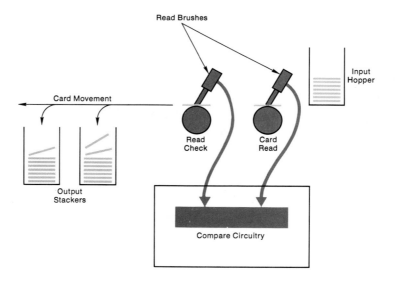

Illustration 8-2. Parallel brush-type reading.

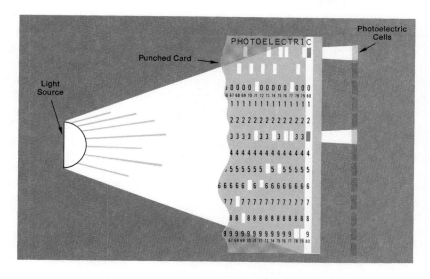

Illustration 8-3. Serial photoelectric reading.

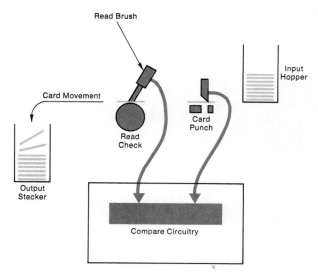

Illustration 8-4. Card-punch operation.

the reading of a punched card, the card-punching function may be performed either serially (column-by-column) or in parallel (row-by-row).

The physical characteristics of card readers and punches vary. They may be separate physical units, or they may be combined into a single unit. The combined units may have separate input hoppers for reading and punching, or they may have only one input hopper for both reading and punching The design of a data processing system may vary because of these physical variations.

The device in Illustration 8-5 has one input hopper and two output stackers. Cards placed in the input hopper can be read or punched, or both.

1. Input hopper
2. Output stackers

Illustration 8-5. Combined card read/punch with one input hopper.

They can be stacked in either of the output stackers. Because this device has only one input hopper, it cannot be used for *reproducing* or for *merging*. On the other hand, since cards are both read and punched in the same feed, it can be used to *intersperse gangpunch* data from one card into succeeding cards. In any event, in the design of a system, the functional capabilities of its input/output devices must be taken into account.

Illustration 8-6 shows one type of combined card read/punch. It has one input hopper for reading, one input hopper for punching, and five output stackers. Two of the stackers can be used for cards from the read-feed; two can be used for cards from the punch-feed; and the middle stacker can be used for cards from either feed. With this device, data from cards in the read-feed can be reproduced into cards in the punch-feed. Cards from

1. Punch input hopper
2. Read input hopper
3. Output stackers

Illustration 8-6. Combined card read/punch.

either feed can be separated into any one of three stackers. And because the middle stacker is common to the read-feed and the punch-feed, cards from the punch-feed can be merged into a deck with cards from the read-feed. In contrast, the card read/punch in Illustration 8-5 cannot be used to carry out any of these functions.

CHECKING FOR ERRORS

To insure the accuracy of input and output operations, input/output devices carry out various types of checks for errors. If these checks were not carried out, computer system processing errors could occur even when CPU operations took place flawlessly. Several types of input/output checks are possible with card readers and punches.

One type of error checking in card reading is called *validity checking*. This is a check of all combinations of punched holes in the card to make sure that they represent valid characters. For example, suppose an 80-column punched card has a combination of a 3-punch and a 1-punch in one of its columns; this is not a valid character in Hollerith coding. Such an error is caught by the circuitry that checks for validity errors. The computer system stops or alerts the operator in some other way that a problem has been encountered.

A second type of check on card reading is shown in Illustration 8-2. As noted in discussion of brush-type readers, cards that are read by this device actually pass through two read stations. The first reading of the cards is compared with the second reading. If the two readings are not the same, an error is indicated. The same principle of checking by comparison is used in many other input/output devices. Recall that, after a card is punched by the card punch in Illustration 8-4, the card passes through a read station. The data punched in the card is read and compared with the data that was intended to be punched. If they are not the same, an error is indicated.

ADVANTAGES AND LIMITATIONS
OF PUNCHED-CARD INPUT/OUTPUT

The basic advantages of punched cards as an input medium stem from the physical characteristics of the card itself. First, data on punched cards is readable by humans, as compared with data on magnetic tape, for example, which is machine-readable only. Since the data on a card is visible, errors are easier to correct than they would be otherwise. Second, cards are relatively inexpensive. Third, they are a relatively durable form of input medium. Fourth, records can be added to or deleted from a card file without processing the remaining portion of the file. This is not possible with magnetic tape. Finally, since the major impetus of card input and output stems from original uses of punched-card equipment, cards are a compatible medium for any other punched-card equipment in use.

Although punched cards are a popular form of input and output, they have many limitations. A serious disadvantage of any card-oriented system is the slow speed of input and output. Card readers are capable of handling from 400 to 1600 characters per second (300 to 1200 cards per minute). Compared to the input speed of magnetic tape, even 1600 characters per second is relatively slow. Punched-card output is even slower because of mechanical movements required at the punch station. Typical speeds of card punches range from 100 to 500 characters per second.

A second disadvantage of punched cards is that they cannot be erased and reused. In contrast, a potential for reuse is one of the basic advantages of magnetic tape, disk, and drum storage. For example, a magnetic tape can be reused in six consecutive jobs, with its contents changing during every job. Third, decks of punched cards are subject to calamities such as being dropped or being inadvertently rearranged. Card records may be sequenced incorrectly or lost. A magnetic-tape file is not subject to such errors because the tape is a continuous medium; each record on a tape is physically attached to the records preceding and following it.

Another disadvantage is the fixed *data density* of a punched card. Since a punched card is fixed in length and only one character can be recorded in a column, the organization of data may be hampered. For instance, if 81 characters of data are to be entered on standard 80-column punched cards, two cards are required. In contrast, with magnetic tape, the data can be packed or the size of the record on tape can be increased to accommodate the data. Finally, as an input or output medium, punched cards are bulky and require large amounts of storage space relative to other media. Thus, the handling and storage costs for punched cards are greater than the costs of keeping the same amount of data on another medium.

In summary, there are a number of variations in card readers and punches that affect the functional capabilities, and, therefore, the design of a system. In addition, there are some variations that affect the speed and reliability of the devices. Finally, circuitry that checks for errors is part of both reading and punching operations. This is necessary to insure the overall accuracy of the processing done by a computer system.

PRINTER OUTPUT

The common functions of a printer are to print one line at a time; to space one, two, or three lines at a time; and to skip to any of 12 punches in a *forms-control tape.* The four major variations in printers are: (1) varieties of forms a printer can print on; (2) number of print positions available on a single print line; (3) number of different characters that can be printed; and (4) type of printing mechanism used for printing. Of these, the first three can affect the design of a system, and the fourth can affect the speed and reliability of a printer.

Perhaps the key variation in printers that affects the design of a system is the types of forms a printer can print on. Most printers print on *continuous forms.* Some can print on *cut forms* such as punched cards or postal cards. Illustration 8-7 shows a printer that can print on both punched cards and continuous forms. The punched cards are fed into and printed on the left side of the machine. Continuous forms are printed on the right side of the machine. When this type of printer is used, punched cards can be printed

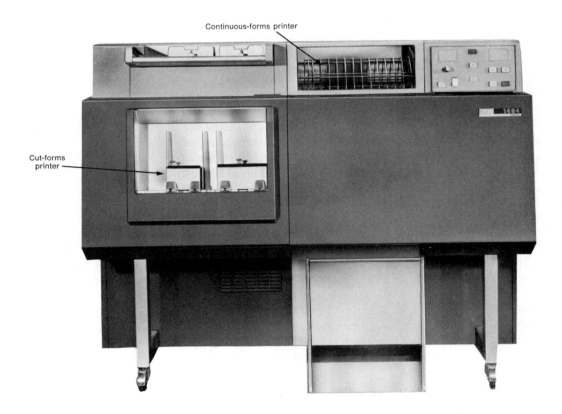

Illustration 8-7. Cut-forms and continuous-forms printer.

and used as output documents such as utility bills. Later, when a bill of this type is returned with a requested payment, it can be processed by the computer as a record of payment. The same punched card is both an output of, and an input to, the system.

The number of print positions that a printer has and the number of different characters that it can print affect the design of output forms. For example, if a printer has 100 print positions, it cannot print a report that is 140 print positions wide. Similarly, if a printer can print only the decimal digits, the alphabet, and certain special characters, it cannot print a report requiring many special characters. Although the characteristics of a printer are not normally a limitation in system design, they must be considered when designing reports.

Among the popular printers of today are those capable of printing 132 and 144 characters per line. The continuous-forms printer in Illustration 8-8, for example, is capable of printing up to 144 characters per line.

To insure accuracy, various checks on printer-output operations are performed. Some of the common checks are:

1. Characters to be printed are examined to make sure the printer is capable of printing them.

Illustration 8-8. Continuous-forms printer.

2. Movements of paper and of printing mechanisms are constantly checked to make sure they are synchronized.
3. Print hammers are checked to make sure they do not misfire.

If an error condition occurs, the computer system halts or alerts the operator in some other way that a problem has been encountered.

There are two principles on which printers are designed just as there are two principles for design of card readers. The distinction in the case of printers is one of character-at-a-time printing versus line-at-a-time printing. *Character-at-a-time printers* include console printers, teletype printers, and matrix printers. Since the console printer provides a special function, it is discussed in Module A, which deals with special-purpose input/output devices. Typical *line-at-a-time printers* are bar, wheel, comb, drum, and chain printers. In this class, the drum printer and the chain printer are the most popular.

The *teletype printer* is used when limited amounts of printer output are expected. It consists of a square which contains the desired characters (see Illustration 8-9). The printing operation is initiated by moving the square across the page from left to right and stopping to position a character. Then, a hammer behind the character strikes the square, causing the character to be imprinted on the page. Since the teletype printer stops for the positioning of each character, its printing speed is extremely slow, generally about 10 characters per second.

The *matrix printer* is based on a design principle similar to that of the scoreboard clock in many football stadiums. It consists of a 5×7 rectangle composed of pins, and certain combinations of the pins are activated to represent characters (see Illustration 8-10). As these pins are pressed against the page, the composite of the character results. Typical speeds of matrix printers approach 900 characters per minute.

The comb printer has one bar that moves horizontally along a line of print from left to right. As the bar moves, hammers behind the desired

A	B	C	D	E	F	G
H	I	J	K	L	M	N
O	P	Q	R	S	T	U
V	W	X	Y	Z		0
1	2	3	4	5	6	7
8	9		#	.	,	/
@	*	♯	&	-	%	$

Illustration 8-9. Teletype square.

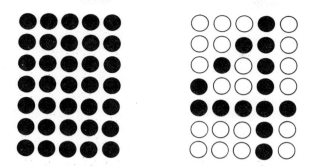

Illustration 8-10. Printer matrix.

characters strike the bar to produce the desired characters at the required positions. After each pass, the bar returns to its original position for the next line of print. Typical speeds of the comb printer approach 150 lines per minute.

The *drum printer* has a cylinder with raised characters on its surface. At each print position, there is a circular band containing all the characters that the printer can print (see Illustration 8-11). The drum rotates at a constant speed, making one revolution for each line of print. As the appropriate character on the drum passes the print position, a hammer at the position strikes the paper against an inked ribbon and then against the character. Drum printer speeds range from 700 to 1600 lines per minute.

The design of a *chain printer,* such as the IBM 3211 printer shown in Illustration 8-8, is based on the concept of a *print chain.* The print chain

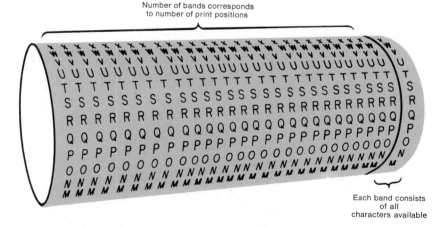

Illustration 8-11. Print drum.

consists of several sets of characters revolving horizontally past all print positions (see Illustration 8-12). As the characters pass the print positions, hammers behind the paper press it against an inked ribbon, which in turn presses against appropriate characters on the print chain, thus printing the characters. Chain printers are capable of producing from 600 to 2000 lines of print per minute.

All of the printing devices discussed thus far are known as *impact printers*. They are typical printers used on computer systems. The term *impact* is appropriate because each printer uses some kind of mechanical printing element to strike the paper on which an output character is to be printed. A newer development is the *nonimpact printer*. Printers belonging to this group use a variety of methods to print output. *Electrothermal* printers use heat to make an image on a special thermal paper. *Electrostatic* printers work much like the typical office copier; some of them can print characters on ordinary, plain paper. The electrothermal or electrostatic printer is often used where a low-cost printer is needed. They are most commonly found on portable terminals and low-cost com-

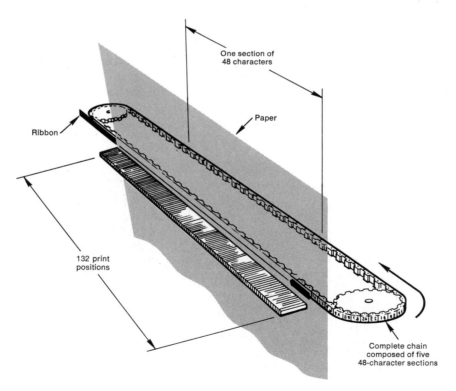

Illustration 8-12. Print chain.

puters. Their silent operation is often a reason for their use, especially in applications where noise might be a problem. Although most electro-thermal and electrostatic printers are relatively slow-speed devices, some are capable of producing 2000 to 5000 lines of print per minute.

Specialized high-speed nonimpact printers have been introduced by several companies. The printer system in Illustration 8-13 can print at speeds as high as 13,360 lines per minute. This printer uses a *laser* and *electrophotographic* technology to attain high speeds. Such a high-speed printer overcomes the primary disadvantage of nonimpact printers: the inability to make carbon copies. Multiple printings of the same page can be made in less time that it takes an impact printer to print one page.

ADVANTAGES AND LIMITATIONS OF PRINTER OUTPUT

An advantage of employing a printer as an output device is that it produces human-readable output. However, printers have a number of disadvantages. First, somewhat like the punched card, printer output is of a fixed size. If a report must be wider than the printer's capability permits, the output must be broken into separate segments and manually aligned. Second, printing is a relatively slow form of output. There are wide variations in printing speeds, but most printers print at speeds of 300, 600, 1200, or 2000 lines per minute.

The nonimpact printer is not used as widely as the impact printer for several reasons. Most of them are not able to make carbon copies of output. They often require special paper that is very expensive. The quality of the nonimpact printed image is often not as good as that produced on impact printers.

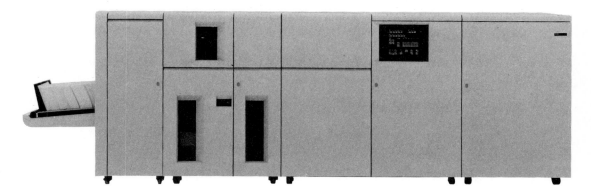

Illustration 8-13. High-speed laser printer.

Summary

1. Punched cards are a basic input/output medium of most computer systems. Card readers and card punches are the input/output devices (peripheral equipment) used to process them. The readers and punches are designed to read and punch data using either a serial (column-by-column) or parallel (row-by-row) method. To read the holes in a card, some card readers use a brush-type mechanism while others use a brushless, or photoelectric, mechanism. In addition to reading and punching cards, a combined card read/punch may be capable of reproducing, merging, or interspersed gangpunching.

2. A card reader performs two checks on data received as input. First, it performs a validity check to determine whether all the combinations of punched holes represent valid characters. Then it performs a second read to insure the accuracy of the reading operation.

3. The advantages of punched cards include human readability, low cost of cards, relative durability of cards, flexibility of card decks, and ability to use cards with other punched-card equipment. Disadvantages of punched cards include slow input/output speeds, fixed data density, and relatively high storage and handling costs. In addition, cards are not erasable; they cannot be reused for new data.

4. Printers can print on continuous forms and/or cut forms. They can be classified as either character-at-a-time, such as console, teletype, and matrix printers, or line-at-a-time, such as comb, drum, and chain printers. They also differ in the number of print positions available per line.

5. The typical printers used on computer systems are known as impact printers. Nonimpact printers are a newer development. They use a variety of methods to print output, including heat, electrostatic, and laser techniques. Their low cost and silent operation make them popular for many applications. Their chief disadvantage is the inability to make carbon copies.

6. The principle advantage of printer output is that it is human-readable. The disadvantages of printers include fixed output size and relatively slow print speeds.

Magnetic Tape
Input and Output

Magnetic tape, in appearance, looks much like the tape in a tape recorder. It has two major parts: the *base,* which is a plastic material, and the *magnetic coating,* which consists of a *ferric oxide.* These parts are bonded together by a thin layer of adhesive. While the plastic base of magnetic tape represents the bulk of the tape, the magnetic coating is the essential ingredient allowing magnetic tape to serve as an input/output medium. Data is recorded on the surface of the tape in the form of magnetized areas, combinations of which correspond to letters, numbers, and special characters. The areas are analogous to the holes that represent data in punched cards.

A reel of magnetic tape can hold as much data as can be punched into several hundred thousand cards. A typical speed at which a magnetic tape can be read is 320,000 characters per second—the equivalent of 4000 punched cards.

Magnetic tape is wound on a reel called the *file reel,* or *supply reel,* in much the same way that motion-picture film is placed on a reel. Generally, a reel of magnetic tape is ½ inch wide and 2400 feet long. However, there are magnetic tapes that are ¾ inch or 1 inch wide. The length of the tape can, of course, be determined by its purpose and may range from 50 to 3600 feet. Illustration 9-1 presents a reel of tape and a blow-up of a section of the tape showing its composition.

A small strip of reflecting material is placed at each end of a magnetic tape. The strip at the beginning of the tape is called the *load-point marker.* It indicates to the computer the beginning of the usable portion of the tape. The strip at the end of the tape is called the *end-of-reel marker.* It tells the computer where the end of the tape is located so that the tape is not run off the reel and processing delayed accordingly. These markers are on opposite sides of the tape to insure that the computer can distinguish between them. They are sensed when they pass under a light source, and they reflect light into photoelectric cells assigned to the markers. The file markers and the photoelectric cells are shown in Illustration 9-2.

DATA REPRESENTATION ON TAPE

Generally, there are two forms of coded data representation on tape. Illustration 9-3 shows one of them: 6-bit BCD code with a seventh bit for parity checking. The short vertical lines on the tape represents areas that are magnetized and are equivalent to on bits. The spaces represent areas on the tape that are not magnetized and are equivalent to off bits. Each of the seven horizontal rows on tape is called a *track.* The tracks correspond to the seven bits of BCD coding: B-, A-, 8-, 4-, 2-, and 1-bits plus the parity, or check, bit. Each character consists of the combination of bits in one vertical column of the tape. For example, the first character in Illustration 9-3 is the number 0, which consists of an 8-bit and a 2-bit; the check bit is off because this tape uses even parity. Because there are seven vertical positions in which there can be on bits, this tape is known as *seven-track tape*.

In addition to seven-track BCD coding, nine-track tape codes are used. As the term *nine-track* implies, these codes are used with tapes having nine vertical positions, or tracks. They are the most common type of tapes. In each set of vertical positions (byte) on a nine-track tape, one EBCDIC or ASCII character, two 4-bit BCD digits, or one 8-bit true binary number can be coded.

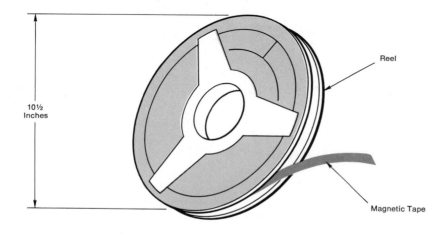

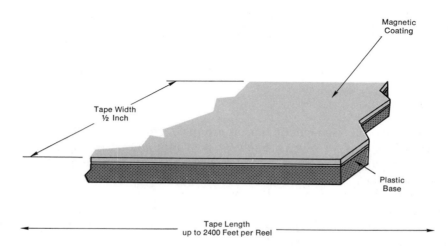

Illustration 9-1. Tape characteristics.

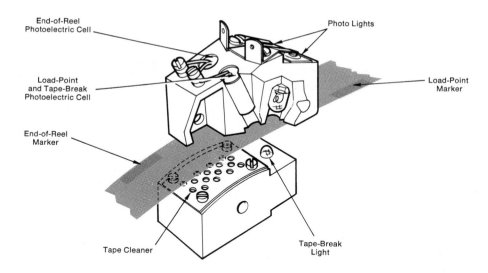

Illustration 9-2. File marking and sensing.

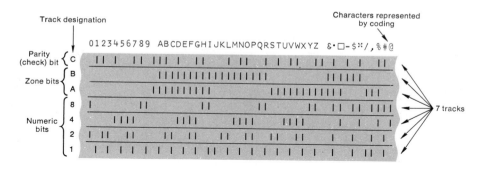

Illustration 9-3. BCD coding on seven-track magnetic tape.

Data is stored on magnetic tape as groups of characters (or bytes) called *physical records,* or *blocks.* Each block, while composed of characters, also represents one or more *logical records*—the data grouping known to a user program.

The number of characters in a block can vary from few to many. Data storage on magnetic tape is not restricted to 80 characters as on the standard punched card. Consecutive blocks on the tape are separated by spaces in which no data is recorded. These spaces are called *interblock gaps,* or *IBGs.*

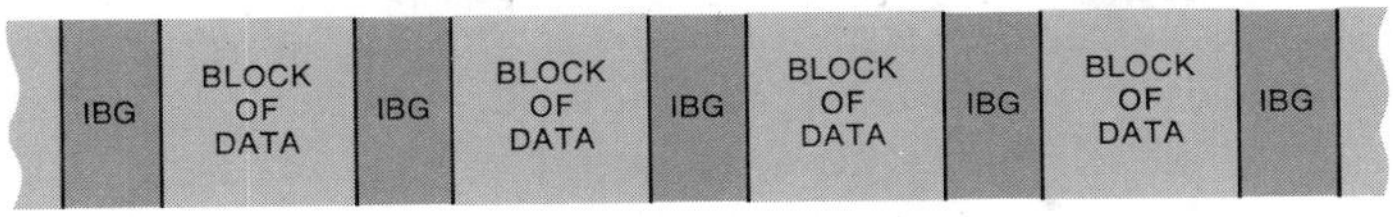

Illustration 9-4. Section of tape with four blocks
of data and interblock gaps.

When a tape is read during the execution of a program, all of the data between two IBGs is read by a single read instruction. If each block is 100 characters (or bytes) long, a single read instruction reads 100 characters of data. The IBGs are necessary because of this stop and start type of operation. They provide the space required to stop the passage of tape over the read/write heads of the tape drive. Since reading and writing are performed at a constant speed, a portion of the IBG is used for the tape to gain speed when a read/write operation begins. The width of the IBGs varies from 0.6 inch to 0.75 inch, depending on the type of tape unit and whether the tape is seven- or nine-track. Illustration 9-4 shows four blocks of data and the gaps that separate them.

THE TAPE DRIVE

A tape drive is shown in Illustration 9-5. This device reads and writes the magnetized areas on a tape. When this device reads data from tape, the data is not affected. That is, the reading operation is not destructive. When data is written on tape, any data previously recorded on the affected area of the tape is replaced by the new data. Therefore, the writing operation is destructive.

Illustration 9-6 demonstrates the arrangement of reels on a tape drive. The file reel (supply reel) that is to be read or written has been mounted on the left side, while the *machine reel (take-up reel)* has been mounted on the right. The *vacuum column* for each reel (see Illustration 9-5) allows slack tape to be pulled from the reel. These columns are necessary because the reels rotate at such high speeds that the tape would snap if slack were not provided. The tape is threaded through a mechanism called the *read/write assembly* (an enlarged schematic of which appears in Illustration 9-6) and anchored on the machine reel. Some tape drives require manual threading of the tape, but other tape drives do this automatically.

When the tape is processed, it moves from left to right through the read/write assembly and onto the machine reel. On some tape drives, the tape must be rewound onto the file reel before it can be read or written again. Other tape drives are capable of reading the tape while the reel is moving in the reverse direction (right to left) also, so no rewinding operation is required.

The reading operation is accomplished by individual *read/write heads*. There is one head for each track on the tape. The reading portion of the head senses the small magnetized areas and, in conjunction with the other reading assemblies, converts these areas into characters. Since data is recorded on the tape serially, the reading operation is performed serially. The writing operation follows a similar pattern. Instead of sensing mag-

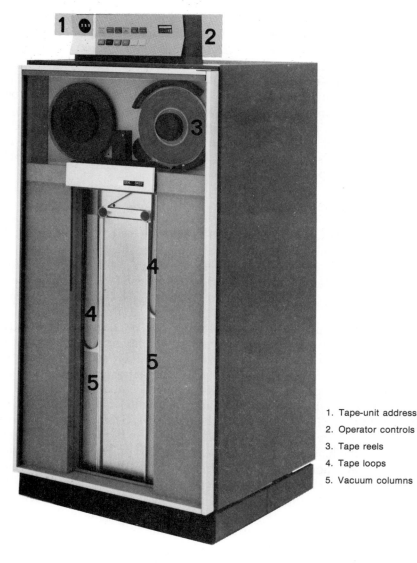

1. Tape-unit address
2. Operator controls
3. Tape reels
4. Tape loops
5. Vacuum columns

Illustration 9-5. Tape drive.

netized areas, a write head places magnetized areas on the tape, replacing any data already there.

The basic programmed functions of a tape drive are to read and write data on a tape. In addition, the tape can be rewound, backspaced, and skipped ahead (over faulty sections of tape) under control of a program.

To insure the accuracy of tape reading operations, a computer system, in conjunction with its tape drives, carries out three checks for accuracy. One kind of check is dependent upon whether or not the read/write heads are

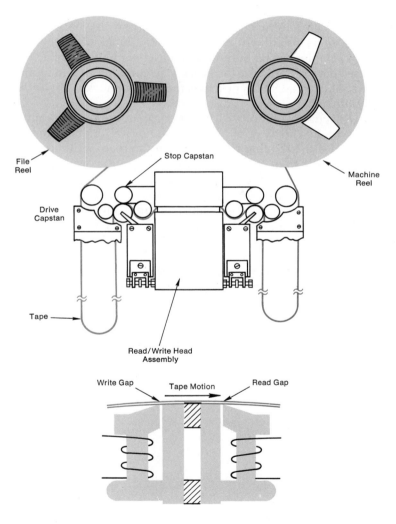

Illustration 9-6. Schematic drawing of a tape drive and a read/write head.

single-gap or dual-gap. Many tape drives have a dual-gap read/write head capability. Data is written at the write gap and then read at the read gap for verification. Thus, this type of head offers a distinct advantage over the single-gap read/write head, which lacks this capability.

A second kind of check is the *vertical parity checking* performed on each character of data that is read into storage (see Chapter 7). In addition, *horizontal parity checking*, or *longitudinal parity checking*, is carried out during tape reading. In this kind of checking, the last byte in every block of data written on tape is a *longitudinal check character*, or *LCC*. This check character has bits that are set on or off to make the total number of bits in each track in a block either odd or even, depending on whether the check is for odd or even parity. Illustration 9-7 shows a block of 20 characters and the LCC for the block. The individual characters have odd parity and the LCC insures that each track in the block also contains an odd number of on bits. When data is read by a tape drive, the data is checked for both vertical and horizontal parity.

To insure accuracy of tape writing operations, data is read immediately after it is written. This is possible because the writing mechanism immediately precedes the reading mechanism in the read/write assembly. The data that is read is then compared with the data that was intended to be written on the tape. If they are not the same, an error is indicated.

Unlike input and output errors on a card system, tape reading and writing errors can sometimes be corrected without interruption of processing. When a reading error is detected, for example, the computer system branches to a programming routine for handling errors. This routine causes the tape to be backspaced one block and read again. It is possible that on the first reading there was a piece of dust or dirt on the tape surface that caused an error. If it was wiped off in passing through the read/write assembly, the second reading may take place without interruption. If so, the computer continues to execute the program as if no error had been indicated. If not, the computer branches to the error routine again. This routine may backspace and re-read the tape as many as 100 times before alerting the computer operator that an error has occurred.

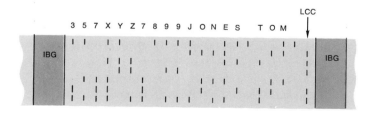

Illustration 9-7. Vertical and longitudinal parity checking.

The same type of error procedure is followed when a writing error is detected. The tape is backspaced, and the computer system tries to write the block again. If the writing takes place without error on this second try, the computer continues to execute the program. Only after many tries does the error routine skip over the faulty section of tape that cannot be written on (this has the effect of making one long interblock gap) and continue farther down the tape. Because errors are corrected in this way, writing errors should not cause the computer system to stop unless a large portion of the tape's surface is damaged or otherwise unusable.

To prevent records from being destroyed in error, detailed written instructions for each processing step are prepared for the computer operator. Among other things, these instructions tell which tapes are to be mounted on which tape drives and whether the tapes are to be read or written on. The operator then checks the label on the outside of each reel to make certain that it holds the tape specified in the instructions. If the tape is to be written on, the operator places a *file-protect ring* on the back of the tape reel before mounting it. Such a ring is shown in Illustration 9-8. If a program tries to write on a tape drive that does not have a file-protect ring, a writing error occurs and no writing takes place. The requirement for this ring helps to prevent records from being destroyed in error.

Another technique to prevent the destruction of records is called *label checking*. In this case, the label is not on the outside of the reel; it is part of the tape itself (an 80-byte record preceding the first data record of a file). This record, or *header label,* contains such items as file name, date the file was created, and date after which it is permissible to write on the file. The label is checked by a programming routine that is executed before records are read or written. The routine reads the header label and checks to make certain that the tape is the right tape and that it is mounted on the correct drive. After the label check, if all is well, the program continues. If not, the program prints out an error message, and the tape is not processed.

The computer determines the end of a file by means of a *trailer label,* a special record following the last data record on the file. This 80-byte record contains control information, such as the number of records in the file.

THE SPEED OF TAPE INPUT/OUTPUT OPERATIONS

One measure of the speed of magnetic tape reading and writing operations is the *transfer rate* of the tape drive. This rate is the maximum number of bytes of data that can be read or written on a tape per second. It depends upon the speed at which the tape moves past the read/write heads (called the *transport speed*) and the number of bytes, or characters, that are recorded per inch along the length of the tape (called the *density*). A common transport speed is 200 inches per second. Some typical tape densities are 556, 800, 1600, and 6250 bytes per inch (BPI, or bpi). Many tape drives have a *dual-density* capability. If a tape drive has this capability, its read/write heads can write on a magnetic tape in either of two densities. A common dual-density is 1600/6250 BPI.

The transfer rate of a tape drive is calculated by multiplying the transport speed times the density. As an example, suppose that a tape drive, with a transport speed of 200 inches per second, reads tapes with a density of 1600 bytes per inch. The transfer rate of this tape drive is 1600 times 200, or 320,000, bytes per second. To appreciate this speed, consider that this book could be read by such a tape drive in less than 10 seconds.

Although the transfer rate of a tape drive is a good indication if its speed, this figure is somewhat misleading. Actually, when a tape drive reads blocks of data, it stops each time it comes to an interblock gap. Therefore, when blocks are being read or written, a certain amount of time is spent stopping and starting at each interblock gap. This is called *start/stop time.*

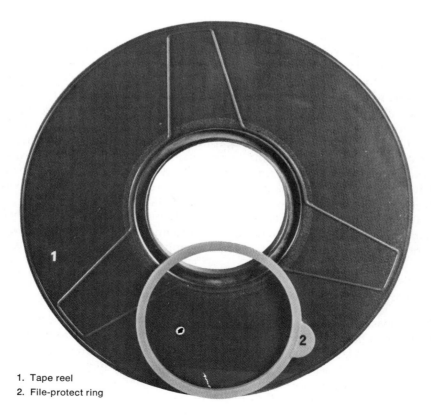

1. Tape reel
2. File-protect ring

Illustration 9-8. File-protect ring.

The total amount of time required to read or write a given number of blocks is the sum of the time spent reading or writing the data plus the time spent starting and stopping at the interblock gaps.

To appreciate the effect of start/stop time on reading and writing speeds, assume that a tape drive has a transfer rate of 320,000 bytes per second and a start/stop time of three *milliseconds* (.003 second). If this tape drive is used to read 6000 blocks and each block is 100 characters long, how long will it take?

In this problem, a total of 6000 times 100, or 600,000, bytes of data are to be read. Since the transfer rate is 320,000 bytes per second, the total time for reading the data is 600,000 divided by 320,000, or 1.88 seconds. As for start/stop time, there are 6000 interblock gaps and passing over each takes .003 second. The total start/stop time is 6000 times .003, or 18, seconds. Therefore, 1.88 plus 18, or a total of 19.88 seconds, are required to read the 6000 blocks. To say it another way, 18 seconds are spent in stopping and starting the tape, and only 1.88 seconds are spent in reading the data.

Up to this point, each block (physical record) has been assumed to contain only one logical record. For reasons that will become obvious, normally more than one logical record is included within each block. For example, blocks of 10 logical records can be recorded on tape. In this case, the records are called *blocked records,* and the tape is said to have a *blocking factor* of 10. Illustration 9-9 represents blocked records with a blocking factor of four. A tape may have a blocking factor of one (one logical record per block); the records on such a tape are unblocked.

In the example above, the reading of 6000 unblocked records, each record 100 characters long, took 19.88 seconds. Suppose the 6000 records were blocked, 10 to a block. How would this affect the total input time? Since 10 records, instead of one, would be recorded between interblock gaps, the total number of gaps to be passed over would be reduced from 6000 to 600. Otherwise, the problem is the same as the preceding one. The total input time would be 1.88 seconds (for reading data) plus 1.8 seconds (600 times .003), or 3.68 seconds. In other words, by blocking the records in this manner, the input time would be reduced from 19.88 seconds to 3.68 seconds. If the blocking factor were increased to 100, the reduction in input time would be from 19.88 to 2.06 seconds.

While certain figures were used in the above illustration, they do not represent all of the capabilities of magnetic tape. The transport speed,

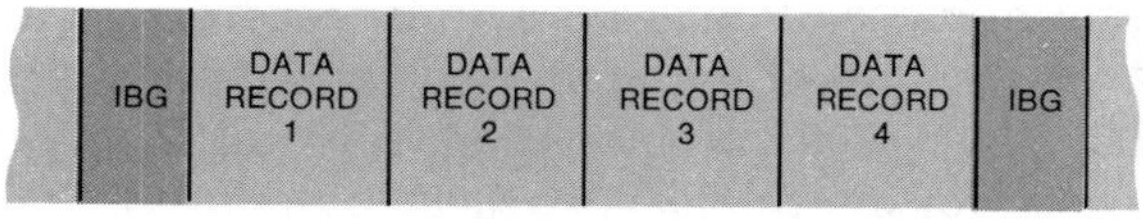

Illustration 9-9. Block of records with a blocking factor of four.

which was given as 200 inches of tape per second, can also be 120, 320, 470, 780, or 1250 inches per second. The number of bytes that the tape drive is capable of reading or writing, which was stated as 320,000 bytes per second, may range from approximately 41,700 to 1,250,000 bytes per second. Finally, the density, which was given as 1600 bytes per inch, can also be 556 or 6250 bytes per inch. Therefore, when the speed of tape input/output operations is to be calculated, a primary consideration is the type of tape drive utilized.

Although blocking records improves tape input/output speeds, it has one major limitation. Since all of the data between two IBGs is read during a single read operation, the input area of storage must be at least as large as the block of data. For example, if 100-character records are blocked 10 to a block, the input area in storage must be large enough to hold 1000 characters. If a program is to read two input tapes and write two output tapes and each block of data is 1000 characters in length, the program requires 4000 positions of storage for input and output areas. The amount of storage that can be set aside for input and output areas must be considered when determining whether (or how) records should be blocked.

THE CAPACITY OF TAPE REELS

To figure the maximum capacity of a reel of tape, one must know two characteristics of the tape: its length and its density. If, for example, a 2400-foot tape has a density of 1600 bytes per inch, the maximum capacity of the tape is 2400 feet times 12 inches times 1600 bytes per inch, or a total of 46,080,000 bytes of data. This total is roughly equivalent to the amount of data that can be recorded on 576,000 punched cards.

The capacity of a tape is reduced by the interblock gaps separating the data on the tape. As noted earlier, a typical length for interblock gaps is 0.75 inch. At a density of 1600 bytes per inch, each of these interblock gaps takes up the equivalent of 1200 bytes of data. To figure the total length of tape that a given number of records will take up, one must calculate the length of tape used for data and for interblock gaps. Since the gaps on tapes are wasted space, blocking records increases the capacity of a length of tape.

Suppose, for example, that 8000 unblocked records are to be recorded on tape and each record contains 100 characters. If the tape has a density of 1600 bytes per inch and an interblock gap of 0.75 inch, how many inches of tape will be required?

Since the total number of characters to be recorded is 800,000 and the density is 1600, the length of the tape used for data is 500 inches (800,000 divided by 1600). Since 8000 interblock gaps separate the 8000 records, 6000 inches will be used for interblock gaps (8000 times 0.75). Therefore, a total of 6500 inches of tape will be required for these 8000 records. Twelve times as much tape will be used for interblock gaps as for data.

If the records are blocked 10 to a block, the only thing that changes is the number of interblock gaps required; only 800 will be needed instead of 8000. Therefore, the total length of tape required for the same amount of data will be 500 plus 600, or 1100 inches. And if the blocking factor is 100, the data will require only 560 inches of tape. In other words, by increasing the blocking factor, the capacity of a tape is increased. Remember, however, that records can be blocked only within the limits of a computer's available storage.

ADVANTAGES AND LIMITATIONS OF TAPE AS AN INPUT/OUTPUT MEDIUM

The primary advantage of magnetic tape as an input or output medium is the speed with which data can be transferred. Tape provides a means through which data becomes extremely accessible to the computer. In conjunction with the input and output speeds, which are desirable in themselves, this additional capability also saves computer time. Since the computer performs better than any input or output device yet discussed, the closer the operating speeds of the input and output devices to the speed of a computer, the more time is saved. Second, magnetic tape possesses the advantage of low storage cost. In comparison to punched cards, magnetic tape is capable of storing a mass of data in a relatively small space. This is possible because of the high density that can be achieved on tape. Third, magnetic tape is reusable. Even though data has been written on a tape, the tape can be completely erased, or updated data can be written over old unwanted data. Fourth, the cost of tape is less than that of punched cards. A single 2400-foot length of magnetic tape costs approximately $15. To record the amount of data that can be placed on a single tape on cards would require several boxes of cards. Fifth, the header label placed at the beginning of a tape can be used as a security device. Normally, a serial number is included in the header label. It is difficult to access the tape without knowing this number. Therefore, if this number is not made available, the chances of gaining access to the data on the tape or of destroying its contents are reduced. Finally, magnetic tape can be used either online or offline. When online, the tape is under the direct control of the computer. Offline means that, while the tape may be stored in the computer room, the computer does not have access to it. Thus, an online tape may contain frequently used programs or data; an offline tape may contain information saved for historical purposes.

There are three primary limitations of magnetic tape. First, the data coded on magnetic tape is not readable by humans. Since the contents of a tape cannot be read by a programmer or an operator, the data on a tape may have to be printed before an error can be located. Second, data on tape can be organized only in a *sequential* manner. This means that individual items on a tape cannot be accessed in a direct fashion. The tape must be scanned from its beginning to locate a specific data item. Generally, processing data in this fashion is relatively slow when compared to processing data on magnetic disk or drum. Finally, magnetic tape may be influenced by environmental factors. Such problems as dust, dirt, high or low temperatures, humidity, and electrical fields cause errors in the processing of data on tape. Dust and dirt on magnetic tape may cause the read head to misread characters. Temperature fluctuations and humidity may cause distortions of the tape or cause it to become brittle so that breakage occurs. Electrical fields or magnetic currents may alter the magnetized areas on the tape. Even static electricity caused by the soles of a person's shoes rubbing a nylon carpet, if discharged into a reel of tape, can cause the tape to be erased. Therefore, extreme care should be exercised in the handling and storage of magnetic tape to insure the accuracy of its contents.

AN EXAMPLE OF MAGNETIC TAPE UTILIZATION

A typical computer system can perform processing that is impossible on a typical card-oriented system. Many of the functions that are carried out by punched-card equipment in a card system are done by the computer itself in a tape system. The system design for tape processing is significantly different from that for card processing.

Illustration 9-10 is a system flowchart for the basic processing of an order-writing, billing, inventory, and accounts receivable application. It represents six processing steps during which a combined invoice and shipping-order form is printed, and inventory (item) and accounts receivable (customer) master records on tape are brought up-to-date. The first step is keypunching and verifying; the other five steps are computer processing runs. In the system flowchart, the ☐ symbol indicates a computer run and the ◯ symbol represents a magnetic-tape file.

Sales orders serve as the source documents in this system; they are used in the keypunching and verifying of item cards. The intent is to record in punched cards the data pertaining to the line items on the orders. This includes the customer number and other identifying information plus quantity ordered and item number for each item. It does not include item description or unit price because this data can be added to the transaction records from master records during subsequent processing.

Although this transaction data can be punched one line item to a punched card as it would be for a punched-card system, it can also be

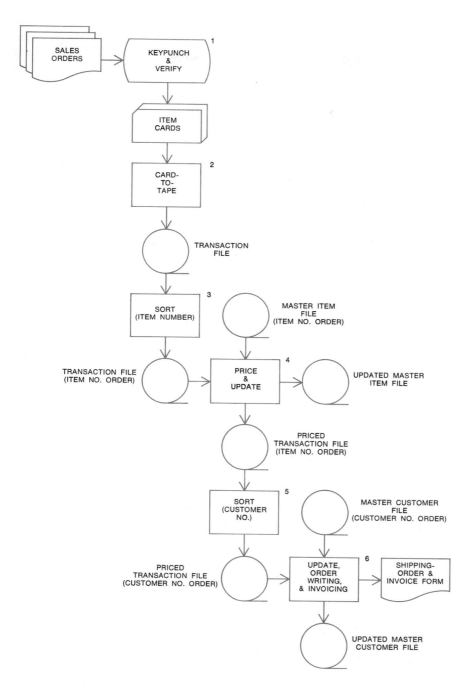

Illustration 9-10. System flowchart for a tape system.

punched several line items to a card. When this method is used, the punched cards are called *spread cards* and the volume of cards to be processed by the system is reduced. Illustration 9-11 is an example of a spread card in which customer number, order number, and order date are punched in the first three fields of the card as identifying information. Thereafter, quantity ordered and item number are punched for up to six line items. If more than six line items are ordered by a single customer, additional spread cards must be used.

Regardless of which type of punched card is used (the unit-record or the spread card), the second step in the system is to convert the punched-card data to data on tape. This is done in a *card-to-tape-run*. At the end of this step, each record on the tape will have five fields: customer number, order number, and order date (these identify each record); and quantity ordered and item number (these represent the transaction). The records may be either blocked or unblocked on the tape. Illustration 9-12 shows a portion of the tape with a blocking factor of four.

Step 3 is a sort run. Although a single input tape and a single sorted output tape are shown, more than two tape drives are required for sorting. It is possible to use only three tape drives, but four are normally used, to increase the speed of the sorting operation. The input tape with the records in the original sequence is mounted on one of the drives. During the sort, each of the tapes on the four drives may be written on, or read from, several times. On completion of the sort, one of the drives holds the output tape with records in item-number order. This sorting process may be very complex from a programming point of view, but the programming effort is easily justified; the ability to sort tape records into a desired sequence is a very important characteristic of tape systems.

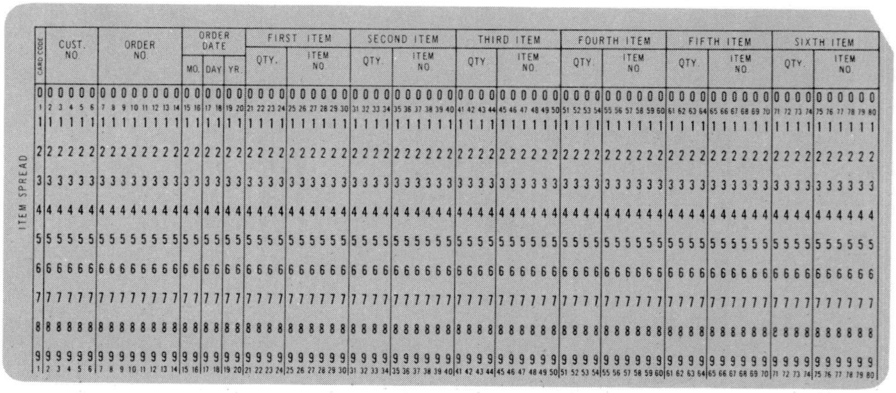

Illustration 9-11. Spread card.

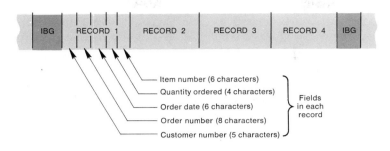

Illustration 9-12. Blocked transaction records.

Step 4 in the system is designed to do two things. First, additional data is added to the transaction file so that it can be used to print the line items of the shipping-order and invoice form. This additional data includes item description, unit price, and whether the items will be shipped or back-ordered. Second, the master item file (inventory file) is brought up-to-date. The records in the master item file have the format indicated in Illustration 9-13. The fields in each master item record that may be affected during this update process are the on-hand field (it will be reduced by the number of items shipped) and the back-ordered field (it will be increased by the number of items ordered when no inventory is available to be shipped).

It should be clear now why step 3 in Illustration 9-10, the sorting operation, is required before step 4 can be accomplished. The transaction records have to be sorted into item-number order so that they are in the same sequence as the master item records before they can be processed against the master item file.

Step 4 has two input tapes and two output tapes. The input tapes contain the transaction records (the transaction file) and the master item records (the old master file). The output tapes contain the priced transaction records (the priced transaction file) and the updated master item records (the new master file). After this processing run, the new master file is the same as the old master file except that the on-hand and/or back-ordered fields in certain records are brought up-to-date. The priced transaction records (one of which is shown in Illustration 9-14) have the same basic data as the sorted transaction records plus five fields derived from the master item

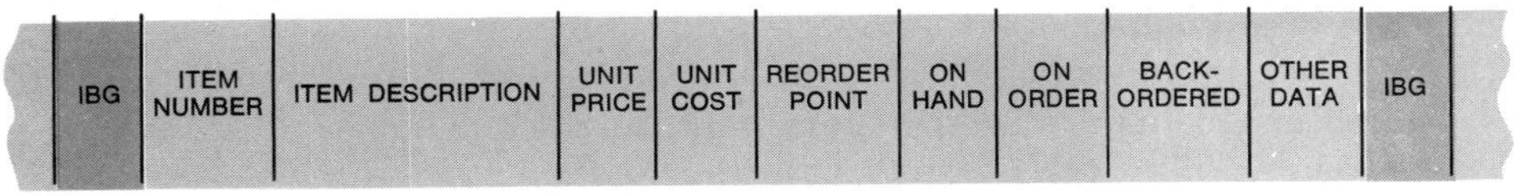

IBG	ITEM NUMBER	ITEM DESCRIPTION	UNIT PRICE	UNIT COST	REORDER POINT	ON HAND	ON ORDER	BACK-ORDERED	OTHER DATA	IBG

Illustration 9-13. Master item record.

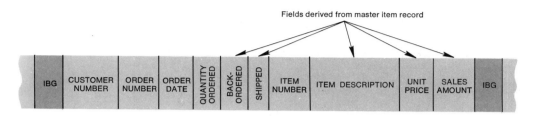

Illustration 9-14. Priced transaction record.

records. The priced transaction records now contain all of the data needed to print the line items of invoices.

The processing in step 4 takes place by reading into storage both a master item record and a transaction record. If the master item record has the same item number as the transaction record, any affected fields in the master record (on-hand and/or back-ordered) are brought up-to-date. A priced transaction record is assembled and written on the priced transaction file. Then the next transaction record is read into storage. When all transactions for a master record have been processed, the updated master record is written on the master file. On the other hand, if there are no transactions for a master record, the record is written on the new master file exactly as it was on the old one. Because a relatively small percent of the master records may be affected in an update run, many master records may simply be copied from the old master file to the new one.

In step 5 the priced transaction records are sorted into customer-number order in preparation for the processing run of step 6. Since the master customer file (accounts receivable file) is in customer-number order, the priced transaction file must be sorted into that same sequence. Once again, although only one input tape and one output tape are shown on the flowchart, all tape drives on the system are normally used by the sort program.

The inputs to the processing run of step 6 are a master customer file (old master) and the priced transaction file. The outputs of this run are the shipping-order and invoice form, plus an updated master customer file (new master). The master customer records contain data needed to print the heading of the shipping-order and invoice form (such as customer name and address, terms, and shipping instructions) plus accounts receivable data (such as total amount owed, and amounts owed over thirty, sixty, and ninety days). After the heading of the output form is printed from the data in the master customer record, the line items are printed from the data in the priced transaction file. At this stage, the invoice total is calculated, printed on the shipping-order and invoice form, and used to bring up-to-date the customer's accounts receivable data. Then the updated customer record is written on the new master file. Because many customers will not have ordered any items, many customer records can simply be read from the old master file and written, unchanged, on the new master file.

Restating this point, card records are converted to tape records in card-to-tape runs. The tape records are first sorted into the order of the master files to be updated and then processed against these master files. Printed reports can be prepared during master updates or later in separate processing runs. At the end of the six steps illustrated in the flowchart, the updated master item file, the updated master customer file, and the priced transaction file are ready for further processing. For instance, the master item file could be processed by the computer to prepare an inventory-management report. Similarly, the master customer file could be used to prepare an aged accounts receivable report. The priced transaction file could be used to prepare sales analysis reports.

DISCUSSION

When tape and card systems are compared, it is obvious that tape systems have several advantages. First, tape records can be read and written faster than card records. Second, a tape can contain a large number of characters while a card is limited to 80. If more than 80 characters must be recorded, additional cards are required. Third, a tape system usually requires fewer steps than a card system for comparable amounts of processing. For example, the tape system in Illustration 9-10 requires six steps to update two master files and print one output document. A similar card system might require eight or more steps for this processing. Fourth, data and programs can be handled more easily when recorded on tape. Consider, for example, the difference between putting 8000 cards in a card reader and mounting one reel of tape on a tape drive. An experienced operator can mount a tape on a drive in 10 to 15 seconds.

On the other hand, tape systems present complications that are not found on card systems. First, programming for a tape system is more difficult than programming for a card system. Because tape-processing runs often involve multiple input and output files, the processing within the program is not as simple as reading a card, processing it, and writing a line on the printer. Multiple input and output areas are required, as well as more complex programming logic. In addition, error-handling routines are required for tape input and output operations, but not for card operations. Remember, for example, that if a tape reading error is detected, the tape is backspaced and the operation is retried. Finally, if logical records are blocked—say, 10 to a block—they must be assembled in an output area in storage before a write operation is performed. Similarly, when a block of logical records is read into storage, the program must keep track of which logical record in the block is next to be processed.

A second complication of tape processing was mentioned earlier: Data on tape cannot be read or decoded by an operator. If an error occurs during a processing run, it is difficult to determine whether the error resulted from programming or from inaccurate data. A program that prints the contents of tapes on the printer must be available. Such programs are called *tape-to-printer programs*. Because an operator can decode data that is punched in cards, such programs are not necessary for card systems.

Third, adding, changing, or deleting records in a tape file is relatively difficult. In a card system, a master record in a card file can be changed by keypunching a new record and replacing the old record in the card file with

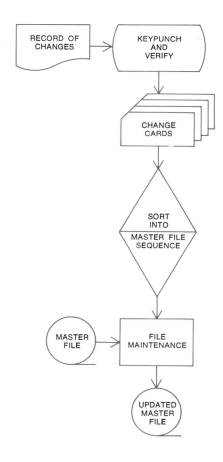

Illustration 9-15. System flowchart for file maintenance.

the new record. In a tape system, special programs, called *file-maintenance programs,* must be executed to add, change, or delete records. Normally, the changes to be made to master records in a tape file are keypunched into cards, sorted, and then processed against the master file by the file-maintenance program. This approach is flowcharted in Illustration 9-15.

Also mentioned earlier was the fact that records on tape can be influenced by environmental factors. Because the surface of a tape can become damaged or dirty, records on tape can become unreadable. In addition, tape records can be destroyed by writing other data over them. Suppose, for example, that a company's current accounts receivable master tape was mounted by mistake on a tape drive used for the output of an inventory-update program. When inventory data was written on the tape, the accounts receivable master records would be destroyed. Can you imagine the loss to the company?

Regardless of the precautions taken, records are destroyed or do become unreadable. To handle this problem, a systems designer plans for *backup* —some way of creating again records that have been lost. In a tape system, the most common backup procedure is to keep the old master and the transaction tapes when a new master tape is written. Then, if the new master tape is destroyed, it can be re-created by repeating the processing of the transactions against the old master records. For greater security, the two preceding master files and transaction tapes for each master file used in a system are kept. Then, even if the two most recent master files are destroyed, they can be re-created from the earlier versions of the file. This method of backup is called the *grandfather-father-son method* because, for every up-to-date master file (the son), the two preceding master files (the father and the grandfather) are kept.

In summary, a tape system can be an efficient system because of the speed, record flexibility, system design, and ease of handling data. However, the tape system introduces certain complications for the operator, programmer, and systems analyst. In addition, since most tape systems have multiple tape drives, the total cost of the system tends to be significant. To facilitate the additional tape input/output operations, more internal storage for input/output areas is generally required. This often leads to a search for a method of utilizing the entire system, computer storage as well as magnetic tape capacity, efficiently.

Summary

1. A magnetic tape is similar in appearance to the tape used in a tape recorder. It is composed of a base and a magnetic coating bonded together with an adhesive. Areas on the tape's surface can be magnetized.

2. Data is represented on magnetic tape in two ways. A seven-track tape employs a 6-bit BCD code with a seventh bit as a parity bit. Nine-track tape uses a code such as EBCDIC with a ninth bit as a parity bit. The vertical columns on a tape are used to represent characters; the horizontal rows, stretching the length of the tape, are called tracks.

3. When data is recorded, it is recorded as groups of characters called blocks. Blocks are separated from each other by interblock gaps (IBGs).

4. A tape drive is the device that employs magnetic tape as an input/output medium. It has a file reel, vacuum columns, a read/write assembly with a read/write head for every track and photoelectric cells that sense file markers, and a machine reel.

5. To insure that data is properly recorded within a block, a longitudinal (horizontal) parity check is performed. At the end of each block, the bits of a longitudinal check character are set on or off to create either an even parity or an odd parity in all tracks in the block. Since each character is checked vertically as well, all data is checked both horizontally and vertically within each block.

6. To provide security, a file-protect ring is inserted on the back of the tape reel when data is to be written on a tape and removed when data is not to be written. Label checking is performed on the first record (header label) of the tape to verify that the tape is the one desired.

7. The speed of tape reading and writing is called the transfer rate and is measured in number of bytes per second. The number of bytes that can be recorded per inch of tape is called density and is measured in bytes per inch (BPI). The transfer rate is determined by multiplying the density by the transport speed, which is the number of inches of tape passing the read/write heads per second. The start/stop time of a tape drive is the time required to stop and start again at an interblock gap between blocks of records.

8. The major advantages of magnetic tape are the input/output speeds with which data can be transferred, low storage cost, reusability, the cost of tape versus the cost of punched cards, labels as security devices, and the online/offline capability of tape. Disadvantages include lack of human readability, the requirement for sequential organization of data, and the susceptibility of tape to environmental factors influencing its ability to retain the data recorded on it.

CAREER PROFILE

Edward Fowlks
I/O Media Specialist

IBM Corporation

Background Experience

I was a Liberal Arts major at Fresno State College. I became interested in computer programming, but there was no CS (computer science) curriculum at Fresno State. I decided to interview with some companies where I could work into this field and was hired by IBM as a mail clerk. Within six months I was the lead man. Then I went into data processing as a computer set-up person. In that job I learned how a computer worked and what programmers and operators did. After about a year, I became a trainee in computer operations. After another six months I became an operator. A year later I became senior operator where I remained for about five years before taking my present position as a media specialist. In terms of my education, I attended night school for a time and have about two years left to graduate.

Primary Job Responsibilities

My main responsibilities are controlling the two forms of media: tapes and disks. We service the users as far as the hardware—the machine, itself—is concerned. I coordinate the work activities of eight people. My job is to see that they do their jobs. As the technical expert, I have to answer anything that comes up involving tapes or disks or know where to locate the answer fast. If equipment malfunctions, it is my duty to ascertain what the problem is and the fastest way of correcting it. If it's minor, I fix it myself. If not, I call a field engineer. I also must see that vital records are stored weekly in the vault. On a typical day, I first meet with my counterpart on the previous shift and find out if there are problems that I will need to handle. An important responsibility I have is to see that communications between all shifts are consistent. I then process requests for disk packs. I check the inventory daily. This is my most critical function—keeping the entire inventory under control. The bulk of the day is spent in solving problems reported by users to my manager. I go out and contact the operator, find out what took place, if it was a bad tape, determine why, and so on. Finally I document the incident, and report back to my manager.

What Has Made You Successful?

I have made use of the IBM mini-courses, which take only 30 minutes and cover everything from the 3033 computer to how to be a good I/O operator. These courses help me right now, on the job—that's critical. For a time I had my own business. It failed but it gave me a better understanding of the needs of a business operation like IBM. The effort I put into my education, including full-time night school before I owned my business, really paid off on the job. Right now I am interested in self-education. I read my manuals at home, and I read a lot of articles on data information. Eventually, I intend to finish my formal education.

CHAPTER 10

Mass Storage Devices

THE DISK PACK

DATA REPRESENTATION ON DISK

THE SPEED OF DISK INPUT/OUTPUT OPERATIONS

AN EXAMPLE OF MAGNETIC DISK UTILIZATION

ADVANTAGES AND LIMITATIONS OF
DISK INPUT/OUTPUT

OTHER DIRECT ACCESS INPUT/OUTPUT DEVICES
The Magnetic Drum
The Mass Storage Subsystem

Although tape systems can process large amounts of data at high speeds, they have two major limitations. First, because the records in a tape file must be in sequence before they can be processed, a tape system requires many sorting steps. For example, before a master file can be updated by a transaction file, both files must be in the same sequence. Therefore, one or both of the files may have to be sorted before processing. Second, when a tape master file is updated, all of the records in the file must be read from the old master tape and written on a new one. Therefore, if a tape master file has 1000 records and only 100 of them are affected by a day's transactions, 900 records must be read and written simply because they are in the file.

As noted in Chapter 9, a computer can access a record in a tape file only after scanning all preceding records in the file. In contrast, it can locate a record in a file on a direct access device without reading all preceding records in the file. With the *direct access method,* it is possible to go directly to desired records and thus process only affected master records during a master-file update. The requirement for sorting is reduced or eliminated. For example, if 100 records of a 1000-record master file are to be updated by a day's transactions, only 100 master records need be read and written. The time required to execute the update program depends on the number of records affected by transactions, not on the number of records in the master file.

One *mass storage device* that can be used in direct access processing is the magnetic disk storage unit. While this mass storage device does not represent all of the devices that can be used in direct access processing, it does represent the most commonly used devices. This chapter deals primarily with magnetic disk, but the concepts and characteristics presented apply to all direct access devices and systems. In the latter part of the chapter, other direct access devices are mentioned to demonstrate other techniques employed in mass storage.

THE DISK PACK

Illustration 10-1 shows a single disk pack (top) and the mounted disk packs and the disk drives (bottom) of a magnetic disk storage unit. A disk drive is the part of the device that reads and writes data; a disk pack contains the data that is read or written. When it is in operation, this disk drive holds one or more disk packs that rotate continuously at a constant speed. Each disk pack can be removed, and another disk pack can be mounted in its place. Thus, the illustration depicts one of a class of disk drives with removable disk packs (that is, of the *removable-disk* variety). There are some models of disk drives to which disks are permanently attached. This class of disk drive is said to be of a *fixed-disk* variety. Most users prefer removable disk packs because the number of magnetic disk storage units they have available is much less than the number of disk packs required to store data. Some users do not have this data storage problem and thus rarely change disk packs. These users prefer fixed-disk storage units because fixed disk packs are capable of storing between 40 and 60 percent more data per disk than comparable removable disk packs.

The disk pack pictured in Illustration 10-1 consists of 11 metal disks mounted on a central spindle. Twenty of the 22 surfaces of these 11 disks are coated with a material that can be magnetized. Data can be recorded

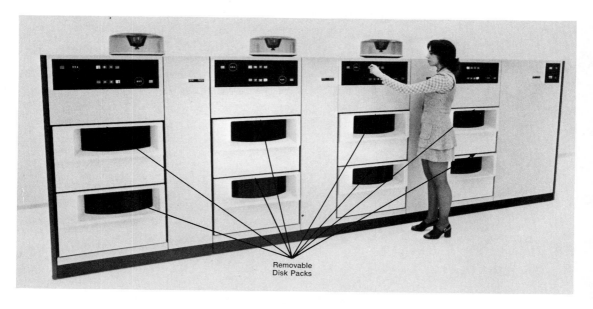

Removable
Disk Packs

Illustration 10-1. Disk pack (top) and disk storage unit (bottom).

on all surfaces of the disks except the top surface of the top disk and the bottom surface of the bottom disk. These two surfaces are blank for protection purposes and because they are apt to be scratched. Of course, the number of disks in a disk pack may vary. For example, there are some disk packs with only five disks, and there are others with 100 disks. Also, the sizes of disks may vary from approximately 1-1/4 to 3 feet in diameter. For example, the IBM 3336 disk pack is 15 inches in diameter and 7 inches deep. Its weight is approximately 20 pounds, so it is easily movable. There are spaces between the disks in a pack. These spaces allow for the read/write heads of the disk drive.

Each of the recording surfaces of a disk is divided into a series of concentric circles on which data can be recorded. These circles are called *tracks*. Illustration 10-2 is a schematic top view of a recording surface that comprises 200 tracks. When a disk pack is to be used by a certain program, it is mounted on the appropriate disk drive and the drive is switched on. The disk pack then begins to rotate. When it reaches the appropriate speed,

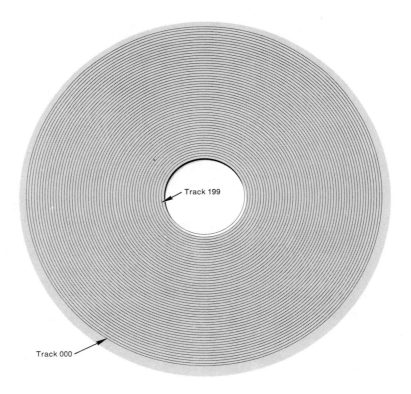

Track 199

Track 000

Illustration 10-2. Top view of a disk surface.

it is ready to be read from or written on. When data is read from the pack, the data is unaffected. When data is written on the pack, it replaces any data previously stored on the same area of the pack.

To read from or write on the disk pack, the disk drive uses an *access mechanism* with one or more *read/write heads*. If multiple read/write heads are used, only one of the heads can operate at a time. Each head can either read or write, but no head can do both at once. Illustration 10-3 shows the read/write heads and access mechanism of a disk drive. While some disk drives utilize one read/write head for each recording surface of the disk pack, other disk drives are designed to employ only one read/write head per disk surface which positions itself on each disk as required.

To operate on all tracks of the recording surfaces, the access mechanism moves back and forth either hydraulically or electrically on a line toward the center of the disk pack. All of the read/write heads of a multiple-head mechanism move at once. At one setting of the access mechanism, all of the read/write heads are on the same tracks of the recording surfaces. For example, the access mechanism could be positioned at the seventieth

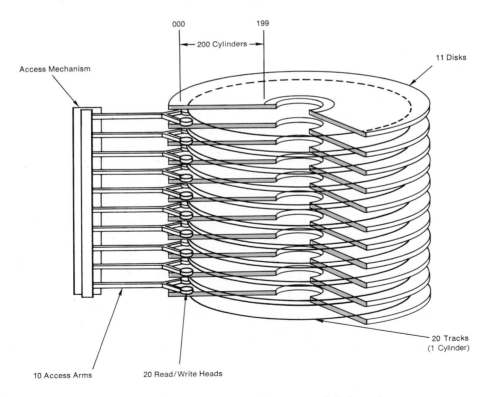

Illustration 10-3. Access mechanism and disk pack.

track on each of the recording surfaces. Then each of the read/write heads could operate on data in the seventieth track of the corresponding disk surface. The tracks that could be operated on at one time make up the seventieth *cylinder* of the disk pack. To say it another way, a cylinder consists of all tracks that can be read or written on in a single setting of the access mechanism. The access mechanisms on some disk drives allow each read/write head to be positioned independent of the others. With a single read/write head or independent read/write heads, the concept of a cylinder is not as well defined.

DATA REPRESENTATION ON DISK

Characters, and records composed of the characters, are recorded on a single track as strings of magnetized bits. Illustration 10-4 represents a section of one track of a recording surface in which several characters are recorded. The 1s indicate magnetized areas, or on bits. The 0s represent unmagnetized portions of the track, or off bits. Although the tracks get smaller as they get closer to the center of the disk pack, each track can hold the same amount of data because the data density is greater on tracks near the center.

A track can hold one or more records. The records on a track are separated by gaps in which no data is recorded, and each of the records is preceded by a *disk address*. This address indicates the unique position of the record on the track and is used to directly access the record. Illustration 10-5 shows a track on which three records have been recorded. Because of the gaps and addresses, the amount of data that can be stored on a track is reduced as the number of records per track is increased. However, as with tape, records on disk can be blocked. Only one disk address is needed per block, and fewer gaps occur. Hence, this technique increases the amount of data that can be written on one track.

Some disk drives use parity bits on the individual bytes of data and a longitudinal check character after each record or block of records as a check on the accuracy of disk input. Other disk drives do not use either of

Illustration 10-4. Section of one track of recording surface.

these parity checks. Instead each record or block of records is followed by two 8-bit bytes called *cyclic check characters,* or *CCs.* These characters are generated when a record is written on the disk pack, based on the bit combinations of the data in the record. Later when the record is read, new cyclic check characters are generated and compared with those on the disk pack. If the compared characters are not equal, an error has occurred. This method of checking input data catches at least as many errors as the combination of individual parity bits and longitudinal check characters. It may catch more.

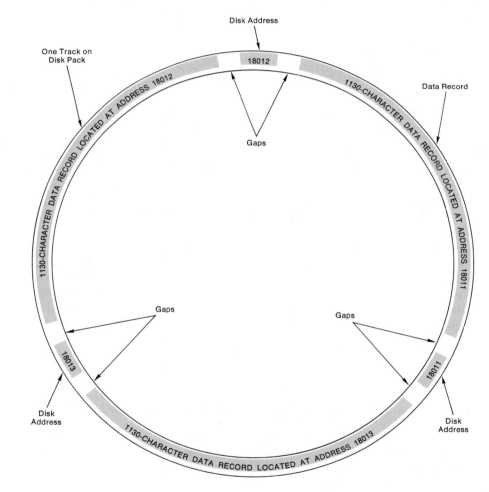

Illustration 10-5. Three records on a track.

THE SPEED OF DISK INPUT/OUTPUT OPERATIONS

The speed at which a magnetic disk operates (*access time*) depends on three factors: (1) head positioning, (2) head switching, and (3) rotational delay. When a specific record is requested, the first response by the disk drive is to position a read/write head over the track at which the record is located. The speed with which this *head positioning* is performed depends on the number of read/write heads, the number of tracks that each head can access at a single position, and the distance the access mechanism has to be moved. Of course, the ideal situation so far as speed is concerned is to have a read/write head for every track on the disk. Some disk drives have this capability. This eliminates the time required to position the head, but it involves much hardware.

Head switching is the process of activating the appropriate read/write head so that data can be transferred from or written on the disk. Since this action takes place at the speed of electricity, the time required for it is considered to be negligible.

Rotational delay is the amount of time that it takes the disk drive to locate the desired data on a track. The time required depends entirely on the rotational speed of the disk, which may range from 40 to 1000 revolutions per minute. An average of one-half revolution is used for the amount of rotation, because, in reality, one complete rotation, part of a rotation, or zero rotations may be required to find the data. If the read/write head is positioned directly over the record that contains the data, no rotation is necessary.

After a read/write head has been positioned over the required record, the *data transfer speed* becomes the focal point. Data transfer speed is measured in terms of the amount of time required to read or write a record, that is, to transfer data to or from the central processing unit. Average access times for typical magnetic disk drives range from 20 to 60 milliseconds (thousandths of a second), while data transfer speeds range from 156,000 to 806,000 bytes (characters) per second. The storage capacities of these disk packs vary widely—from 7.25 million to 317.5 million characters.

AN EXAMPLE OF MAGNETIC DISK UTILIZATION

Suppose, in this example, a computer system having direct access capabilities is to prepare a combined shipping-order and invoice form from an original sales order and maintain inventory and accounts receivable master files. What steps are required to prepare the form and to update records of the inventory (item) and accounts receivable (customer) master files?

Illustration 10-6 is a system flowchart for the basic processing in this system. It consists of two steps and requires two master files: the item file and the customer file. A master item record contains such data as item number, item description, unit price, unit cost, reorder point, stock on hand, stock on order, and items back-ordered. A master customer record contains such data as customer number, customer name and address, shipping instructions, payment terms, and amount owed. These files can be stored on the same disk pack or on two disk packs. One or two disk drives are needed, depending on whether one or two packs are used. The processing steps are the same in either case. (Note the symbol for disk input/output: ⬚ .)

In step 1 of the system, item cards are keypunched from the original sales orders, then verified. These cards can be unit-record cards (one card per line item) or spread cards (several items per card). If spread cards are used, the number of cards required by the system is less than it would be otherwise. The data that is keypunched is the identifying information for each item ordered (item number and quantity ordered).

In the second step of the system, the keypunched item cards are processed by the computer. These cards do not have to be sorted before they are processed. In this single processing run, the item records are checked to see whether the items ordered are in stock. the combined shipping order

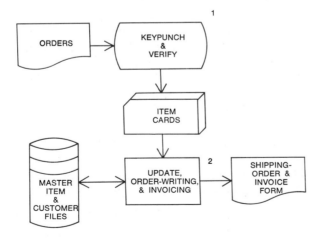

Illustration 10-6. System flowchart for a direct access system.

and invoice is printed with back-ordered items so indicated, and the item (inventory) and customer (accounts receivable) records on disk are updated. Because of the direct access capabilities of the disk, only the master records affected by transactions are processed. If the item cards are spread cards, the basic processing steps in the program are as follows:

1. An input card is read.
2. The master customer record with the same customer number as the input card is directly accessed and read from disk.
3. The heading on the shipping-order and invoice form is printed from data in the customer record and in the input card (customer name and address, customer number, order number, order date, shipping terms, special instructions, and so on).
4. The master item record corresponding to an item named on the input card is directly accessed and read from disk.
5. The data for the first line item on the invoice is printed. Item number, item description, and unit price are taken from the master item record. Quantity ordered for the item is taken from the input card. However, if there is not enough stock on hand, the quantity ordered is printed in the back-ordered portion of the shipping form. To calculate the price for this line item, quantity shipped is multiplied by unit price.
6. The new stock-on-hand balance for the item is calculated, and the updated master item record is written on the disk in its original location.
7. If more than one item is ordered by the customer, processing, like that for the first item on the order, is repeated for each of the remaining items. In short, the master item record is read, a line item is printed, and the updated master item record is written back onto the disk.
8. When there are no more line items to be processed for the customer, the invoice total (and any discounts) are calculated, and the total line of the invoice is printed.
9. At this point, the balance owed by the customer is increased by the amount of the invoice, and the updated customer record is written on the disk in its original location. Then processing continues with the next spread card in the input deck.

   In short, both master item (inventory) and master customer (accounts receivable) records are updated as the shipping-order and invoice form is printed. Only the master records affected by the item cards are read and written. On the other hand, any master item record may be read a number of times during program execution. If, for example, one item is ordered by 100 different customers, the master item record must be read 100 times.

ADVANTAGES AND LIMITATIONS OF DISK INPUT/OUTPUT

As previously mentioned, magnetic disk drives offer the potential of directly accessing data stored on a magnetic disk. This is the primary advantage of the magnetic disk over input media such as punched cards and magnetic tape, which are sequentially organized and processed. Without this capability, online, realtime processing cannot be effectively achieved. (The realtime concept is discussed in Chapter 16.)

Another basic advantage of magnetic disk is the speed at which data can be transferred to and from the central processing unit. While magnetic disk units have not yet achieved the transfer speeds of the magnetic drum (discussed below), they have surpassed magnetic tape devices in this respect.

Perhaps the most critical disadvantage of magnetic disk is that it does not usually provide for backup. When data is recorded on a magnetic disk, only one copy is normally made. In comparison, when magnetic tape is used as the input/output medium, an extra copy of the tape can be provided with relative ease, thus insuring that the data is protected from accidental erasure or destruction. Further, the magnetic tape cannot be written on unless a file-protect ring is properly installed.

Another disadvantage of magnetic disk is its cost. Consider, for example, the relative costs of magnetic disk and tape. As stated previously, a reel of magnetic tape costs approximately $15. Most disk packs cost between $400 and $1150.

Another limitation (or possibly, advantage, depending on how one views the problem) is one of system design and the difficulties that may be encountered in programming a system to operate according to its design.

File organization is a major system design consideration. A file can be organized in any one of three ways on a direct access device. Besides the *direct* organization, records can be stored in sequence on a direct access device. For example, on a disk device, record number 1 of a *sequential* file is stored in the cylinder 1, track 1, and record 1 location; record number 2 is stored in the cylinder 1, track 1, and record 2 location; and so on. When reading records from a sequential file, access-mechanism movement is minimal because all of the records in one cylinder are read before records are read from the next cylinder. Since direct access devices normally have fast transfer rates, records arranged sequentially can be read and written at relatively high speeds. Sequential records on a direct access device can be sorted using only that device, in contrast to a tape system where three tape drives are required to sort data, even when the records to be sorted are initially contained in one file on one tape drive.

A third kind of file organization, called *indexed sequential,* allows records to be retrieved sequentially or by direct access, depending on the program. In this method, the records are stored sequentially on the direct access device. In addition, a table (index) is kept that indicates the approximate location of each of the records stored on the device. To process the records on a direct access basis, a program looks for a record number in the table, determines the approximate location of the record on the device, and searches for the record at that location.

The problem of the system designer is to choose the best of these methods (direct, sequential, or indexed sequential) for each file stored on a direct access device. Since each method has advantages and disadvantages, the choice is difficult. For example, although direct organization may be best for an invoicing run such as the one shown in Illustration 10-6, it may be difficult to prepare management reports from directly organized master files. (How could an inventory report in item-number sequence be prepared from the directly organized master inventory file?)

In addition, a directly organized file requires additional storage space on the direct access device because of the problems in computing unique device addresses for records. In contrast, a sequential file permits full use of the storage allocated for it on the device. However, such a file has the disadvantages of other sequential files: (1) sorting is a common requirement, and (2) if only a few of the records in a master file are affected in a processing run, many records are processed unnecessarily.

Indexed sequential file organization combines the advantages of both direct and sequential organizations. However, run times for direct access processing of an indexed sequential file are likely to be longer than they would be if the file were organized on a direct basis. In any event, the problem of the system designer is to choose an organization that keeps processing times down, not just for a single processing run, but for all of the runs in which the file will be used.

In summary, direct access systems offer advantages not found in sequential processing systems. Direct access systems also require programming and systems considerations that are not required by sequential systems. Perhaps the most significant difference between direct access and sequential systems is that a direct access system can retrieve records from a master file more quickly than a sequential system can. Managers can "inquire" into files in a direct access system for current information. For instance, if a credit manager wants information on a customer account, the customer's number can be keyed on an input/output device that resembles a typewriter. Under program control, the computer system can, in milliseconds, retrieve the customer's record from a direct access device and print the contents of the record on the typewriterlike unit. Because of its *inquiry* capability, the direct access system makes possible a management information system. In contrast, in a sequential system, before the desired record could be retrieved for processing, all records prior to the desired record in the file would have to be read. Such an approach would be highly impractical.

OTHER DIRECT ACCESS INPUT/OUTPUT DEVICES

The Magnetic Drum

The magnetic drum is another type of direct access device (see Illustration 10-7). Although it was developed before magnetic disk storage, the

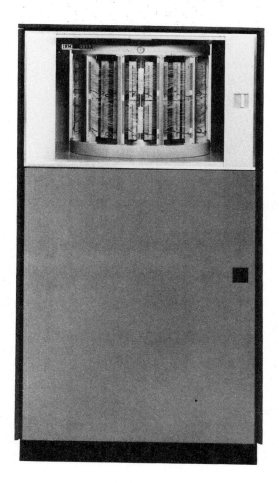

Illustration 10-7. Drum storage device.

use of the magnetic drum as a secondary storage device has dwindled in recent years. The primary reason for this dwindling usage is that the drum has a limited storage capacity—a result of the design of the device. The recording medium of the device is a *drum,* or *cylinder,* which is coated with a magnetically sensitive material. This drum is permanently fixed to the device. While a magnetic disk pack generally is removable, allowing additional data to be written or read, a magnetic drum is not. The magnetic drum is still employed in some installations because of its primary advantage: the fast input/output speeds at which the device operates.

The drum is similar to a magnetic disk in that its surface is divided into tracks (see the schematic diagram in Illustration 10-8). These tracks form circular bands around the drum, which rotates at a constant speed. The coded representation of data in Illustration 10-8 follows a pattern similar to that used on a seven-track magnetic tape. The tracks can be assigned to

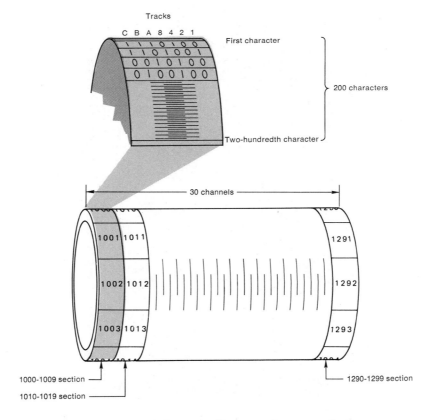

Illustration 10-8. Schematic diagram of a magnetic drum.

channels as in the illustration. This illustration, when compared to Illustration 10-7, points out one of the basic differences in various types of magnetic drum devices. The drum in the schematic diagram is in a horizontal position while the drum in the previous illustration is vertical.

The basic functions of the read/write heads of a magnetic drum (see Illustration 10-9) are to place magnetized areas on the drum during the writing operation and to sense these areas during the reading operation in the same general manner that these functions are performed when magnetic tape or disk is used. A second major difference in the design of magnetic drums is the number of read/write heads employed. Some drums employ only one read/write head which services all tracks on the drum. The head moves back and forth (or up and down) over the surface of the drum as required. Other drums, employing multiple read/write heads, have one principle advantage over drums of the single-head type: Since one read/write head is assigned to each track, no read/write head movement is required. That is, the time required for head positioning is zero. The only significant time required when reading or writing is the rotational delay that occurs in reaching a desired record location.

Data can be recorded on a magnetic drum by either of two methods: serial or parallel. A drum on which data is written in parallel is read in parallel; another type of drum uses serial reading and writing. These methods are similar to the ways of reading punched cards, which were discussed in Chapter 8.

Since there is wide variation in the design of magnetic drums, the speeds at which the writing and reading of data can be performed vary greatly as well. The speed of drum rotation ranges from approximately 6000 revolutions per minute (10 milliseconds per revolution) for high-speed drums to about 600 revolutions per minute (100 milliseconds per revolution) for

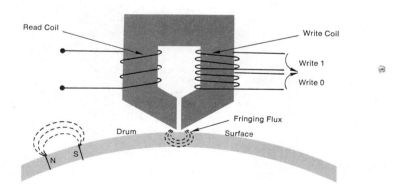

Illustration 10-9. Magnetic drum read/write head.

larger drums. Since the faster rotating drums are usually smaller than other drums, less data can be recorded on their surfaces. In addition, these smaller drums are usually more expensive because of the mechanics required to achieve accurate data transfers at high speeds. Some of these high-speed drums are capable of transferring over one million characters of data per second, which is roughly equivalent to reading a stack of cards 8 feet high in one second. The storage capacities of magnetic drums range from 20 million to more than 130,000 million characters.

The Mass Storage Subsystem

A third type of direct access device is the mass storage subsystem, such as the IBM 3850, which was introduced in 1974. The 3850 uses fist-sized data cartridges to store data; each is about 2 inches in diameter and 4 inches long, and can hold up to 50 million bytes of data (see Illustration 10-10). Inside the system, the cartridges are stored in a honeycomblike arrangement of cells (see Illustration 10-11).

When a program calls for a certain file or a portion of a file, one of two cartridge accessors is automatically instructed to retrieve the needed cartridge from its cell and mount it at a read/write station if it is not already mounted at the station. The cartridge is opened, and the contents of the 3 ×

Illustration 10-10. Data cartridge.

Illustration 10-11. 3850 "honeycomb."

770 inch tape strip contained therein are transferred to a 3336 disk pack for computer use. This process is called *staging*. After processing is completed, only altered records are written back to the tape strip.

Perhaps the greatest advantage of the 3850 Mass Storage Subsystem is economy of data storage. The subsystem can store from 35 billion to 472 billion bytes of data; the maximum is roughly equivalent to the data stored in a 47,200-reel tape library. (In 1975, Control Data Corporation introduced its 3850 Mass Storage Subsystem providing 16 billion bytes of online storage. Its capacity was declared to be about the same as that of 6400 reels of tape or 200 big disk packs.) The system can end practically all manual handling of tape reels and disk packs and greatly lower the cost of maintaining a library. An important security aspect is that extensive data files can be kept in one place. The 3850 can be located up to 200 feet away from the computer and can be equipped with special features to detect the presence of any foreign magnetic device, to sense fire and fumes, and to trigger a fire suppression system (if the user chooses to provide one). Access to data in the 3850 subsystem is controlled through password-protection programming.

Perhaps the largest potential for the 3850 exists among the multitude of magnetic-tape users. Although the 3850 subsystem provides direct-access capabilities, it is not well suited to random retrieval. The staging process described above involves a significant amount of physical movement, and access times are long when such movement is required. For records stored and processed sequentially, the frequency of staging is lower than it might otherwise be. But some users have determined that they can transfer data from 6250-BPI magnetic tapes faster than it can be transferred from the 3336 disk packs that provide online access to 3850 data. For organizations with massive amounts of data, economies of storage media and storage space may be determining factors.

Summary

1. Magnetic disk drives, magnetic drum units, and mass storage subsystems are direct access devices employing slightly different recording media. Data is recorded on a disk pack by a disk drive, on a magnetically sensitive cylinder by a magnetic drum unit, and on a magnetic strip retrieved from a cartridge in a mass storage subsystem.

2. Disk drives are characterized as either fixed-disk or removable-disk drives, depending on whether or not the recording medium (magnetic disks) can be removed. Each disk is composed of concentric circles called tracks. Disk packs for removable-disk devices come in many varieties. They differ in number and size of disks employed as well as in number of tracks per disk. The data recorded on these tracks by one or more read/write heads of an access mechanism is composed of a disk address and a record or block of records. The corresponding tracks of each disk in a disk pack are called a cylinder.

3. The speed at which a magnetic disk operates (access time) depends on three factors: head positioning, head switching, and rotational delay. Head positioning is the time required to position a read/write head over the required track. Head switching is the time expended to activate the read/write head in preparation for an input/output operation. Rotational delay is the time required to locate a record once the head has been positioned and activated. To maintain the accuracy of data on magnetic disk, cyclic check characters are placed at the end of each record or block of records.

4. Mass storage devices permit a variety of file organizations, including direct, sequential, and indexed sequential arrangements.

5. While the magnetic disk is the most commonly used mass storage medium, both magnetic drums and mass storage subsystem devices have especially useful functions. Magnetic drums are noted for their speed while mass storage subsystem devices are known for their low cost and large storage capacity.

Special-Purpose Input and Output Devices

CHARACTER RECOGNITION INPUT DEVICES
Magnetic Character Readers
Optical Character Readers
Optical Bar Codes

DATA COMMUNICATION

TERMINALS
Touch-Tone Devices
Voice-Response Units
Visual Display Devices
Hard-Copy Devices
Point-of-Sale Devices
Intelligent Terminals

KEY-ENTRY DEVICES
Key-to-Tape Devices
Key-to-Disk Devices

OTHER INPUT/OUTPUT DEVICES
Paper Tape and Paper Tape Devices
Console Printer-Keyboard
Computer Output Microfilm
Floppy Disk Devices

In Chapters 8, 9, and 10, several of the more commonly used input/output media and devices are discussed. Other input/output devices, although not as commonly used, are more appropriate in certain situations. Some of these devices are discussed in this module.

CHARACTER RECOGNITION INPUT DEVICES

With the development of electronic data processing systems, there came a realization that wide use could be made of input devices capable of reading data that could also be read by people. The processing of billions of checks and an inestimable volume of other notices—insurance billings, magazine subscription renewals, invoices, manufacturing routing slips, utility bills, and so forth—could be simplified by the use of characters recognizable by both people and machines. Two input devices that can read such characters are magnetic character readers and optical character readers.

Magnetic Character Readers

In 1955, the American Bankers Association (ABA) began to study the problem of how to automate the processing of a continuously increasing volume of checks. A major consideration of the individuals studying the problem was the realization that any approach to the electronic processing of checks had to be widely supported by the banking industry. A bank may handle a check written on an account in another bank. The check then may be handled by one or two Federal Reserve Banks. Finally, it is processed by the bank handling the account.

After considering several alternatives, the individuals studying the problem proposed that certain data be coded on checks in *magnetic ink*. This approach had three advantages:

1. A check could be used as an input medium to the computer, or the data on it could be transferred to another medium for later processing.

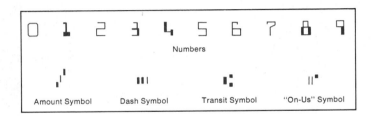

Illustration A-1. E-13B type font.

2. The data required in processing could be coded on checks of varying lengths, widths, and thicknesses.
3. The coded data would be easily readable by people.

The proposal to use magnetic ink was accepted by the American Bankers Association membership. Three committees (one representing the American Bankers Association, another representing the Federal Reserve System, and a third representing the computer manufacturers) were formed to study the problem of what *type font* (a complete set of type of one size and face) should be adopted. After several months of study, the E-13B type font was adopted, primarily because it was easily readable by people as well as by machines. As reflected in Illustration A-1, the E-13B type font is composed of 14 characters. Since no alphabetic characters are

Illustration A-2. Magnetic character inscriber.

included, the kind of data that can be processed using this type font is limited. However, the type font serves a significant purpose: It allows the banking industry to efficiently and effectively process billions of checks each year.

The first bank to receive a check must copy the amount of the check on the check in machine-readable form. This is accomplished by means of a *magnetic character inscriber (MCI)* like the one shown in Illustration A-2.

A *magnetic character reader (MCR)* is shown in Illustration A-3. This device reads the E-13B type font characters inscribed on a check (see Illustration A-4). A second important labor-saving feature of this specialized input device is its ability to sort magnetically inscribed checks by account number in offline operations. The characters composing each account number are magnetized as the checks are fed through the MCR. These characters are then read by a sensing mechanism. During a sorting operation, the reader sorts the checks into sort pockets. By repeated passes of checks through the machine, the checks can be grouped and routed to

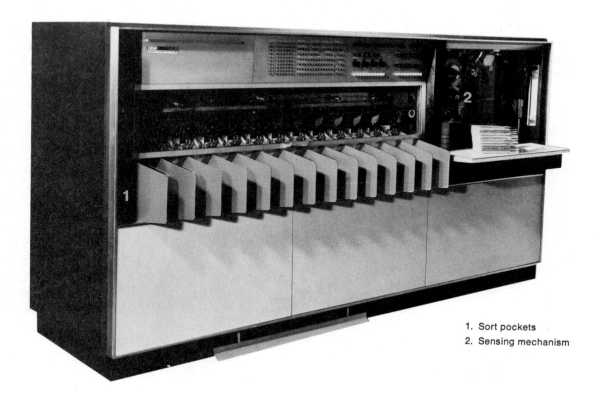

1. Sort pockets
2. Sensing mechanism

Illustration A-3. Magnetic character reader.

their sponsor banks. In each sponsor bank, a MCR is used as an input device to a computer system. Thus, the sorting function of the MCR assists a bank in updating customer accounts and returning checks to the individuals who wrote them. This device is basic to the banking industry's timesaving method of processing large volumes of daily transactions.

The MCR is used by most banks today. Many savings and loan associations are also using this machine. The extensive use of this device is due to (1) the coordinated efforts of the American Bankers Association and the various manufacturers of magnetic character readers, and (2) the fact that the Federal Reserve Banks will not handle checks through regular bank channels unless they are inscribed with magnetic ink characters. The British Bank Association has also accepted the E-13B type font as a standard.

Optical Character Readers

It is expected that the *optical character reader* (OCR) will become as widely used for data entry as the magnetic character reader is, in the banking industry. Optical character readers can read printed uppercase and lowercase alphabetic characters, numeric characters, bar codes, and certain special characters from handwritten, typed, and printed paper

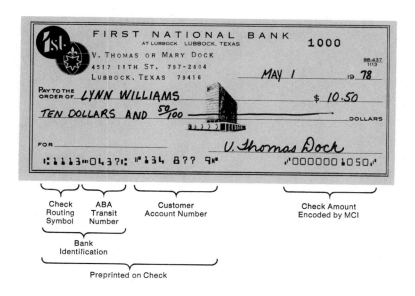

Illustration A-4. Use of the E-13B type font on a check.

documents. The specific characters that can be read and whether the characters must be handwritten, typed, or printed depends upon the type of OCR being used. The purpose of the reading operation is to translate the source data into machine language. The data may be either entered directly

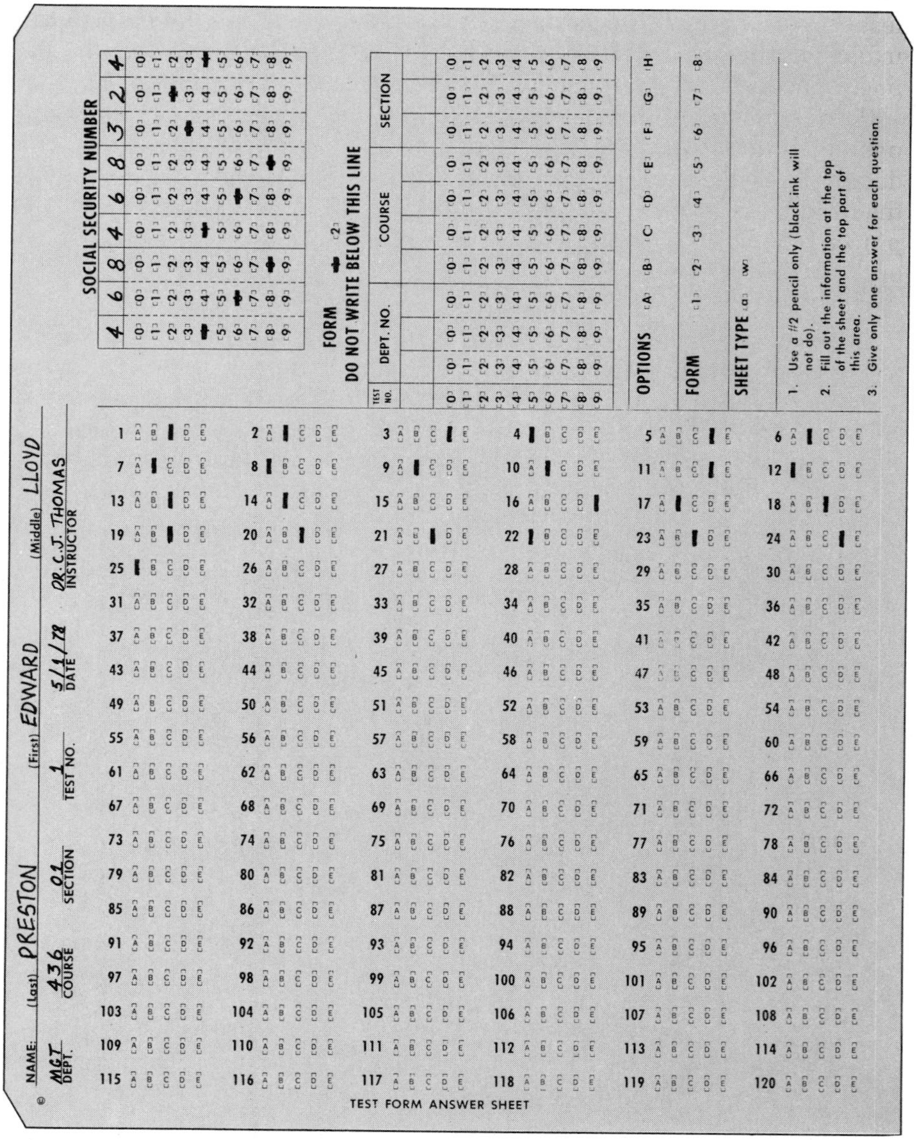

Illustration A-5. Test-scoring sheet with optical marks.

into the computer or transferred directly to punched cards, magnetic tape, or paper tape for later processing by the computer. Thus, no special step to transcribe data from source documents to an input medium is needed; the time between receipt of data and entry of that data into the computer system is less accordingly.

Optical-mark recognition.   Optical marks are commonly used for scoring tests. Illustration A-5, for example, shows a typical test-scoring sheet. It is marked by the person taking the test and can be read by an *optical-mark page reader.*

Illustration A-6 shows an optical-mark page reader. Such a device can operate in two ways: (1) it can be online to the computer system and read data into computer storage, or (2) it can be attached to a card punch. When the reader is attached to a card punch, cards are punched, read, and processed by the computer system. When online to a computer system, an optical-mark page reader can read up to 2000 documents an hour. Although

Illustration A-6. Optical-mark page reader.

this rate is slow when compared with that of other input devices, the overall speed of the system may be excellent because the necessity for manual keying of data is eliminated.

Besides test scoring, optical-mark documents can be used for applications such as order-writing, inventory control, insurance policy rating

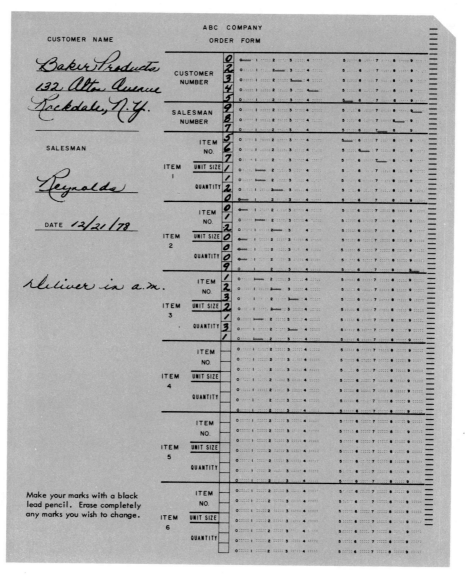

Illustration A-7. Order-writing form.

surveys, questionnaires, and payroll. Illustration A-7, for example, shows a source document for an order-writing application. In this application, the order clerk marks the customer number and salesman number for each order, and the item number, unit size, and quantity for each item ordered. The document then has all of the data required for processing the order, and it can be read and processed by the computer system.

One of the problems in designing a system that uses an optical-mark document is designing the document itself. It must be designed so that it can be understood and completed easily by the people who use it. If it is not, errors may result—more perhaps than would occur in using a traditional source document and keypunching from it. These errors may then be spread throughout any master files updated during subsequent processing.

Optical-character recognition. Other kinds of optical character readers can read optical characters. These characters have a slightly irregular typeface as shown in Illustration A-8. They consist of the letters of the alphabet, the 10 decimal digits, and several special characters. The characters can be printed by accounting machines, computer printers, cash registers, adding machines, and typewriters.

Illustration A-8. Optical characters.

Optical character recognition devices can read data on either cut forms (for example, sales slips) or continuous forms (such as cash-register tapes), depending on the model. Usually, the machines that can read cut forms can be used offline to sort them. Some optical character recognition devices can read optical marks as well as optical characters. In this case, the source documents can contain both optical characters and optical marks.

An application well suited for optical character recognition is accounts receivable. For example, Illustration A-9 shows a utility bill with printed optical characters. On the left side of the bill are spaces for optical marks. If the bill is returned with full payment, the document is processed as receipt of payment. If the bill is returned with partial payment, a clerk marks the amount of the partial payment on the left of the document before it is processed. Use of this document eliminates the need for manual keying of data.

Handwritten characters. Finally, some optical character recognition devices can read handwritten data as well as optical characters. Specifically, they can read certain precisely written letters and numbers. Illustration A-10 shows some handwritten characters that can be read and some that cannot. Like other optical character recognition devices, most handwriting-readers can be used to sort cut forms as well as to read data into computer storage.

Because handwriting is a basic form of recording data, handwriting-readers can be used in many different applications. For instance, a handwritten sales slip can be read and processed by the computer as the

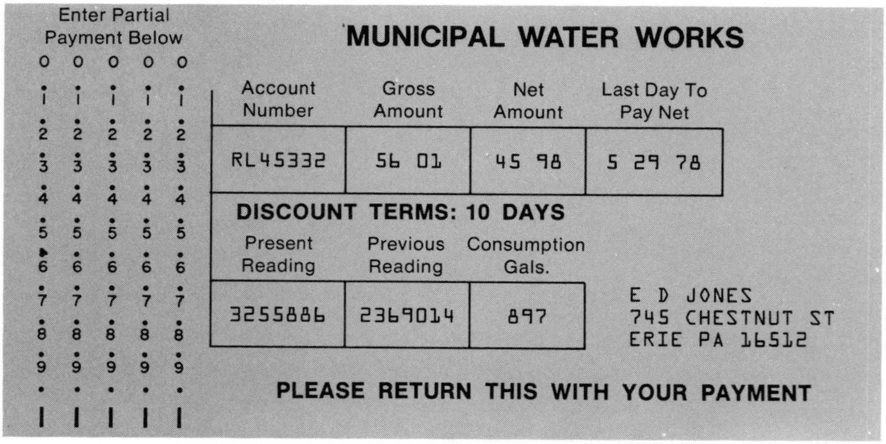

Illustration A-9. Utility bill with optical characters and optical marks.

basic input to accounts receivable and inventory-control applications. A copy of the sales slip can be given to the customer as a record of sale.

The diversity in typed, printed, and handwritten characters causes optical character readers to encounter some difficulty in reading source documents. This is reflected by the fact that a small percentage of the source documents is rejected. Also, characters are read but incorrectly identified in a very small percentage of the source documents. Fewer and fewer of these errors are occurring for two reasons: (1) the expanding use of a standard type font (OCR-A), which is recognized by the American National Standards Institute (ANSI), on source documents, and (2) improved optical scanning techniques.

Optical character readers are used in many diverse areas. For example, they are used in credit card billing, utility billing, and the reading of adding machine and cash register tapes, and by the post office. The use of optical character readers should continue to increase and expand as improved scanning techniques result in fewer source documents being rejected, fewer characters being identified improperly, the reading speed of readers increasing, and the cost of readers decreasing.

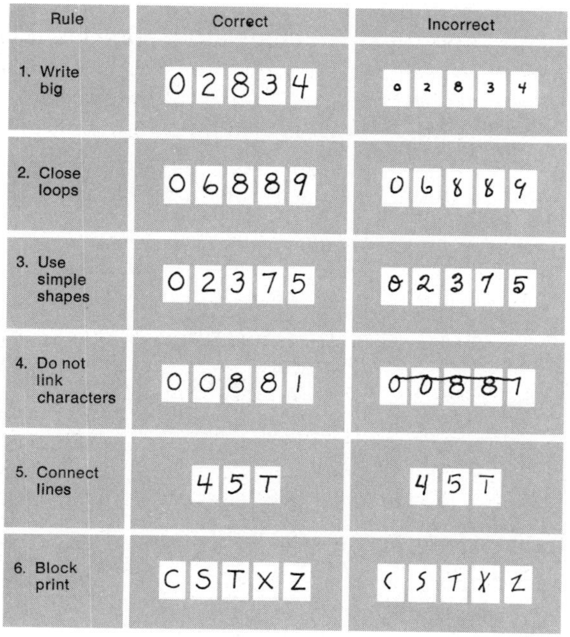

Rule	Correct	Incorrect
1. Write big	0 2 8 3 4	0 2 8 3 4
2. Close loops	0 6 8 8 9	0 6 8 8 9
3. Use simple shapes	0 2 3 7 5	0 2 3 7 5
4. Do not link characters	0 0 8 8 1	0 0 8 8 1
5. Connect lines	4 5 T	4 5 T
6. Block print	C S T X Z	C S T X Z

Illustration A-10. Handwritten characters.

Optical Bar Codes

Optical bar codes were first used by railroads in 1967 for automatic rail car identification. Similar bar codes were introduced in grocery stores in 1973. The bar codes usually included characters readable by people (see Illustration A-11).   Many retailers are installing optical bar-code readers that can read special bar codes that identify merchandise. One code is called the *Universal Product Code (UPC)*. When marked on an item, it consists of 10 pairs of vertical bars representing the manufacturer's identity and the identity code for the item. Over 85 percent of the products sold in supermarkets bear this code. The code can be read by passing a hand-held wand reader over it. The data that is read is entered into a cash register terminal which prices and identifies the item. (See Illustration A-12.) Other types of bar codes are used on merchandise tags attached to retail items. The processing is similar: A clerk waves a wand reader over the tag and a coded description of the item is recorded.

DATA COMMUNICATION

The devices used to enter data into a computer are often close to it. However, under some circumstances this arrangement may not be efficient; it may even be impossible. An illustration of this problem may be seen in the assembly line operation of an automobile manufacturer where data concerning the progress of specific steps in the operation must be provided as input to a computer. Obviously, it is impractical to have the computer near the assembly line. It is also impractical to physically transport the data to a computer facility elsewhere every time the steps are performed. If the computer facility is located in a city several hundred

Illustration A-11. Optical bar codes.

miles away, such a procedure is impossible. It takes too long. Thus, a means of relaying data to the computer (and in some cases, receiving a reply) is needed. The data must be entered into the computer as it is generated, regardless of the distance between the point of origin and the computer.

The addition of these kinds of capabilities to computer systems did not necessitate a vast redesign of computers. Existing telephone, telegraph, and microwave installations were suitable for data transmission with only minor modifications of existing hardware. In most cases, all that was required was the implementation of devices to convert data at the point of origin into electrical impulses that could be transmitted over telephone lines. Then the impulses could be modified at the computer facility for input to the computer. The data could be transmitted in either *serial* (one bit at a time) or *parallel* (one character at a time) mode. As further explained in Chapter 16, *data communication* is simply the electrical transfer

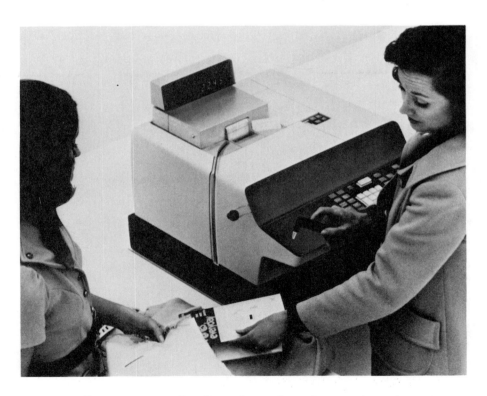

Illustration A-12. Reading a bar code with a wand reader.

of data from one point to another. This type of data transmission can occur at rates of 300 to 3000 cycles per second.

A *data set* is the device that converts data to either transmit it from its point of origin or receive it at its destination. The encoding of data for transmission as electrical impulses is called *modulation*. The decoding of data when it reaches the computer facility is called *demodulation*. Therefore, data sets are sometimes called *modems* (modulation-demodulation devices). One such device is the *data phone* in Illustration A-13. It uses existing telephone lines to link the computer with data at a distant (*remote*) location.

The number and type of remote devices in a system depends upon the number of points from which transmission of data is required, the volume of data to be transferred, the transmission quality desired, the timing of transmissions (peak and slack periods of transmission), and the transmission speed required. A number of these remote devices (sometimes called *terminals*) can be connected to the computer through a channel (discussed in Chapter 14).

Illustration A-13. Data phone.

TERMINALS

As the number and variety of computer applications increase, the need to communicate with the computer from remote locations becomes more evident. To satisfy this need to "converse" with the computer, a variety of remote devices have been developed to allow the input of data to the computer facility and/or the output of information to the user. Among these devices are touch-tone devices, voice-response units, visual display devices, hard-copy devices, point-of-sale terminals, and a group of devices commonly known as "intelligent terminals."

Touch-Tone Devices

Touch-tone devices are designed to use existing telephone communication links. The telephone service companies, particularly the American Telephone and Telegraph Company, have played a large part in the development of these terminals, primarily because of the potential business increase for the telephone companies. Business organizations have readily adopted these devices because they can use existing telephone lines in their businesses. Only minor adjustments in the service connections are required. This type of data-transmission medium has proven very accurate and reliable. However, as a group, the touch-tone devices are low-speed data transmission devices.

There are many devices in the touch-tone category. Among the more prominent in this class are:

- The Card Dialer. This device employs a modified telephone-type connection capable of reading data from prepunched plastic cards. Its transmission rate ranges up to 8 or 9 characters per second.

- The Call-A-Matic. This device also uses a modified telephone-type connection, but it uses a magnetic belt (similar to magnetic tape) to store data. The call-a-matic magnetic belt has the basic advantage of all magnetic media in that it is capable of storing relatively large amounts of data in relatively little space.

- The Touch-Tone Audio Terminal. When touch-tone telephone dialing was developed, a third type of terminal was introduced. This one has audio capabilities. It is triggered by sound frequencies rather than by punched holes or patterns on magnetic belts. While the devices above require prior coding of a punched card or a magnetic belt, the audio terminal translates the sound frequencies into electrical impulses and transfers data by keying the characters on a keyboard. The touch-tone terminal in Illustration A-14 can be used to enter data from either a touch-tone keyboard or a magnetic strip on a plastic card. The touch-

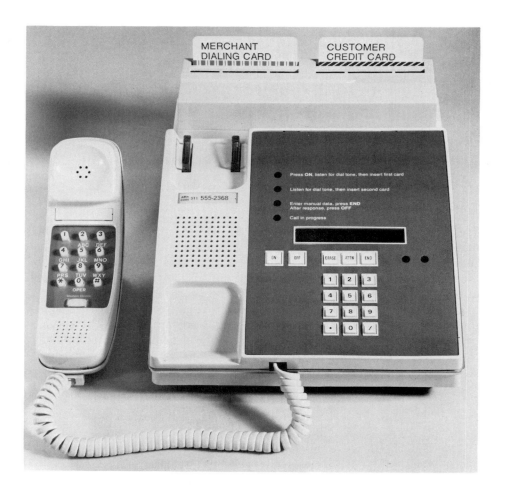

Illustration A-14. Touch-tone terminal with a slot
reader for credit cards.

tone audio terminal has an additional advantage in that some models are
portable. The data transfer rate of this device averages 5 to 7 characters
per second.

Voice-Response Units

The voice-response unit can be connected to telephone lines or to lines
especially installed for the voice-response unit. Since this device is typically utilized for output only, it is sometimes called a *voice-output* or

audio-response unit. However, voice data entry terminal systems that are computer based and can be programmed to recognize voice input are available. As an output device, the voice-response unit is limited only by the coded vocabulary preselected for it by the system designer. The output speed of this type of device is limited to about 1 or 2 words per second.

Visual Display Devices

The visual display device, commonly referred to as a *CRT* (cathode-ray-tube), is used in many computer systems for both input and output.

Illustration A-15. Visual display device.

The display unit in Illustration A-15 has a screen similar to that of a television set. This device can display both alphameric and special characters. It also has a keyboard similar to a typewriter for data entry.

These units do not produce printed output. They are often called *soft-copy devices*, a term used to contrast them with devices that produce printed output, often called *hard-copy devices*. CRT devices have several advantages over hard-copy devices. They are silent in operation and have a much higher display speed (up to 10,000 characters per second). In some applications, a quick response to an inquiry is needed but a printed record is not necessary. The CRT is well suited for this type of use. In cases where a printed copy of the display on the screen is needed, a microfilm unit or a printer can be attached to the CRT. When used in such applications as airline reservations, car rental reservations, and credit card verification, CRTs are often called *inquiry/response stations.*

Another type of CRT is the *graphic display device.* (See Illustration A-16.) It can perform all of the functions mentioned for the visual display device and can present graphs and line drawings. Both types of CRT devices may be equipped with light pens. The operator directs a beam of light from the light pen onto the CRT screen to enter data. The operator either points the light pen at a certain spot on the screen or draws on the screen to enter the data. If data is entered into one of these devices from the keyboard, each character is displayed on the screen for visual check-

Illustration A-16. Graphic display device.

ing by the operator. This allows the operator to make corrections to the data before forwarding it to the computer.

CRT devices can be located at a central computer facility with connections to the computer made by cable, or they may be at locations several thousand miles away. The major disadvantage of visual display devices is that no permanent record is written when information is received or data is transmitted. This can be overcome by attaching a microfilm unit or a printer to the CRT as suggested above.

Hard-Copy Devices

As mentioned in the previous section, devices that produce printed output like that of a typewriter are referred to as hard-copy devices. They are used in applications where printed output is needed. As a class they are much slower than CRTs and more noisy in operation. There are many different types of these devices, and they use a variety of printing methods. Some do *impact* printing similar to a typewriter, while others do *nonimpact* printing using a thermal process.

Portable hard-copy devices are becoming increasingly popular. A portable terminal like the one in Illustration A-17 can be connected directly to

Illustration A-17. Portable hard-copy device.

the computer or communicate with it via a telephone line. Such a device is especially useful when it is necessary for the user to communicate with the computer from remote locations. For example, a business representative may need information from a central computer while on a business trip. The representative can dial the number of the computer from a telephone, and then insert the telephone handset in a special holder in the terminal to communicate with the computer.

Point-of-Sale Devices

Many retail operations use remote terminals capable of performing the functions of a cash register while recording all of the sales data. These terminals are commonly referred to as *point-of-sale (POS) terminals*. A typical terminal is shown in Illustration A-18. Such devices usually include a keyboard for entry of sales data, a display panel to show the price, a cash drawer, and a cash receipt printer. All POS terminals are designed to allow operators to use them without much training. A message panel or a series of lighted keys directs the operator when entering a transaction. Often a wand reader is included and used by the operator to read either the Universal Product Code on boxes, cans, and packages or other bar code on merchandise tickets, thus eliminating keyboard entry. The POS terminals are an essential part of a source-data collection system that provides important inventory and sales information for the retailer. When the POS terminals are connected to a central computer, this information is immediately available.

Intelligent Terminals

Intelligent terminals are being developed at a rapid pace. An intelligent terminal differs from other terminals in at least one very important way: An internal processor performs specific functions for the operator. Among these functions are data editing, data conversion, and control of other terminals. Many applications now use intelligent terminals. One of the most widely used applications is the POS system mentioned above. Among the newer uses of intelligent terminals are the automatic tellers or cash-dispensing terminals used by some banks. Terminals like the one in Illustration A-19 can be placed at various locations in a community. For example, many banks provide 24-hour deposit and withdrawal services by means of these terminals.

The remote terminal is one of the most widely used computer input/output devices. As more transaction-oriented computer systems are in-

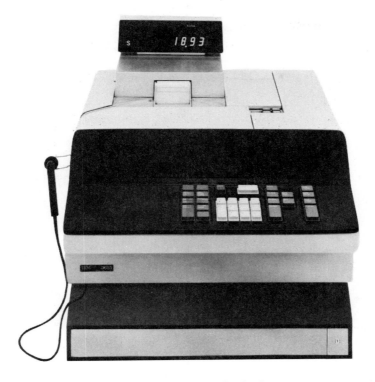

Illustration A-18. Point-of sale device.

stalled, the use of these types of terminals will increase. More and more communications with computers will be handled this way, and more and more data will be captured as transactions occur. The development of low-cost processors has made it feasible to make most terminals intelligent. This will make data entry and retrieval easier for the user.

KEY-ENTRY DEVICES

The most widely used method of data entry today involves key-to-storage devices. There are two basic types of key-to-storage devices: key-to-tape and key-to-disk. A *key-to-tape* device can be a single unit that replaces a keypunch machine, while a *key-to-disk* device typically comprises several keyboard units. Both of these devices are used to record data that will be processed by a computer at a later date; that is, they prepare the data offline. This is in contrast to the terminals just discussed, which operate online. As they record data, they also transmit it directly to the computer.

Illustration A-19. Intelligent terminal.

Key-to-Tape Devices

Magnetic tape can be produced as a by-product of some operation (typing or keypunching) or directly by a keying operation. A key-to-tape device consists of a keyboard for entering data, a buffer storage area that temporarily holds the data for an accuracy check, and a magnetic tape unit. After data is keyed onto the tape, the tape is rewound, and the same device can be used to verify the data. The verified data can then be read by a computer system.

Although keying data onto tape does not reduce or eliminate the keying of source data, it has several advantages over keypunching and verifying cards. First, there is no movement of cards to slow the key-to-tape operation; the operator can work faster when using this device than when using a card punch. Second, the handling of cards is eliminated. Third, magnetic tape units have higher input speeds than card readers do.

Key-to-Disk Devices

The key-to-disk devices are another popular method for key entry of data. A key-to-disk system includes multiple keyboard terminals connected to a computer and a magnetic tape unit and magnetic disk drive. (See Illustration A-20.) The number of keyboard terminals can range from 2 through 64. They usually have display screens to assist operators in entering data correctly. As data is entered at a keyboard, it goes through

Illustration A-20. Key-to-disk data entry system.

Illustration A-21. Key-to-floppy-disk data entry device.

the computer, which edits and validates the data and then stores it on a magnetic disk. Key-to-disk systems use the magnetic disk as temporary storage to allow more effective operator control in formatting and editing the data. The computer then writes all of the data on magnetic tape for later input to another computer for processing. In most cases, the final output of the key-to-disk system is a magnetic tape. These systems are most often used to prepare large amounts of data for processing on either medium-size or large computers.

A second type of key-to-disk system allows one or more operators to key data directly onto a flexible disk, more commonly called a *floppy disk*. One such device is shown in Illustration A-21. Such systems can be connected directly to a computer while the data is keyed, or keying can be done as a separate function. This type of key-to-disk device is often used with mini-computer systems (discussed in detail in Chapter 11). The floppy disk is commonly used for data storage.

OTHER INPUT/OUTPUT DEVICES

Paper Tape and Paper Tape Devices

Punched paper tape, like punched cards, can be used as both an input and an output of a computer system. A continuous strip of the paper is wound on a reel and punched with combinations of holes that represent data. There is a great similarity between this method of representing data and the coding of data on magnetic tape. In fact, the principles on which magnetic tape and paper tape units operate are the same. (While paper tape is emphasized here, it should be noted that plastics and metals are used in the same fashion.) Illustration A-22 shows a reel of paper tape and one of

A Reel of
Paper Tape

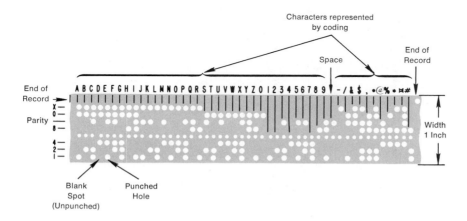

Illustration A-22. Paper-tape coding scheme.

Illustration A-23. Paper tape reader (above) and punch units (below).

the punched-hole coding schemes that can be used with paper tape. In this coding scheme, each column of punches represents one character, and the coding scheme corresponds closely to 6-bit BCD (see Chapter 7). In addition to this coding scheme, there are paper-tape codes that use five, six, and seven vertical punching positions.

Paper tape can be read at speeds ranging from 350 to 2000 characters per second. The latter rate is equivalent to reading approximately 1500 cards per minute. Data can be punched into paper tape at the rate of 20 to 60 characters per second. However, paper tape has one rather obvious limitation: Once data is punched into the tape, it cannot be erased (as data on magnetic tape can). Corrections can be made only by splicing, and the tape cannot be reused for new data. Illustration A-23 shows two units; one is a paper tape reader (upper portion) and the other is a paper tape punch (lower portion).

There are several advantages to using paper tape as an input or output medium. First, it is an inexpensive means of recording data, less expensive than even punched cards (which require more storage space). Second, paper tape is often punched as a by-product of some other operation. For example, a paper tape punch might be attached to a cash register to record all transactions that occur each day. At the end of the day the tape can be removed and sent to a computer facility for processing. Third, as an input/output medium for terminal operations, paper tape is well adapted for transmitting data over telegraph lines. Western Union, a proponent in the development of paper tape as a data-transmission medium, uses paper tape. The tape serves as one additional communication medium and provides for the storing of much data on a single reel. Paper tape and paper tape devices can satisfy certain requirements that no other terminals are designed to satisfy.

CONSOLE PRINTER-KEYBOARD

The printer-keyboard in Illustration A-24 is both an input and an output device. It is usually close to a panel of lights and switches called the *console,* from which overall control of an executing program is exercised. When it is used as an output device, it prints one character at a time like a typewriter. This printing takes place under control of an executing program. When it is used as an input device, data is keyed on the keyboard and then read into computer storage under control of an executing program. In some computer systems, the console output device is a CRT instead of a printer. This allows relatively fast display of messages to the operator. The time the computer must wait for a response to a message may be reduced accordingly. Some computer systems provide both a CRT and a slow-speed printer for console output. The console operator can select items to be printed.

Because the console printer-keyboard is an extremely slow input/output device, it is used primarily for communication between the operator and the computer system. Programmed messages to the operator are printed as output. Responses from the operator are keyed as input. Suppose, for example, the logic of a program detects that one of the data cards in an input deck is not in sequence. The program prints CARDS NOT IN SEQUENCE on the console printer-keyboard, halts, and waits for a reply from the operator. After the operator adjusts the cards in the input deck so that they are in sequence, he or she keys in a response such as OK on the keyboard. The response is read and processed by the executing program. If

Illustration A-24. Console printer-keyboard.

the response is an acceptable one, the program continues processing. This same type of communication can be used to alert the operator of other error or exceptional conditions in the system and to give instructions.

Computer Output Microfilm

Photographing and placing computer output on microfilm, referred to as *computer output microfilm*, or *COM*, is being used by an increasing number of organizations. Using COM can reduce the cost of producing reports in several ways. There are reductions in paper costs and in the costs associated with handling and storing computer reports. The costs of producing computer reports have accelerated over the past few years due to paper costs and the increasing number of reports an organization generates. Printing an increasing number of reports consumes increasing amounts of computer time. This can be reduced significantly using COM. Reports placed on microfilm take much less storage space, and less handling is required when a report needs to be retrieved.

The increased cost of mailing computer reports has also been a major reason for companies to switch to COM. Microfilm can be mailed at a fraction of the cost of printed reports. The reports on microfilm can be printed at the receiving end if needed.

The process of placing reports on microfilm is shown in Illustration A-25. Computer reports are placed on magnetic tape, which serves as input to a microfilm processor. The microfilm can be viewed with a microfilm reader or used to produce printed reports as needed.

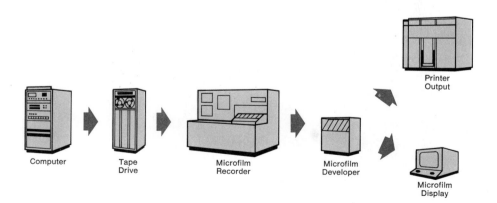

Illustration A-25. Recording computer output on microfilm.

The use of COM will continue to increase as organizations continue to seek ways to reduce costs and yet meet the need for additional reports.

Floppy Disk Devices

The floppy disk was introduced in 1973 for use in the key-to-disk systems discussed previously. Soon after, manufacturers began making floppy disk devices for use on minicomputers. The floppy disk drive is now one of the most popular input/output devices on minicomputers (see Illustration

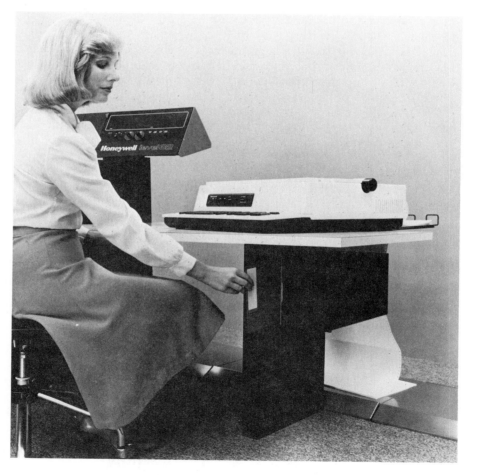

Illustration A-26. Minicomputer with floppy disk input/output.

A-26). It is also used on intelligent terminals and in some larger computers to store control programs. The small business computers discussed in Chapter 11 frequently use floppy disks for data storage. They offer the advantage of direct access storage at a very low cost. A floppy disk can be purchased for as little as $5.00 and may store up to 500,000 characters.

Summary

1. Character recognition input devices fall into two categories: magnetic character readers and optical character readers. Magnetic character readers are capable of distinguishing magnetically inscribed characters of the E-13B type font. In addition, documents on which magnetic characters are inscribed can be sorted offline. The result is faster processing of documents. Optical character recognition equipment can be used to read handwritten, typed, and printed documents, optical marks, and bar codes. This allows data to be entered into a computer system without the intermediate process of transcribing it from source documents to an input medium.

2. The advantages of character recognition input are: (1) data can be input directly from documents or stored on some other medium for later processing, (2) the characters can be recorded on documents of varying widths, lengths, and thicknesses, and (3) the coded data is easily read by humans.

3. Data communication devices became necessary because of the time required to physically transport data from its point of origin to the computer facility. These devices allow data to be transmitted over existing transmission media such as telephone or telegraph lines. To accomplish this, data sets (modems) were devised to transmit the data as electrical impulses from the point where it is created (modulation) and to decode the data at the computer facility (demodulation).

4. There are many devices that may serve as remote terminals to provide input or receive output from a computer. Among the devices are touch-tone devices, voice-response units, visual display devices, hard-copy devices, point-of-sale terminals, and intelligent terminals. Each satisfies distinct needs for data entry and transmission.

5. Key-to-tape and key-to-disk devices are the most widely used form of data entry. They allow formatting and editing of data as it is recorded.

6. A by-product of terminal operations, in some circumstances, is a punched paper tape containing valuable data. The paper tape, while similar in nature to magnetic tape, represents a very inexpensive input/output medium for a computer system. It is easily adapted for use in transmitting data over telegraph lines.

7. A console printer-keyboard is used directly with the computer to relay information to the operator from the computer, and to the computer from the operator, while a program is executing.

8. Computer output on microfilm is being used by an increasing number of organizations to reduce the costs associated with computer reports. Microfilm offers several advantages as an output medium; it requires less storage space, mailing costs less, and paper usage is less. Printed reports can be generated from microfilm when needed.

9. The floppy disk drive is a very popular input/output device on small computer systems because it offers direct access storage capability at a low cost. Many low-cost computer systems use floppy disks as their only data storage medium.

CHAPTER 11

Computer Systems

MICROCOMPUTER SYSTEMS

MINICOMPUTER SYSTEMS

SMALL COMPUTER SYSTEMS

MEDIUM-SIZE COMPUTER SYSTEMS

LARGE COMPUTER SYSTEMS

THE SIZE OF COMPUTERS AND SCOPE
OF THE COMPUTER INDUSTRY:
A RESTATEMENT AND COMPARISON

The past decade has seen a tremendous growth in both the types of computers being produced and the number of manufacturers making them. There are now over 50 manufacturers producing a wide variety of computers, ranging from complete microcomputer systems that cost less than $2000 to large computers that cost millions of dollars.

In the past decade, there has been a tenfold increase in the number of computers installed. A good percentage of this total has been due to the minicomputer. The introduction of the minicomputer has led many new companies to enter the computer manufacturing field, and, by contrast, General Electric, RCA, and Xerox Data Systems have stopped manufacturing computers.

As technological advances are made, the size and cost of computers continue to drop while their capability increases. Consider that a computer job that cost $14 to process and took 375 seconds of computer time in 1955 can now be processed for less than .25¢ and in 5 seconds. The recent advances in microelectronics have significantly reduced the time needed to design and build new computer systems, thus accelerating the development of computers. Because of these improvements in computer cost and performance, computers are being used in many new applications. Many of these new applications use the newest development in computers, the microprocessor. The *microprocessor* is a development of microelectronics, a miniaturized version of a computer central processing unit. It becomes a microcomputer when it is combined with input/output devices, a storage unit, and an internal clock for timing operations.

Traditionally, computer power has been centralized, and data has been collected and brought to a central computer for processing. A major reason for this has been the high cost of the computer and the special facilities needed to house it. With the introduction of the microcomputer and the minicomputer, there has been an increase in the decentralization of computer power. This has been possible because of the low cost of these computers and because they do not require special facilities.

The distinction between the various categories of computer systems is not always clear. In this chapter, the general categories of microcomputer, minicomputer, small, medium, and large computer systems are recognized and described. Some of the basic characteristics of the various categories of computer systems and their applications are discussed.

MICROCOMPUTER SYSTEMS

The development of the microcomputer began in 1971 when the first computer processor based on microelectronics was introduced. Since that time there have been a number of improvements in the microcomputer, and it has had a tremendous impact on the computer industry. A microcomputer uses a processor that is from 100 to 1000 times smaller than a comparable central processing unit built in 1970. Its primary advantage besides size is its low cost in comparison to other processors.

A typical microprocessor consists of a chip of silicon containing over 50,000 transistors. It is capable of performing more than 100,000 operations per second. The microprocessor in Illustration 11-1 has about the same processing power as the central processing unit contained in a first-generation computer costing over $500,000. Yet the cost of this micropro-cessor is less than $10, and a complete microcomputer system using this microprocessor costs less than $2000.

Illustration 11-1 is an enlarged view of a microprocessor chip, which is actually about 1/10-inch square. An entire computer using this chip could be placed on this page. When packaged with a power supply, it looks as shown in Illustration 11-2.

The low cost of microprocessors is due not only to their size but also to the method by which they are produced. The wafer in Illustration 11-3 is about 4 inches in diameter. Each square on the wafer is a microprocessor. The technology that made the minicomputer possible has also been the basis for the microprocessor. It is called *large scale integration* or *LSI*. LSI

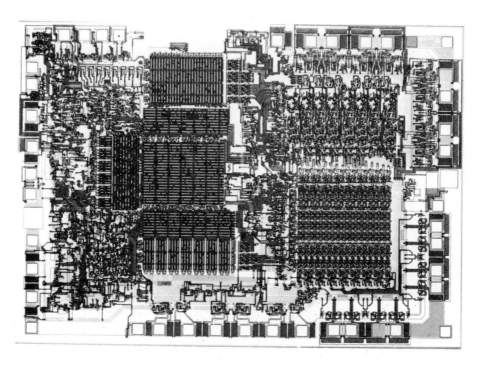

Illustration 11-1. Microprocessor on a chip.

Illustration 11-2. Complete microprocessor and microcomputer.

Illustration 11-3. Wafer containing a number of microprocessors.

is the process of placing thousands of electronic components and transistors on chips. Intel Corporation, the pioneer in microprocessors, used LSI to produce in one year a hundred times more transistor devices than had been produced since the transistor was invented over two decades ago.

While the microprocessor is a direct descendant of the LSI technology used in the minicomputer, it is not likely to replace the minicomputer processor for some time. The average microprocessor is 3 to 10 times slower than the processor of a minicomputer. Its slow processing speed is a major disadvantage in many application areas. However, there are a variety of applications that do not require high processor speeds. It is in these areas that microprocessors can be used. Since its introduction, the microprocessor has appeared in a variety of computer hardware. It is used in desk-top computers, pocket calculators, compact business machines, check processors, cash registers, credit card verification systems, and computer input/output devices such as printers and terminals.

One of the largest applications of the microprocessor in business data processing has been in the area of computer terminals. One popular system uses microprocessor-based cash register terminals to collect and refine data before it is transmitted to a central computer. Each terminal performs the functions of a cash register and also verifies credit cards while collecting sales data. Such systems are called *point-of-sale* (POS) systems. They are being used by many large retailers to lower inventory costs, improve customer service, and provide timely sales information for management. Module A discusses these systems in more detail.

The portable computer is another development based on the microprocessor. For example, the desk-top computer in Illustration 11-4 is designed to provide problem-solving capabilities to the individual user. It is not much larger than an office typewriter, yet it is a complete computer. A variety of input/output devices are often used on portable computers. A keyboard is used for entry of data or programs. A visual display screen or a printer can provide output. The portable computer can also be linked to other computers to either send or receive data.

Most portable computers are offered together with a variety of ready-to-use computer programs in such areas as statistics, mathematics, and business and finance. With some of these machines, a computerized language course is provided to instruct users on how to use the specific language available with the machine. Most portable computers can be purchased for less than $10,000. They can be used in a wide variety of ways in both small and large organizations.

The rate at which the microprocessor is used in business data processing applications will accelerate along with the trend toward decentralized processing. Its potential application in other areas seems limited only by the resourcefulness of users and the rate at which it continues to drop in price.

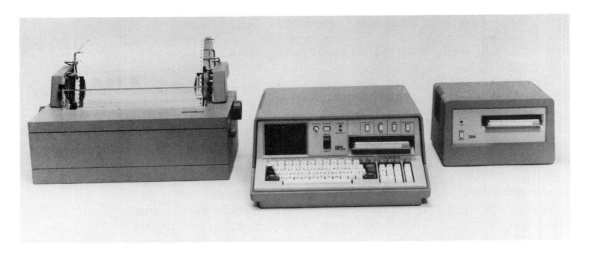

Illustration 11-4. Desk-top portable computer.

MINICOMPUTER SYSTEMS

The minicomputer market began to develop in the early 1960s when a few manufacturers provided a rather limited line of systems. The large growth of manufacturers and of installed systems in the late 1960s resulted from the demand for a low-cost computing machine capable of performing functions ranging from those of a desk-top calculator to the control of production processes in manufacturing. By definition, a minicomputer is a digital computer, compact in size, with limited internal storage, a monthly rental price of $300 to $1200, and a purchase price of $2000 to $50,000. The characteristics of minicomputer systems vary widely depending on their cost and application. Many of the characteristics of the minicomputer equal those of larger computers. Through the use of LSI circuits and new memory technology, designers have been able to achieve processor speeds and data rates close to those of medium-size computers. A typical minicomputer system like the one in Illustration 11-5 includes display terminals, a printer, and magnetic disk storage. A minimum system may be purchased for under $20,000, but systems are often higher.

In manufacturing plants, the control of production processes and quality-control testing by minicomputer makes it possible to produce better products more economically. Many manufacturing plants produce products through a continuous production process. Where such products are developed, minicomputers can be installed to control the production process, monitoring it and making any changes necessary to insure a uniform

Illustration 11-5. Minicomputer system with terminals.

product. In a steel mill, for example, the continuous production of sheet steel can be monitored by a minicomputer. It detects any changes in the thickness of the steel and makes corrections in the production process accordingly.

The role of the minicomputer continues to expand. Through 1975, systems control and data monitoring had accounted for about 50 percent of all minicomputer usage. This usage is expected to drop to about 40 percent by the end of the decade. Minicomputers of this type will be most prevalent in highly automated factories, refineries, and transportation systems.

By the mid-1970s the minicomputer had become one of the fastest growing computer markets. With the maturing of the minicomputer, manufacturers began to place more emphasis on customer support. Early users of minicomputers often found themselves with a computer and a set of instruction manuals and little else. Support services now include high-level programming languages, application programs (so users need not write all their own programs), and customer education on system use.

The cost and size of minicomputers continue to drop at significant rates, while capability increases, because of the use of LSI chips. Some of the lower-priced minicomputers have microprocessors as internal components. It is predicted that the microcomputer will replace the low end of the minicomputer market in the next few years. With lower prices and expanded capability, business users have become the major growth area for the minicomputer. Over the next five years the fast-growing minicomputer market is expected to triple in size. Sales will exceed 5 billion dollars with the business user contributing the main portion of this growth.

Businesses have used minicomputers in several ways in addition to process control applications. These include: (1) replacement of manual or mechanical data processing systems; (2) use as a remote entry device to a larger computer; (3) replacement of a large computer; and (4) to augment a larger computer.

Many small businesses that have used traditional manual methods of data processing or accounting services are installing minicomputer systems. The continual drop in the cost of minicomputers has made them a feasible alternative to manual data processing systems. In many cases, a

Illustration 11-6. Transaction-oriented minicomputer.

minicomputer system can reduce data processing costs and/or provide more relevant information for business decision-making. An increasing number of minicomputer manufacturers are making systems specifically designed for small businesses. These manufacturers commonly call the systems *small business computers*. The small business system may contain a minicomputer or a microcomputer, but it is still referred to as a small business computer.

The lowest-cost small business computers are usually *transaction-oriented systems*. Data is entered through a keyboard and processed concurrently; that is, data entry and processing are a combined operation. A typical transaction-oriented system (like the one in Illustration 11-6) includes: a keyboard for data entry; a display screen for operator verification of data entered and for display of processing results; a printer to provide a copy of the results; and a magnetic disk unit for auxiliary storage. The main disadvantage of these systems is their slow operating speed. Because data is entered by an operator at a keyboard, this operation is limited by the keying speed of the operator. The overall speed of the system is limited accordingly. Typically, low-speed printers are attached to these systems to keep costs down, but they are adequate, considering the operator's data entry speed.

Transaction-oriented systems are designed to be operated by individuals who have little data processing background, but who are familiar with the applications being processed. The computer manufacturer or a vendor often provides all of the computer programs needed to perform the common applications of small businesses. These include packages for such applications as invoicing and billing, order entry, accounts receivable, and payroll. The small business may use these programs rather than hire programmers. However, if programs are needed for specific applications, the cost of developing them or of having them developed may exceed the cost of the computer. Several computer manufacturers are addressing this need by providing programming packages for specific types of small businesses. A small business computer system may include a number of special industry application programs. Examples are programs for the construction industry, food and paper wholesaling, office product suppliers, hospitals, and membership organizations and associations.

The increased capability of small business computers, along with lower processing costs and simpler operating procedures, will accelerate the use of computers in small businesses in the years to come. As the costs of a business continue to rise and governmental reporting requirements continue to increase, more businesses will turn to the small business computer to remain competitive and profitable.

As a remote device for a larger computer, a minicomputer in a branch location of a business can refine and condense data to be entered into a central computer by means of a data-transmission facility. Remote input/

output devices linked to a central computer have been used for *remote job entry* for some time. Remote job entry allows the transfer of large amounts of data to a central computer and the return of the results of processing to the remote location. In many systems, the minicomputer acts as the remote job entry terminal and is used also for *local processing* (that is, some processing is done at the remote location).

A business that is using a central computer to serve the needs of several branches may find that it is more practical and economical to replace the central computer with minicomputers at the branches. This is especially likely if the functions of the branches are not closely related. However, the complete decentralization of computing power in a business is not as likely to occur as is another method of data processing called *distributed processing*. In a distributed processing system, minicomputers are placed at points in the organization where data originates. The data can be processed and retained locally, or it can be passed to a central computer. Distributed processing is discussed in more detail in Chapter 16.

As new data processing applications in a business require additional computing power, adding minicomputers may be preferable to increasing the size of the central computer. This allows the minicomputers to be dedicated to specific functions, yet they can still be linked to the central computer if needed.

Some computer professionals believe that completely distributed processing, which eliminates the central computer and links all of the minicomputers in a system so that they can exchange data and programs, will appear in the future. While this may be possible in a few years, it is likely that a central computer augmented with minicomputers will be used in many businesses for some time.

Illustration 11-7. Cartridge tape drive

The minicomputer can support many of the input/output devices found on larger computers. Typically, slower, lower-cost versions of printers, magnetic tape units, and magnetic disk units are used. Both the tape cartridge and the tape cassette are often used for data storage. A tape cartridge and tape drive are shown in Illustration 11-7. The tape cassette is like those used on common tape recorders. It has a storage capacity of about 150,000 characters. Both cassette and cartridge tapes offer an inexpensive and compact method of data storage.

A very popular disk unit uses a flexible disk in a plastic envelope. (See Illustration 11-8.) The diskette, or floppy disk as it is commonly called, is about 8 inches square and can hold up to 500,000 characters. Because the floppy disk offers many of the advantages of larger disk units, it will be a popular storage medium for some time.

The overall processing capability of the minicomputer is far less than that of a larger computer. One reason for this is the smaller set of instructions that the minicomputer can perform. The basic set of instructions built into the minicomputer do not usually include functions like division and multiplication. Instead, these functions are performed by software called subroutines. This requires more processing time than if the functions were performed directly by the hardware.

Illustration 11-8. Floppy disk.

A number of minicomputer manufacturers offer *microprogramming* capabilities or *microprograms* to overcome the lack of certain basic instructions. Microprograms can be placed in a special storage area in the central processing unit to perform functions not available directly in the hardware. The purpose, then, of a microprogram is to carry out some function that would otherwise be accomplished by a subroutine. The primary advantage of using a microprogram is that it can perform the function much faster than would be possible if a subroutine were used.

The special storage area for microprograms can be either a *read-only memory (ROM)* or a *programmable read-only memory (PROM)*. The ROM is programmed by the manufacturer and cannot be altered by the user. The PROM is programmed by the manufacturer, but it can be reprogrammed for special functions. Users do not normally write microprograms, but it is possible. Microprogramming will continue to be used in minicomputers for some time. It greatly expands their versatility.

Without question, the minicomputer will play an important role in computer applications over the next decade. As time passes it will become more difficult to tell the difference between minicomputers and larger computers. Already the top-of-the-line minicomputer has as much computing power as many of the small and medium-size computers.

SMALL COMPUTER SYSTEMS

A small computer system typically includes a general-purpose digital computer with a storage capability slightly larger than that of a minicomputer. It supports a variety of input/output devices. There is a wide range in both price and performance of small computer systems.

The small computer system is often *batch-oriented*. Data is collected in a separate step before it is submitted to the computer for processing. Punched-card input and output are common. Typical users of these systems have used punched-card systems in the past and then upgraded to card-oriented small computers.

For the business that is using a punched-card system for data processing, the small batch computer can offer an increase in system processing speed, greater flexibility in the use of the system, and better management information. It may offer a reduction in equipment cost. Often a small batch computer system can be justified in a business using punched-card data processing, just by its potential for reducing data processing costs.

A small business acquiring a computer for the first time has the choice of using either a small transaction-oriented minicomputer or a small batch computer. Often a decision is made on the basis of the applications to be processed and the cost. A business with a small amount of data entry in relation to processing might start with a transaction-oriented minicomputer system. When data entry begins to consume the major portion of computer usage, the system can be replaced by a small batch system. In a small batch system, the data can be recorded on punched cards, magnetic tape, or magnetic disk, independent of the computer. The recorded data can be processed on the computer when it is available.

In 1969, the introduction of a new small computer, the IBM System/3, renewed the interest in punched-card computer systems. The System/3 was aimed primarily at businesses using punched-card equipment or manual data processing methods. It is based on the use of a 96-column card, the first new punched-card design in over 50 years. Several models of System/3, namely a card system, a disk system, and a keyboard-oriented disk system, have been developed. A typical configuration of a System/3 disk system is shown in Illustration 11-9.

The basic configuration of the System/3 card system includes a central processing unit, a multi-function card machine, and a 100-lines-per-minute printer. The card system is attractive to the punched-card data processing user who has a variety of applications, none of which requires a large amount of processing. The card system can be used to punch, sort, collate, read, and print the contents of cards, thus eliminating the need for separate pieces of equipment for these functions.

Other manufacturers have introduced small batch computer systems that accept 96-column cards. The system in Illustration 11-10 uses 96-column cards and cassette tapes for data input. This system uses magnetic disk storage for files, thus reducing the need for a large number of card

Illustration 11-9. System/3 computer with disk storage.

Illustration 11-10. A small batch computer system using magnetic disk
storage, cassette tapes, and 96-column cards.

files. Systems such as these offer several advantages over transaction-
oriented minicomputers.

1. Several jobs can be run concurrently, through *multiprogramming*
   (a capability discussed in Chapter 14). This allows more work to be
   accomplished in less time.
2. High-speed, high-capacity disk storage allows quick access to data files.
3. A larger variety of input/output devices are available and their operating speeds are higher.
4. A larger number of application programs for different types of organizations are available. These include programs for retailing, manufacturing, banking, hospitals, and educational institutions.
5. High-level programming languages such as COBOL, RPG II, and FOR-
   TRAN are available for program development.
6. Both batch processing and transaction-oriented processing can be accomplished on the same system.

Small batch computer systems are considerably more expensive to install and run than transaction-oriented systems. The batch system may cost well over $100,000 to purchase and requires trained programmers and operators. The higher-speed input/output devices used on these systems are a major reason for their higher cost. The cost of programming, when suitable programs are not available, often exceeds the cost of the computer system.

The potential market for small computers appears to be large. Over 10,000 System/3 computers have been installed. It is estimated that in the next five years the total number of small computers installed will exceed 100,000 units. Contributing to this total will be many former punched-card equipment users and many first-time users of automated data processing.

How does a business decide whether it needs a minicomputer or a small batch computer system? If a small business changed to computer data processing in the 1960s, it may have started with a minicomputer. The point at which a small computer should be acquired is not fixed. A business must determine its processing needs and then select the system to best meet those needs, with consideration given to cost and performance.

The small batch computer has a place in the large business. Since the need for computing power is not always easy to satisfy with one large computer, it is often necessary to provide several small computers within branches or divisions of a business. A small computer can be used at each branch or division for all of its major data processing needs. When necessary, the small computer can be used as a terminal to a larger computer. Many manufacturers make small computer systems. Among them are Burroughs, Honeywell, IBM, National Cash Register (NCR), Univac, and Digital Equipment Corporation (DEC).

MEDIUM-SIZE COMPUTER SYSTEMS

A medium-size computer system can be used for a wider variety of applications than a small batch computer system can. Medium-size computers have faster operating speeds and larger storage capacities. They can support a large number of high-speed input/output devices. Typically, medium-size computers are used for applications that require large amounts of batch processing and many files. Multiprogramming is available so a number of batch jobs can be run at one time. For example, a group of batch jobs running concurrently might include: a payroll program, an inventory master file update, a customer billing program, and an accounts receivable program. These programs could be accessing files on different magnetic disk and/or magnetic tape units at the same time.

These systems are capable of supporting batch processing along with remote job entry and multiple users at remote terminals, at the same time.

All of the major programming languages are usually supported, and extensive software is usually available. A combined hardware and software feature called *virtual storage* or *virtual memory* is usually available. Virtual storage makes it appear that the computer has more main storage capacity than is actually physically present. This allows the computer to process programs that would otherwise be too large to fit in main storage. When a programmer is writing programs to be run on a computer with virtual storage, the program size need not be limited. (The way in which virtual storage functions on a computer will be discussed further in Chapter 15.)

The medium-size computer can support a management information system and its associated data bases. A data base requires extensive file capacity and should be maintained on a magnetic disk for fast access. Terminals may be provided in management offices so that executives can make inquiries to obtain current information. These systems can also support research and development and scientific applications requiring large amounts of disk storage and fast processor speeds.

Such systems cost from $5000 to $20,000 a month to rent and up to $1,000,000 to purchase. This wide range in price results partially from the expandability of the systems. For example, a business may start with a system that has 150,000 bytes of storage, two disk drives, a card reader, and

Illustration 11-11. A medium-size computer system
with disk and tape storage.

a 1300-lines-per-minute printer. As the data processing needs of the business increase, the system may be expanded to include 512K bytes of storage, several more disk drives, and an additional printer.

Illustration 11-11 is a medium-size computer system with tape and disk storage. The disk storage capacity of this system is expandable to over 1-1/2 billion characters. Its main storage capacity may be up to 1 million bytes. Such a system rents for about $12,000 to $15,000 per month; it can be purchased for about $700,000.

LARGE COMPUTER SYSTEMS

The large computer system offers the ultimate in operating speed and storage capacity. A typical system has a storage unit capable of storing millions of bytes and operating at speeds measured in nanoseconds. These systems rent for $40,000 to $250,000 or more per month; they cost millions of dollars. Large businesses use these systems for many of the functions mentioned above for medium-size systems but the processing volume is much greater. The large computer system in Illustration 11-12 has several banks of main storage, multiple input/output devices, and disk and tape storage.

Most large computer systems use some type of virtual storage. There are often two or more central processing units within a system, allowing simultaneous processing of jobs. This is called *multiprocessing*. In addition to providing faster processing, the system can be set up to allow one processor to take over for another if one fails. Multiprocessor systems are

Illustration 11-12. A large computer system.

often used for applications that are time-dependent such as airline reservation systems and credit card verification systems. Large computers that multiprocess can also support multiprogramming. Each processor in a multiprocessing system can act like a single computer and run a number of jobs concurrently.

Management decision-making tools, such as simulation, can be used on large computer systems. Through mathematical techniques, for example, various activities of a business that would normally occur over many months or years can be simulated in hours. For example, a business may be considering the installation of a new inventory-control system to achieve better control of items in stock. Before converting to the new system, several years of inventory activity can be simulated to verify that the system will be an improvement over current methods of handling inventory. A large computer system may support a very sophisticated management information system.

The large computer system is also well suited for scientific and engineering work. Its speed and size allow it to do mathematical computations that are not practical or possible on other computer systems. The engineering research and development processing necessary for the creation of new products can often be accomplished on the large computer system used for other data processing functions of the business.

A distributed processing system can be based on a large computer that has a number of minicomputers or small computers attached. The large computer processes jobs that are too large for the other computers and maintains the large data files of the organization. Often the large computer acts as a routing agent to interconnect smaller computers so they can share information.

THE SIZE OF COMPUTERS AND SCOPE OF THE COMPUTER INDUSTRY: A RESTATEMENT AND COMPARISON

Since 1954, over a hundred different computer models have been designed and built. A computer is generally classified as a microcomputer, minicomputer, small, medium-size, or large computer. This classification is not necessarily an indication of physical size. Rather, it is usually a general price-scale categorization. Average monthly rental prices are considered by the computer industry to be an acceptable means of classification. As indicated by Illustration 11-13, the average monthly rental price of a computer is approximately one-fiftieth of the average purchase price. Basic models in each computer size classification can be purchased within the price range shown. The total cost of a computer system in any of these size classifications increases as more hardware and/or software are added.

Computer size	Average monthly rental price range, including maintenance	Purchase price range
Microcomputers		$ 1,500- 10,000
Minicomputers	$ 300- 1,200	2,000- 50,000
Small	1,200- 5,000	50,000- 200,000
Medium	5,000- 20,000	200,000-1,000,000
Large	20,000-250,000	1,000,000-5,000,000

Illustration 11-13. Rental and purchase price ranges of computers.

Through 1955, several hundred computer systems were installed. In contrast, through 1960, 5400 computer systems were installed; through 1965, 23,000 computer systems were installed; through 1970, 90,000 computer systems were installed; through 1975, 210,000 were installed; and by 1980, it is estimated that about 566,000 computer systems valued at $60 billion will have been installed.

Many computer companies are engaged in the design, construction, and installation of computer systems. The industry leaders for the minicomputer market and for larger systems are shown in Illustration 11-14. Digital

Larger computers	1976 sales in millions of dollars	Share of market
IBM	$7,200	66.1%
Sperry-Univac	790	7.3
Burroughs	700	6.4
Honeywell (HIS)	680	6.2
NCR	340	3.1
Control Data (CDC)	265	2.6
Minicomputers		
Digital Equipment (DEC)	$ 710	38 %
Hewlett-Packard	304	16
Data General	179	10
Honeywell (HIS)	112	6
General Automation	79	4
Texas Instruments	58	3

Source of statistics: International Data Corp.

Illustration 11-14. Industry leaders for larger systems and minicomputer systems.

Equipment Corporation is the leading supplier of minicomputers, holding 38 percent of the market. By 1980 they expect to double their sales. The leading supplier of larger computers is IBM, with about 66 percent of the market. Sperry-Univac is second in this market with approximately 7 percent.

In recent years, emphasis has been placed by American computer firms on the building of minicomputers and small computers. This emphasis is primarily a response to the strong desire of small and medium-size businesses to change to electronic data processing. The result of this emphasis is reflected by the fact that in terms of the distribution of computers, about 3 percent are large systems, 14 percent are medium-size systems, and small and minicomputer systems make up the remainder.

Summary

1. Computer systems come in a variety of sizes and price ranges. Each can satisfy the data processing needs of numerous business applications.

2. Microcomputers are based on microprocessors that are constructed on chips less than 1/4-inch square. Microcomputers are used in a variety of applications including process control systems, minicomputers, portable computers, and intelligent terminals. Due to their low cost and size, they promise to become the major computer advance of the decade.

3. Minicomputers are compact in size. They vary greatly in price and performance. The minicomputer is used in ways such as: control of production processes; a replacement of manual or mechanical data processing methods; a remote terminal to a large computer system; a transaction-oriented small business system; and in a distributed processing system. Microprogramming is now offered on some minicomputers to overcome limitations in the hardware. The floppy disk is a popular low-cost storage medium used with these computers. One of the fastest growing markets for the minicomputer is the small business system. Many small businesses are installing these systems as they convert from manual data processing methods.

4. Small computers have larger storage unit capacities and faster operating speeds than minicomputers. They are well suited to handling larger amounts of data. These systems use a variety of input/output devices. Of these, the most common are devices that handle punched cards. Small computers are well suited for batch processing, where data is collected in a separate step before it is submitted to the computer.

5. Medium-size computer systems, because of their internal storage capabilities and the use of virtual storage, can support a wider range of business data processing applications than either the minicomputer or the small computer. They often support batch processing, users at remote terminals, and remote job entry at the same time. Also, they are capable of supporting a wider variety of high-speed input/output devices than smaller computer systems are.

6. Large computer systems are used by large businesses to process large amounts of data on a regular basis. They are capable of supporting large management information systems. In addition to the types of applications performed by other computer systems, large computer systems can be used for mathematical simulations and scientific applications where the internal operating speed of the computer is critical. A large computer can serve as the main computer in a system that includes minicomputers or small computers that do distributed processing.

CAREER PROFILE

Paul C. Ely, Jr.
Vice President and General Manager

Computer Systems Group
Hewlett-Packard

Background Experience

Even as a teenager, I was very much inclined toward technical things such as building radios. I attended Lehigh University, studying engineering physics, and was graduated in 1953. I started

working for Sperry-Gyroscope Company in a department making test equipment for radar systems. My ten years there were essentially spent in engineering-type activities, working mainly on government contracts. For the last two or three years, however, I was involved in a small effort Sperry made to use their technology to build test equipment for commercial sale. In 1962 I began my career with Hewlett-Packard as an engineering project leader. During that time, I got my Master's Degree in Electrical Engineering from Stanford University. About 1964 I was made engineering manager for what was then the Microwave Division. Two years later Hewlett-Packard invented its first minicomputer. I had some very strong, enthusiastic ideas about how the computer could help us build automated microwave test systems. When we did, in fact, get the first pilot-run computer and build a system out of it, my real involvement with computers began. In 1968, I became general manager of the Microwave Division, where I remained until 1973 when I was asked to take over HP's computer effort. In recent years, our computer business has grown dramatically. When I began five years ago, there was one division and now there are eight. The computer effort is almost 40% of Hewlett-Packard's total business.

Primary Job Responsibilities

The Computer Systems Group designs, manufactures, and markets a broad range of computers, computer systems, and computer peripheral products used in industry, science, education, medicine, and business. I manage roughly 5,000 people directly related to the division. In addition, there are another 4 or 5 thousand employees in the administrative structure who work directly with our computer programs, so my work involves a large number of people spread out all over the world. My primary responsibilities are to oversee our strategy. This is complicated by two facts: the rapid advancements in computer technology and the constantly changing nature of the market. Because our portion of the computer industry is averaging about 30% growth per year, it is a challenge to foresee all the problems that that kind of growth can create and, in fact, to do the things that make it possible for our organization to share in the growth that is available in the market. The other complicating factor pertains to the market—who our customers are, how they are using our products, and who our competitors are. These elements change almost monthly. That may sound like an exaggeration but in the last eighteen months, I would guess that half of our computer customers have been new to us and they are often using our products in new ways. In addition, two-thirds of our competitors are new to us, with new kinds of products. These are two of the challenging situations that create substantial strategic and even tactical problems for me. In a typical 10- to 12-hour day at work, nearly 90% of my time is spent talking with somebody. I am either in a one-to-one conversation or in a meeting with a number of people discussing issues of strategy, the day's operating problems, tomorrow's tactics, or I am possibly meeting with a group of customers visiting our facilities. The occasions I have to think and reflect take place only when I am away from the office.

What Has Made You Successful?

At the most fundamental level, I would say desire combined with curiosity. What seems to separate people generally is not the quality of their education or the level of their intelligence, but their willingness to use the tools that they have to achieve some purpose. That's the desire part. Curiosity is the unwillingness to leave something unexplained. These qualities are essential to success and, I think, are possible to develop. My education was also extremely helpful in my career. My choice of engineering physics was particularly helpful because it is a curriculum that provides virtually all the academic basis for most of the other engineering disciplines. Practical stuff, today, is obsolete by the time you get out of school, or within a few years, but the academic truths, the underlying theories, remain. With this foundation, it is easier to adapt to the rapid changes of technology. Returning to get my Master's Degree reinforced my belief in the need to be studying and reading and learning constantly. Another thing I have found very helpful is the stimulation and learning I get from people around me. I have found that it is better to be in an organization where almost everybody is a top performer as opposed to being some place where you feel you ought to succeed because the general performance level is not that good. It's very hard to grow and develop if you don't have people around you who know more than you do about something. At Hewlett-Packard these people are often my peers and people who work for me.

Computer Programming and Design

Program Flowcharting

PROGRAM FLOWCHARTS

PROGRAM FLOWCHART SYMBOLS AND USAGE

PROGRAM LOOPS

USE OF CONNECTORS

SPECIALIZED FLOWCHART SYMBOLS

FLOWCHARTING AIDS

The use of a computer to solve business data processing problems requires that a procedure be developed for the computer to follow in solving the problem. A computer is a powerful machine; however, it is capable of doing only what it is directed to do. This direction is provided by a *computer program,* which is a series of instructions that the computer executes, or carries out.

The preparation of a computer program also involves following a procedure. The problem must first be defined. This definition must include an analysis of the data elements within the source documents that will be used by the program and of the data elements that will constitute the desired reports or other output from the program.

Once the problem has been defined and sample layouts of any reports or records have been created, the program that will produce these reports or records must be prepared. As seen in Chapter 3, the *system flowchart* is a tool that can help clarify the relationships that exist between several applications in a business system; it is a graphic representation of the system and the flow of data through the system. But details as to how processing will occur in the system are not specified in a system flowchart. Rather, processing details are provided in *program flowcharts.* The general relationship between system and program flowcharts is shown schematically in Illustration B-1.

Normally, a detailed program flowchart is prepared for each program required for an application. There are no standards as to the amount of detail to be included in program flowcharts. If an application is complex, two levels of program flowcharts may be prepared. One flowchart describes the main processing steps, and several others provide more exacting details of these steps.

The flowchart that describes the main processing steps in a data processing application is often called a *modular program flowchart.* Each major step is considered a *module.* A module can represent a complete program or a part of a program such as a subroutine, depending on the complexity of the application. Each module can be represented by a *detailed program flowchart.* It describes the individual steps that are necessary for the solution of the problem. The modular flowchart provides a clear picture of the application without the clutter of the detailed processing steps. This makes it easier for the programmer to determine whether or not all of the major processing steps have been identified before creating any detailed flowcharts.

Compare the modular flowchart in Illustration B-2 with the detailed flowchart. The main steps needed for a customer billing application are shown in the modular flowchart. The detailed flowchart shows the steps for calculating a customer bill. There are advantages in flowcharting and designing programs in this manner. Large programs can be divided into manageable sections. Several programmers can be assigned to complete

SYSTEM FLOWCHART   MODULAR PROGRAM FLOWCHART

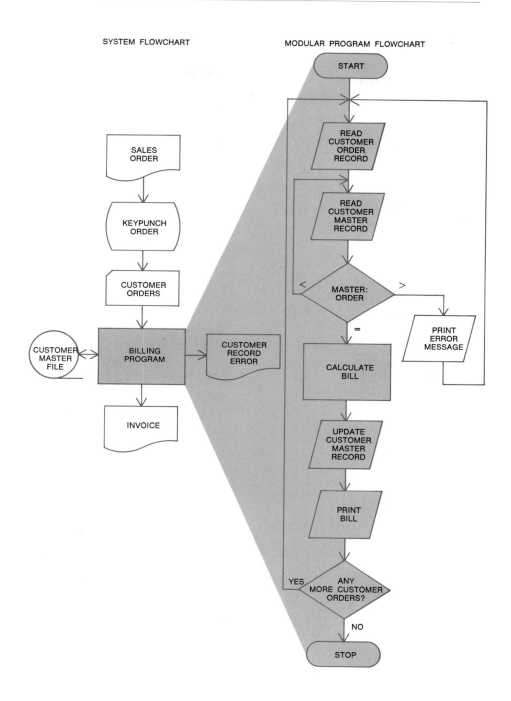

Illustration B-1. System and program flowcharts.

MODULAR PROGRAM FLOWCHART

DETAILED PROGRAM FLOWCHART

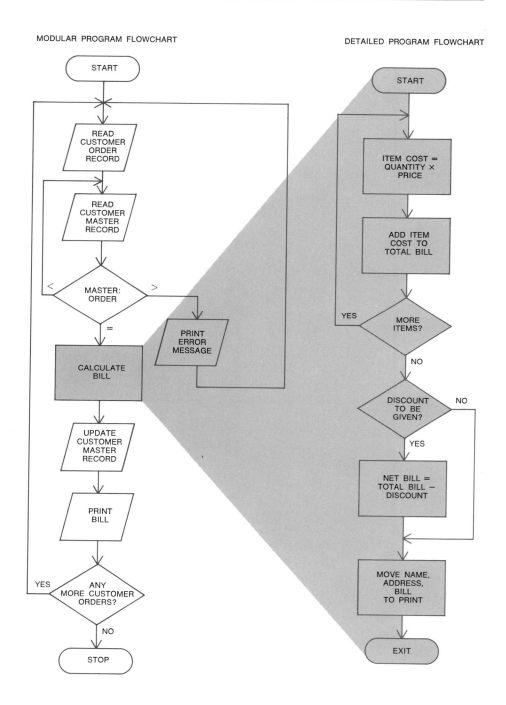

Illustration B-2. Modular and detailed flowcharting.

specific processing modules. Each of these modules can be flowcharted, developed, and tested to insure it is correct before it is combined with other modules.

The programmer uses a program flowchart to prepare a program (in effect, a series of instructions representing the steps in the flowchart). After the programmer has written the program, and it has been recorded on an input medium, it is ready to be compiled, tested, and debugged. *Compiling* is the process of translating the programming language into a machine-readable language. *Debugging* is the process of finding program errors and correcting them so that the program runs correctly. This is often a very challenging and time-consuming activity. *Testing* consists of running the program with input data that simulates, or is a representative sample of, the real data that will be processed by the program.

PROGRAM FLOWCHARTS

A program flowchart, the pictorial representation of the steps necessary to solve a problem, is sometimes called a *logic diagram* or *block diagram*. The detailed steps of problem solution can be seen clearly when displayed on a program flowchart. The purpose of a program flowchart is to represent by use of symbols the processing that should take place in a program. In other words, a program flowchart shows the detailed steps within the program and the order in which the steps are to be performed. It indicates the "logic" of a program. By studying the flowchart, a programmer can analyze the logic and determine whether a reasonable plan for the solution of the problem has been developed. The flowchart must be detailed enough to serve as a guide when coding the program and as a reference when testing and debugging it. The flowchart also serves as documentation of the program, either for future modifications of the program or for use by other personnel in the business.

Flowcharts contain symbols that represent basic functions or operations. Each symbol represents an instruction or a series of instructions that the computer must execute to solve a problem. In an attempt to standardize these symbols, the *American National Standards Institute (ANSI)* has adopted a set of symbols that are widely used and accepted by programmers. Some variations exist in data processing installations that have developed their own sets of symbols. The ANSI system flowchart symbols were shown in Illustration 3-1 of this book. The ANSI program flowchart symbols are shown in Illustration B-3.

PROGRAM FLOWCHART SYMBOLS AND USAGE

The *terminal symbol* (the leftmost symbol in Illustration B-4) is used to indicate the beginning or end of a program flowchart. Additionally, it is

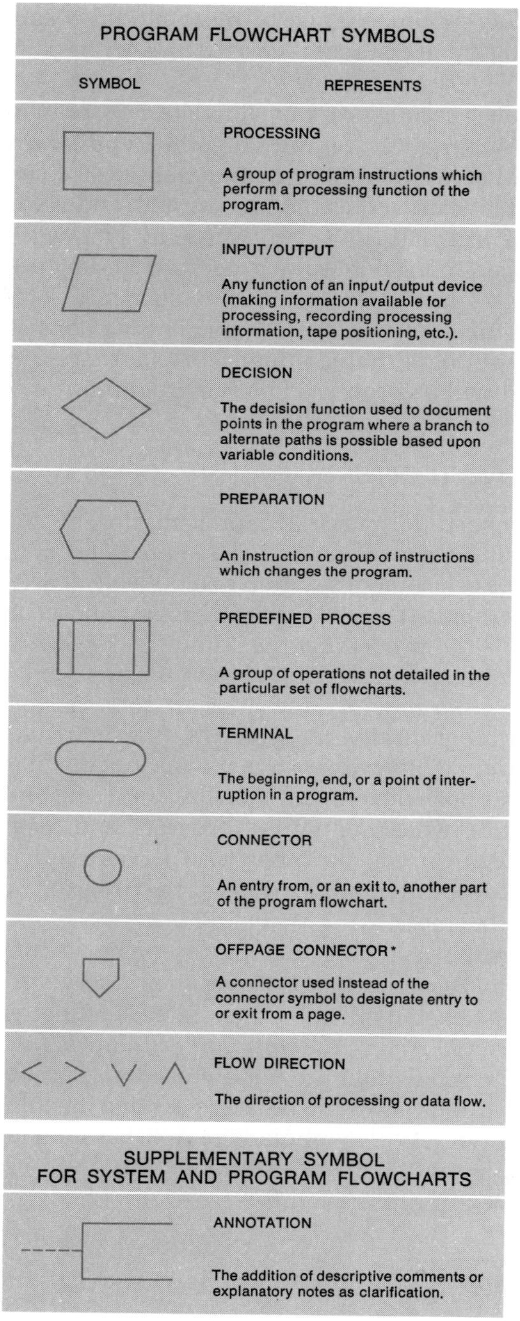

PROGRAM FLOWCHART SYMBOLS

SYMBOL	REPRESENTS
	PROCESSING A group of program instructions which perform a processing function of the program.
	INPUT/OUTPUT Any function of an input/output device (making information available for processing, recording processing information, tape positioning, etc.).
	DECISION The decision function used to document points in the program where a branch to alternate paths is possible based upon variable conditions.
	PREPARATION An instruction or group of instructions which changes the program.
	PREDEFINED PROCESS A group of operations not detailed in the particular set of flowcharts.
	TERMINAL The beginning, end, or a point of interruption in a program.
	CONNECTOR An entry from, or an exit to, another part of the program flowchart.
	OFFPAGE CONNECTOR * A connector used instead of the connector symbol to designate entry to or exit from a page.
< > ∨ ∧	**FLOW DIRECTION** The direction of processing or data flow.

SUPPLEMENTARY SYMBOL FOR SYSTEM AND PROGRAM FLOWCHARTS

	ANNOTATION The addition of descriptive comments or explanatory notes as clarification.

*IBM usage only

Illustration B-3. Program flowchart symbols.

used to show any pause in a program because of an error condition or for operator action.

Within the terminal symbol (or any other flowchart symbol) is a brief comment about the function or activity that is to take place. When additional comments are needed for clarification, an *annotation symbol* is used as shown at the right in Illustration B-4. It is connected to the symbol for the function by a broken line as in the illustration.

Any input or output function is represented by the *input/output symbol* (Illustration B-5). For input this symbol usually represents reading a record from some input device. For output the symbol represents writing the results of processing on an output device. Only one input/output function should be represented by one symbol. On most flowcharts, there are at least two input/output symbols.

Direction-of-flow is indicated by a *flowline* and an arrowhead (Illustration B-6). Generally, the flowchart is drawn from the top of the page to the bottom, starting at the left of the page and continuing to the right if needed. The symbols on the flowchart are connected by flowlines. An arrowhead must be used on any flowline providing for a direction-of-flow other than from the top or the left. Arrowheads can be used on all flowlines to improve clarity.

A processing step completed by the computer is represented by the *process symbol* (Illustration B-6). Any data manipulation, such as a calculation or moving data from one location to another, is processing. One process symbol may represent one operation, for example, "Multiply Hours by Rate." More than one operation can be represented by a process symbol when the operations are related; for example, "Compute Gross Pay" in Illustration B-6 may represent several calculations.

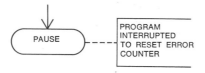

Illustration B-4. Terminal and annotation symbols.

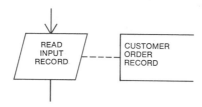

Illustration B-5. Input/output symbol.

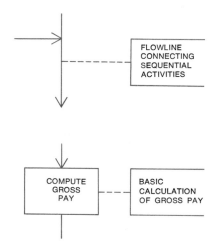

Illustration B-6. Flowline and process symbols.

The steps in a program flowchart are executed in order unless the sequence is altered by a decision process. This alteration of program sequence by *branching,* or transfer of control, allows great flexibility. The program logic may be quite complex in applications where extensive branching is used.

Testing for one or more specific conditions that may be encountered during program execution is represented on a program flowchart by the *decision symbol* (Illustration B-7). Generally, one decision or test is represented by a decision symbol; however, multiple alternatives can be indicated. As in Illustration B-7, the flowlines that exit the decision symbol must be labeled to identify the outcomes of the test that they show.

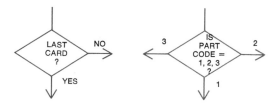

Illustration B-7. Decision symbol.

Given two numeric quantities, X and Y, their possible relations can be expressed as follows:

X is equal to (=) Y
X is not equal to (≠) Y
X is less than (<) Y
X is less than or equal to (≤) Y
X is greater than (>) Y
X is greater than or equal to (≥) Y

Tests are often stated in terms of the relationship between two numeric quantities, or data items, as shown in Illustration B-8.

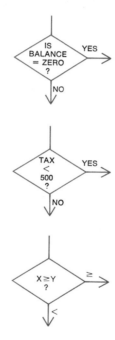

Illustration B-8. Relational tests.

PROGRAM LOOPS

The ability of the computer to repeat a series of instructions that it executes is called *looping*. As an outgrowth of the repetitive execution, a *program loop* is formed. Such a loop is shown in Illustration B-9. The flowchart describes a program that prepares a printed listing of an inventory file on punched cards. It repeats a series of instructions by branching back to the first instruction.

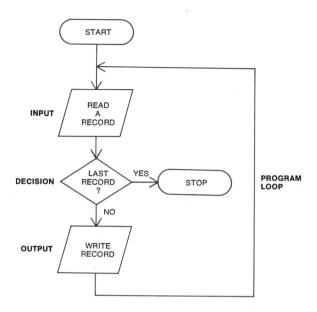

Illustration B-9. Program loop.

Every program loop should contain an exit point so that the repeated execution of the loop can be terminated, either to continue with other processing or to stop. In Illustration B-9, the exit point is the test that determines whether the last record has been read. If so, the loop is terminated. Using a last record test to terminate processing is a common practice when the number of records to be processed is unknown. Generally, the last record in the file contains, not data, but rather some indication that it is the last record. Since it is not a data record, it is not processed as one. For this reason, the last record read by the program in Illustration B-9 is not written to the output file.

The flowchart in Illustration B-10 uses the same inventory file to prepare a listing of current inventory balances for items in stock. Each card record contains the old balance on hand from the previous month and any issues and receipts for the current month for one item. It is necessary to add all of the receipts, if any, to the previous balance, and then subtract any issues to arrive at a current balance for the item.

A record is read, and a test is made to see whether it is the last record in the file. If it is not, a test is made to see whether there are any receipts for the item. If there are, they are added to the previous balance in a process step. If there are not, the process step is omitted; a branch is made to the next test. A test for issues is made, and a similar process step is executed or

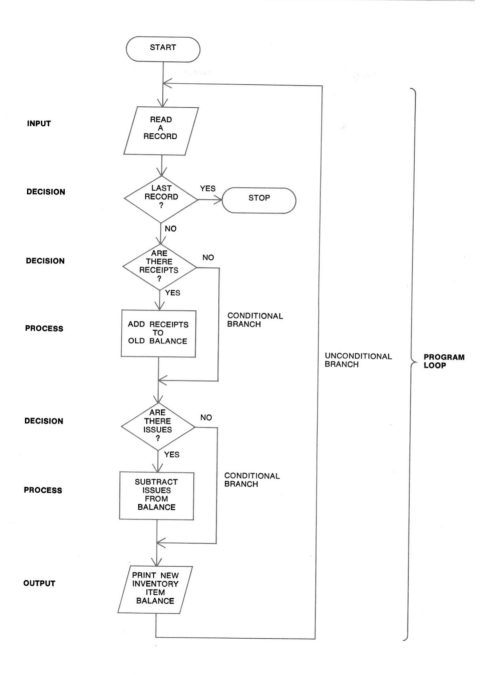

INPUT

DECISION

DECISION

PROCESS

DECISION

PROCESS

START

READ
RECORD

LAST
RECORD

YES

NO

ARE
THERE
RECEIPTS
?

NO

YES

ADD RECEIPTS
TO
OLD BALANCE

CONDITIONAL
BRANCH

UNCONDITIONAL
BRANCH

PROGRAM
LOOP

ARE
THERE
ISSUES
?

NO

YES

SUBTRACT
ISSUES
FROM
BALANCE

CONDITIONAL
BRANCH

PRINT NEW
INVENTORY
ITEM
BALANCE

Illustration B-10. Inventory listing flowchart.

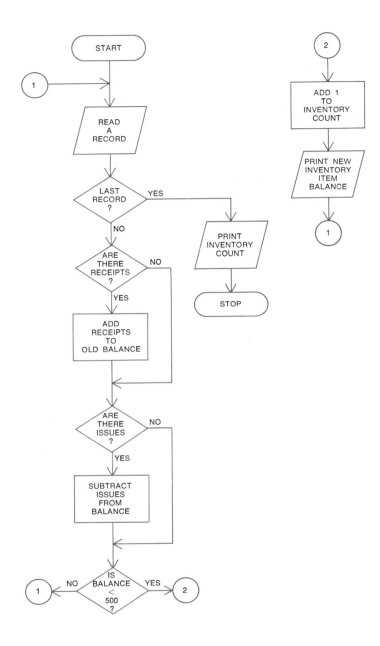

Illustration B-11. Modified inventory listing flowchart.

branched around. The last step prints the current inventory balance for the item. This completes the processing cycle for a record. A return to the read step occurs at this point. The entire loop sequence is repeated if any data records have not been processed.

Two types of branching are used in this example: conditional and unconditional. A *conditional branch* requires that a condition be met before the branch occurs. In this example, the tests for receipts and for issues are conditional branches. The *unconditional branch* is always taken when it is encountered. Here it occurs after the balance for an item is printed.

USE OF CONNECTORS

More complex flowcharts often involve multiple loops and additional branching. They may be several pages long. To reduce the number of flowlines on a flowchart and improve clarity, a *connector symbol* is often used to connect an exit from one part of the flowchart to an entry on another part of the flowchart. Some installations use a special *off-page connector* when the exit and entry points are on different pages of the flowchart.

Illustration B-11 is a modification of the inventory listing flowchart. It shows the logic required to print a listing of only the items with balances below 500 units. A total count of these items will be printed at the end of the inventory listing. This total is determined by adding one to an inventory count each time a balance is printed.

Several connector symbols are used instead of flowlines in Illustration B-11. In each case, corresponding exit and entry connectors have the same number, and arrowheads show the direction-of-flow.

The flowcharts in Illustrations B-10 and B-11 are similar. Other flowcharts could have been drawn to show how to provide the same output but use different steps in doing so. There is usually more than one way to flowchart a problem and still arrive at a correct solution. Problem solving is a creative process. If two programmers flowchart the same problem, their flowcharts are likely to differ even if they provide identical results.

SPECIALIZED FLOWCHART SYMBOLS

Several specialized flowchart symbols are shown in Illustration B-12. The *predefined process symbol* ▯ represents a group of operations that are not defined on the program flowchart. These operations may be another program that is used by the main program. They may be a subprogram,

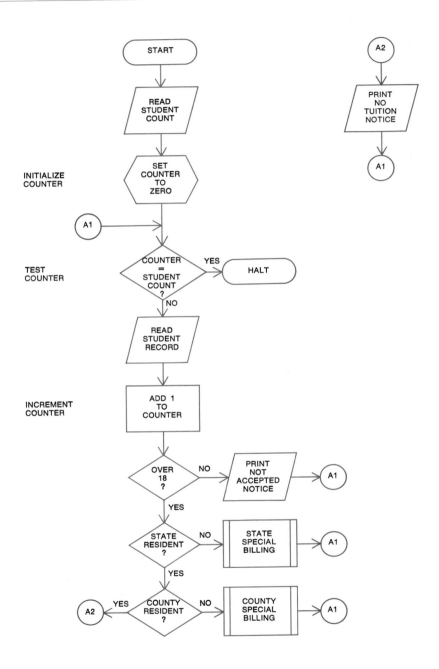

Illustration B-12. Specialized flowchart symbols.

which is simply a series of instructions that may be executed several times but is not a part of the main program.

The *preparation symbol* ⟨   ⟩ is used to indicate a step such as setting a location to zeros or to a maximum value, or setting a binary digit position to 1 or 0 for use as a switch that determines whether or not a branch is made during execution of the program. The flowchart in Illustration B-12 shows how to determine whether or not a student is eligible for enrollment, and if so, what tuition the student should pay, based on residence considerations. This flowchart contains a counter that is used to control the number of times a program loop is repeated. The essential elements of the program loop are: (1) initializing the counter, (2) incrementing the counter, and (3) testing the counter to see whether or not a particular limit has been reached. Either incrementing or testing may follow initialization of the counter, depending on the logic preferred by the programmer who constructs the flowchart.

The use of counters is a common practice in programming. In this program, the counter that controls the number of times the loop is executed, at the same time, controls the number of student records that are processed. The counter is initialized to zero in the preparation step, then tested to see whether its value equals the limit (student count) that has been read as input.

Each time a student record is read, one is added to the counter and a comparison is made to see whether the counter is equal to the student count. Records for students requiring special billing for tuition are handled by special series of instructions represented by the predefined process symbols on the flowchart. The connectors on this flowchart contain letters and numbers for reference, which is a common practice.

When a counter is used to control processing, the limit of the counter can be provided in any of several ways. The flowchart in Illustration B-12 uses a limit that is read as input. Another way to provide a limit is to state the limit in the program. This approach is used in the flowchart in Illustration B-13.

The flowchart in Illustration B-13 shows how to process a file of records containing monthly sales in sequence by branch office to determine the annual sales total for each of 25 branches in a retail chain. Twelve monthly sales records are to be processed for each branch. The counter used for the branch limit is set to 25 and the counter used for months is set to zero in preparation steps; both of these counters are used to control program

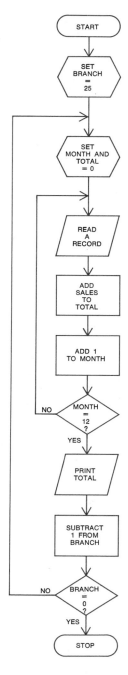

Illustration B-13. Nested loop.

loops. The data field that is used to accumulate the annual sales total for a branch is also set to zero. It is added to repeatedly in determining each branch total.

After a record is read and the monthly sales are added to the annual sales total for a branch, the counter for months is incremented and then tested for a value of 12. This program loop is repeated 12 times. Then the annual sales total for the branch is printed.

The counter for the branch limit is reduced by one after each branch total is printed. The loop controlled by this counter is repeated until the counter equals zero. Then processing halts.

The program described in Illustration B-13 contains one loop that is entirely within another; that is, all steps in the loop controlled by the counter for months are also within the loop controlled by the branch counter. Such a loop is called a *nested loop*.

FLOWCHARTING AIDS

Several flowcharting aids are available to the programmer. The *flowchart template* contains all of the flowchart symbols as cutout forms that can be traced neatly on a flowchart. Flowcharts can be prepared on any type of paper; however special *flowchart worksheets* are available for this purpose. Illustration B-14 shows a flowchart on such a worksheet.

When the flowchart worksheet is used in preparing a flowchart, certain conventions should be followed. Each rectangle is identified by a letter and number so that connectors can point to specific rectangles. If a connector symbol refers to a rectangle on another page, the number of the page is written to the left of the connector. There are no such references on the flowchart in Illustration B-14, because this flowchart is contained on only one page. However, if such a reference were needed, it could be written as shown below. This symbol indicates that this particular path of a program continues at B5 on page 6 of the flowchart.

In preparing a modular program flowchart on a flowchart worksheet, individual modules can be cross-referenced as shown in Illustration B-15. All of the main processing steps or modules are represented by symbols that use striping at the top to show the names of detailed flowcharts. The page on which the detail begins is indicated above the upper left corner of each symbol. The modular flowchart for the main module refers to all of the major processing routines, but ideally it consists of not more than one flowchart worksheet. A detailed flowchart consisting of one or more flow-

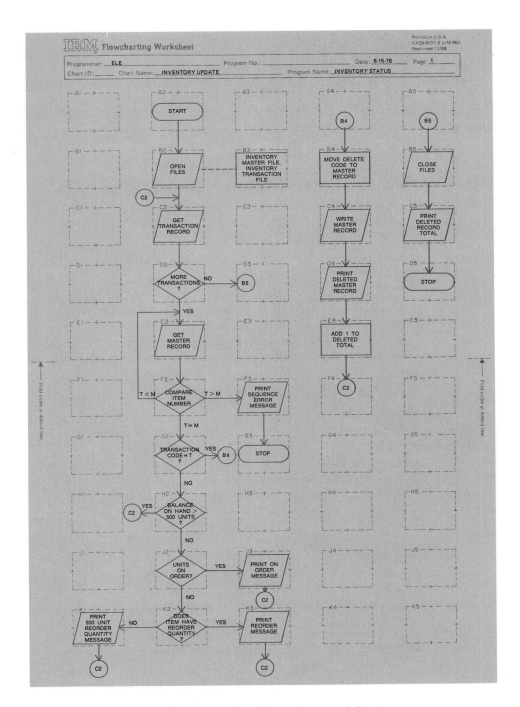

Illustration B-14. Flowchart worksheet.

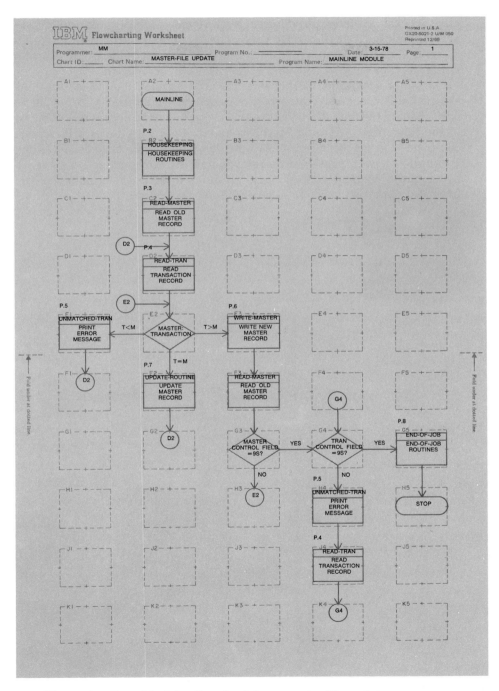

Illustration B-15. Modular flowchart for a master-file update program.

chart worksheets is required for each referenced module. (For another example, look back at Illustration B-2. The "Calculate Bill" module would normally be represented with striping like the modules in Illustration B-15.)

Computer programs that prepare flowcharts from detailed instructions are available. Generally, the programmer sketches out the basic logic to be described on the flowchart. This is expressed in a form acceptable as input to the flowchart program. The flowchart program produces a flowchart complete with machine versions of the flowchart symbols as output. Such *automated flowcharting* allows revisions to the flowchart to be made by a computer. Manual redrawing is eliminated. This saves considerable time and makes it easier to keep the flowchart current.

Summary

1. System and program flowcharts are tools used in defining procedures for solving problems in business data processing. A system flowchart is a graphic representation of the flow of data and work through a business data processing system. A program flowchart is a graphic representation of a series of steps necessary to solve a problem.

2. A modular flowchart can be used to describe the major processing steps in an application. Each major step, or module, can be described on a detailed flowchart.

3. The basic symbols used on most program flowcharts are the terminal, input/output, flowline, process, decision, and connector.

4. Each symbol on a program flowchart contains a brief description of the function or actions to be performed. The annotation symbol should be used when additional comments are needed for clarification.

5. A program or subprogram that is not defined on a program flowchart can be represented by the predefined process symbol.

6. The preparation symbol is used to indicate processing steps that change the program.

7. The flow in a flowchart should be from top to bottom and from left to right. Where flowlines are numerous, connectors should be used for clarity.

8. Program testing is represented by the decision symbol. It allows for alternate paths of flow. A change in direction of flow based on a decision is called a conditional branch. When program testing is not involved in a branch, the branch is unconditional.

9. Program loops are often based on conditional branching. One type of program loop uses a counter to control the number of times the loop is executed. The counter is initialized, then tested for a limit and modified within the loop. The processing steps in the loop are repeated until the limit of the counter is reached.

10. Several flowcharting aids are available to the programmer. These include the flowchart template, flowchart worksheets, and computer programs for flowchart preparation.

The Programming Cycle

When a programming project has been agreed upon, a number of rather well-defined steps should be taken to create a useful and efficient program. Among the steps that should be taken are: (1) recognizing and defining the problem, (2) planning the solution to the problem, (3) selecting an appropriate language, (4) coding the program, (5) debugging and testing the program, and (6) program documentation and maintenance. The flow of these steps is shown in Illustration 12-1. In most cases, the required tasks are the responsibilities of several individuals, such as the manager, the systems analyst, and the programmer. Each performs a different function. In some instances, however, the majority of the tasks fall to a programmer or a team of programmers. In an educational environment, a student may perform all of them.

RECOGNIZING AND DEFINING THE PROBLEM

Before a problem can be defined, there must be a realization that the problem exists. Often, the problem stems from the desires of management personnel to obtain more information with which to make better decisions. For example, the production supervisor may request information related to the efficiency of the present configuration of machinery. In another case, the corporation president may ask for a breakdown of the financial standing of the firm. In each of these situations, the existence of a problem is realized; if a decision is made to use the computer to solve the problem, the programming cycle is initiated.

The definition of the problem, sometimes called *system analysis and design* (see Chapter 3), comprises a number of interrelated tasks. The first task is to lay out a clear and concise statement of the problem. Second, if required data is not readily available, a method for acquiring the data must be devised. Third, the basic formats of input and output should be established, as should the structure of related files. Fourth, if necessary, the problem should be divided into component parts. Finally, the basic procedures for the project should be outlined.

The Problem Statement

Developing an accurate statement of the problem is probably the most important step in problem definition and in the development of a program. In an educational setting, most of the problems encountered by students are well-defined. In a business environment, this is not usually the case. If the problem is loosely or improperly defined, the resulting program may not solve the problem at all; it may serve only as a waste of time and money. However, if good judgment is exercised, and a clear definition established, a solution to the problem can usually be obtained.

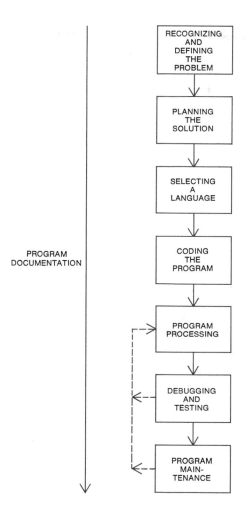

Illustration 12-1. Programming cycle.

In addition to the problem statement, the objectives and goals of the program that is to satisfy the problem requirements should be set forth in a clear and concise manner. In this way, misinterpretation is minimized. After the programmer or analyst (depending on the structure of the firm) has developed a complete statement of the problem, he or she should consult with the individual or group who is to use the information, or results. If the definition satisfies the problem requirements, the next phase of program development can begin.

Acquiring Data

The next stage in the analysis of a problem is the acquisition of data. This phase depends entirely upon the problem to be solved. If the objective is market research, for example, the source of the data is external to the firm. The important point is that some plan for collecting, recording, editing, organizing, and processing the data must be established. Caution must be exercised in collecting the data so that the resulting *data bank* accurately depicts the actual situation. If the data that is accumulated is irrelevant to the problem, no program—not even an accurate, precise one—can arrive at a correct answer. In such a situation, a simple truth applies: *GIGO* (*garbage-in/garbage-out*).

Establishing Formats

The next stage in the development of the program is to design functional input, output, and file formats. The input form should be designed for ease

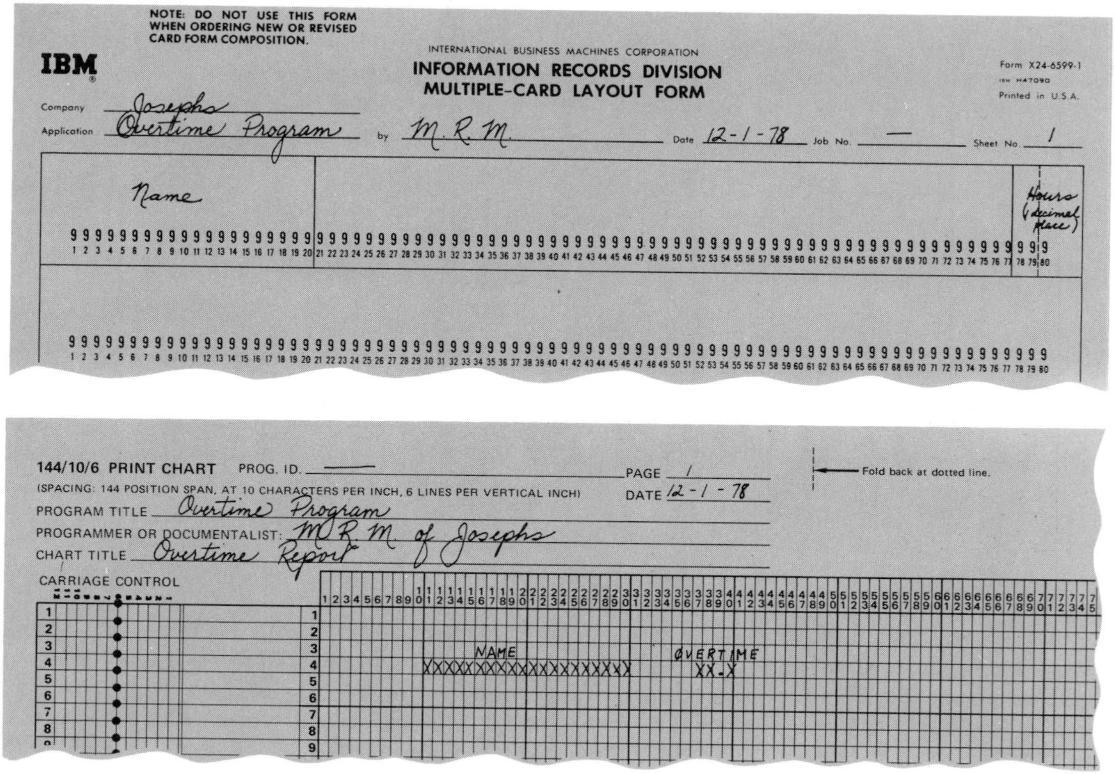

Illustration 12-2. Multiple-Card Layout Form and Print Chart

of recording as well as ease of processing. The output should be designed to accurately depict the results in a way that enhances the information and promotes understanding.

Illustration 12-2 shows two documents used by programmers in designing input and output formats. The first document is a *Multiple-Card Layout Form*. It gives the formats of the input cards for a program. In this example, the format for the one type of card used as input to an Overtime Program is given on the form. Columns 1-20 of each card are the name field, and columns 78-80 are the hours field, accurate to one decimal place. If necessary, one Multiple-Card Layout Form can be used to give the formats for up to six types of cards.

The second document in Illustration 12-2 is the left-hand portion of a *Print Chart*. It shows 75 of the 144 print positions representable on a complete chart of this type. The Print Chart indicates the specific horizontal print positions to be used for information printed on a report. In this example, print positions 11-30 are used for the employee's name, and 37-40 are used for overtime hours. Print position 39 of 37-40 is reserved for a decimal point.

In designing the layout of files, a number of requirements must be dealt with. For example, if a file is to be maintained on magnetic tape, such items as the recording mode, the block size, the number of characters per record, the retention cycle, the number of items to be maintained, and the volume number of each reel should be stated. Illustration 12-3 shows a document called a *Record Format,* which is one kind of storage layout form; it gives the format of one type of record on a magnetic-tape file. When used properly, it provides information relevant to the organization and handling of the file.

The Structure of the Problem

The fourth phase of problem definition is to determine the component parts of the problem. Under some circumstances, a problem can be divided into segments, each of which is part of the final solution. The problem, and its solution, may be structured either *serially,* with the output of one segment serving as the input to the next, or *in parallel,* with segments designed to execute simultaneously. If a problem can be subdivided, the final results may be achieved more quickly, assuming that personnel are available to code the various segments. In some cases, a problem cannot be subdivided.

Establishing Procedures

The final phase of problem definition is the establishment of procedures. The procedures may pertain to several diverse items, each of which is

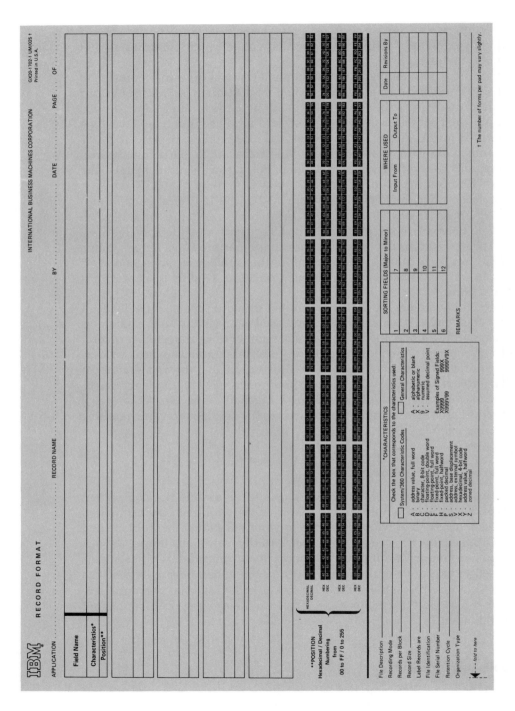

Illustration 12-3. Storage layout form.

important to the final results. For example, a special form may be devised to preserve accuracy of the data which is gathered. A staffing projection assigning the responsibility for each segment to a specific individual or team may be developed. Finally, a timetable for program (and project) completion may be established. Thus, the procedural phase considers the project organization. Its purpose is to determine how to make smooth, efficient progress toward stated objectives.

PLANNING THE SOLUTION TO THE PROBLEM

After the problem has been defined, the planning for its solution can begin. This step determines the layout of the program. It should coincide with the next step, which determines the language to be used in programming. The language should be selected at this point because it is one of the factors determining the ease or difficulty with which a solution can be worked out.

In the planning stage, the programmer finalizes the design of the input and output records. From this, the programmer determines the logical processes by which the program will accept and produce the records. Then, how the program will provide the desired final results is planned out.

The programmer employs many tools to describe the sequence of steps in the program. Probably the most commonly used aid is the *program flowchart*. The purpose of the program flowchart is to represent, by use of symbols, the processing that should take place in the program. It indicates the instructions that should be executed repeatedly by looping and the conditions under which the program should branch. By constructing a program flowchart and then studying it carefully, a programmer can analyze the logic of a program and determine whether a reasonable plan for the solution of the problem has been worked out.

A simplified flowchart for an Overtime Program is shown in Illustration 12-4. The basic symbols on this flowchart are the essence of flowcharting. The parallelogram ⟋⟋ represents an input or output operation. It normally appears where a read, write, or punch operation should occur. The rectangle ▭ stands for a processing operation. It may be either an arithmetic or a data-movement operation. The diamond ◇ represents a decision. The flowlines represent the direction-of-flow, which is generally from top to bottom and left to right on a flowchart. One symbol on a flowchart can represent one or more instructions of the program. (An extended discussion of program flowcharts is given in Module B.)

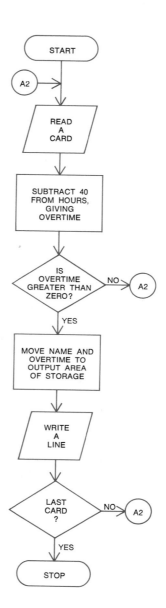

Illustration 12-4. Program flowchart for an overtime program.

This planning activity is the final step before the actual preparation of the program. If any alterations are to be made to the basic definition of the problem, they should be made at this point. Delaying such changes beyond this point creates major difficulties and seriously impedes the completion of the project.

SELECTING A PROGRAMMING LANGUAGE

Coinciding with the plan for the solution of the problem should be a survey to determine which language should be used in programming. A selection must be made in the planning stage because it often affects the solution to the problem. The program flowchart for a solution in one language may differ from that for another. The specific considerations in selecting a language are discussed in detail in Chapter 13.

PROGRAM CODING

After the solution to the problem has been planned and an appropriate language has been selected, the program can be coded. Program coding is the process of translating the planned solution to the problem, depicted in a program flowchart, into statements of the program. The program flowchart acts as a guide to the programmer as he or she describes the logical processes involved in the problem through the medium of a programming language.

The program is usually written on a *coding form*. Several forms are shown as examples in Illustration 12-5. These coding forms are designed to simplify the task of coding. The basic advantages of proper use of coding forms are:

1. They depict the basic structure and some of the characteristics of the language for which they are designed.
2. They tend to reduce clerical errors in coding.
3. They make the keypunching task easier.
4. They assist in the organization and identification of the program.

During the coding phase, the programmer may encounter an operation depicted on the program flowchart for which there is no practical implementation in the chosen language. If so, program development must regress to the planning stage so that an alternative solution can be proposed. After the program is coded, it is keypunched into cards (one card for each line of code on the coding form) and desk-checked (see below). Then it is submitted to the computer.

PROGRAM DEBUGGING AND TESTING

No program development task is complete until debugging and testing procedures have been carried out. The care exercised in this step (or the lack of it) may significantly affect the worth of the program.

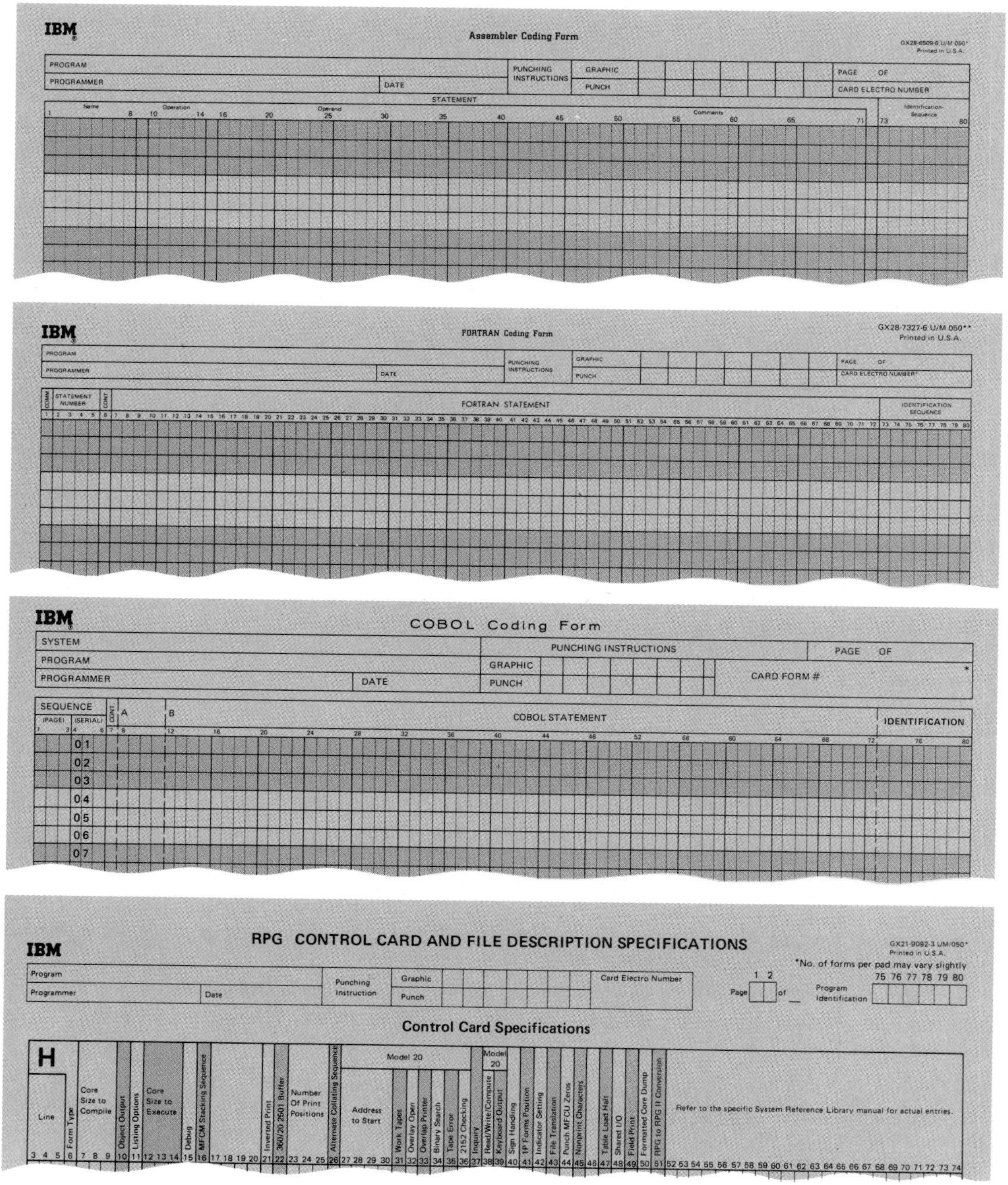

Illustration 12-5. Some commonly used coding forms.

Debugging

A program seldom executes successfully the first time. If the program contains any degree of complexity, it normally contains a few errors (bugs) as well. Debugging is the process of locating and correcting programming errors. These errors may be due to faulty logic in the design of the program. They may also be caused by mistakes in coding.

There are two basic levels of debugging. The first level, called *desk checking,* is performed after the program has been coded and keypunched. Its purpose is to locate and remove as many logical and clerical errors as possible. Then the program is read into the computer and processed by a *language translator.* The function of the language translator is to convert the program statements written by the programmer into the binary code of the computer. As a part of this translation step, the program statements are examined to verify that they have been coded correctly. If errors are detected, a series of *diagnostics* referred to as an *error message list* is generated by the language translator. With this list in hand, the programmer enters the second level of debugging.

The error message list helps the programmer to find the causes of errors and make the necessary corrections. At this point, the program may contain keypunching errors, as well as other clerical errors and logical errors that were not detected in the desk-checking process. The diagnostics provided by the language translator should enable the programmer to eliminate most, if not all, of the clerical errors and some of the logical errors.

After the corrections have been made, the program is again read into the computer. If the program still contains errors, the language translator again generates diagnostics. Corrections are made, and the program is resubmitted. This procedure continues until an *error-free run* (a run in which no diagnostics are generated) is achieved. The programmer should not assume that the program is truly error-free because logical errors and clerical errors of a nature that the language translator cannot detect may still exist. But, at this point, testing begins.

Testing

The purpose of testing is to determine whether a program consistently produces correct or expected results. A program is normally tested by executing it with a given set of input data, for which correct results are known. However, one run represents only one test of the porgram. The extent of testing may depend on the amount of time available for testing (the recipient of the information may be willing to forego complete testing because he desperately needs the results). In addition, there may be little money available for testing. In short, the amount of testing is usually determined by balancing the cost of testing against the penalties of acting on incorrect information.

In a typical test of a program, the test procedure is broken into three segments. First, the program is tested with inputs that one would normally expect for an execution of the program. If the results of this test run correspond to the expected results, the second test run is made. Valid but slightly abnormal data is injected to determine the capabilities of the program to cope with exceptions. For example, the minimum and maximum values allowable for a sales-amount field may be provided as input to verify that the program processes them correctly. In the third segment, invalid data is inserted to test the program's error-handling routines.

When a program is designed to replace an existing system or procedure (whether it is another program or a manual operation), *parallel runs* may be set up as a part of the test procedure. Each parallel run entails using both the old and the new systems and determining whether the systems yield identical results. Generally, several of these runs are made over a period of time. For example, if a company is preparing to shift from a manual accounting operation to a computer program designed to perform the same function, both systems may be used for six months to verify that the program is capable of replacing the manual operation.

Now, suppose that the results of test runs are not adequate. If the distortions are rather minor in nature, minor bugs may be the cause. The programmer may use any of three alternatives to locate minor errors. First, the programmer may *trace* the processing steps manually to find the errors. In effect, the programmer may pretend to be the computer, following the execution of each statement in the program and noting whether or not results are as expected. For example, if a statement multiplies hours worked by rate of pay, is the field reserved for the result defined correctly and large enough to hold any result that may be calculated?

As a second alternative, the programmer may use *tracing routines* if such routines are available for the language in which the program is coded. This approach has at least one advantage over the first one: It takes less time. Furthermore, the computer performs the tracing operation, and it is not susceptible to human error.

Finally, the programmer may use a *storage dump,* which is a printout of the contents of computer storage locations. By examining the contents of various storage locations, the programmer can determine the instruction at which the program halted. This is an important clue to finding the error that caused the halt to occur.

If major inadequacies are noted during test runs, a return to the planning stage may be necessary. A program may never be completely error-free because some routines may never be executed, some branches may never be taken, or the data provided as input may never cause a malfunction. To test all possibilities may be next to impossible. Even so, testing is a necessary and useful process. The debugging and testing step in the programming cycle may be as costly and time-consuming as both the planning and coding steps, but it is an essential one.

PROGRAM DOCUMENTATION AND MAINTENANCE

Documentation of the program should be developed at every step of the programming cycle. Documentation in the problem-definition step should include a clear statement of the problem and the objectives of the program (what the program is designed to accomplish). The source of the request for the program and the persons approving the request should be identified.

Documentation in the second step (planning the solution to the problem) should include flowcharts or other descriptions of the program logic, and descriptions of input, output, and file formats. The language selected and why it was selected should be pointed out. Documentation in this stage should also include a full and complete statement of the hardware requirements for the program.

Documentation in the program-coding step should include the number of personnel involved, their names, the segment of coding for which each is responsible, and the amount of time spent in coding the program.

The documentation of a program may include two additional components. First, a *user's manual* may be prepared to aid persons who are not familiar with the program in applying it correctly. This manual should contain a description of the program and what it is designed to accomplish, the details of the input records, and the essence of the output produced. A second component, an *operator's manual,* may be developed to assist the computer operator in successfully running the program. This manual contains (1) instructions about starting, running, and terminating the program, (2) messages that may be printed on the console printer-keyboard and their meanings (see Module A), and (3) setup and takedown instructions for files.

The documentation should be such that it provides all necessary information for anyone who comes in contact with the program. First, it may help supervisors in determining the program's purpose, how long the program will be useful, and future revisions that may be necessary. Second, it simplifies program maintenance (revising or updating the program). Third, it provides information as to the use of the program to those unfamiliar with it. Fourth, it provides operating instructions to the computer operator.

Although program maintenance is not a part of documentation, it is heavily dependent on it. The programmer is likely to use the documentation of a program whenever program maintenance is required. As an example, assume that a company uses a payroll program to calculate the wages of its workers. Further assume that the income tax rates, the basic wage rate, the premiums for life insurance, and the base for computing old age and survivors' insurance (OASI) are included as constants in the program. Program maintenance is required whenever any of the constants must be changed. If the program has been documented properly, the location of each of the constants is easy to determine. From this, it is a rather simple task to alter the program by replacing an old rate with a current one, thus updating the program. However, if the program is not documented properly, the programmer may spend hours searching through the program for one of the rates. The importance of documentation cannot be overemphasized because the long-range success or failure of the program may depend on it.

Summary

1. The programming cycle consists of a set of rather well-defined steps. Among them are: (1) recognizing and defining the problem, (2) planning the solution to the problem, (3) selecting an appropriate programming language, (4) coding the program, (5) debugging and testing the program, and (6) program documentation and maintenance.

2. Defining the problem, sometimes called system analysis and design, includes making a clear and concise statement of the problem; devising a scheme for acquiring the necessary data; establishing the basic formats for input, output, and related files; breaking the problem into component parts; and outlining the basic procedures for the project.

3. Planning the solution to the problem consists of identifying the basic logical processes required to solve the problem. One basic tool employed in this area is the program flowchart. It outlines what is to be done by the program.

4. Selection of an appropriate programming language is a crucial step; it must not be taken lightly. A language selection must be made in the planning stage because it often affects the solution to the problem.

5. Program coding is the process of translating the planned solution to the problem, which may be depicted in a program flowchart, into statements of the program. Often, programmers use coding forms to simplify the coding process.

6. Program debugging and testing are the means by which the program is checked for correctness. This may be done by executing the program with test data. If an existing system is being replaced, parallel runs may be made.

7. Program documentation is essential throughout the programming cycle. With proper care, it can contribute to the continuing success of the program.

8. Program maintenance is a continuing process whereby existing programs are revised or updated to meet current needs. Programmers usually refer to program documentation when performing program maintenance. Their work is much easier when proper documentation is provided.

CAREER PROFILE

Pamela Pitts
Analyst Programmer III

Federal Reserve Bank

Background Experience
I was a keypunch operator for several years before deciding that, in order to reach higher career levels in the computer field, I needed more education. I then enrolled at Golden Gate University and majored in accounting. While in school, I worked at night as a keypunch operator and technical assistant. I was later promoted to associate programmer and then programmer. My accounting background was useful not only because of the technical involvement, but also because of my general interest in business applications. I have worked at many firms in San Francisco, including a mining company, a software company, and the Federal Reserve Bank. My keypunch and computer operations experience give me a good background and understanding of the "inner workings" of the field.

Primary Job Responsibilities
I am principally responsible for maintaining the effectiveness of the existing systems and analyzing the requests for systems modifications that are submitted by users. As a programmer, I interface a great deal with users, both making sure they are satisfied with what they have, and trying to identify anything that can make their work more efficient. I also supervise and aid the junior programmers. I work with the other programmers on testing and development and try to increase their productivity. I develop detailed systems designs and specifications and also lead the installation and testing of projects. My group, the Branch Services section, is responsible for developing, maintaining, and enhancing the bank's systems.

What Has Made You Successful?
I have developed confidence in myself because of my varied work experience in computer operations. Also I have taken advantage of the excellent in-house training at the Federal Reserve. Here, education isn't an option, it's a requirement. In addition to video, audio, and in-house courses, the Federal Reserve pays tuition for related courses at other institutions such as Golden Gate. In addition, I read a great deal in my spare time. Before starting my job, I read extensively about the Federal Reserve Bank so that I would have the necessary information to interact with users. I think the important thing is not to be afraid to do a little extra work to gain experience. Experience is the key to success.

Top-Down Program Design and Structured Programming

TOP-DOWN PROGRAM DESIGN

DOCUMENTATION AND DESIGN AIDS
HIPO Diagrams
Pseudocode

STRUCTURED PROGRAMMING
Sequence Structure
Selection Structure
Loop Structure

DISCUSSION

In recent years, data processing personnel have been searching for ways to improve program design techniques to reduce the costs of program development and maintenance. With the use of traditional methods of program design, programming costs have continued to rise in relation to computer hardware and software costs. Many programmers consider programs to be personal creations. Programmers with this viewpoint often write programs that are complex and obscure. Such programs are hard for other programmers to understand. Even the original programmers may find their own programs difficult to understand months later. Such programs are also difficult to maintain, especially if they become the responsibility of another group of programmers. One new approach to program design and coding that is receiving widespread attention is called *top-down program design*. It can provide the following benefits:

1. Program standardization is improved because design is emphasized.
2. Programmers are more productive; they write more program instructions per day and make fewer errors.
3. Program complexity is reduced; as a result, programs are easier to read, write, debug, and maintain.

TOP-DOWN PROGRAM DESIGN

When top-down program design is used, a program is divided into segments called *modules*. Each of these modules is independent of other modules in the program and performs a separate function. Emphasis is placed on the main functional modules first because they contain the highest-level control logic and are the most critical to the success of the program. These modules are designed, coded, and tested. Then the next-lower-level modules are created in the same manner. In this way, most of the details of the solution plan are left until the lowest-level modules are designed. Thus, a program developed by using a top-down design consists of a series of modules created and related in a treelike (hierarchical) structure.

The treelike structural relationship between modules in a top-down-designed program can be shown in a *structure chart*. The structure chart shows each module and its functional relationship to other modules. The flow of control is from the highest-level module to the lowest-level modules (top-down). Each module is called, or invoked, by a next-higher-level module.

Illustration C-1 shows a structure chart with one level of processing modules. This structure chart is based on the update, order-writing, and invoicing portion of the system flowchart for the tape system shown in Illustration 9-10. The main module controls the execution of each processing module directly below it in the hierarchy. Thus, after the execu-

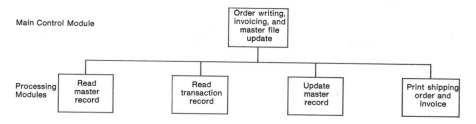

Illustration C-1. Structure chart for update, order-writing, and invoicing program.

tion of each processing module ("Read master record" through "Print shipping order and invoice"), control returns to the main module before the next module is executed.

There can be as many levels of processing modules as needed in a program. Two more levels of processing modules have been added to the update, order-writing, and invoicing program in Illustration C-2. Notice that the "Update master record" module is now both a processing module and a control module; it causes the execution of the "Write new master record" module. The "Write new master record" module is also a processing and control module; it controls two processing modules directly

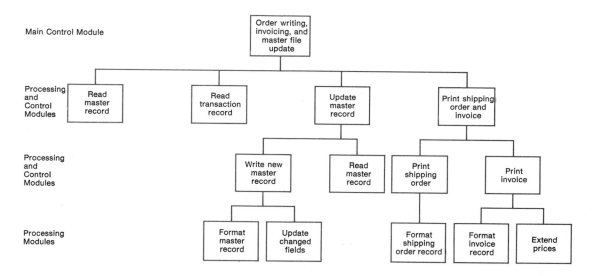

Illustration C-2. Structure chart for update, order-writing, and invoicing program with three levels of processing modules.

below it. As this example suggests, a structure chart can be an effective alternative to a system flowchart when top-down program design is used.

Some basic guidelines should be followed when using top-down design to develop program modules. Each module should have only one entrance and one exit point so that the flow of control is easy to follow. The segmentation of a program should be done so that the program modules relate to each other in a treelike manner with control passing from the top down. Each module should represent a single program function. For example, each module in Illustration C-1 does a single stated function (read master record, read transaction record, and so forth). Each module should not exceed one page of program code, that is, about 50 lines. When a module is contained on one page, program readability is enhanced because it is not necessary to look through several pages of code to understand the function of the module. Many programmers have found that modules limited to a single page each are easier to test and debug than programs coded in the traditional manner.

The higher-level modules of a program are coded and tested first. These are followed by the next-lower-level modules. When a module is tested, it calls (attempts to execute) the modules that it controls (the modules directly below it in the hierarchy). Since these lower modules are not yet coded, *dummy modules* must be created for testing purposes. Each dummy module takes the place of an actual module and passes control back to the higher-level module that calls it so that testing of that module's function can be completed.

By coding and testing a program in this manner, each level of modules is debugged and tested before the next lower level. As each lower-level is debugged and tested, the higher-level modules are tested again. This insures that the most critical, main modules are tested the most. For instance, in developing the program in Illustration C-2, the "Update master record" module would be coded and tested before the "Write new master record" module and the two modules below it. The "Update master record" module would be tested again as each lower-level module was tested.

By coding and testing each module separately and from the top down, the programmer can more readily isolate errors to specific modules. The task of finding errors is also simplified because the programmer need only look at the one page of code for each suspect module. The result is that the program is fully tested when the lowest-level modules are completed. Using traditional methods of program design, the programmer often must work with an entire program, possibly thousands of lines of code, to isolate, locate, and correct errors.

DOCUMENTATION AND DESIGN AIDS

During the initial design phase of a program development project, each major module is identified and then further subdivided into lower-level modules. It has already been shown that a structure chart can be used to identify and show relationships between program modules. After the structure chart has been completed, and possibly redrawn several times, the detailed program design must be completed. This requires that each module shown in the structure chart be designed in enough detail to allow it to be coded in a programming language. A program flowchart could be used for this purpose. Several other design aids are also available. The detail of a specific program module can be expressed using HIPO (Hierarchy plus Input-Process-Output) diagrams and pseudocode.

HIPO Diagrams

A HIPO diagram can be used as both a program design aid and the documentation for a completed program. A complete HIPO package includes diagrams that graphically describe each program module, from the general to the detail level. The number of levels of HIPO diagrams that must be prepared for an application depends on its complexity. When HIPO is used together with a structure chart, the structure chart is called a *visual table of contents*. An *overview diagram* like the one in Illustration C-3 is prepared for each module shown in the visual table of contents. The diagram shows the inputs, outputs, and processing for a module. If the module passes control to a lower-level module during its processing, so that it can perform a certain processing step (function), that step is boxed in the

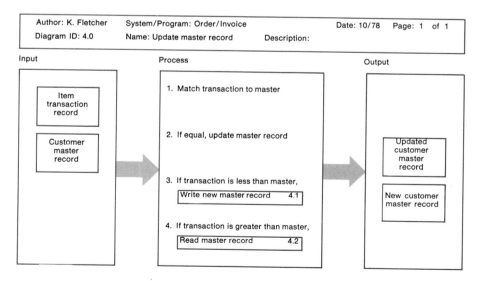

Illustration C-3. HIPO diagram for "Update master record" module.

"Process" portion of the diagram. (See steps 3 and 4 in Illustration C-3. Note that the referenced modules are identified as lower-level modules to this module in Illustration C-2.) *Detail diagrams* are prepared as necessary to further describe the modules shown in the visual table of contents. The complete HIPO package is the basis for coding the program and is also the final documentation of the program.

Thus, HIPO documentation can serve the manager who needs an overview of a program, other designers and programmers who are responsible for related programs, and programmers who must locate specific functions in the program so they can be changed.

Pseudocode

Pseudocode is a program design aid that serves the function of a program flowchart in expressing the detailed logic of a program. It has been recognized for some time that a program flowchart is often an inadequate tool for expressing the control flow and logic of a program. By using pseudocode, programmers can express their thoughts as English-language statements. These statements can be used both as a guide when coding the program in a specific programming language and as documentation for review by others. Because there are no rigid rules for using pseudocode, the programmer can express the logic of the program in a natural manner; there is no need to conform to the rules of a particular programming language at this stage. A series of "structured words" is used to express the major program functions. These structured words are the basis for writing programs using a technique called structured programming.

STRUCTURED PROGRAMMING

An approach to programming that is being discussed widely is called *structured programming*. This approach (1) facilitates program development, (2) improves program clarity—the ease with which a person unfamiliar with the program, including possibly the original programmer, can read the code and determine what is occurring, and (3) simplifies program debugging.

A structured program is written using only three basic control structures: sequence, selection, and loop. Each of these structures has a single entry point and a single exit. The program listing is easy to read because there is no random branching (forward or backward) from one part of the program to another part. Since control flows from top to bottom, the listing can be read more or less like a book. The program logic is easy to follow.

Sequence Structure

The *sequence structure* is simply recognition of the fact that program statements are generally executed in the order in which they are stored in the computer. Thus in Illustration C-4, the statements in function A will be executed before the statements in function B.

As indicated in the flowchart, control simply flows from function A to function B. This is good programming practice. Branching to another function should be avoided. One of the objectives of structured programming is to eliminate branches out of a sequence structure. When there are branches, it is often difficult for the programmer to follow the program logic. Therefore, program debugging and maintenance are harder.

Selection Structure

The *selection structure* allows a choice between two program paths based on a true or false condition, as shown in Illustration C-5. If the test is true, function A is done; if false, function B is done. The selection structure is also called the IF-THEN-ELSE pattern. It can be expressed directly in many programming languages.

Loop Structure

The *loop structure* provides for performing a function *while* a condition is true.

The basic form of this structure is called the DO-WHILE or WHILE-DO pattern. It is shown in Illustration C-6. The flow of control in the DO-WHILE loop can be described as "*do* function A *while* condition B is true."

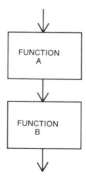

Illustration C-4. Sequence structure.

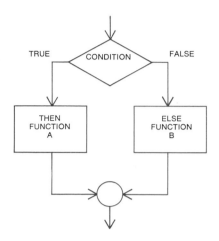

Illustration C-5. Selection structure (IF-THEN-ELSE).

In this type of structure, function A may never be executed because condition B may be false when it is first tested.

A variation of the loop structure is the DO-UNTIL pattern. In this pattern, the processing steps in the loop are executed at least once (see Illustration C-7). The pattern here is "*do* function A *until* condition B is true."

Structured programming can be used with programming languages available today. It is easier to implement the basic patterns of structured programming in some languages than in others. These languages include statements that represent directly some or all of the patterns. In the other languages, a number of statements may be required to represent each pattern.

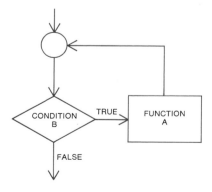

Illustration C-6. Loop structure (DO-WHILE).

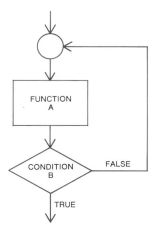

Illustration C-7. Variation of the loop structure (DO-UNTIL).

Illustration C-8 is an example of a program expressed in pseudocode form. The structured-programming control structures to be used in the program are represented by the keywords that are capitalized. The functional details are written in lower case. A portion of the Procedure division of a structured COBOL program coded from this pseudocode is shown in Illustration C-9.

```
Open files
Read first record (heading)
Initialize program variables
DO WHILE more text records
   Read text record
   DO WHILE more words in text record
      Extract next text word
      Search word table for extracted word
      IF extracted word found THEN
         increment word's occurrence count
      ELSE insert extracted word in word table
      ENDIF
      Increment words-processed count
   ENDDO (end of text record)
ENDDO (all text records processed)
Print word table and summary information
Close files
Terminate program
```

Illustration C-8. Pseudocode for word-frequency analysis program.

```
            PROCEDURE DIVISION.
            WORD-FREQUENCY-MAIN-ROUTINE.
                PERFORM INITIALIZATION.
                PERFORM TEXT-PROCESSING
                    UNTIL LAST-RECORD-PROCESSED.
                PERFORM PRINT-TABLE.
                PERFORM TERMINATION.
                STOP RUN.
        *
            INITIALIZATION.
                OPEN  INPUT  INPUT-FILE
                    OUTPUT PRINT-FILE.
                READ INPUT-FILE INTO HEADING-LINE-TEXT.
                MOVE 0 TO WORDS-PROCESSED.
                MOVE 0 TO UNIQUE-WORDS.
                PERFORM INITIALIZE-WORD-TABLE.
        *
            TEXT-PROCESSING.
                READ INPUT-FILE AT END
                    MOVE 1 TO LAST-RECORD-PROCESSED.
                PERFORM EXTRACT-NEXT-WORD
                    UNTIL LAST-WORD-PROCESSED.
        *
            PRINT-TABLE.
                MOVE WORDS-PROCESSED TO HI-WORDS-PROCESSED.
                MOVE UNIQUE-WORDS TO HI-NUMBER-OF-WORDS.
                MOVE 99 TO PRINT-LINE-COUNTER.
                PERFORM TABLE-PRINT-LOOP
                    VARYING TABLE-INDEX FROM 1 BY 1
                        UNTIL TABLE-INDEX = NUMBER-OF-ENTRIES.
        *
            TERMINATION.
                CLOSE  INPUT-FILE
                    PRINT-FILE.
        *
        INITIALIZE-WORD-TABLE.
            •
            •
            •
        EXTRACT-NEXT-WORD.
            •
            •
            •
            PERFORM TABLE-SEARCH
                UNTIL HIT-OR-EOT.
            •
            •
        TABLE-PRINT-LOOP.
            •
            •
            •
        TABLE-SEARCH.
            •
            •
            •
```

Illustration C-9. COBOL Procedure Division coding of the higher-level modules of the word-frequency analysis program.

DISCUSSION

Structured programming has come to mean more than the use of the control structures just discussed. Most programmers find that to use structured programming effectively, they must design their programs using a top-down approach. A goal of top-down program design is to create independent program modules. Each module is to have one entry point and one exit point. This goal can be achieved using structured programming. Thus, these techniques are often used together. Top-down program design, top-down coding, top-down testing, the use of pseudocode for documentation, and structured coding are a set of techniques that programmers generally refer to as structured programming. The goal of all of these techniques is to make programs easier to write, read, debug, and maintain, thus making programmers more productive. The techniques are now being used with positive results by a number of data processing installations.

Summary

1. Traditional methods of program design and coding rely primarily on the creativeness of the programmer. They have often resulted in programs that are complex and difficult to read. New program design and coding techniques have been developed in an effort to reduce program development and maintenance costs. Among these techniques are top-down program design and structured programming.

2. The focus of top-down program design is to divide a program into functional modules. The programmer designs the main module first and then designs lower-level modules. The programmer uses structure charts to show the program modules and their relationships. The purpose of a structure chart is to provide a clear view of the flow of logic in a program and the connection and purpose of each program module.

3. When using a top-down approach, the programmer codes the higher-level modules first and tests them. Then lower-level modules are coded and tested. Program debugging is easier because errors can be isolated to specific modules.

4. New documentation methods and design aids to be used with top-down program design have been developed. One way to describe the input, processing steps, and output of a module is to create a set of HIPO diagrams.

5. A program can be developed using pseudocode as a guide. The program is first written in pseudocode. In this step, the programmer represents the structured logic of a program but avoids the details of a specific programming language. The pseudocode then performs the function of a program flowchart when the program is written in a programming language (the actual code).

6. Structured programming is a set of techniques using control structures for program coding. The control structures simplify program coding and establish coding standards that make programs easier to read. The three basic control structures are sequence, selection, and loop.

CHAPTER 13

An Overview of Programming Languages

MACHINE LANGUAGE

MACHINE-ORIENTED ASSEMBLER
(SYMBOLIC) LANGUAGE

MACRO-INSTRUCTIONS

HIGH-LEVEL PROGRAMMING LANGUAGES
Procedure-Oriented and
Problem-Oriented Languages
FORTRAN
COBOL
BASIC
RPG

LANGUAGE SELECTION

Now that the reader has a basic understanding of the components of a computer system and of the programming tasks required to direct it, the types of computer languages and their characteristics should be discussed. If computer languages did not exist, a computer would be nothing more than a relatively expensive piece of machinery. The computer hardware must be applied in conjunction with computer software before the major benefits of this tool can be realized.

As noted in Chapter 6, the development of computers can be divided into generations that roughly correspond to specific developments of computer hardware. The same division can be applied to the development of specific types of computer languages. The first generation of computer languages is represented by *machine languages,* which are closely tied to the design of the computer. In the second generation, *machine-oriented assembler (symbolic) languages* were developed and *macro-instructions* came into use. The third generation is marked by the creation of several *high-level programming languages.* These languages can be divided into (1) *procedure-oriented languages* such as FORmula TRANslator (FORTRAN), COmmon Business Oriented Language (COBOL), and Beginners' All-purpose Symbolic Instruction Code (BASIC); and (2) *problem-oriented languages* such as Report Program Generator (RPG).

MACHINE LANGUAGE

Machine languages were first developed during the infant stage of computer development. They are closely tied to specific machines (that is, types of computers). Thus, the term *machine language* denotes the principle characteristic of these languages. A machine language consists of instructions that vary with the requirements and the design of the machine being used.

A machine-language instruction includes an *operation code (op code)* and an *operand* (usually, the address(es) of data on which an operation is to be performed). Since the computer stores every instruction in binary form, in absolute terms, a machine-language instruction consists of a string of zeros and ones (although an octal, hexadecimal, or binary coded decimal equivalent may be used in coding). The programmer must write an instruction to control each operation to be performed. Therefore, a *one-to-one relationship* exists between the instructions coded by the programmer and the performance of operations by the computer. The complete list of instructions is known as an *object program.*

The relationship between machine-language instructions (the object program) and the computer is shown in Illustration 13-1. An object program can be executed by a computer without first being translated to make

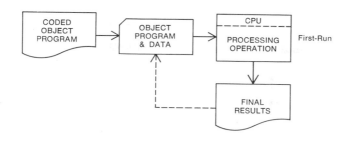

Illustration 13-1. Processing cycle for a machine-language program.

it machine-understandable. The instructions are keypunched and loaded into main storage to control subsequent processing steps. No translating process is necessary because the object program can be acted upon by the computer.

There are, however, a number of obvious disadvantages in the use of machine language. First, the programming aspects of a machine-language program are extremely tedious. As a programmer writes the program, the addresses of storage locations containing data to be operated on, as well as the addresses of instructions in the program, must be recorded. Such clerical details, in addition to the design of the program itself, keep the programmer occupied.

Second, besides keeping track of addresses, the programmer has to remember numeric op codes. The programmer has to write the numeric op code for each operation that the computer must perform.

Third, if an error is discovered in the results produced by the program, the programmer has to tediously examine each instruction in order to find the point where the error occurred. If a correction entails more than removal of keypunching errors, any addition to, or deletion from, the program may mean that all instructions from the location of the error to the end of the program have to be changed. Since machine-language instructions are normally executed sequentially, from first to last, without interruption, the address of each instruction from the point of the insertion or deletion must be altered to reflect the modification. Any references to these instructions throughout the program must be changed.

Fourth, the programmer is not able to use any parts of previously written programs when coding a new program. Each program is written totally independent of any other program with which the programmer is familiar. If this were not the case, considerable time could be saved in coding.

Finally, the programmer must have a detailed knowledge of the computer on which the program is to be executed. If the type of computer is changed, the programmer must become familiar with the new machine, and any existing programs must be rewritten for the new machine.

All of these disadvantages can probably be summed up by saying that the design and development of a machine-language program is very time-consuming and, consequently, extremely expensive. The use of machine language for today's applications is impractical.

There are two basic advantages in using machine language. First, it is an extremely efficient method of using the storage capacity of a computer. Second, the speed of processing is aided by the fact that no conversion (from another computer language to machine language) is necessary. However, the disadvantages of machine language so outweigh its advantages that the coding of programs in machine language is practically non-existent today.

MACHINE-ORIENTED ASSEMBLER (SYMBOLIC) LANGUAGE

Because machine-language programming was tedious, time-consuming, and costly, efforts were made to alleviate the coding problem. In the early 1950s, the problem was partially solved by the introduction of a machine-oriented assembler (symbolic) language. The use of assembler language was possible because of a software aid called an *assembler program,* or *assembler.* The assembler program performed the task of recording (remembering and using) the address of each unit in the program, thus relieving the programmer of many clerical tasks previously required. In addition, the assembler allowed the use of symbolic names, or *mnemonics* (abbreviations of Englishlike words and acronyms), instead of numerical designations, for machine operations.

An assembler-language instruction is broken into three distinct segments. As shown in Illustration 13-2, the first segment is the *label,* or tag. It represents the first storage location of the instruction to which it is attached. The label serves two purposes: (1) as an aid to the programmer in locating specific instructions in the program coding, and (2) as a point of reference when branching within the program is required.

The second segment of an assembler-language instruction is the op code (operation code). While labels can be mnemonics, the major advantage of the use of mnemonics is in the area of op codes. A set of mnemonics to be used as op codes is explicitly defined within the assembler language. These symbolic names replace their numerical counterparts in machine language. READ, ADD, and COMP (rather than strings of digits) may represent the input of data, the addition of data, and the comparison of two data fields, respectively. The programmer soon becomes familiar with the mnemonic op codes, and the burden of memorizing and writing numerical representations of operations is removed.

A COMPLETE INSTRUCTION		
LABEL	OP CODE	OPERAND

Illustration 13-2. Parts of an assembler-language instruction.

The third part of an assembler-language instruction is the operand. It contains the addresses that are relevant to the op code of the instruction. In machine language, the addresses are given in binary form, but in assembler language, the addresses are stated in decimal or mnemonic form. Since the programmer does not have to write actual (also called absolute) addresses, this task is much easier. The programmer specifies (or reserves) the first storage location used for the program. The assembler assigns other addresses sequentially from the given point of reference.

The one-to-one relationship between an instruction and an operation exists in assembler language as in machine language. However, the one-to-one relationship takes on an additional meaning in assembler language: There is only one line of coding for each instruction. A single machine-language instruction may require many lines of coding.

One additional technique is used to provide the program with data and constants. It is called a *declarative operation,* or simply a *declarative.* It is similar to the assembler-language instruction described above (sometimes called an *imperative*) in that it contains a label and operands. But it differs from an imperative instruction in that it contains a declarative op code. The op code signals the computer that data is to be placed in storage at the address stated in the operand. No action is performed on the data until it is referred to by an imperative instruction in another part of the program.

All of the instructions of an assembler-language program, organized into one unit, are called a *source program.* A source program differs from the object program derived from machine-language instructions in that it must be translated into machine language before it can be executed by the computer. As Illustration 13-3 shows, the source program enters the central processing unit (CPU) and is translated into its object-program counterpart under the supervision of an assembler program.

The conversion from assembler language to machine language takes place in two parts. First, the mnemonic op codes used in the source program are replaced by machine-language equivalents. The assembler performs this step by referring to a table composed of all available mnemonic op codes and the corresponding machine-language operations. Second, the addresses used in the source program, which are stated as decimal digits or mnemonics, are transformed into equivalent actual addresses.

In addition to the object program, the assembler provides an error message list (recall "Program Debugging and Testing" in Chapter 12). It can detect errors due to violations of *syntax* (the grammatical correctness of instruction structure), instructions that are out of sequence, references to nonexistent parts of the program, and illegal mnemonic op codes. In some cases, the assembler is designed to overlook minor errors such as one wrong letter in a mnemonic op code. The assembler either corrects or accepts these minor errors. It continues to scan the source program and detects possible errors, but it may not generate an object program. Under most conditions, the errors are of such a nature that the object program, if generated, would be worthless to the programmer. The error message list provides a means by which the programmer is alerted to errors. The programmer can correct the errors and resubmit the source program.

When the source program satisfies all checks made by the assembler during translation, the object program is generated. It can be used in the second stage of attaining final results. This time the object program is executed; that is, problem-related data is provided as input, and processing takes place. The computer enacts the machine-language operations and generates the final results, or output.

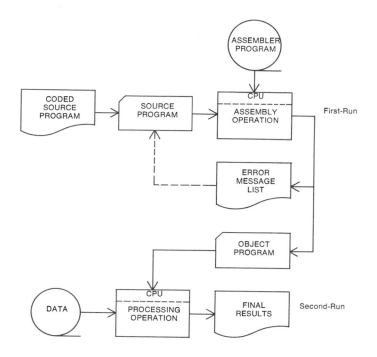

Illustration 13-3. Assembly of an assembler-language program.

There are a number of advantages to using machine-oriented assembler language rather than machine language. First, the programmer can employ easy-to-remember symbolic names, or mnemonics, in place of machine-language operation codes. In addition, the use of labels, or tags, makes the task of referring to instructions (say, for branching) easier. Second, the assembly operation provides an error message list that can be used in making corrections to the source program. Finally, since the computer adjusts addresses automatically when the source program is translated (assembled), the program can be modified without having to rewrite many instructions as is often the case with a machine-language program.

Although assembler language saves vast amounts of programmer time and effort previously required for clerical tasks, it shares one major disadvantage with machine language. The programmer is still not able to use parts of previously written programs in a new program. Each instruction has to be written individually.

MACRO-INSTRUCTIONS

To eliminate the necessity to write one line of coding for each operation, macro-instructions were introduced. Programmers noticed that many series of instructions appeared repeatedly in different programming projects. These instructions were always in the same sequence and were designed to accomplish the same objective in each use. As a result, a specific sequence of assembler-language instructions, or *routine,* was established for each objective and placed in a library of *macros* (macro operation codes). Then when a specific routine was required in a program, the programmer inserted a certain macro-instruction to cause the routine in the library to be referred to. The macro-instruction generated a number of assembler-language instructions. This broke the one-to-one relationship between the programmer's lines of coding and computer operations that existed previously.

A basic advantage of macro-instructions is that the use of a macro reduces the duplication of instructions and, therefore, the amount of coding required on the part of the programmer. A second advantage, derived from the reduction in coding, is that there is less chance of error.

Of course, there may be some highly repetitive routines for which no macro-instructions exist, but the programmer is not at a complete loss in this situation. The programmer can write new macros and insert them into the library of macro operation codes. The macro-instructions defined in this manner can be used just like others, whenever they are required.

HIGH-LEVEL PROGRAMMING LANGUAGES

Assembler language represents the second stage in the development of programming languages. It is closely related to machine language and is thought of as a *low-level programming language*. After assembler language and macro-instructions, a number of languages were developed. Developers of these languages took the idea of macro-instructions one step further; they created complete macro-instruction languages. Every statement (instruction) in these languages generates one or more routines to perform needed operations. As a group, the languages are known as *high-level programming languages* because they are not closely related to machine instructions. In fact, a programmer does not have to have a detailed knowledge of a computer in order to write programs in a high-level language.

Recall that an assembler-language program (also called a source program) is translated into machine language (an object program) by an assembler (see Illustration 13-3). The procedure of translating a source pro-

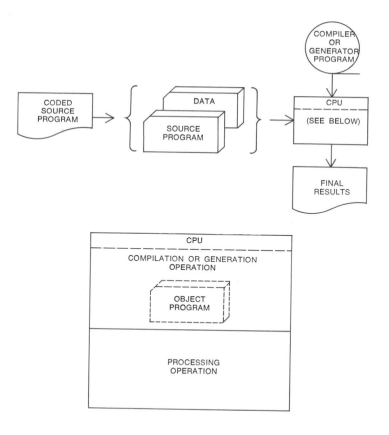

Illustration 13-4. Compilation or generation of
a high-level-language program.

gram of a high-level language into machine language (an object program) is very similar. It is shown in Illustration 13-4. The assembler is replaced by a *compiler* or *generator,* depending on the high-level language used. A compiler examines a program statement written by the programmer and converts it into one or more machine-language instructions. When using a generator language, the programmer does not write program statements; rather, the programmer describes what is needed in more general terms, through specifications. The generator creates the instructions needed to provide the desired results.

Since a specific compiler or generator is developed for each high-level programming language, the language may also be called either a compiler language or a generator language. Like an assembler, both compilers and generators are software aids. They are usually written by computer manufacturers and made available with computers.

The processing steps of high-level languages differ from those of assembler language. The basic difference is that the data for a high-level-language program is often submitted with the source program, whereas it is maintained separately for an assembler-language program. The translation process also differs. While it is possible to compile or generate the source deck (data and source program, punched into cards) and produce an object deck (object program, punched into cards), the object program is usually stored within the CPU for subsequent use rather than punched into cards. Thus, with one submission of the program, assuming that all serious errors have been eliminated, the final results of program execution can be obtained.

Procedure-Oriented and Problem-Oriented Languages

The separation of high-level languages into *procedure-oriented languages* (such as FORTRAN, COBOL, and BASIC) and *problem-oriented languages* (such as RPG) was noted at the beginning of this chapter. Basically, a procedure-oriented language consists of a system of computational procedures designed to solve a problem, whereas a problem-oriented language is descriptive in nature; it is used to describe problems. All high-level languages that require a compiler are procedure-oriented languages. As a group, however, high-level languages are sometimes referred to as problem-oriented (in contrast to machine-oriented). They are designed for ease of use in problem solving.

There are many basic advantages of high-level programming languages. First, as previously mentioned, these languages reduce the amount of coding. Second, they are easy to learn. Third, they are *machine-independent;* that is, programs written in any of these languages can be executed on a wide range of computers with little or no alteration. Fourth, the programs are easy to document since special provisions for documentation accompany each language. Finally, they are easy to update or maintain because revisions are possible without extensive rewriting of affected code.

High-level languages possess at least two disadvantages. First, high-level-language programs usually take longer to execute than comparative low-level-language programs. The translation process is extensive and generates many machine-language instructions. Second, some of the machine operations that a computer is capable of performing are not implemented in high-level languages. These languages have been designed around basic, commonly employed routines, and some operations have been deemed impractical to implement because of a general lack of need. But, these languages are constantly undergoing updates and changes, so this disadvantage may not be as critical in the future.

FORTRAN

In the mid 1950s, a group of men, headed by John Backus of IBM, was organized to create a computer language that would easily lend itself to arithmetic computation. By 1956, they had developed a language known as FORTRAN (an acronym for FORmula TRANslator). A FORTRAN compiler containing 25,000 lines of coding was ready to be tested. More than two years of effort and an estimated investment of over $2 million had been expended on the project.

In 1957, the first tests of the new compiler were conducted. By the end of that year, a number of minor errors had appeared. This prompted IBM to release a new version of the language, called FORTRAN II, in 1958. The same year, IBM also released a new FORTRAN compiler system as a complement to new hardware developments. Other computer manufacturers began to develop versions of FORTRAN to accompany their machines. Among these were FORTRAN IV, FORTRANSIT, and FORTO-COM. It became obvious that standardization was necessary to bring uniformity into programmer training and to aid in the interchange of programs. In 1962, the United States of America Standards Institute (USASI), now called the *American National Standards Institute (ANSI)*, took on the task of standardization. Out of this, in 1966, came two standard versions of FORTRAN. First, ANSI Basic FORTRAN, which is similar to FORTRAN II, was proposed. Second, ANSI FORTRAN, which is similar to FORTRAN IV, was introduced. The computer manufacturers followed this lead, and compilers capable of translating ANSI Basic FORTRAN and ANSI FORTRAN have been developed for most computers. Significant properties of both versions of the language, collectively referred to as FORTRAN, are discussed below.

The initial purpose of FORTRAN has not changed even though many versions of the language have been offered. The original definition of the language, *THE FORTRAN Automatic Coding System of the IBM 704 EDPM,* is as valid today as it was when stated in 1956:

> "The FORTRAN language is intended to be capable of expressing any problem of numerical computation. In particular, it deals easily with problems containing large sets of formulas and many variables, and it permits any variable to have up to three independent subscripts. However, for problems in which machine words have a logical rather than numerical meaning it is less than satisfactory, and it may fail entirely to express some such problems. Nevertheless, many logical operations not directly expressible in the FORTRAN language can be obtained by making use of provisions for incorporating library routines."

Thus, FORTRAN has evolved into a scientific-mathematical language, basically algebraic or algorithmic in nature. As such, the language is especially adaptable to research applications or analysis of problems in engineering, science, and business (for example, operations research or statistical analysis). However, there are some applications, especially in business, to which FORTRAN is not particularly well suited. In situations where large volumes of input and output must be dealt with, or extensive file maintenance is required, other languages should be considered.

The basic element in a FORTRAN program is the *statement* (which corresponds to an instruction in assembler language). The types of statements that can be included in a FORTRAN program are divided into four categories: (1) input, (2) assignment, (3) output, and (4) control. An *input statement* causes data recorded on an external medium, such as punched cards, magnetic tape, or magnetic disk, to be accepted by the computer. One basic type of input statement—the READ statement—is available in FORTRAN.

An *assignment statement* causes the computer to perform some computational or logical operation. Normally, a statement of this type consists of at least three parts: a receiving field, the symbol $=$, and an expression containing one or more operators and operands. Consider the arithmetic assignment statement $A = B + C$. Here A is the symbolic name which acts as a receiving field, B and C are symbolic names used as operands, and the symbol $+$ is an operator. Obviously, many different assignment statements can be created by varying the expression portion of the statement $(B + C)$. Other symbolic names, operators, or constants such as 1.0, 22., and the like, can be included. The receiving field can also be changed.

An *output statement* causes data that is stored internally to be recorded on some external medium, such as printer paper, punched cards, or magnetic tape. There are three basic types of output statements, the WRITE, PRINT, and PUNCH statements, which perform this type of operation.

Finally, FORTRAN *control statements* include the GO TO, IF, DO, and STOP statements. These statements cause the computer to branch from the normal sequence of operations, make comparisons of values, perform looping operations, and stop executing the program, respectively.

A FORTRAN program to process up to 100 employee pay records and print a listing of the results is shown in Illustration 13-5. The program contains at least one statement from each of the four basic types (input,

```
IBM                                        FORTRAN Coding Form                    GX28-7327-6 U/M 050**
                                                                                  Printed in U.S.A.
PROGRAM    EMPLOYEE WAGES                                                          PAGE 001 OF 002
PROGRAMMER V. THOMAS DOCK

C    THIS PROGRAM CALCULATES THE WEEKLY WAGES OF THE EMPLOYEES OF THE XYZ COMPANY
1    WRITE (6,1)
     FORMAT ('1', 'EMPLOYEE NAME', 3X, 'HOURS WORKED', 2X, 'HOURLY RATE
    1', 2X, 'GROSS WAGE', 2X, 'FEDERAL INCOME TAX', 2X, 'STATE INCOME
    2AX', 2X, 'SOCIAL SECURITY TAX', 1X, 'RETIREMENT', 1X, 'NET WAGE')
     DO 6 I = 1,100
     READ (5,2,END=7) NAME1,NAME2,NAME3,NAME4,HRSWRK,HRRATE
2    FORMAT (4A4,7ZO.F2.0,7Z5,F3.2)
     IF (HRSWRK .LT. 41) GO TO 3
     OHOURS = HRSWRK-40.
     OWAGE = (OHOURS*HRRATE*1.5)
     GRWAGE = HRRATE*40.+OWAGE
     GO TO 4
3    GRWAGE = HRSWRK*HRRATE
4    FIT = GRWAGE*.0627
     SIT = GRWAGE*.0175
     SST = GRWAGE*.0520
     RETIRE = GRWAGE*.06
     WAGNET = GRWAGE-(FIT+SIT+SST+RETIRE)
     IHRWRK = HRSWRK
     WRITE (6,5) NAME1,NAME2,NAME3,NAME4,IHRWRK,HRRATE,GRWAGE,FIT,SIT,
    1SST,RETIRE,WAGNET
5    FORMAT ('0', 4A4, 5X, I2, 10X, '$', F4.2, 7X, '$', F6.2, 10X, '$',
    1F5.2, 12X, '$', F4.2, 15X, '$', F5.2, 7X, '$', F5.2, 5X, '$', '$',
```

```
IBM                                        FORTRAN Coding Form                    GX28-7327-6 U/M 050**
                                                                                  Printed in U.S.A.
PROGRAM    EMPLOYEE WAGES                                                          PAGE 002 OF 002
PROGRAMMER V. THOMAS DOCK

    2F6.2)
6    CONTINUE
7    STOP
     END
```

Illustration 13-5. A FORTRAN program.

assignment, output, and control). The numerals 1 and 2 are placed in column 6, the continuation column, of continuation lines for statements that are longer than one coding line.

COBOL

Up to the late 1950s, no computer language particularly suited to business applications had been developed. Assembler language and various special languages valid only with specific computers were being used to solve business problems. In May of 1959, the Federal government of the United States, through the Department of Defense, decided to sponsor a committee to develop a language especially applicable to problems in a business environment. At first, this idea met with opposition. But the government stood firm in its determination to create such a language and pointed out to computer manufacturers that the government was the largest single purchaser of computing equipment.

Under the guidance of the government, a committee was formed in 1959 to study the needs of business and develop an appropriate computer language. Representatives of business and of universities served as committee members. By December of 1959, the original specifications for COBOL (an acronym for COmmon Business Oriented Language) were completed. They were printed by the Government Printing Office in 1960. The design committee became known as *CODASYL (COnference of DAta SYstems Languages)*. The first version of the language became known as COBOL-60.

To encourage full compliance with the project, in 1960, the Department of Defense announced that no lease or purchase contracts would be made for computers that did not possess the characteristics required for a COBOL compiler. Therefore, through some governmental pressure, computer manufacturers adopted a policy of designing their equipment so that COBOL compilers could be used.

Succeeding versions of COBOL were labeled by the year in which CODASYL made updates to the original specifications (1961, 1964, and 1965). Because of the many versions of COBOL available at different installations, the development of COBOL approached the same state as the development of FORTRAN. Therefore, ANSI again took on the challenge of setting up standards for a computer language. In 1968, ANSI (in conjunction with computer manufacturers and users) released American National Standard (ANS) COBOL. In 1974, the language definition was expanded; that is, a revised ANS COBOL standard was agreed upon.

COBOL offers several advantages. It is considered to be machine-independent. It employs much of the vocabulary of the business world and is written in Englishlike terms. Since it is Englishlike in nature, it tends to be self-documenting. No additional comments are necessary in a COBOL program. The program can be understood by programmers and by other business personnel as well. The language is relatively easy to learn. The COBOL compiler reduces the programming burden and provides diagnostics (error messages) that make program debugging easier. COBOL is well suited for the input and output operations commonly associated with business enterprises. Finally, the language can process alphabetic or alphameric information; this capability is extremely important because a significant portion of business data comprises other than numeric characters.

In keeping with the Englishlike nature of COBOL, the structure of the language is comparable to that of a book. The basic element of a COBOL program is the *sentence* (the COBOL counterpart to the statement in FORTRAN). The next level in the structural hierarchy of the language is the *paragraph*. It is followed by *sections* and *divisions,* in order as named.

There are four divisions in a COBOL program. They are, in order of their occurrence in a program: (1) the IDENTIFICATION DIVISION, (2) the ENVIRONMENT DIVISION, (3) the DATA DIVISION, and (4) the PROCEDURE DIVISION. The IDENTIFICATION DIVISION identifies a program by requiring that, at a minimum, it be assigned a name (see 001,02, page 1 line 2 in Illustration 13-6). Additional information such as the author of the program, the installation at which it was written, the date it was written, the date it was compiled, security requirements, and remarks concerning the program may be provided. The COBOL program in Illustration 13-6 reads input and writes output similar to that of the FORTRAN program in Illustration 13-5. The IDENTIFICATION DIVISION of the program contains valuable program documentation.

The ENVIRONMENT DIVISION has two primary functions. First, it describes the type of computer that will compile (001,12) and execute (001,13) the program. Second, it relates each file used in the program with the input device from which the file is to be read (001,18) or the output device on which the file is to be written (001,19). The DATA DIVISION describes in great detail all of the data to be processed by the program. It also shows the relationships that exist between data (002,03-11; 002,12-24 and 003,01-09; 003,12-23; and 004,01-23). The PROCEDURE DIVISION contains the statements that instruct the computer in detail as to the specific operations it is to perform and the order in which it is to perform them (005,02-21 and 006,01-21).

BASIC

The acronym BASIC is derived from the term *Beginners' All-purpose Symbolic Instruction Code.* BASIC is similar to FORTRAN in many

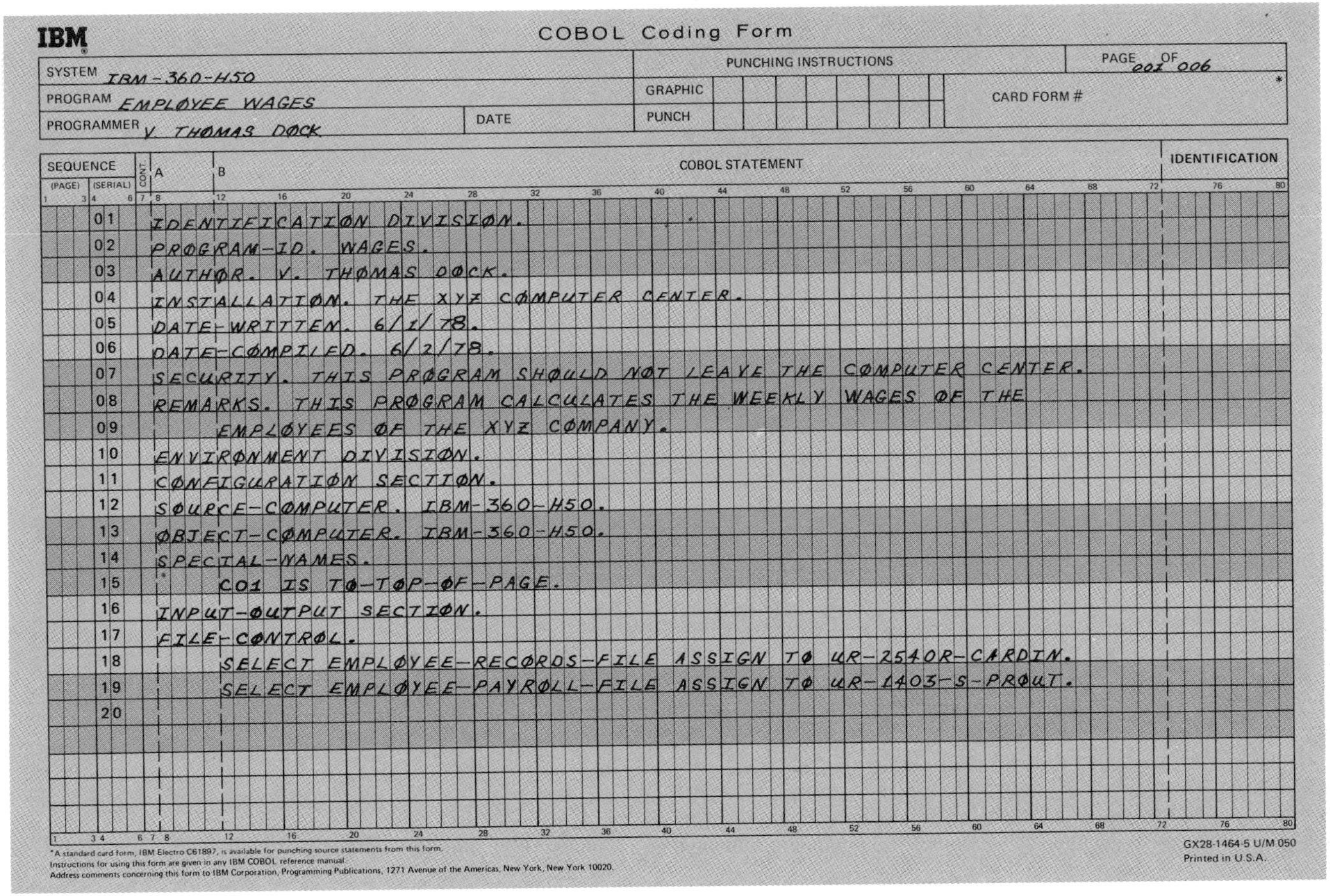

IBM COBOL Coding Form

SYSTEM IBM-360-H50
PROGRAM EMPLOYEE WAGES
PROGRAMMER V. THOMAS DOCK
DATE
PUNCHING INSTRUCTIONS: GRAPHIC / PUNCH
PAGE 001 OF 006
CARD FORM #

SEQUENCE (PAGE) (SERIAL) | CONT. | A | B | COBOL STATEMENT | IDENTIFICATION

```
01 IDENTIFICATION DIVISION.
02 PROGRAM-ID. WAGES.
03 AUTHOR. V. THOMAS DOCK.
04 INSTALLATION. THE XYZ COMPUTER CENTER.
05 DATE-WRITTEN. 6/1/78.
06 DATE-COMPILED. 6/2/78.
07 SECURITY. THIS PROGRAM SHOULD NOT LEAVE THE COMPUTER CENTER.
08 REMARKS. THIS PROGRAM CALCULATES THE WEEKLY WAGES OF THE
09          EMPLOYEES OF THE XYZ COMPANY.
10 ENVIRONMENT DIVISION.
11 CONFIGURATION SECTION.
12 SOURCE-COMPUTER. IBM-360-H50.
13 OBJECT-COMPUTER. IBM-360-H50.
14 SPECIAL-NAMES.
15          C01 IS TO-TOP-OF-PAGE.
16 INPUT-OUTPUT SECTION.
17 FILE-CONTROL.
18          SELECT EMPLOYEE-RECORDS-FILE ASSIGN TO UR-2540R-CARDIN.
19          SELECT EMPLOYEE-PAYROLL-FILE ASSIGN TO UR-1403-S-PROUT.
20
```

*A standard card form, IBM Electro C61897, is available for punching source statements from this form.
Instructions for using this form are given in any IBM COBOL reference manual.
Address comments concerning this form to IBM Corporation, Programming Publications, 1271 Avenue of the Americas, New York, New York 10020.

GX28-1464-5 U/M 050
Printed in U.S.A.

Illustration 13-6. A COBOL program.

IBM

COBOL Coding Form

SYSTEM IBM-360-H50

PROGRAM EMPLOYEE WAGES

PROGRAMMER V. THOMAS DOCK

DATE

PUNCHING INSTRUCTIONS

GRAPHIC

PUNCH

CARD FORM #

PAGE 502 OF 006

*

SEQUENCE	CONT.	A B	COBOL STATEMENT
01		DATA DIVISION.	
02		FILE SECTION.	
03		FD EMPLOYEE-RECORDS-FILE	
04		LABEL RECORD IS OMITTED.	
05		01 CARD-RECORD.	
06		02 EMPLOYEE-NAME	PICTURE A(15).
07		02 FILLER	PICTURE X(4).
08		02 HOURS-WORKED	PICTURE 99.
09		02 FILLER	PICTURE XXX.
10		02 HOURLY-RATE	PICTURE 9V99.
11		02 FILLER	PICTURE X(53).
12		FD EMPLOYEE-PAYROLL-FILE	
13		LABEL RECORD IS OMITTED.	
14		01 PAYROLL-RECORD.	
15		02 FILLER	PICTURE X.
16		02 EMPLOYEE-NAM	PICTURE A(15).
17		02 FILLER	PICTURE X(6).
18		02 HOURS-WORK	PICTURE 99.
19		02 FILLER	PICTURE X(8).
20		02 HOUR-RATE	PICTURE $9.99.
21		02 FILLER	PICTURE X(8).
22		02 GROSS-WAGE-OUT	PICTURE $$99.99.
23		02 FILLER	PICTURE X(22).
24		02 FEDERAL-INCOME-TAX-OUT	PICTURE $$9.99.

IDENTIFICATION

"A standard card form, IBM Electro C81897, is available for punching source statements from this form.
Instructions for using this form are given in any IBM COBOL reference manual.
Address comments concerning the form to IBM Corporation, Programming Publications, 1271 Avenue of the Americas, New York, New York 10020.

GX28-1464-5 U/M 050
Printed in U.S.A.

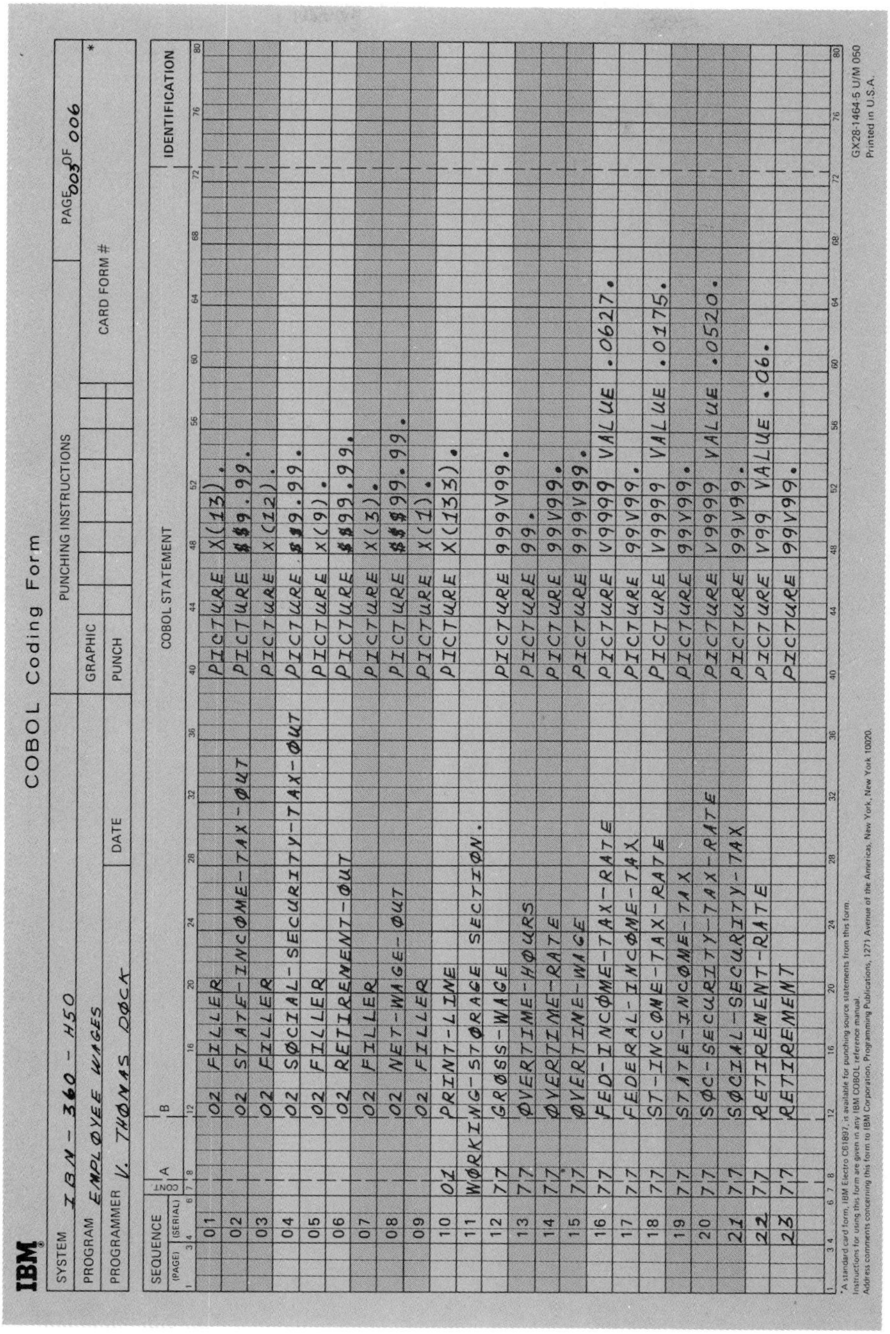

COBOL Coding Form

SYSTEM: IBM-360-H50
PROGRAM: EMPLOYEE WAGES
PROGRAMMER: V. THOMAS DOCK
PAGE 003 OF 006

Seq	COBOL Statement
01	02 FILLER PICTURE X(13).
02	02 STATE-INCOME-TAX-OUT PICTURE $$9.99.
03	02 FILLER PICTURE X(12).
04	02 SOCIAL-SECURITY-TAX-OUT PICTURE $$9.99.
05	02 FILLER PICTURE X(9).
06	02 RETIREMENT-OUT PICTURE $$99.99.
07	02 FILLER PICTURE X(3).
08	02 NET-WAGE-OUT PICTURE $$$99.99.
09	02 FILLER PICTURE X(1).
10	01 PRINT-LINE PICTURE X(133).
11	WORKING-STORAGE SECTION.
12	77 GROSS-WAGE PICTURE 999V99.
13	77 OVERTIME-HOURS PICTURE 99.
14	77 OVERTIME-RATE PICTURE 99V99.
15	77 OVERTIME-WAGE PICTURE 999V99.
16	77 FED-INCOME-TAX-RATE PICTURE V9999 VALUE .0627.
17	77 FEDERAL-INCOME-TAX PICTURE 99V99.
18	77 ST-INCOME-TAX-RATE PICTURE V9999 VALUE .0175.
19	77 STATE-INCOME-TAX PICTURE 99V99.
20	77 SOC-SECURITY-TAX-RATE PICTURE V9999 VALUE .0520.
21	77 SOCIAL-SECURITY-TAX PICTURE 99V99.
22	77 RETIREMENT-RATE PICTURE V99 VALUE .06.
23	77 RETIREMENT PICTURE 99V99.

Illustration 13-6. A COBOL program (continued).

COBOL Coding Form

SYSTEM: IBM-360-H50
PROGRAM: EMPLOYEE WAGES
PROGRAMMER: V. THOMAS DOCK
PAGE OF: 001 006
CARD FORM #

PUNCHING INSTRUCTIONS
GRAPHIC
PUNCH

```
01   01 HEADING-1.
02      02 FILLER          PICTURE X VALUE SPACE.
03      02 EMP-NAME        PICTURE A(13) VALUE 'EMPLOYEE NAM
04   -  'E'.
05      02 FILLER          PICTURE XXX VALUE SPACES.
06      02 HRS-WK          PICTURE A(12) VALUE 'HOURS WORKED'
07      02 FILLER          PICTURE X VALUE SPACE.
08      02 HR-RAT          PICTURE A(11) VALUE 'HOURLY RATE'.
09      02 FILLER          PICTURE X(4) VALUE SPACES.
10      02 GRS-WGS         PICTURE A(10) VALUE 'GROSS WAGE'.
11      02 FILLER          PICTURE XX VALUE SPACES.
12      02 FED-INC-TAX     PICTURE A(18) VALUE 'FEDERAL INCO
13   -  'ME TAX'.
14      02 FILLER          PICTURE X VALUE SPACE.
15      02 ST-INC-TAX      PICTURE A(16) VALUE 'STATE INCOME
16   -  'TAX'.
17      02 FILLER          PICTURE X VALUE SPACE.
18      02 SOC-SEC-TAX     PICTURE A(19) VALUE 'SOCIAL SECUR
19   -  'ITY'.
20      02 FILLER          PICTURE X VALUE SPACE.
21      02 RTRM1           PICTURE A(10) VALUE 'RETIREMENT'.
22      02 FILLER          PICTURE X VALUE SPACE.
23      02 NT-WGS          PICTURE A(9) VALUE 'NET WAGES'.
```

*A standard card form, IBM Electro C61897, is available for punching source statements from this form.
Instructions for using this form are given in any IBM COBOL reference manual.
Address comments concerning this form to IBM Corporation, Programming Publications, 1271 Avenue of the Americas, New York, New York 10020

GX28-1464-5 U/M 050
Printed in U.S.A.

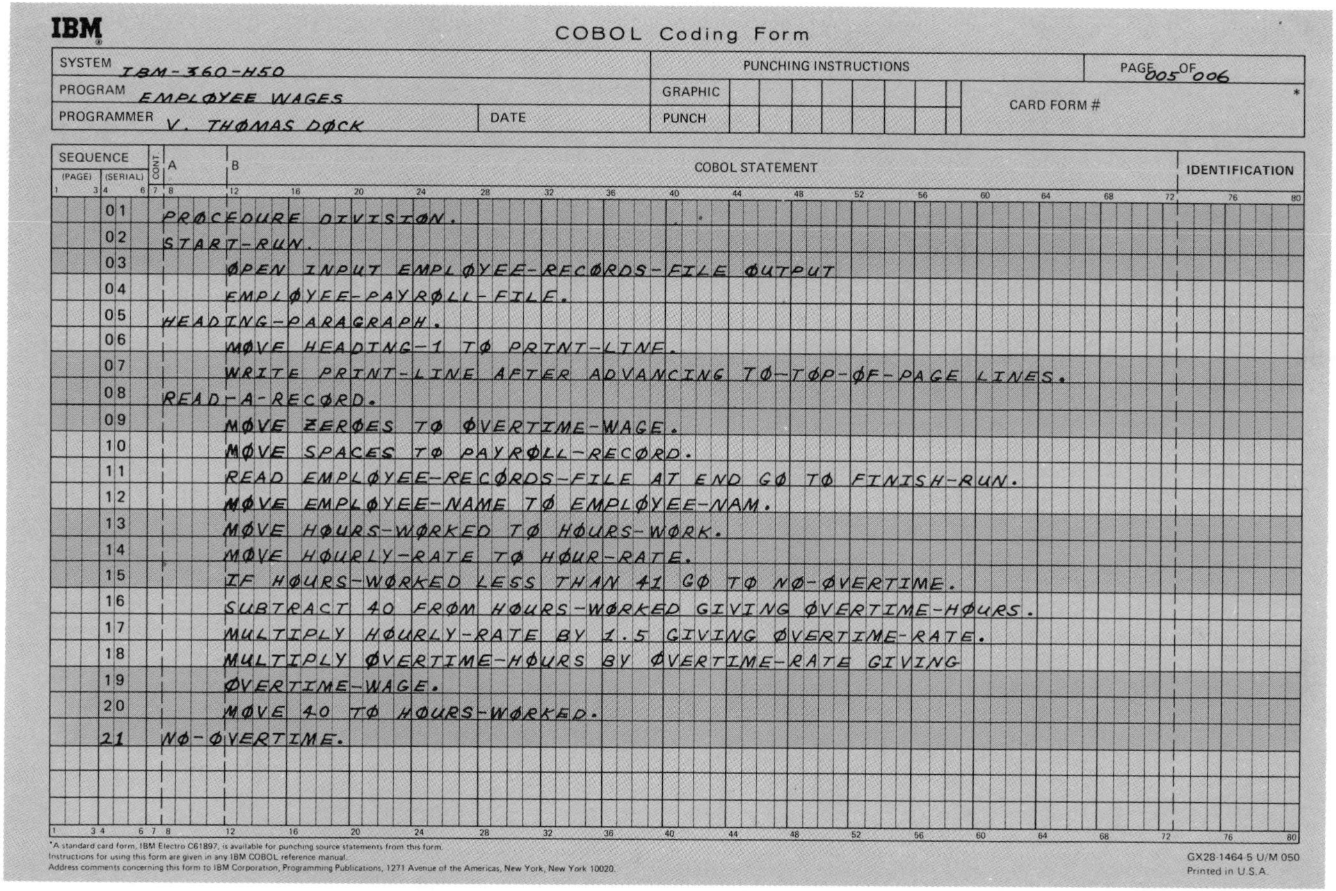

IBM COBOL Coding Form

SYSTEM IBM-360-H50
PROGRAM EMPLOYEE WAGES
PROGRAMMER V. THOMAS DOCK
DATE

PUNCHING INSTRUCTIONS
GRAPHIC
PUNCH
CARD FORM #

PAGE 005 OF 006

```
01   PROCEDURE DIVISION.
02   START-RUN.
03       OPEN INPUT EMPLOYEE-RECORDS-FILE OUTPUT
04           EMPLOYEE-PAYROLL-FILE.
05   HEADING-PARAGRAPH.
06       MOVE HEADING-1 TO PRINT-LINE.
07       WRITE PRINT-LINE AFTER ADVANCING TO-TOP-OF-PAGE LINES.
08   READ-A-RECORD.
09       MOVE ZEROES TO OVERTIME-WAGE.
10       MOVE SPACES TO PAYROLL-RECORD.
11       READ EMPLOYEE-RECORDS-FILE AT END GO TO FINISH-RUN.
12       MOVE EMPLOYEE-NAME TO EMPLOYEE-NAM.
13       MOVE HOURS-WORKED TO HOURS-WORK.
14       MOVE HOURLY-RATE TO HOUR-RATE.
15       IF HOURS-WORKED LESS THAN 41 GO TO NO-OVERTIME.
16       SUBTRACT 40 FROM HOURS-WORKED GIVING OVERTIME-HOURS.
17       MULTIPLY HOURLY-RATE BY 1.5 GIVING OVERTIME-RATE.
18       MULTIPLY OVERTIME-HOURS BY OVERTIME-RATE GIVING
19           OVERTIME-WAGE.
20       MOVE 40 TO HOURS-WORKED.
21   NO-OVERTIME.
```

"A standard used form, IBM Electro OEI 897, is available for punching source statements, from this form.
Instructions for using this form are given in any IBM COBOL reference manual.
Address comments concerning this form to IBM Corporation, Programming Publications, 1271 Avenue of the Americas, New York, New York 10020.

CX28-1464 5 U/M 050
Printed in U.S.A.

Illustration 13-6. A COBOL program (continued).

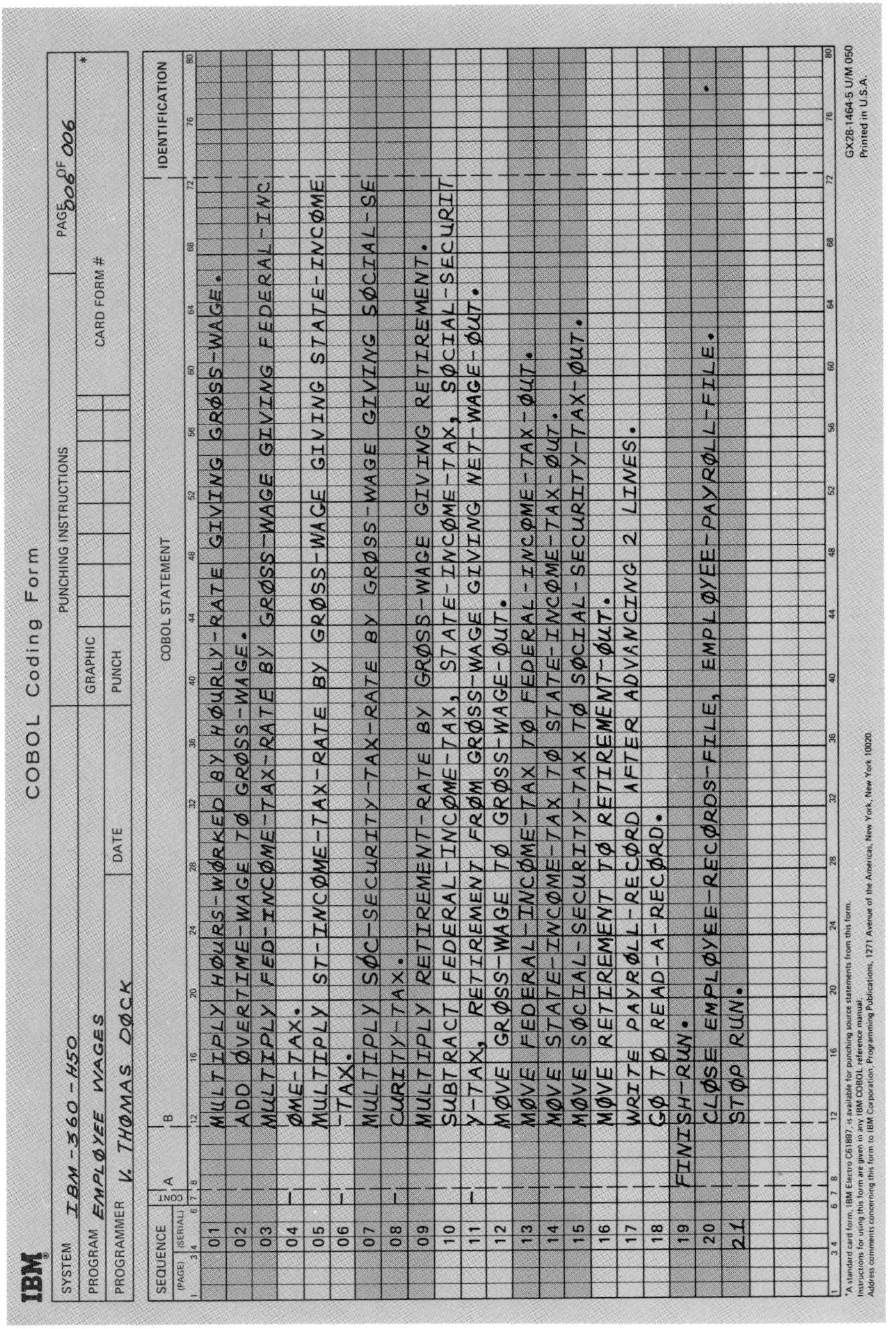

IBM COBOL Coding Form

SYSTEM: IBM-360-H50
PROGRAM: EMPLOYEE WAGES
PROGRAMMER: V. THOMAS DOCK
PAGE 006 OF 006

```
01   MULTIPLY HOURS-WORKED BY HOURLY-RATE GIVING GROSS-WAGE.
02   ADD OVERTIME-WAGE TO GROSS-WAGE.
03   MULTIPLY FED-INCOME-TAX-RATE BY GROSS-WAGE GIVING FEDERAL-INC
04   OME-TAX.
05   MULTIPLY ST-INCOME-TAX-RATE BY GROSS-WAGE GIVING STATE-INCOME
06   -TAX.
07   MULTIPLY SOC-SECURITY-TAX-RATE BY GROSS-WAGE GIVING SOCIAL-SE
08   -CURITY-TAX.
09   MULTIPLY RETIREMENT-RATE BY GROSS-WAGE GIVING RETIREMENT.
10   SUBTRACT FEDERAL-INCOME-TAX, STATE-INCOME-TAX, SOCIAL-SECURIT
11   Y-TAX, RETIREMENT FROM GROSS-WAGE GIVING NET-WAGE-OUT.
12   MOVE GROSS-WAGE TO GROSS-WAGE-OUT.
13   MOVE FEDERAL-INCOME-TAX TO FEDERAL-INCOME-TAX-OUT.
14   MOVE STATE-INCOME-TAX TO STATE-INCOME-TAX-OUT.
15   MOVE SOCIAL-SECURITY-TAX TO SOCIAL-SECURITY-TAX-OUT.
16   MOVE RETIREMENT TO RETIREMENT-OUT.
17   WRITE PAYROLL-RECORD AFTER ADVANCING 2 LINES.
18   GO TO READ-A-RECORD.
19   FINISH-RUN.
20   CLOSE EMPLOYEE-RECORDS-FILE, EMPLOYEE-PAYROLL-FILE.
21   STOP RUN.
```

Illustration 13-6. A COBOL program (continued).

respects. It is an easy-to-learn high-level programming language, offering both numeric and alphabetic capabilities. The language was originally developed in the 1960s at Dartmouth College. It can be used for a variety of educational, engineering, mathematical, statistical, and business applications. The language is widely used by problem solvers working at terminals.

BASIC is an *interactive* (conversational) language. This feature of the language has several implications. First, a program and data can be entered into the computer, in parts, from a terminal. Second, the computer can request additional data during execution of the program. Third, one or more of the program statements can be changed from the terminal before execution of the program is completed. Thus, program statements and data can be changed, added, or deleted during execution of a program. Finally, the programmer is in continuous direct communication with the computer. Because the BASIC language is most often used in a system having data communication capabilities, the language is discussed in more detail in Chapter 16. Specific features of the BASIC language and programming problems to be solved using BASIC are given in Appendixes A and B.

RPG

As stated earlier in this chapter, Report Program Generator (RPG) is a problem-oriented language. The language was initially designed to generate programs whose outputs are business-oriented, printed reports. An RPG program is a description of a report to be produced. Based on the description (specifications), a generator program (normally, provided by the computer manufacturer) creates a program to produce the report. Today, RPG can also be used for other types of processing. For example, it can be used to create and maintain files stored on magnetic disk or magnetic tape.

The RPG language is designed to duplicate the logic of punched-card equipment. Thus, it is the primary programming language for small computer systems that are typically installed as replacements for punched-card data processing systems. An early example was the IBM System/3. The RPG language is also used on medium-size and large computer systems. In general, the RPG language is *upward compatible;* that is, with only minor modifications, an RPG program can be translated and executed on a computer system that is faster and has more internal storage than the computer system for which it was written. While RPG is not the primary programming language for medium-size and large computer systems, it is often used in business data processing applications for which it is particularly suitable.

The programmer who uses RPG must describe the input and output files to be used in the program, define the significant fields of input records, set up any calculations or logical operations to be performed, and define the report or output records to be created. To prepare an RPG program, five forms may be used. These are: (1) File Extension Specifications, (2) File Description Specifications, (3) Input Specifications, (4) Calculation Specifications, and (5) Output Specifications. An RPG program to read input and provide output similar to that of the FORTRAN and COBOL programs discussed earlier is shown in Illustration 13-7.

Several entries are common to all RPG specifications forms: Page, Program Identification, Line, Form Type, and Comments. The page entry (punched-card columns 1 and 2) is located in the upper right corner of each form; it can be used with the line number assigned to each specification line (columns 3, 4, and 5) to provide program sequence information. A program code name can be entered in the program identification field (columns 75-80). Comments can be entered on any specifications form by placing an asterisk (*) in column 7 of a specification line as has been done in the example program.

Generally, the RPG specifications forms are coded in the order that they will be arranged in the source deck: File Extension, File Description, Input, Calculation, and Output Specifications. The File Extension Specifications are prepared only when tables or disk files are to be used.

In the example program, two files are defined on the File Description Specifications form. The first file (CARDIN) is the card input file containing employee pay records. The length of the records in the file is defined (80) and the type of input device that will read the file is indicated (an IBM 1442 Card Reader). The output file (PRINT) will be printed on a 132-characters-per-line printer.

The specific fields that will be used from records in the CARDIN file are defined on the Input Specifications form. Each field is identified by its starting and ending locations and is given a name. The coding on line 010 causes each input record to be checked to see whether or not it contains a character in column 20; if it does not, then no further processing of the record occurs.

The calculations needed to determine values for the output report are described on the Calculation Specifications form. None of these calculations occurs until an input record is read. This is specified by the indicator 35 (columns 10 and 11), which also appears on the Input Specifications form (columns 19 and 20). These corresponding numbers indicate that the data to be used in the calculations comes from records in the CARDIN file. The hours worked (HOURS) are compared to 40; if the hours worked exceed 40, the overtime pay (OTIME) is calculated; otherwise, only regular pay (GROSS and GROSS1) is calculated. Then deductions are calculated.

The specifications for the output report to be created from the PRINT output file are given on the Output Specifications form. Each heading line (constant) and each field that is to be printed are defined. The editing needed for each field is specified.

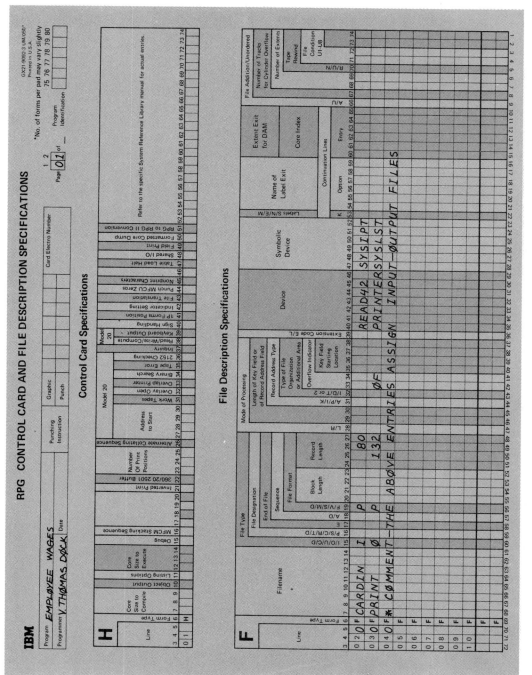

Illustration 13-7. A RPG program.

IBM

RPG INPUT SPECIFICATIONS

GX21-9094-2 U/M 050*
Printed in U.S.A.

| Program | EMPLOYEE WAGES |
| Programmer | V. THOMAS DOCK |

Punching Instruction — Graphic / Punch

Card Electro Number

Page 02 of ___ Page 1 2

75 76 77 78 79 80 — Program Identification

Line	Form Type	Filename	Sequence	Number (1-N)	Option (O)	Record Identifying Indicator or **	Position	Not (N)	C/Z/D	Character	Record Identification Codes	Field Location From	To	Decimal Positions	Field Name
01	I	CARDIN	AA			35	20	N	C						
02	I											1	15		NAME
03	I											20	21	0	HOURS
04	I											25	27	2	RATE
05	I	*COMMENT—THE INPUT FIELDS FOR THE TIME CARD RECORD ARE DEFINED													

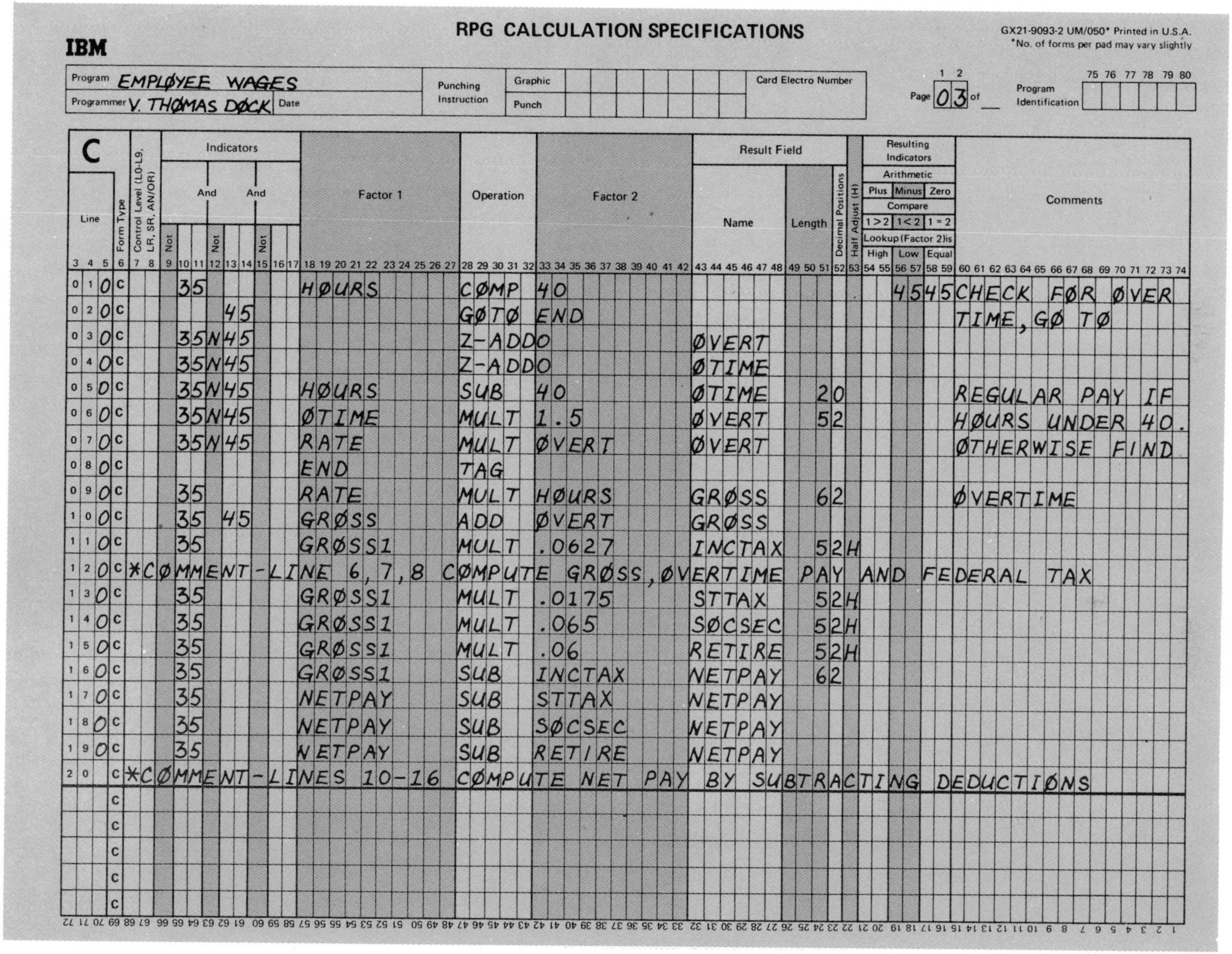

IBM — RPG CALCULATION SPECIFICATIONS — GX21-9093-2 UM/050* Printed in U.S.A. *No. of forms per pad may vary slightly

Program: EMPLØYEE WAGES
Programmer: V. THØMAS DØCK
Page 03

Line	Form Type	Indicators	Factor 1	Operation	Factor 2	Result Field Name	Length	Decimal Positions	Half Adjust (H)	Resulting Indicators	Comments
010	C	35	HØURS	CØMP	40					4545	CHECK FØR ØVER
020	C	45		GØTØ	END						TIME, GØ TØ
030	C	35N45		Z-ADD	0	ØVERT					
040	C	35N45		Z-ADD	0	ØTIME					
050	C	35N45	HØURS	SUB	40	ØTIME	2	0			REGULAR PAY IF
060	C	35N45	ØTIME	MULT	1.5	ØVERT	5	2			HØURS UNDER 40.
070	C	35N45	RATE	MULT	ØVERT	ØVERT					ØTHERWISE FIND
080	C		END	TAG							
090	C	35	RATE	MULT	HØURS	GRØSS	6	2			ØVERTIME
100	C	35 45	GRØSS	ADD	ØVERT	GRØSS					
110	C	35	GRØSS1	MULT	.0627	INCTAX	5	2	H		
120	C	*CØMMENT-LINE 6, 7, 8 CØMPUTE GRØSS, ØVERTIME PAY AND FEDERAL TAX									
130	C	35	GRØSS1	MULT	.0175	STTAX	5	2	H		
140	C	35	GRØSS1	MULT	.065	SØCSEC	5	2	H		
150	C	35	GRØSS1	MULT	.06	RETIRE	5	2	H		
160	C	35	GRØSS1	SUB	INCTAX	NETPAY	6	2			
170	C	35	NETPAY	SUB	STTAX	NETPAY					
180	C	35	NETPAY	SUB	SØCSEC	NETPAY					
190	C	35	NETPAY	SUB	RETIRE	NETPAY					
20	C	*CØMMENT-LINES 10-16 CØMPUTE NET PAY BY SUBTRACTING DEDUCTIØNS									

Illustration 13-7. A RPG program (continued).

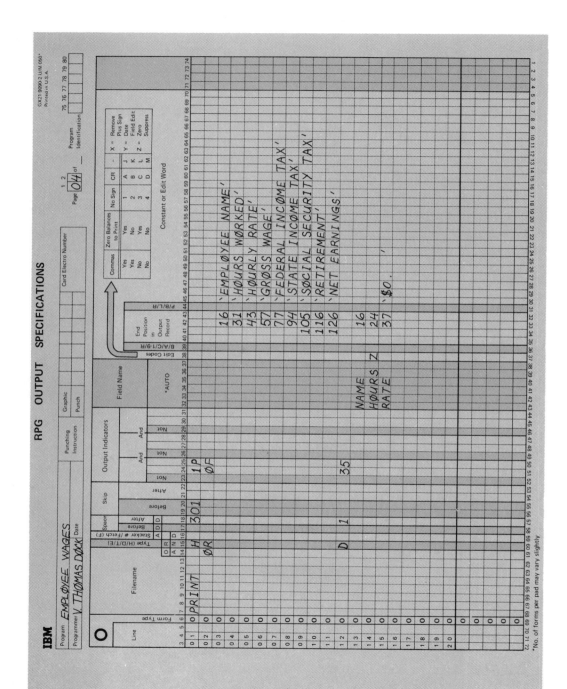

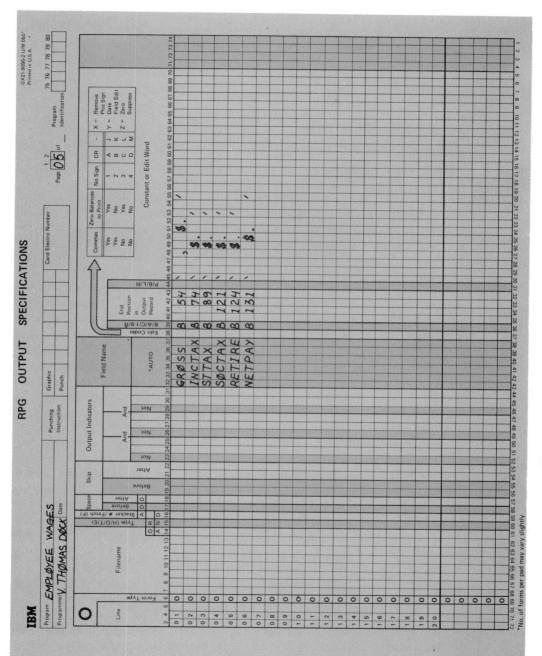

Illustration 13-7. A RPG program (continued).

By now it should be evident that RPG is not *free-form*. Each specification line entry must be placed in certain columns of the line. RPG cannot be free-form because the specifications that the programmer writes are the generator program's only guidelines in creating a complete program to perform the processing steps required.

LANGUAGE SELECTION

The importance of selecting an appropriate programming language during the planning stage of the programming cycle was stressed in Chapter 12. How does one decide whether an assembler language, FORTRAN, COBOL, RPG, or some other programming language should be used in coding? Generally, the basic question of which language to select can be viewed from three aspects: (1) the purpose of the program and the frequency of execution, (2) the time and money required to design and code a program in a particular language, and (3) the availability of a particular language.

The purpose of the program and the frequency of execution are considerations that emphasize the speed with which a program can be executed. Under most circumstances, if two programmers of equal talent were to write programs to solve the same problem, one using an assembler language and the other a compiler language, the program written in assembler language would execute faster and require less storage space. Although the coding of an assembler-language program often requires more time and money than the coding of an equivalent program in a compiler language, if the program is to be run repeatedly, the savings in computer time and storage requirements may more than compensate for the extra coding costs. Furthermore, many factors indicating specific machine operations are easily programmed in an assembler language but are either not available or impractical to program in a compiler language. Therefore, if the nature of the program is such that a number of executions of the program are expected or if particular features of machine operations are needed, as assembler language is normally the best choice for the program. If program efficiency is the deciding factor, an assembler language is usually adopted.

The second aspect of the selection question is basically one of the preparation cost of a program. As suggested above, one of the basic weaknesses of assembler language is the amount of time required for coding. Compiler languages do not share this weakness. The effort involved in coding, correcting, and documenting a program is minimized when a compiler language is used. This implies that if the nature of the program is such that it is likely to be revised from time to time, a compiler language has an advantage over an assembler language. Any alteration of an assembler-language program may necessitate extensive rewriting.

An additional advantage of a compiler language is that it is somewhat machine-independent, This means that it can be employed on any of several types of computers. In contrast, an assembler language is machine-oriented (and, therefore, machine-dependent); it is designed for one particular type of machine. If a program is coded in an assembler language and then the computer is changed, but the need for the program continues, the entire program must be rewritten for the new machine.

The final aspect of the selection question is one of language availability. This question is primarily concerned with compiler or generator languages (since a particular assembler language can be used on only a certain type of computer). Before a particular high-level programming language is chosen, the capability to execute programs written in that language on the computer in use should be verified. If the purchase (or rental) of a compiler or generator program is anticipated, the costs should be weighed relative to the benefits of being able to use the language in programming.

The familiarity of programmers with any language that is considered for selection should be assessed accurately for the particular installation. If involved programmers have not had previous experience with a language, the training costs and the ease of adapting to the language should be estimated. The time required for such training and adjustment should be factored into the selection process.

Although choosing a language for a program might seem to be a relatively simple task, it is not as straightforward as one might assume. A great deal of effort should be expended in the selection of a language because, ultimately, it may determine the worth of the program.

Summary

1. Programming languages, much the same as computer hardware, were developed in phases, or generations. Machine language was the first to be introduced. Assembler language and high-level programming languages followed.

2. Machine languages are machine-dependent in that programs written in a machine language can be executed only by computers for which the language was designed. Thus, a program written for one computer cannot be executed by another computer unless it is of the same type. Machine languages are very tedious and time-consuming to use. However, once written, programs in machine language execute quickly and use a minimum amount of internal storage.

3. Assembler languages represent the next development. They are structurally similar to machine languages but they permit the programmer to use symbolic names rather than numerical representations of operations. This reduces coding time and the amount of information the programmer has to remember. Assembler-language programs are processed by an assembler, which translates the assembler-language (source) program into a machine-language (object) program.

4. The third level of development of computer languages involved macro-instructions. These instructions contain macro operation codes. They are used by the programmer to cause often repeated series of assembler-language instructions to be inserted in a program, thus reducing the amount of coding necessary on the programmer's part.

5. The next level of computer languages includes high-level programming languages such as FORTRAN, COBOL, BASIC, and RPG. While some of these languages are considered to be procedure-oriented, they may all be called problem-oriented languages. These languages are generally machine-independent and satisfy specific needs. For example, FORTRAN and BASIC were designed to satisfy engineers' and scientists' needs for mathematical computation while COBOL and RPG are more suited to business data processing. All these languages reduce the amount of coding necessary for programs, compared with assembler-language programs, and require little in-depth knowledge about the computer on which the programs are to be executed. They do, however, take longer to execute (after translation) than an equivalent program initially written in machine or assembler language. Despite this handicap, high-level programming languages are in widespread use today.

CAREER PROFILE

Kenneth Long
Senior Programmer-Analyst

United Airlines

Background Experience

I graduated from California State Polytechnic College in 1960 with a Bachelor of Science in Technical Arts. In the Army Security Agency in Germany, I was a tabulating equipment operator. I enjoyed it. After discharge, I looked for work in the manufacturing industry but I felt that the long-range career opportunities were unpromising. My introduction to data processing in the Army triggered my interest in that area as a career so I entered the Automation Institute in Sacramento. I took a year-long course brushing up on tab equipment operation and studying several programming languages. Upon completion, United Airlines offered me a job where I started as a tab operator. Three months later I was a computer operator and in another three months I became a programmer trainee, taking programmed instruction in COBOL. During this time I did the run manuals for the IBM 1410 to 360 conversion and prioritized testing for other programmers and analysts. Later, I began programming in our Inventory Systems Group. And, in 1973, I took over most of the programming responsibility for the Turbine Shop Systems.

Primary Job Responsibilities

My title is Senior Programmer-Analyst/Team Leader. As a team leader, I direct the work of four programming assistants, plan their workloads, assign tasks, and carry out the maintenance of turbine shop programs. The Turbine Shop at United performs overhaul, rework, and safety maintenance on the airplane engines. They take the engines off the wing, inspect them, and send parts through various plating, milling, and inspection sections and then reassemble them. We maintain systems covering all these procedures. Additionally, we are responsible for issuing notification when engines are due for inspection. I interface with the accounting and inventory departments, providing them with information related to the jobs being done in the turbine shop. A typical day for me would begin with reviewing the previous night's production reports, and rescheduling any activities that have presented problems. I would also check the status of work assignments being done by my programming team. The rest of the day I would spend writing programs.

What Has Made You Successful?

We have quite a few opportunities at United for furthering our education. The company offers programming courses and programmer productivity courses that teach you to complete more work in a given time. I take advantage of these and, in addition, have just finished a course in Main Event Management which helps me organize people's work in a better way. Working with other analysts at United is also very educational. Off the job I try to relax as much as possible as there can be very stressful times in this work. I pursue several hobbies which help me to unwind. Additionally, I belong to an organization that sends me as a delegate to the Fair Board of San Francisco where I help shape policy. Although this is separate from my work, it allows me to meet and work with professionals in other occupations and helps me develop listening qualities (which is important for an analyst) and the ability to question other people's decisions in a tactful way.

An Overview of Systems

CHAPTER 14

Overlapped Systems

OVERLAPPED PROCESSING

TYPES OF OVERLAPPED PROCESSING

Prior to the introduction of third-generation computers, computer systems could perform only one operation at a time. Thus, one of the inefficiencies of first-generation and second-generation computer systems was that some of their components were idle for long periods of time, even while the system was running. As shown in Illustration 14-1, a typical card system read a card, processed it, and printed an output line on the printer. It then repeated this sequence for the next card. Assume a 600-cards-per-minute reader and a 600-lines-per-minute printer were included in the system. Allow .05 second to process each record, or card. The line graph in the illustration represents the relative amounts of time required for each of the operations. At these rates, the card reader and the printer were each used 40 percent of the time and the CPU—the most expensive component of the computer system—was used only 20 percent of the time.

In an effort to reduce the idle CPU time, third-generation input/output devices are buffered. A *buffer* is a storage device used to compensate for the difference in rates of flow of data from one device to another or from an input/output device to the central processing unit.

With faster input/output components, the input/output percentages may change, but the components still are idle part of the time. Illustration 14-2 shows similar processing for a tape system with 320,000-characters-per-second tape drives (1600 BPI × 200 inches-per-second). In this program, an 80-character record was read, processed, and written on a tape. Assuming .002 second for processing each record (a faster CPU than the one on the card system described), the line graph in the illustration represents the relative amounts of time the components of the tape system were in use. In this case, the CPU was used about 80 percent of the time, but each tape drive was used only about 10 percent of the time.

To reduce the time that components are idle, third-generation computer systems *overlap* input and output operations with processing. For exam-

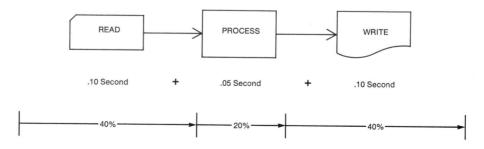

Illustration 14-1. Card-system processing.

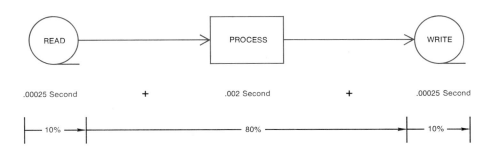

Illustration 14-2. Tape-system processing.

ple, an overlapped card system can read a card, process a card, and print a line—all at the same time. Similarly, an overlapped tape system can read a tape record, process a tape record, and write a tape record—all at the same time. By overlapping operations in this way, the components of a computer system are used a greater percentage of time and the computer system can do more processing in less time.

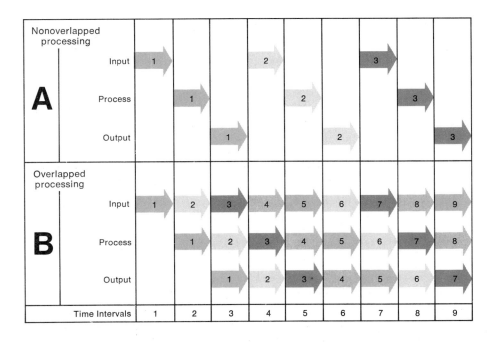

Illustration 14-3. Overlapped and nonoverlapped processing.

OVERLAPPED PROCESSING

Illustration 14-3 demonstrates the difference between nonoverlapped and overlapped processing. Nonoverlapped processing is shown in part A, and overlapped processing is shown in part B. In both cases, equal amounts of time (one time interval) are required to read a card, to process the data, and to print a line. At the end of the nine time intervals, then, three records have been read, processed, and written by the nonoverlapped system. Each of the components of this system (card reader, CPU, and printer) is in use 33 percent of the time. In the same amount of time (nine intervals), nine records have been read, eight have been processed, and seven have been written by the overlapped system. After the first two time intervals, each of the components is used 100 percent of the time.

Overlapping is possible because many of the access cycles that take place during an input/output operation are not used by the computer system. Take, for example, a card reading operation on a computer with a 1-byte access width and a 2-microsecond access speed. When the card reader reads an 80-column card, 80 access cycles (or 160 microseconds) are required to transfer the data from the card reader to main storage (one access cycle for each character of data read). However, at 1200 cards per minute, a card reader takes .005 second for each card read, the equivalent of 25,000 access cycles. During the reading of one card, then, 25,000 minus 80, or 24,920, access cycles are not used by the computer system. The idea behind overlapping operations is to use these wasted access cycles for other input/output or CPU operations. For example, 100 access cycles could be used for printing a line while the card is being read. The remaining access cycles could be used for executing instructions in the CPU. (To review access cycles, see "The Execution of Program Statements" in Chapter 7.)

This idea of wasted access cycles applies to high-speed input/output operations in the same way that it applies to card input/output or printing operations. Suppose, for example, that a tape is read at the rate of 50,000 bytes per second on a computer system with a 2-microsecond access speed and a 1-byte access width. At 50,000 bytes per second, each byte takes 20 microseconds to be read, but only 2 microseconds to be transferred into storage. Therefore, 18 microseconds, or the equivalent of nine access cycles, are wasted for each byte of data read. These cycles can be used for other input/output or CPU operations.

A nonoverlapped system does not make use of additional access cycles because it has no way of executing more than one instruction at a time. The control unit of the CPU controls the execution of instructions (including input/output instructions), one after another. In contrast, an overlapped system has special devices, called *channels,* that control the execution of input/output instructions, thereby freeing the CPU's control unit to exe-

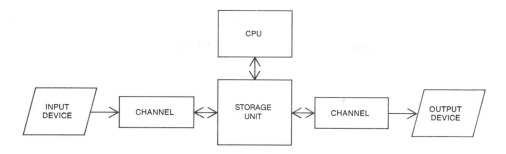

Illustration 14-4. Computer system components
with overlap capabilities.

cute other instructions of a stored program. Thus, at any given time, the
control unit of the CPU can control the execution of internal operations;
one channel can control the execution of an input/output operation; and
another channel can control the execution of another input/output operation. In this way, some of the access cycles that are wasted on a nonoverlapped system can be put to use.

Illustration 14-4 represents the components of a card system that has two
channels. Although the storage unit is often considered part of the CPU,
it is represented here as separate from the CPU. The CPU consists of the
control unit and the arithmetic/logic unit and is connected to the storage
unit. The channels are between the storage unit and the input/output
devices. During overlapped processing, each channel moves data to and
from storage as it executes input/output instructions, and the control unit
of the CPU moves data to and from storage as it executes instructions. If a
channel and the control unit require an access cycle at the same time, the
channel has priority. Suppose, for example, that a channel has to move a
byte of data from a card reader to the storage unit, but the CPU is in the
midst of accessing an instruction into its control unit. The CPU stops for
one access cycle, the byte of data is moved from the channel to storage,
and the CPU resumes operations where it left off. During overlapped
processing, then, access cycles can be used alternately by the channels
and the CPU.

A channel can have one or more input/output devices attached to it, and
a computer system can have one or more channels attached to it. The
number of operations that can be overlapped depends on the number of
channels on the system because each channel can control only one input/
output operation at a time. The types of operations that can be overlapped
depend on the arrangement of the input/output devices on the channels.

Illustration 14-5 shows a system that has two channels and can, therefore, overlap two input/output operations with processing. For example,

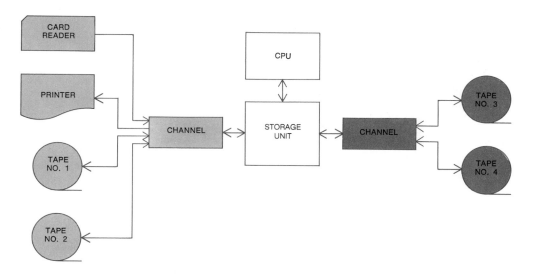

Illustration 14-5. Overlapped tape system.

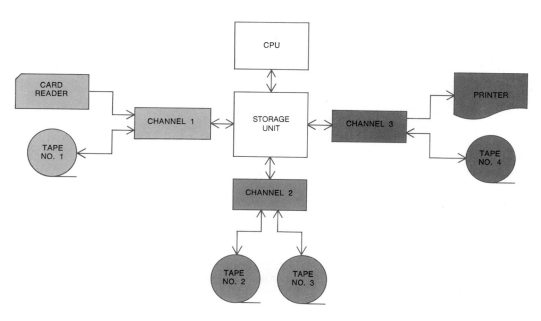

Illustration 14-6. Three-channel computer system.

card reading and writing on tape 3 can be overlapped, but card reading and printing cannot be overlapped. In contrast, Illustration 14-6 represents a system with three channels. It can overlap three input/output operations with processing. Card reading can be overlapped with printing. Tape operations on tapes 1, 2, and 4 can take place at the same time. However, a tape reading operation on tape 2 cannot be overlapped with a tape writing operation on tape 3. The input/output devices must be on different channels if their operations are to be overlapped.

Because an overlapped system requires channels, it costs more than a nonoverlapped system. In addition, an overlapped system raises special programming considerations. For instance, instead of reading an input record, processing it, and writing an output record, a program for overlapped processing must start by reading two input records. This means that two input areas must be assigned in storage. The first input record is read into one input area. Then, while the second input record is read into the other input area, the first input record can be processed. Throughout the program, processing must switch back and forth between the two input areas. Since these same ideas apply to output areas in storage, the overlapped program is not a simple straightforward program. The additional expenses (equipment and programming) are justified by the increased processing potential of the overlapped system.

TYPES OF OVERLAPPED PROCESSING

Although Illustration 14-3 shows equal times for input, processing, and output, this representation is unrealistic. Actually, input, processing, and output times would probably not be equal. In this case, even though a system overlapped operations, some of the components of the system would be idle part of the time—sometimes the CPU, sometimes one or more of the input/output devices.

Illustration 14-7 represents overlapped processing for a program that: (1) reads unblocked tape records as input; (2) processes the records; and (3) prints lines of output (one for each record) on a printer. In this system, the printer operations take twice as long as the tape operations and four times as long as the CPU operations. As a result, after seven intervals, the printer is in use 100 percent of the time, the tape drive 50 percent of the time, and the CPU 25 percent of the time. Because the speed of the program depends on the speed of the slowest input/output device, such a program is said to be *input/output bound*. If output is changed from the printer to a tape unit, the program is still input/output bound, but to a lesser extent. Illustration 14-8 shows the amount of overlap when a second tape unit is used instead of the printer. Eight output records have been written, in the

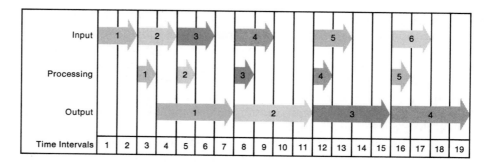

Illustration 14-7. Input/output-bound tape-to-print program.

amount of time that the printer in Illustration 14-7 completed only four. Since most business programs read and write relatively large amounts of data and perform relatively little processing, most business programs are input/output bound.

If the speed of a program is limited by the speed of the CPU, the program is said to be *process bound.* The process-bound program in Illustration 14-9 can be speeded up only by increasing the speed of the CPU operations. In this program, each of the input/output units is in use about 66 percent of the time, while the CPU is in use 100 percent of the time.

To increase the use of the components of a computer system during execution of an input/output-bound program or process-bound program, some systems run two or more programs in internal storage concurrently. This is called *multiprogramming.* The idea is to combine the execution of two input/output-bound programs, or of one input/output-bound program with a process-bound program. Then, whenever the CPU is idle during the execution of one program, it can branch to an instruction in the second

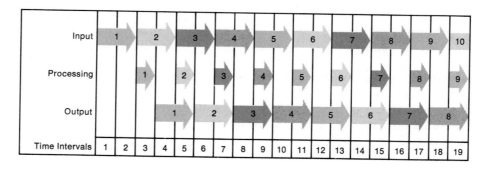

Illustration 14-8. Input/output-bound tape-to-tape program.

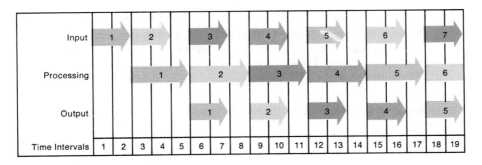

Illustration 14-9. Process-bound program.

program. Illustration 14-10, for instance, represents the execution of two input/output-bound programs on a multiprogramming system. At the start, the first two input records for each program are read into the storage unit. After the first input record for program A is in the storage unit, the CPU begins processing this record. The CPU finishes this processing at the end of interval 3. It would have to wait until the end of interval 4 if program A were the only program in the storage unit. Because program B is also in the storage unit, the CPU branches to this program and processes its first

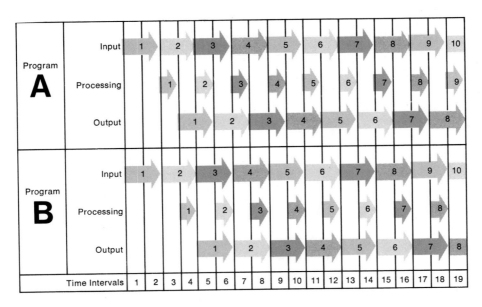

Illustration 14-10. Multiprogramming two input/output-bound programs.

input record. The computer system continues switching back and forth between the programs throughout the execution of the programs. Because of multiprogramming, the two programs are executed in about the same amount of time as would otherwise be required for one of them.

An added cost of a multiprogramming system is additional channels. In Illustration 14-10, for example, the input/output operations for two programs are overlapped rather than the input/output operations for one program. Twice as many channels (in this case, four) are required. A second added cost is additional storage capacity. Because two or more programs are read into the storage unit at one time, the multiprogramming system must have more storage capability than a computer system that processes single programs. In addition, multiprogramming requires extra system programming considerations. Specifically, programming routines must be written for branching back and forth between the programs in the storage unit. If, by multiprogramming, the computer system can do proportionately more processing than it could otherwise do, these additional costs are justified.

Summary

1. Even though a computer system is running, it may have components that are in use only a fraction of the time. For this reason, overlapped systems were developed.

2. The idea underlying overlapped processing is to use the access cycles that are normally wasted during input/output operations. Channels control input/output operations and thus free the CPU for other processing. Input, processing, and output can be overlapped. The number of operations that can be overlapped depends on the number of channels on the system.

3. Input/output-bound and process-bound programs (even when overlapped) permit computer-system components to be idle. Multiprogramming is an attempt to increase the use of idle components by executing two or more programs at the same time. In this case, the computer system switches back and forth between the programs whenever the CPU is required to wait for the completion of an input/output operation.

CHAPTER 15

Introduction to Operating Systems

AN OPERATING SYSTEM AND
STACKED-JOB PROCESSING

AN OPERATING SYSTEM AND
THE PROGRAMMER

VIRTUAL STORAGE
Sharing the Internal Storage Unit
Sharing the Computer

At one time, computer manufacturers designed a computer, then decided what programming support, such as assemblers or compilers, should be supplied with it. When designing third-generation computer systems, however, they faced the fact that the programming support, or software, was almost as important as the equipment, or hardware. Then they began to design software in conjunction with hardware. The result is that the hardware of a system and an *operating system* to support it are now developed integratedly. The operating system is a group of programs designed to maximize the amount of work the system can do. The programs of the operating system are usually written and supplied by the computer manufacturer. Specifically, the operating system is designed to reduce the amount of time that the computer and other system components are idle, and to reduce the amount of programming required on the part of a computer user.

AN OPERATING SYSTEM
AND STACKED-JOB PROCESSING

Before operating systems were developed, a computer system stopped when it reached the end of a program. The operator then made ready the input/output devices to be used by the next program and loaded the program into storage. During this time, the computer system was idle. If a computer system ran many programs during a day, it was likely to be idle a large part of the time. For example, if 40 programs were scheduled per day, with a 3-minute delay between programs, the computer system was idle two hours per day.

With an operating system, the operator does not load the programs that are to be executed. Instead, the operator places a deck of *job cards* in the card reader at the start of the day. Thereafter, the computer system loads and begins executing programs (jobs) according to the job cards. The computer system does not stop at the end of a program. Instead, it reads the job cards for the next program to be executed. It loads the program into storage, usually, from tape or disk. Then it branches to the first instruction of the program. These operations are done under the direction of *control programs* that are part of the operating system. In short, the computer assists the operator, thus reducing the time required to load programs and increasing the amount of time the computer system can do productive work. This processing of a stack of jobs, rather than one job at a time, is called *stacked-job processing*.

Illustration 15-1 shows job cards for a stack of five jobs to be processed. For each job, two or more cards in the stack indicate which program is to be run and which input and output units are to be used (for example, the reels of tape required for the particular job and the tape drives on which they should be mounted). If a job is going to read data from punched cards, the data deck is placed behind the job cards for the job in the stack of jobs. For example, jobs 2 and 3 in the illustration read data from cards.

During stacked-job processing, a control program called the *supervisor* (or *monitor*) resides in storage. When a program that is executed comes to an end, it branches to the supervisor program. At this stage, the supervisor could read the job cards for the next program, process them, and load the next program into storage. However, a supervisor program is not usually designed to do all this. Instead, the supervisor loads a *job-control program* into storage. (See Illustration 15-2.) The job-control program reads and processes the job cards for the next program to be executed. When this processing is finished, control passes back to the supervisor program. The supervisor loads the next program, which was identified by the job cards, and branches to it. By using a job-control program, instead of having the supervisor do all of the work, operating-system designers have reduced the number of computer storage locations required for the supervisor. The job-control program occupies main storage only when loaded to read and process job cards.

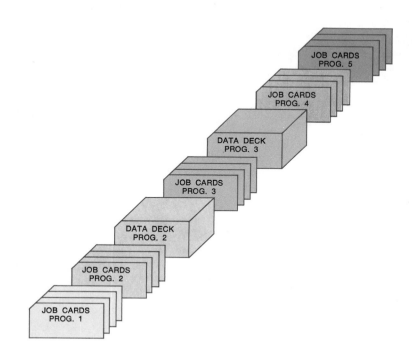

Illustration 15-1. Job cards for a stack of jobs.

The input/output device from which programs are loaded into main storage is often called the *system residence device.* This device must be directly available (online) to the computer at all times. It contains all programs to be run by the computer—both application programs (billing, sales analysis, and so on) and programs that are part of the operating system. Although the system residence device can be a magnetic tape unit, it is more commonly a direct access storage device. Because of its direct access capability, a direct access device eliminates the need to sequentially search for programs as is required when the programs are stored on tape. In addition, a direct access device has a relatively fast transfer speed. Therefore, less time is required to load programs into storage.

To illustrate how stacked-job processing can eliminate idle computer time, consider the execution of six jobs as described in Illustration 15-3. They are to be executed on a system that consists of a CPU, a card reader, a

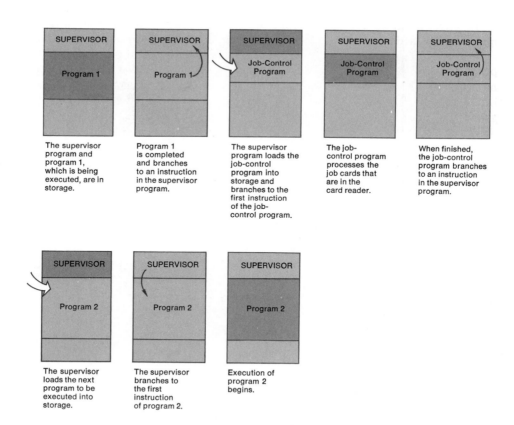

Illustration 15-2. Job-to-job transition using control programs.

card punch, a printer, six tape drives, and two disk drives, one of which is the system residence device. The purpose of scheduling these six jobs is to enable the operator to make ready the input/output devices for one job while another job is running. By so doing, the operator helps make it possible for the computer system to execute all six jobs without stopping.

The operator begins by placing cards for the six jobs in the card reader, mounting a tape on tape drive 1, and starting the computer system. While the first program (a card-to-tape program) is running, the operator mounts tapes on tape drives 2, 3, 4, 5, and 6 in preparation for the second job in the stack. At the end of the first job, the operating system reads program 2 (a sort program) and begins executing it. This program sorts the records originally mounted on tape drive 1, using the five tape drives 2 through 6. During execution of the program, the operator mounts the inventory disk pack on disk drive 2 in preparation for job 3. The computer system can then go to job 3 without having to stop. Continuing in this manner, the computer system can execute all six jobs without stopping.

In some cases, it is impossible to schedule jobs so that the operator can make ready the input/output devices for one job while another job is running. Then the computer system must stop, regardless of stacked-job processing. Similarly, the computer system must stop if an operator mounts the wrong tape on the wrong drive or fails to make ready an input/output device required by a program. In this case, the supervisor generally prints a message to the computer operator indicating which device requires attention. For example, the message

M 182,A12345,PAYROLL

may mean that a reel of tape with the label A12345 is required by the program named PAYROLL, and should be mounted on tape drive 182. As soon as the operator responds to this message, the computer system can resume processing.

The principles of stacked-job processing apply to multiprogramming systems as well as to systems that handle only one job at a time. In a multiprogramming system, however, the supervisor and other control programs of the operating system do more than has been shown so far. For example, various control programs keep track of available storage and determine whether some of the programs in a stack of jobs can be multi-programmed. Then, when programs are run simultaneously, programming routines in the supervisor program handle the switching from one program to another. Because of this operating system help, multiprogramming is less difficult than it would be if each computer user had to control these tasks through user-written programming routines.

In addition to the type of stacked-job processing illustrated thus far, an operating system can do much more. For example, it is possible for one card to indicate to the operating system that it should run a stack of jobs for

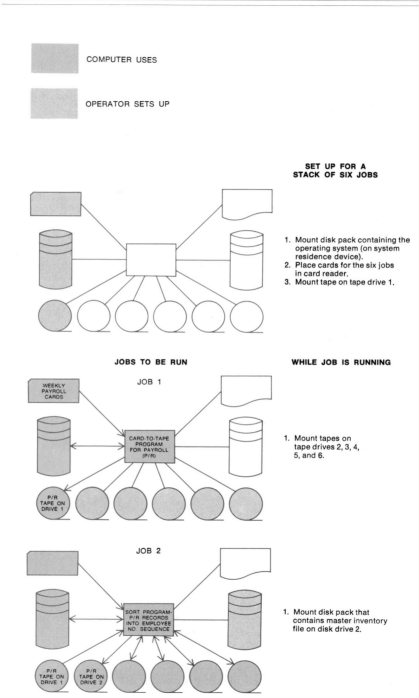

COMPUTER USES

OPERATOR SETS UP

**SET UP FOR A
STACK OF SIX JOBS**

1. Mount disk pack containing the operating system (on system residence device).
2. Place cards for the six jobs in card reader.
3. Mount tape on tape drive 1.

JOBS TO BE RUN

JOB 1

WHILE JOB IS RUNNING

WEEKLY PAYROLL CARDS

CARD-TO-TAPE PROGRAM FOR PAYROLL (P/R)

P/R TAPE ON DRIVE 1

1. Mount tapes on tape drives 2, 3, 4, 5, and 6.

JOB 2

SORT PROGRAM- P/R RECORDS INTO EMPLOYEE NO. SEQUENCE

P/R TAPE ON DRIVE 1

P/R TAPE ON DRIVE 2

1. Mount disk pack that contains master inventory file on disk drive 2.

Illustration 15-3. Six jobs run without operator intervention.

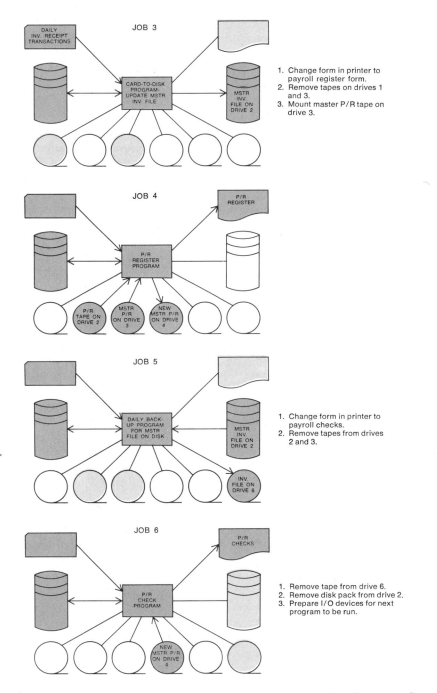

Illustration 15-3. Six jobs run without operator intervention (continued).

which job information is already stored as part of the operating system. This means that the operating system, rather than data processing personnel, can then schedule the jobs. As the programs in the stack are executed, the operating system can print out messages to the operator indicating which input/output devices should be made ready. The result of such an operating system is that the computer does the detailed work of keeping track of which programs are to be run and in what order, and which input and output files are needed.

Regardless of the amount of detail handled by control programs for stacked-job processing, the cost of these programs must be considered. For instance, a system residence device is required. So is enough additional main storage to hold the supervisor program and any other programs or routines that must be resident in main storage. These additional costs must be justified by the increased productivity of the computer system.

AN OPERATING SYSTEM
AND THE PROGRAMMER

The programs and programming routines of an operating system help to reduce the time and expense of programming. In particular, language translators, utility programs, and an Input/Output Control System (IOCS) are stored in a *program library* for general use. Such programs and routines are provided on computer systems without operating systems, but programs are not processed on a stacked-job basis.

Typical *language translators* are assemblers, compilers, and generators. Their value, as discussed in Chapter 13, is in reducing the programming time required to prepare object programs. Some operating systems include many language translators; others have only one assembler and one high-level-language compiler.

Utility programs are generalized programs that perform necessary but routine jobs in an electronic data processing system. A sort program, for example, is a utility program. Sorting is required in most tape systems, and only a few specifications vary from job to job (for instance, record length, location of the field to be sorted on, blocking factor, and number of tape drives to be used). Therefore, one generalized sort program can be used for many sort jobs. To use the sort program, the user supplies coded specifications for the variable factors, or *parameters*. The generalized program is adjusted to deal with them accordingly.

In addition to sort programs, there are several other types of utility programs. Programs that transfer data from one data-recording medium to another are usually utility programs. Examples of these are card-to-tape, card-to-printer, tape-to-printer, and card-to-disk programs. (The use of such programs was introduced in Chapter 7 and mentioned in other chapters.) In addition, some utility programs provide routines for testing programs; others are used to keep programs on the system residence device up-to-date.

An *IOCS* provides the programming for input and output operations, particularly operations involving tape and direct access records. These routines are valuable because input and output routines make up a large portion of a program (commonly as much as 40 percent). One type of input/output routine, for example, checks for tape-reading errors. Such a routine commonly backspaces the tape and attempts to re-read the record when an input error is detected. A typical program may attempt to re-read the record up to 100 times before it gives up and prints an error message indicating that the record cannot be read. This type of error-checking routine must be executed for every program that uses tape input. Besides this type of routine, others are necessary for checking labels on tapes and direct access records, for blocking and deblocking records and, as described in Chapter 14, for keeping track of input/output operations on an overlapped system. When an IOCS is available, the programmer does not need to write programs or routines to do these functions.

To use an IOCS, a programmer must specify, at the start of a program, the characteristics of the files and records that the program uses. Thereafter, the program is coded to accept input records as though they are read from simple sequential files. Whenever a read or write operation is necessary, the programmer codes a one-line macro-instruction (recall Chapter 13). Later, the program is translated into machine language and executed. Dozens of machine-language instructions may be included in the program and executed, in place of each single macro-instruction.

In summary, the language translators, utility programs, and IOCS routines of an operating system are designed to relieve the programmer of common programming chores. This increases the amount of time that the system is available for production by reducing the amount of computer time required for preparing object programs. It allows the programmer to concentrate on applications rather than on programming details.

VIRTUAL STORAGE

Sharing the Internal Storage Unit

Prior to the introduction of the IBM System/370 computer series, programmers generally had to be concerned with internal storage capacity. Each programmer had to make sure that a program and the data for it would fit into the available storage space. If the program was too large, the programmer would segment it. This allowed the first section to be loaded into primary storage and the rest to be kept on secondary storage. After the first section was executed, the second section was written over (overlaid—commonly referred to as overlaying) the first section. Additional sections were processed in a similar manner.

Shortly after the introduction of System/370, in 1971, IBM announced that most System/370 models would have *virtual-storage* (also called *virtual-memory*) capability.

There are two principal methods of implementing virtual-storage capabilities. Generally, both software and hardware are involved. One method is *segmentation,* in which each program's address space (range of storage locations referenced by the program) is split into variable-sized blocks ("segments"). The other method is *paging,* in which physical-memory space is divided into fixed-size physical blocks ("page frames") and programs and data are divided into blocks ("pages") of the same size. Thus, one page of information can be loaded into one page frame.

Segmentation involves breaking a program into logically separable units. For example, one segment may be a subroutine; another may be a data area. An instruction or a data item within the program is identified by a two-part address which specifies the name of a segment and the relative location, or displacement, of the instruction or data item within the segment. The system constructs these addresses and keeps track of the various segments in a *segment table* established for the program in the storage unit. If an executing program tries to refer to a segment that is not in the storage unit, the system intervenes and brings the segment into it (see Illustration 15-4). Burroughs uses the segmentation technique to implement virtual storage operations.

A computer having paging capability is automatically capable of breaking a program into the sequences of instructions called pages. The size of a page may range from that required to store a fairly small number of instructions to that required for a large segment. But all pages in a system are the same size. When a program is to be executed, a single page (or a small number of pages) of that program is brought into the storage unit from the virtual storage area, which is on direct access storage. Pages from several programs can be in the storage unit simultaneously. The computer executes instructions from one program, then from another, and so on (see Illustration 15-5). This ability is especially important if the computer system is operating in a time-sharing mode (about which more is said in Chapter 16).

When a page or segment (depending upon the implementation) not in the storage unit is referenced during program execution, a *missing-item fault* occurs. One method of minimizing the number of faults is by a prepaging or presegmentation technique. When one page or segment is transferred into the storage unit, certain other pages are transferred as well, with the expectation that they are likely to be referenced. Only one *page-in* or *segment-in* operation is needed for the entire group, whereas a separate page-in or segment-in operation would be needed for each referenced page or segment if they were brought in singly. A second method of minimizing the number of faults is by the use of a *demand paging* or *demand segmentation* technique. Each page or segment is loaded into the storage

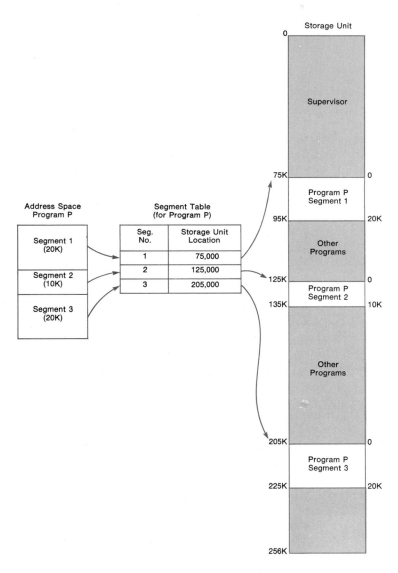

Illustration 15-4. Segmentation.

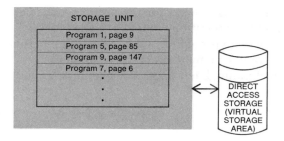

Illustration 15-5. A method for sharing
a storage unit.

unit only when called for as the result of a missing-item fault, and no pages or segments are loaded unless referenced. There may be more page-in or segment-in operations, and the system may operate more slowly because of them, but no pages or segments are brought into the storage unit unnecessarily.

Virtual storage does not provide the user with an actual super-large storage unit. If all of the storage unit is in use when another page or segment is referenced, a replacement operation is necessary. Then, in System/370, for example, the least recently used (LRU) page in the storage unit is replaced. If that page was not modified while occupying the storage unit, it can be overlaid by the needed page, because a copy of the page being replaced exists in the virtual storage area. If the page was modified, however, a *page-out* operation must occur before replacement. This insures that a valid copy of the page will be available on virtual storage the next time it is referenced during program execution.

There is no concise, well-established rule for determining the amount of storage unit space that must be available to support a certain amount of virtual storage space. However, if an executing program is not allocated enough storage unit space, many of the references within it are likely to generate missing-item faults. If a similar situation exists for numerous programs in execution, the system is forced to spend most or all of its time moving pages or segments between virtual storage and the storage unit. This phenomenon is known as *thrashing.* The more thrashing occurs, the more inefficient the execution of programs.

The primary advantage of segmentation, paging, and virtual storage is better utilization of the storage unit. Less space is wasted because no contiguous portion of the storage unit large enough to hold a complete program waiting to be executed is required. The result is that potentially more programs can be executed, which in turn means greater utilization of the CPU and other system components. The greatest disadvantage is increased system overhead—the time it takes to transfer segments or pages from direct access storage and the storage unit space required for the sophisticated software to supervise the segmentation or paging operations.

Sharing the Computer

In either a segmentation or paging system, several programs are in the storage unit at the same time. The computer can be programmed to share processing time among them.That is, multiprogramming can be used.

Either of two methods can be used in deciding when control should be transferred from one program to another in this kind of an environment. One method is to switch control at the end of a very short predetermined period of time, known as a *time slice*. Each program in turn gets its slice of time, if it can use it. This method is very useful for scientific-oriented applications where the time required for any one problem is not known.

An alternative method is to switch control whenever a program currently having control has to wait for an input/output operation to be completed (recall Chapter 14). The program may thus execute and wait many times before its execution is completed. Since business-oriented applications commonly require frequent input/output, and input/output operations are slower than internal processing operations, this method is often used in business data processing.

Summary

1. An operating system is a group of programs designed to increase the productivity of a computer system. Some of the programs of an operating system reduce the amount of idle computer time. Others reduce the amount of programming that must be done by a computer user.

2. The idea behind stacked-job processing is to process many jobs in sequence by letting the computer load and begin execution of programs. This is done by control programs that load programs from a system residence device based on job cards placed in the card reader of the system. By careful scheduling of jobs and processing on a stacked-job basis, the idle computer time between the execution of programs can be reduced or eliminated.

3. The language translators, utility programs, and IOCS routines of an operating system reduce the amount of programming that must be done by a computer user. Because the programmer is relieved of common programming chores, less time and expense are required for programming.

4. To further increase the amount of useful work that can be accomplished by a computer system, virtual-storage capabilities based primarily on segmentation and paging techniques have been developed for current computers.

CHAPTER 16

Introduction to Data Communication

OFFLINE COMMUNICATION SYSTEMS

ONLINE COMMUNICATION SYSTEMS

REALTIME COMMUNICATION SYSTEMS

TIME-SHARING SYSTEMS

DISTRIBUTED SYSTEMS

S ignificant developments in computer hardware and software have reduced the time required for processing data. However, processing is only one part of the data processing cycle. The total cycle consists of data collection, processing, and distribution. It is not surprising, then, that a data processing system may be slow even when the processing portion is fast.

The collection and distribution of business data is often complicated. Many companies have offices in several different locations. Suppose, for example, that a company has five branch sales offices in various cities around the country and a warehouse across town from the home office. Also assume that the branch offices receive customer orders and mail them twice a day to the home office, where they are processed. The resultant shipping orders are printed as output. They are then delivered to the warehouse, where the ordered items are packed for shipping. In this system, the time required for collecting, processing, and distributing the order data may break down like this:

Data Collection
     Waiting for batch of orders in branch office .... 4 hrs.
     Mailing orders to home office .... 24 hrs.
Data Processing
     Keypunching order data .... 4 hrs.
     Processing keypunched order data .... 1 hr.
Data Distribution
     Delivery of shipping orders to warehouse .... 2 hrs.

Data collection and distribution require 30 hours, while processing takes only 5. Even if no time were required for processing, it would still take 30 hours for an order to reach the warehouse.

A *data communication system* is one solution to this problem. It is designed to reduce the time required to collect and distribute data. Specifically, a system with data communication capability provides for the electrical transfer of data from one point in the system to another. (For details, see also Module A.)

Data communication is being used increasingly by organizations. It is estimated that there will be a 1600 percent growth in data communication volume between 1970 and 1980. This is reflected in the fact that approximately 70 percent of the computer systems being installed have data communication capability. It is also estimated that, while there were only 185,000 terminals installed in 1970, by 1980 2-1/2 million terminals will be in use.

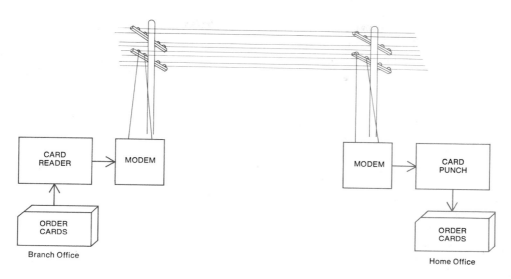

Illustration 16-1. An offline communication system.

Five commonly used types of data communication systems are: (1) off-line systems, (2) online systems, (3) realtime systems, (4) time-sharing systems, and (5) distributed systems. The capabilities available with these systems are described in this chapter.

OFFLINE COMMUNICATION SYSTEMS

Illustration 16-1 is a diagram of a system for transmitting order data from a branch office to the home office of an organization. As orders are received in the branch office, order cards are keypunched and verified. At scheduled times during the day, the data on the cards is read by a card reader, sent over communication lines to the home office, and punched into cards via a card punch. The cards are then transferred manually to a card reader and processed in the home office. This is an example of an offline data communication system.

An offline data communication system requires (1) terminals, (2) communication lines, and (3) modems. *Terminals* are remote devices attached to communication lines to send and/or receive data. The terminals in Illustration 16-1 are devices that read and punch cards, but they could be paper tape readers and punches, magnetic tape units, typewriterlike devices, or visual display devices. The particular device used depends on the volume of data to be transmitted and the speed required of the data communication system. *Communication lines* are commonly telephone or telegraph lines, but they can be other types of lines. These lines can be leased so that the communication system has 100 percent use of them, or they can be used on a dial-up basis, paid for at an hourly rate. Data sets (modulation/demodulation devices; also called modems) are devices that convert data from a data-processing code (in this case, Hollerith code) to one that can be sent over communication lines, and convert the communication code back to a data-processing code. (See also Module A.)

Data is transmitted from one terminal to another in an offline communication system. Transmission can be in either one direction or both directions, depending on the terminals used. Although Illustration 16-1 shows transmission in only one direction, it would be possible (by adding the necessary terminals) to transmit a batch of cards for processing at the home office, and sometime later (after processing) to receive a batch of processed transactions from the home office.

A major value of an offline communication system is that it eliminates delays in transmitting data. In Illustration 16-1, the time for mail delivery is eliminated. However, there are still many delays in the system. For instance, at the branch office there are delays because of waiting for batches to collect, keypunching and verifying, and use of communication lines. At the home office there are delays due to waiting for use of the computer and transferring data manually from the card punch to the card reader attached to the computer. In addition, duplication exists in an offline communication system. In the example, the data that is punched into cards in the branch office is punched again into cards at the home office.

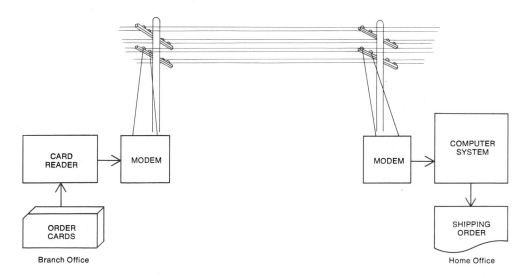

Illustration 16-2. An online communication system.

ONLINE COMMUNICATION SYSTEMS

An online data communication system sends data directly between a terminal and a computer system. Illustration 16-2 represents an online system for processing order data. As in the offline communication system, cards are keypunched and verified in the branch office as orders are received. Then at scheduled times (perhaps twice a day) the data in the accumulated batch of cards is read by a card reader and sent over communication lines to the computer system in the home office. There the data is processed as it is received, under control of the CPU. The result is the same as it would be if the card reader were in the same room as the CPU.

The transmissions of an online communication system (like those of offline) are normally batched, and, depending on the terminals used, can be in one direction or both directions. However, additional equipment is usually required in an online communication system. Some form of secondary storage, such as magnetic tape or magnetic disk, is needed to store the incoming data and the processed results. For example, assume that several branch offices make scheduled transmissions throughout the work day. The transmitted data is stored on magnetic tape by the computer in the home office. Then, one major processing run is made during the evening. The processed results are stored on magnetic tape and then transmitted to each of the appropriate branches in turn in time for the opening of business the following day.

Because data is collected into groups and processed at specific time intervals, this type of system can be called a batch-processing system. The offline system above is also a batch-processing system. In fact, the majority of business data processing takes place in this manner. The disadvantage of using batch processing in a data communication system is that the data files in the system are only as current as the last run to update the files.

The values of the online communication system are the reduction of delays in collecting data at the home office and the elimination of duplication. However, delays at the branch offices, such as waiting for batches to collect and keypunching, still exist. In addition, scheduling the online transmissions of data requires close coordination of the home office and the branch offices. There is often idle computer time. Suppose, for example, that each of five branches is to send data to the home office twice a day. To avoid idle computer time, a branch office must send its data immediately after the preceding branch has finished sending its data. If, when its turn comes, a branch is not ready, idle computer time can result.

REALTIME COMMUNICATION SYSTEMS

A realtime communication system makes possible the elimination of all delays in collecting data and in distributing processed results. It provides immediate two-way communication, processes transactions as they occur, and can respond to unusual processing conditions.

Illustration 16-3 represents the major components of a realtime communication system for processing orders submitted by five branch offices. In this communication system, each branch office has a terminal that can both send and receive data. When it is used to send data, the operator keys the data on the keyboard. The keyed data is either displayed on a screen or printed on paper at the terminal so that the operator can check it. When the terminal is used to receive data, the data is displayed or printed under control of the computer system.

There are two terminals in the warehouse. The first is a visual display device used for communication with the computer system. The second receives data from the computer and is used to print shipping orders. It may be a character-at-a-time printer similar to a typewriter or a high-speed line-at-a-time printer. In the home office, a data set converts the data sent over the communication lines into a data-processing code that can be

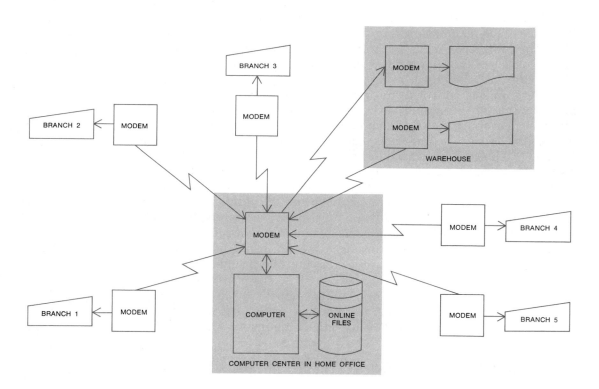

Illustration 16-3. A realtime communication system.

processed by the computer. A magnetic disk contains the inventory and accounts receivable files of the company.

In this type of communication system, when an order is received at a branch office, there is no waiting. The terminal operator keys the order data (customer number, item numbers, and quantities of items ordered) on the terminal. This data is sent over the communication lines to the computer in the home office. The method of verifying the data transmitted depends on the type of terminal and on the program being executed by the computer. After the operator has verified the keyed data by reading it on the screen or the terminal printout, he or she presses a key to indicate to the computer that the data is ready for processing. If the data is not correct, the operator re-keys the data that is in error before signaling to the computer that the data is ready. The computer checks the inventory file on magnetic disk to determine whether the items ordered are in stock. If they are available, the computer sends a response to the branch-office terminal indicating that the order will be filled immediately. If any items are not in stock, the computer supplies the date when the items are likely to be available. Then the branch office can contact the customer (who may be waiting at a phone) to indicate the status of the order. After communicating with the branch office, the computer system processes the order data and prints a shipping order on the terminal in the warehouse.

There are definite advantages to this realtime communication system. The time between receiving an order at a branch office and learning of it at the warehouse is reduced to minutes. In addition, because transactions are processed as they occur, the computer system can respond immediately to unusual situations such as stockouts.

In evaluating a realtime communication system, the additional costs of operating the system must be weighed against the increased value it provides. In general, a realtime communication system necessitates additional equipment, programming, and system design. Among the equipment requirements are communication lines, modems, terminals, and magnetic disk devices.

As a practical consideration, a realtime communication system should have multiprogramming capabilities. (See Chapters 11 and 14.) Consider, for example, that a realtime communication system for order processing must be available throughout the day to process incoming orders. Without multiprogramming capabilities, other processing programs such as payroll and inventory control can be run only on a second shift or by a second computer. Furthermore, although the realtime system must be available continuously, there are times when it is likely to be idle. During the lunch hour, for instance, few orders are apt to be received. Finally, because typewriterlike terminals are slow input devices, thousands of instructions can be executed by the computer system between the periods when any

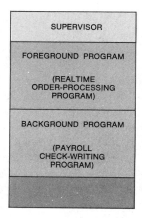

Illustration 16-4. The use of main storage
in a real-time system.

two characters of data are transmitted. Without multiprogramming capabilities, there is no way to use this available computing power (unused
access cycles); hence, it is wasted.

With a large computer system that offers multiprogramming capabilities, the realtime program (in this case, the order-processing program) and
one or more other processing programs can be executed at the same time.
Illustration 16-4, for instance, shows the contents of main storage while a
typical realtime communication system is running. The primary program,
called the *foreground program,* is the realtime program. It has priority over
any other programs in main storage. Whenever data is being sent from a
branch office, this program has control of the computer system. However,
whenever data is not being sent, the secondary program, called the *background program,* is executed. In the illustration, this program is a payroll
check-writing program. To handle the switching back and forth between
the two programs, a supervisor program remains in storage throughout
processing. As in other multiprogramming systems, the CPU executes the
instructions of one of the programs while channels carry out input/output
operations. With the use of multiprogramming, processing programs such
as payroll, inventory-control, and sales analysis can be executed by the
computer system that is available all day for realtime processing.

TIME-SHARING SYSTEMS

Time sharing is a technique that allows several users of a computer
system to use that system on what appears to be a simultaneous basis. Each
user is connected to the system via a terminal and operates independently

of any other user. The time-sharing system gives almost immediate responses to each user; therefore, the users are seldom aware that the system is being shared.

A time-sharing system is generally a multiprogramming system. Several programs are processed concurrently. Typically, a time-slicing algorithm as described at the end of Chapter 15 is set up. Under this approach, each user is allocated a fixed portion of CPU time for processing of his or her program. Because each time slice (*quantum*) is very short, many users can share the system without having to wait for extended periods. As shown in Illustration 16-5, users of one time-sharing system may be inquiring into files, writing computer programs, preparing reports, and entering data from geographically separated terminals at the same time.

An organization may install a time-sharing system on its computer or use time-sharing facilities available for a fee from an external data processing service center. For some organizations, the latter choice may be more

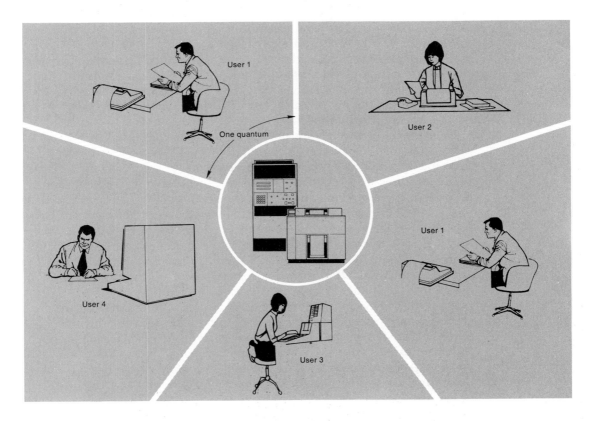

Illustration 16-5. A time-sharing system.

economical than installing a system; a decision favoring one approach or the other must be based on an organization's data processing requirements. The advantage of using an outside service center is that, although certain fixed costs, such as those for acquisition and installation of terminals and communication lines, must be paid by the user, the user is charged for the central processing facilities of the computer system only when they are used to do the user's work. Thus, the user obtains access to a large computer system at a fraction of the cost of installing one internally.

Depending on the data processing requirements of an organization, only one terminal or many may be installed; in the first case, the organization becomes one time-sharing user, together with other organizations using the system. If there is a need for multiple terminals in an organization, such as one for each department, each terminal is, in effect, a time-sharing user.

Various types of time-sharing systems are used in organizations. Some have a series of application programs that can be executed by the user, but not altered; some allow the user to create and use programs; some have one main application and the user merely provides input data for that application; and others are a combination of all of these types with the main application having first priority.

An example of an application that can be executed but not altered is a payroll program for which a clerk enters weekly employee time-card data into a terminal and then requests program execution to print checks. In a second request, the payroll clerk may call for execution of a program to print a weekly payroll report.

An example of a single-purpose system is one that involves teller terminals designed for savings-account applications. When a customer goes into a bank to make a deposit or withdrawal, his or her passbook is placed in the terminal. The keyboard is used to enter such data as the customer account number, amount, and type of transaction. This data is transmitted to the computer, which processes the transaction, computes any accumulated interest, and prints the updated balance in the customer's passbook. Many of these terminals may be online to a computer at the same location or many miles away. Each terminal is operated by a time-sharing user of a realtime communication system designed for the primary purpose of maintaining customer savings accounts.

Time-sharing systems that allow users to create and use their own programs usually provide several programming languages for this purpose. Some of these languages are *interpretive;* that is, they check each program statement as it is entered and point out any errors in the statement. This allows the programmer to edit and debug a program as it is being created. Once the program has been created, it can be executed and/or stored for future use.

One of the most popular time-sharing languages in use today is called BASIC (Beginners' All-purpose Symbolic Instruction Code). As noted in Chapter 12, this language can be learned easily and used to solve many types of business problems. It is usually implemented as an interactive, or conversational, language, which means that it permits interaction between the user at a terminal and the computer during execution of a program.

Illustration 16-6 shows how a BASIC program can be created on a terminal, stored for future use, and then recalled and executed on one kind of time-sharing system. This program computes the compound interest on a user-specified sum of money for a user-specified period of time. The following steps are performed:

1. The user identifies himself or herself to the time-sharing system, giving an account number and a keyword which are automatically typed over to protect the user's account.
2. The program is created and stored under the program name INTEREST.
3. The program is called for, and execution is requested.
4. The program requests the amount of money, interest rate, and time period. After this data is entered, the compound interest is computed and printed.
5. The user signifies the end of processing.

```
                  NAME? martin holland
                  ACCOUNT? ⬛⬛⬛⬛
User              KEYWORD? ⬛⬛⬛
Identification    TERMINAL? p35
                  COMMAND ? clear text
                  COMMAND ? basic
                  :ENTERING STANFORD/BASIC.
                  COMMAND ? collect 10 by 10
                     10.   ? rem computes compound interest on a sum of money for any number years.
                     20.   ? print '   '
                     30.   ? print 'after the # prints, type in input data separated by commas'
                     40.   ? input p , i ,n
                     50.   ? print '  '
                     60.   ? let s = p * ( 1 + 1 ) ** n
                     70.   ? print p 'dollars compounded annually for' n 'years'
Program              80.   ? print 'at' i 'percent interest gives' s 'dollars'
Creation             90.   ? print '  '
                    100.   ? print 'if you wish to try other values type a 1, if not a 9'
                    110.   ? input z
                    120.   ? if z = 9 then 140
                    130.   ? go to 20
                    140.   ? print '******     end of "interest" program      ******'
                    150.   ? print '   '
                    160.   ? end
                    170.   ? ***
Program           #***
Saved             COMMAND ? save interest on sys19
                  "INTEREST" SAVED ON SYS19
Program           COMMAND ? use interest on sys19 clear load
Called            COMMAND ? go

                  AFTER THE # PRINTS, TYPE IN INPUT DATA SEPARATED BY COMMAS
Program           # 1000.00 , .05 , 10
Executed
                    1000 DOLLARS COMPOUNDED ANNUALLY FOR 10 YEARS
                  AT .05 PERCENT INTEREST GIVES 1628.877 DOLLARS
Program
Terminated        9
```

Illustration 16-6. A BASIC program.

DISTRIBUTED SYSTEMS

When several geographically *dispersed,* or *distributed,* computers are connected in a communication network, the term *time-sharing system* is no longer appropriate. The term *distributed system* (network) is used to describe this kind of an environment. A distributed system is like a time-sharing system in that it can be used within a single organization or by several organizations. In either situation, there is a decentralization of processing activity within the framework of a network with system-wide rules. A hierarchy of computers allows much processing and storing of data to be done at or near the origin of the data to be processed. But the important advantages of large, centralized computer systems, such as organization-wide access to basic operational data, are present as well.

The lowest level of processors in a distributed system includes mini-computers or small computers. They have some local data storage and perform local processing. Tasks that are too large or that require data not available in local files are transmitted to a higher-level regional or centralized computer. The highest level in the hierarchy of computers has the capability to process large-scale problems.

Illustration 16-7 shows a basic distributed system. All terminals are interfaced with a smaller computer, which, in turn, is directly linked to a large computer. Additional devices can be linked to the smaller computer to permit data retrieval from files on secondary storage when needed. Such a system can be (and usually is) a realtime system. This capability depends on the availability of direct access storage devices.

As shown in Illustration 16-8, more than one smaller computer can be attached to one large computer. For example, a state university system

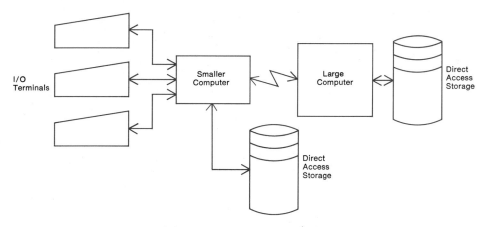

Illustration 16-7. A basic distributed system.

may have a smaller computer at each campus which can be either used alone or linked with a large central computer to operate as part of a distributed system.

System design and programming costs are relatively high for a distributed system because of the greater complexity of the system. A system like the one in Illustration 16-7 or 16-8 requires a complex routine to determine which communication line to process next and how to handle input when several terminals are ready to send data simultaneously. In designing such a system, the systems analyst must determine such things as the maximum number of terminals that the computer system can handle at one time, and the probability that all remote locations will want to send data at the same time. The systems analyst must evaluate the possibility of system overload and provide for any conditions that may occur. In addi-

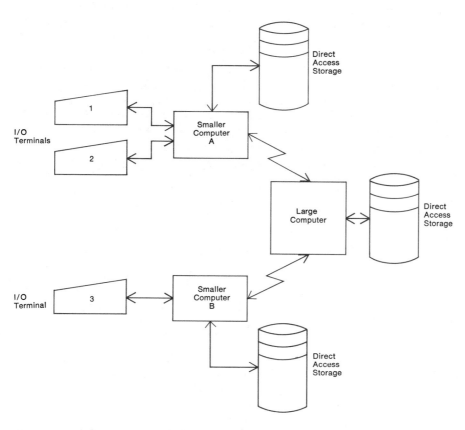

Illustration 16-8. A distributed system with two smaller computers.

tion, the systems analyst must provide an alternative method of handling input that can be used when the computer system is not working because of mechanical failure.

Assume Illustration 16-7 shows an order-processing system. Offsetting the costs of the system are benefits such as improved customer service. In addition to faster order processing, this type of system makes other types of customer service possible—specifically, quick and accurate responses to inquiries. Suppose, for example, that the system were also used for answering accounts receivable inquiries against a master file accessible to the large computer. In this case, a terminal user could key in the customer's account number and transmit it to the large computer. That computer could access the customer's accounts receivable record and send a response back to the terminal. The terminal user could quickly answer the customer's inquiry with up-to-date information.

A distributed system can also make greater management effectiveness possible through updated management information. For example, consider how a distributed system can be used for inventory control. A terminal in each warehouse is used to record receipts of items into inventory. The inventory file on magnetic disk always represents the current inventory balances in the warehouse, not the balances as they were at some time in the past. When an inventory balance falls below its reorder point, a warning is printed out on a terminal in the inventory-control department. Thus, inventory-control personnel know about exceptional conditions when they happen—that is, in realtime. Similarly, distributed systems can be used to provide current information for sales management, production-control management, and any other area of operation where the value of the information justifies its cost.

Summary

1. Processing is only one part of the data processing cycle. The other parts, collecting and distributing data, may be far more time-consuming. Data communication systems are designed to reduce the time required for the collection and distribution of data.

2. Offline data communication requires terminals, communication lines, and data sets. Batches of data are sent from one terminal to another. The electrical transfer of data eliminates the delay of mailing, but does not reduce delays involved in collecting and distributing data.

3. Online data communication is direct transmission of data to the computer system. Such transfer of data reduces some communication delay, because the data is processed directly by the computer as it is received. Scheduling the online transmissions requires close coordination of branch offices with the home office.

4. Realtime systems process transactions as they occur and respond to conditions as they develop with immediate two-way communication. In addition to terminals, communication lines, and data sets, realtime systems require direct access storage devices. For practical reasons, they should have multiprogramming capabilities.

5. Time sharing is a technique that permits several users to share a computer system on what seems to be a simultaneous basis. Each user is connected to the system via a terminal and is allocated a portion of CPU time. Access to a time-sharing system can be on a fee basis through a data processing service center or on a system within the organization.

6. The term *distributed system* (network) is used to describe several geographically dispersed, or distributed, computers connected in a communication network. Besides equipment costs, programming and system design costs are relatively high for such a system. These costs are offset by the value of the information it provides.

CAREER PROFILE

Sherrill Overfield

Chairperson, Data Base
Administration Committee

TRW, DSSG

Background Experience

I graduated with a degree in mathematics from Northern Illinois University and taught school for two years. I wanted, however, to do something else so I applied for programming jobs and was hired by IBM. When I moved to California after a year, I was hired by TRW. They wanted to do their own in-house training, and I had the qualifications they wanted: I could teach and I could understand programming. TRW was involved with IBM's Information Management System (IMS) which was new at the time. In 1970 I took a class in IMS in order to teach our programmers. When my manager took over the entire IMS support effort, I began doing the actual SYSGENing of IMS. We divided into two groups, and I was part of the data base administration support area. During this time I designed some data bases for our education program called skills-base, which are still in use. In 1972 I was appointed coordinator of a new committee made up of a data base administrator (DBA) from each application area. We functioned as an ad hoc committee working on implementing a data base administration concept, setting standards—good ways to recover, solving IMS implementation and application problems, and developing a data dictionary. In 1974, we were given official sanction as a committee reporting to the managers who report to our Vice President.

Primary Job Responsibilities

At TRW, we have two separate programming divisions to support business data processing. One deals with systems programming (implementing operating systems, IMS, hardware, and software). The second is responsible for all application programming. Within this division are all the application programmers

for financial and administrative systems including payroll, accounts payable/receivable. Other areas have responsibility for project management, product systems, and engineering and data systems. Each of these groups has its own DBA. Supporting these areas is my group, Computer Technology. Our primary responsibility is to communicate and interface between the Systems Division (the implementers) and the Applications Division (the programmers). We provide the answers to technical questions related to IMS, the operating system, and programming language. I also am continuing my responsibilities as chairperson of the DBA Committee. A typical day is spent principally in advising, consulting, and teaching. People come to me, for example, with a data base design and ask if it's going to work. I also study and research new developments. We're currently working on our next IMS implementation, so I'm planning the best ways of presenting it to the application areas. Unrelated to IMS, I have responsibilities in entry-level programming training.

What Has Made You Successful?

First, that I had to learn IMS well enough to teach it. Once you've learned how to access an IMS data base, or perhaps any other data base system, designing the call access strategy is going to be the same, no matter what kind of data base you are accessing. Second, the contacts I have had with other IMS users, particularly a group in the Los Angeles area that meets each month. Third, keeping current on data base subjects through journal reading and audio-visual courses, and IMS courses put out by vendors. Perhaps the thing that has contributed most to my success is that I enjoy working with people.

Data Processing Management and the Computer Industry

CHAPTER 17

The Business Organization and the Data Processing Department

THE APPLICATION OF COMPUTERS IN
BUSINESS ORGANIZATIONS

THE SELECTION AND INSTALLATION OF
A COMPUTER SYSTEM
The Cost of the System
The Time Required for Installation
General Practices

THE CONTROL OF A DATA PROCESSING SYSTEM
Top Management Control
Data Processing Department Management Control
Controls during the Processing of Data
The Evaluation of Error Controls

FRAUD

PHYSICAL SECURITY

THE DATA PROCESSING DEPARTMENT
Job Descriptions
The Separation of Functions
The Location of the Data Processing Department
within the Organization

The discussions thus far in this text have centered primarily around the hardware and software characteristics of data processing. An underlying assumption of these discussions has been that the hardware and software are located within the organization.

The discussion within this chapter centers around the decisions to obtain the hardware and software, where they will be located within the organization, and the qualifications that people who are going to work in the data processing department should have.

THE APPLICATION OF COMPUTERS IN BUSINESS ORGANIZATIONS

There are four basic ways in which computers are being used in business organizations to assist management in the accomplishment of organizational objectives. The first way is to print information required to instruct employees concerning how to perform various activities in accordance with the policies of the organization. Thus, computers alleviate a portion of the paperwork that otherwise must be done manually.

A second way in which computers are used in business organizations is to make routine management decisions. For example, a computer can be programmed to detect when the stock quantity of an inventory item is reduced via sales to a predetermined reorder level. It can be directed to print the information necessary to order a certain quantity of the particular inventory item when such a situation occurs.

A third way in which computers are used in business organizations is to provide progress reports with respect to the performance of particular activities. Up-to-date progress reports provide management with the information needed to control the performance of the particular activities.

A final way in which computers are used in business organizations is to provide information about a particular topic in response to management requests for the information. This is the most important way in which computers can be used because a manager is provided the information needed to make correct and timely decisions. This information could be stored in file cabinets, but then it would have to be updated manually. Also, a manual record of what was where would have to be maintained. If a great quantity of information had to be stored, many file cabinets and a large amount of storage space would be required.

THE SELECTION AND INSTALLATION OF A COMPUTER SYSTEM

The fundamental criterion for deciding whether or not to install a computer system in a business organization is whether or not the system will help to increase profits. For a nonprofit or governmental organization, the criterion is whether or not the computer will result in either reduced operating costs and/or significantly improved ability to provide service to customers, clients, or the public.

The installation of a computer system is a major capital expenditure. It requires a substantial initial outlay of resources. It also changes the procedures for processing data. It may alter the operations and management structure of the organization. Obviously, a decision to install a computer system is an expensive and important one; such a commitment should be made only after careful analysis. Consideration of at least the factors discussed below is mandatory.

The Cost of the System

The basic cost considerations involved in acquiring a computer system can be compared to those involved in acquiring an automobile. The initial consideration is whether to purchase or lease the computer system. Most computer systems are leased because this approach provides flexibility with respect to making changes in the computer system (see "Computer Manufacturers" and "Leasing Companies" in Chapter 18).

Most leasing contracts include a provision for regular maintenance. If the computer system is purchased, its maintenance must be performed by specially trained personnel within the data processing department. Alternatively, a contract must be signed with an organization that can provide maintenance. Since maintenance on a computer system is needed only periodically, it is usually less costly to sign a maintenance contract with another organization than to hire maintenance personnel. However, an overriding consideration is how long it will take the maintenance personnel to respond to a maintenance problem. The direct and indirect costs to the organization resulting from the computer system being inoperable ("down") throughout this period of time must be evaluated.

Also, similar to an automobile, the value of a computer system depreciates over time. By leasing the system, the organization avoids assuming the risk of obsolescence. A computer usually becomes *functionally obsolete* before it becomes *operationally obsolete*. That is, since a computer has no moving parts, its "wear-and-tear" is nominal; it need not be traded because of hard use. A computer system becomes unable to perform the type or volume of data processing activity required of it before it becomes unable to actually operate as it was built to operate.

Finally, when acquiring an automobile, any options, such as air conditioning and stereo-radio, are extra-cost items. Their cost is added to the basic cost of the automobile. A similar situation is true when acquiring a computer system. Every equipment component is separately priced, and many desirable features are extra-cost options. Therefore, a basic computer system (with or without various options) can be acquired for any of several prices.

Fortunately, the cost of computer system equipment has been steadily declining since the introduction of computers. Looking at it from another perspective, there have been major improvements in the performance of computer system equipment; more computing power can be acquired without a corresponding increase in cost.

The Time Required for Installation

Complete installation of a computer system requires many months of preparation. As a rough guide, installing a batch-oriented data processing system requires from 12 to 24 months. That is, after the decision is made to investigate the feasibility of installing a computer system, from one to two years may be required to reach the point where the system is satisfactorily processing business data. In some cases, the total elapsed time can be reduced by performing some tasks simultaneously rather than one after another. Even so, a year of selection and preparation activity is probably a minimum. For an inexperienced organization, two years is more reasonable. Adequate planning and preparation time for the final selection and installation of equipment ranges from 8 to 15 months. The time needed depends on the computer installation experience of the organization, the complexity of the system, and related factors. A complex realtime system requires two to three years for the steps from initial investigation to successful operation.

General Practices

While many computer systems in current use are successfully performing data processing activities, others are fraught with problems. The problems are rarely caused by incorrectly functioning equipment. They may be caused by the failure of certain software and/or user programs to correctly instruct the computer. However, the problems are usually caused by the failure of responsible personnel to adhere to one or more of the following general practices during selection and installation: (1) enlist top management's participation and support, (2) develop adequate plans and controls, and (3) consider possible employee problems and take steps to prevent such problems from arising.

Top management's participation and support in the selection and installation of a computer system is a necessary condition for success. Since the installation of a computer system can be disruptive to the organization, the entire organization must understand that top management is solidly behind the new system. Lower levels of management tend to support what is clearly supported by top management.

The installation of a computer system extends over a long period of time. If the installation is not properly planned and controlled, the activities involved in installing the system will not be completed on time. Furthermore, the components of the system will not mesh correctly.

Finally, employees who have not been informed as to the objectives and purposes of installing a computer tend to oppose the computer. The computer system should be installed with due regard for its impact on people in the organization and on organizational operations. Special precautions should be taken to guard against disruptions of operations during installation of the system. The specific process of evaluating a computer system, selecting equipment, and installing the system must be tailored to fit the characteristics of the organization. It is imperative that management consider possible employee problems as a result of the installation of a computer. It is wise to develop and implement a plan of action to solve these problems before they occur.

THE CONTROL OF A DATA PROCESSING SYSTEM

The processing of data is too often carried out with a higher error rate than is desirable because top management does not require that the proper level of error control be exercised. The proper level of control cannot be established or maintained without cost. The manager who understands the problems, methods, and procedures involved in achieving control is able to evaluate the expected results of maintaining it compared to its cost. While there are some control problems in computer data processing that are not found in manual data processing, there are also unique, new control methods and procedures available to the manager because of the capabilities of the computer.

Top Management Control

Within an organization there exists a hierarchy of control of a data processing system. The highest level of control is exercised by the top management and procedures of the organization. Thus, top management has the overall responsibility for the efficient and effective operation of the data processing system. This responsibility should be exercised over the activities involved in four data-processing-related areas. These are:

- *The authorization of major changes in the data processing system.* Top management is responsible for evaluating proposals concerning major changes in the data processing system in terms of costs and benefits. An improved or new data processing system is similar to a large expenditure for an addition to a plant or for equipment; any·proposal for a major change should receive careful scrutiny before resources are committed to the project. The work of the data processing department affects the nature and extent to which other departments must process data. It also affects the information available to them. Top management's understanding and evaluation of any proposed change are necessary for adequate control of the data processing activity. A requirement for top management approval forces data processing management to do adequate preplanning.

- *The post-installation review of the actual cost and effectiveness of the data processing system.* There is a tendency among data processing personnel to underestimate the cost and difficulty of implementing a new or improved data processing system. Top management should follow up on proposals involving changes in the data processing system; they should evaluate the reasons for any deviations from planned cost, planned schedule, and estimated benefit. The assessment of performance resulting from the post-installation review should aid management in evaluating future requests for changes in the system.

- *The review of the organization of the data processing department and the various methods and techniques used to control the data processing activity.* Top management has the responsibility for insuring that competent, adequately trained management personnel are employed within the data processing department. The organization and control practices of the data processing activity should be subject to top management review.

- *The monitoring of the performance of the data processing activity.* Finally, top management is responsible for monitoring the performance of the data processing department and reporting any deviations from expected levels of performance. The monitoring should be guided by established performance standards and reporting procedures. Three areas of performance should be monitored: (1) the cost of data processing activities compared to their expected cost, (2) the frequency and length of delays in meeting processing schedules, and (3) the number of errors detected at various control points.

Data Processing Department Management Control

Below top management, the next level of responsibility for control of the data processing system lies with the manager of the data processing department. Specifically, the data processing manager is responsible for the day-to-day control of activities performed within the department. An inadequate level of control of the data processing system is an indication of a weakness at this level of management.

Although a separation of functions is not always economically feasible in small and medium-size data processing departments, a fundamental aspect of control is to have each of the various data processing functions (duties) performed by a different person within the department. This separation acts as a guard against the possibility of individual incompetence and/or fraud.

Basically, two types of control should be provided for and exercised concerning the data processing activity: (1) *internal data processing control*, which is exercised by the data processing department, and (2) *external data processing control*, which is exercised by one or more individuals independent of the data processing department.

Internal data processing control is concerned with insuring that the processing of data is performed correctly and that no data is lost or mishandled within the department. For example, consider an accounts receivable application. At scheduled intervals, the accounts receivable transactions are processed against the current accounts receivable master file to produce an updated accounts receivable master file. The monetary sum of the transaction records and the prior balances of all master records should equal the total of the new balances of all records on the updated master file.

The external data processing control function can be exercised in several ways. For example, a department that uses the computer, such as the accounting department, can compare manually calculated totals in one or more of the accounting-related files with corresponding totals calculated by the computer. This *balancing to control totals* is an important technique for insuring the accuracy of a data processing system.

Controls during the Processing of Data

The use of a computer system requires new controls for detecting and controlling errors that arise during the use of such a system. Examples of the types of controls required are:

1. Verification procedures to check the conversion of source data into machine-readable form
2. Control totals to detect any loss of data or failure to process data items
3. Computer programs and manual procedures to guard against the misuse of files stored on machine-readable media such as disk and tape
4. Hardware features to detect hardware malfunctions
5. Computer program checks to guard against errors by the operator

In a manual system, internal control relies upon such factors as human alertness and judgment, care, acceptance of responsibility, and division of duties. After the data processing activity is computerized, many controls based on such factors are no longer available. However, a computer program can be an effective substitute for many human controls. For example, in a manual system, a clerk detects an error when an item on a shipping document is not on the applicable price list. In a computer operation, the possibility of a nonmatch such as this must be provided for in the computer program. Once programmed, the nonmatch routine will be executed faithfully by the computer. In most instances, computer checks can be more extensive than those performed manually.

The Evaluation of Error Controls

There are error control procedures to prevent or detect almost any type of error. Despite the availability of these procedures, however, an error such as preparing and distributing a weekly payroll check for $1000 instead of $100 still occurs. In such instances, fundamental controls are not being exercised.

Error controls, like all other controls, require an expenditure of resources. For example, programmed error controls (programmed controls, for short) take up valuable storage positions. These controls need to be part of the data processing system, but there is an associated storage cost.

Before implementing a programmed control of a particular error, the merits of the control should be evaluated. The following questions should be asked:

1. How frequently might the error occur?
2. What are the monetary and nonmonetary consequences of not detecting the error?
3. What is the cost of detecting the error?
4. If the error is missed at this point in the data processing system, will it be detected at a later point?
5. What are the consequences of detecting the error at a later point in the data processing system?

Error controls must also be established to guard against the possibility of human errors. These controls are needed throughout the preparation of a program and the data it is to process, the processing of the data, and the distribution of the results. In fact, the necessity for, and the effectiveness of, specific controls cannot be viewed in isolation. Rather, all of the internal and external data processing controls applicable to a particular application must be considered. The organizational and management environment in which they are applied must be evaluated. All of these factors, in combination, determine the quality of the control exercised over and during the processing of data.

FRAUD

In addition to control procedures that insure the accuracy of processed data, control procedures must be established to safeguard the data against *fraud*—the manipulation of data for unfair or unlawful purposes. The protection of data against fraud is related to the protection of data for accuracy. Procedures can be set up with this goal in mind.

First, a duplicate copy of all data sent to the data processing department should be kept by the individual sending the data. The copy should be retained a specified, appropriate period of time—at least, until after the data is known to have been processed successfully.

Second, any changes or errors in the data or in the program that processes the data should be reported directly to the data processing manager. In addition, for certain types of changes to data, advance approval from the data processing manager should be required.

Third, in a centralized organizational structure, the data processing department can be isolated so that it will not be directly subjected to undue pressure from a powerful or large user who wishes to make improper program runs. Any request for processing, especially one concerning funds or supplies, should be stated in writing and signed by an authorized manager. Unfortunately, small organizations cannot make effective use of this procedure.

PHYSICAL SECURITY

Finally, control procedures against the unauthorized use of data must be developed. The data processing department handles various types of information, some of which is vital to the survival of the organization. One way to control confidential output is to retain it on a tape or disk and to keep the tape or disk in a safe until a printout is needed. This method protects the output against fire, theft, or easy access for duplication. If necessary, similar procedures can be established for programs and data files. Access to the safe should be authorized only by the data processing manager.

To minimize accidental loss of data during processing, several control steps can be taken:

1. Files should be clearly labeled to identify their contents.
2. In the case of tape storage, the file protect ring should be removed from the tape reel. This helps to prevent the accidental writing of data on the tape when the reel is mounted on a magnetic tape unit.
3. Duplicate (backup) copies of programs and data files should be preserved a specified period of time for reference or substitution in case original files are lost or destroyed.

4. Insurance against fire or loss of replaceable equipment and supplies, as well as fidelity insurance to protect the organization from employees' dishonesty, should be obtained. Although the number of losses resulting from dishonest employees is not large, the concentration of a large amount of vital data under the jurisdiction of relatively few persons makes fidelity insurance necessary.

THE DATA PROCESSING DEPARTMENT

The data processing department is an important department within an organization for two basic reasons: (1) the expense involved in maintaining the components of the computer system, and (2) the role of the department as a service department with respect to the receiving, processing, and storing of data, and the distribution of results to management or other individuals or groups. If this function is not performed correctly, the activities of the organization may be impaired seriously.

A data processing department should be managed according to the same basic management principles as other departments within the organization. There are, however, several organizational features and operating procedures that are unique to the data processing department.

Job Descriptions

A job description gives the title of the position being described and outlines the functions that should be performed by an individual holding that position. Such a description should be prepared for each position within the data processing department. The number and types of positions vary somewhat among data processing departments, but the following general job descriptions cover the most common ones.

Data processing manager.   The manager of a data processing department is responsible for the overall planning, organizing, staffing, directing, and controlling of the data processing activity. Thus, the data processing department manager should possess the same basic managerial skills as the managers of other departments within the organization.

Many persons now holding positions in data processing management have been promoted from within their departments, after having acquired the necessary background and experience. However, an increasing number of organizations are recruiting college graduates who are not presently members of their organizations for this position. Anyone who desires a career as the manager of a data processing department should complete the requirements for a college degree. In many instances, a master's or Ph.D. degree is generally required. The type of college degree needed for this position is somewhat dependent upon the nature of the data processing performed by the department. A business administration degree with a primary concentration in data processing and some practical experience is appropriate for a manager of a business-oriented data processing department. A scientific, mathematics, or statistics degree with a minor concentration in computer science and some practical experience is appropriate for a manager of a scientific-oriented data processing department.

As the number of data processing personnel and the magnitude of the data processing activity increase, it becomes necessary for a data processing manager to have one or more assistants. Some of the more common assistant supervisory positions are:

- The manager of systems and procedures, in charge of all system analysis and the maintenance of the program library
- The manager of programming, in charge of all programming, debugging, testing, and maintenance
- The manager of operations, in charge of all activities concerned with the use of equipment and the scheduling of data processing jobs

Systems analyst.   When a decision is made to computerize a business data processing function (say, the preparation of an organization's payroll), the programmer(s) responsible for coding the programs within the system must be given certain information. Providing the information is a responsibility of the systems analyst. The systems analyst evaluates the present system, determines the information required from the system, and designs data processing procedures for providing that information. Then the analyst outlines the system and prepares system specifications to guide the programmer(s) in writing the programs required.

The type of educational background that a systems analyst should possess is somewhat dependent on whether the analyst works within a business-oriented or scientific-oriented data processing department. The kinds of system studies to be performed also affect this consideration. In general, however, a college graduate with a background of management, computer science, and mathematics should find excellent opportunities for employment and advancement as a systems analyst.

Data base administrator.   The data base administrator (DBA) is primarily a manager. A person in this position should have a good foundation in data processing and in the business of the organization, but a technical background equivalent to that of a computer specialist is not required. That is, the DBA must have the technical background needed to make management decisions. Other personnel within the data processing department can be expected to have the practical experience needed to implement them.

The DBA must manage the DBA staff to insure orderly development of data base projects, to satisfy data base users, and to plan for future data base requirements. The DBA must plan and budget the staff and available data base resources. As conflicts arise, these resources must be reallocated to achieve maximum organizational benefits. Finally, the DBA is responsible to upper management for data base projects. Periodic reporting and negotiation for resources to accomplish present and planned activities are a part of this responsibility.

A college graduate with a background in management and in data processing is a potential candidate for this position. Since many organizations are just beginning to take advantage of data base technology, and the position of data base administrator is a relatively new one, there are numerous opportunities for qualified individuals.

Programmer. A programmer prepares a program flowchart for each computer program required in the system designed by the systems analyst. The programmer codes the logic of the program flowchart in the appropriate language, debugs and tests the program, and provides any additional program documentation required.

Programming requires a logical mind, an attention to detail, an ability to determine the procedure required to solve a problem, and a knowledge of the computer language used to code the program.

Some sophisticated, highly specialized, business-oriented or scientific-oriented applications require a formal educational background in a particular area. Generally, however, a four-year college degree is not required to obtain a good programming job. Anyone who desires to work as a programmer in a business-oriented data processing department should obtain some formal education that emphasizes appropriate business administration courses; accounting, mathematics, and statistics courses are desirable. Anyone who desires to work as a programmer in a scientific-oriented data processing department should obtain some formal education emphasizing computer science and mathematics courses. All programmers should have some college-level education, if possible, because (1) some employers use the attainment of, or failure to attain, a college degree as the major basis for considering (or not considering) programming applicants, and (2) a general educational background assists programmers in understanding the structure and activities performed by an organization.

Operations librarian. An operations librarian controls, stores, and issues data files, programs, and operating procedures for computer processing according to schedule or need. A person in this position also maintains records of the files stored on tape and/or disk in the library for subsequent processing or historical purposes. The librarian transfers backup files to, and retrieves them from, alternate storage site(s). Finally, the librarian is responsible for the file purging system and controls the periodic cleaning and conditioning of magnetic tapes and, as required, disk packs.

Anyone who desires to work as an operations librarian should have at least a high school diploma and be familiar with basic data processing concepts. In addition, it is desirable that the individual have high-level clerical aptitudes, particularly, in recordkeeping and coding skills.

Computer operator. A computer operator operates the computer according to the general operating procedures of the department and any particular operating procedures required for successful execution of individual programs. The operator must be alert to detect any operational problems that arise during the processing of a program and take appropriate action accordingly.

A person desiring to be a computer operator should have at least a high school diploma. Formal training can be obtained through a private business or technical school, a community or junior college, or, in some instances, a high school. A basic part of any formal training should be on-the-job experience.

Keypunch or key-entry device operator. A keypunch or key-entry device operator prepares data for entry into a computer by transcribing the data from source documents to either punched cards or magnetic disk or magnetic tape. Keypunching requires a high level of manual dexterity, alertness, and practical thinking. Formal keypunch training can be obtained through a private business or technical school, a community or junior college, or, in some instances, a high school.

The Separation of Functions

As the job descriptions above indicate, at least seven unique job categories exist within data processing departments. A point made earlier is that the functions within these jobs should be performed by different individuals. Although a complete separation of functions is not economically feasible in many small and medium-size data processing departments, the systems analyst, programmer, and computer operator should be different persons. If all three positions cannot be held by different persons, it is especially important that at least the systems analyst and the programmer be different persons. This separation of functions has one advantage mentioned earlier: The possibilities of incorrect processing of data and/or fraud are reduced. Another advantage is that operational efficiency within the department is increased since the functions require different levels of training and skill.

The Location of the Data Processing Department within the Organization

The data processing department may be located in any of several places within the organization. The most common approach is to have the manager of the data processing department report to the chief financial or accounting officer, say, the vice president of finance, the treasurer, or the controller. There is a growing tendency to move the manager of the data processing department to a higher position in the organization. In cases where the department is a service center for many departments, the possibility of conflict over the scheduling of the computer and the design of common files requires that the data processing manager be on the same organizational level as the managers of the departments being served.

Summary

1. There are many applications of computers in a business organization. Generally, they can be grouped into four categories. First, the computer is used to instruct employees and reduce the amount of paperwork required. Second, the computer is used to make routine management decisions. Third, it is used to produce progress reports. Finally, it provides information concerning a particular topic in response to management requests for the information.

2. Some of the considerations for the selection and installation of a computer system include the cost of the machine plus any options that are deemed important, the time required to install the system, and other general practices such as enlisting top management's support, developing adequate plans and controls, and anticipating possible employee problems.

3. The overall responsibility for the control of the data processing department belongs to top management. They are responsible for authorization of major changes, review of cost and effectiveness, review of the organization of the data processing department and the techniques used to control the data processing activity, and monitoring the performance of the data processing activity.

4. Control during the processing of data is an important phase of any data processing activity. This may include verification procedures to check the conversion of source data into machine-readable form, control totals to detect any loss of data or failure to process data items, computer programs and manual procedures to guard against misuse of files, hardware error detection features, and checks to guard against operator errors.

5. Some levels of error control, though possible, may not be feasible in a system. Some considerations when determining feasibility are: how frequently the error occurs, the monetary and nonmonetary consequences of not detecting the error, the cost of detecting the error, the probability of detecting the error at a later point in processing, and the consequences of detecting the error at a later point.

6. Data processing department control procedures must be established to safeguard data against fraud—the manipulation of data for unfair or unlawful purposes. In addition, the physical security of data must be established by developing control procedures to prevent its unauthorized use.

7. The data processing manager has responsibility for the overall control of activities within the data processing department. Other positions within the data processing department exert varying degrees of control over the functioning of the department. Some of the positions which are subordinate to the data processing manager are the systems and procedures manager, the programming manager, the operations manager, the systems analyst, the data base administrator, the programmer, the operations librarian, the computer operator, and the keypunch or key-entry device operator. Each of these individuals is concerned with a given aspect of the overall performance of the data processing department and tends to exercise control over a corresponding sphere of interest.

CAREER PROFILE

Ronald Clemens
Applications Manager

Stanford Center for Information Processing
Stanford University

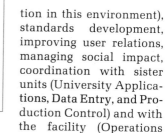

Background Experience

I graduated from Bucknell University in 1958 with a BA in English literature. In the Army, I spent six months as a programmer on a classified crypto-graphic/communications project. Later I worked as a programmer for TWA in a group which developed an online passenger reservation system. Five years followed as a systems engineer and programmer for IBM. This period, during which I worked on a variety of projects, including the creation of operating systems software, simulation, and doing support for systems engineers in the field, was very good career development. I next looked at health care and was hired as systems analyst for Columbia Presbyterian Medical Center. I designed an online patient information system and managed six programmers through the project. This experience laid the groundwork for my work here at Stanford which I have enjoyed for the last four years.

Primary Job Responsibilities

Stanford Center for Information Processing (SCIP) is a department of the university that provides services to a number of Stanford communities. Within SCIP, I manage a small computing group (sixteen applications pro-grammers/analysts and two administrative assistants) with the job of providing effective data processing to Stanford University Hospital. Our involvement is primarily with finan-cial applications—patient accounting and general accounting. We also give administra-tive support to specialized departments in the hospital such as Medical Records. My major concern is with the performance of our appli-cations group. My tasks are those normally found in a technical management position: planning, communication, resource alloca-tion, recruiting, hiring, maintaining training and motivating personnel, budgeting and tracking expense, marketing (a reduced func-tion in this environment), standards development, improving user relations, managing social impact, coordination with sister units (University Applica-tions, Data Entry, and Pro-duction Control) and with the facility (Operations and Systems Programming), and performing staff work in support of my management and department. The main aspect of my work is people—in my own group and in the user area. In a typical day I handle perhaps half a dozen phone calls from users who report, for ex-ample, that something hasn't gone quite right, that something has gone well, or that some-thing has gone differently. I keep in touch with production services throughout the day and through the evening sometimes to check that our production work is going well. I might talk to three or four of my people to check where they are on something or to give them direction and certainly to take an interest in their work and to learn from them. Apart from that, there are meetings inside SCIP, with users, or at the department head level in the hospital.

What Has Made You Successful?

Stanford University offers courses covering general skills such as time management and particularized courses for supervisors and managers. I have taken some of these courses and also computing classes geared to our own facility through SCIP. I work in a group of highly motivated and skilled individuals and learn from them every day. Nearly everything I learn from interpersonal relations has ap-plication in my work. The skill I never learned in school and have learned as a worker is working in a group. Most of our successes come from group efforts. Social change inter-ests me. I find that I can make it happen where I work and that it is accepted—often valued—by my employer. Success for me means, above all, being myself.

Social Implications of the Computer

INFORMATION PROCESSING

DECISION MAKING

AUTOMATION

INDIVIDUALITY AND THE COMPUTER

PRIVACY AND THE COMPUTER

THE CONTROL OF COMPUTER SYSTEMS

THE FUTURE

Today we are facing a revolution—the computer revolution, fostered by the emergence of the computer as one of the most significant inventions of this century. With the Industrial Revolution, machines performed many of the functions that humans had used muscles for. In the computer revolution, the computer is performing many of the functions of the brain. The ability of the computer to store, retrieve, analyze, and make decisions about information gives it powers once thought to be uniquely human. The sheer speed of the computer makes it impossible for humans to compete with it in performing many tasks. Some tasks beyond human solution just because of the time involved in their solution can now be solved by the computer. Its potential use in society seems unlimited. New applications are being identified constantly. The effects of its use are being felt in many ways.

Just as the automobile created many problems for society, so has the computer. Because the computer is such a general-purpose tool, it has the capability to help solve many of the problems that it creates. In fact, the computer offers the potential for solution to many of the problems facing our society today. It is one of the most universal tools available.

The impact of the computer has been experienced by society in many ways. Some people have greeted it with enthusiasm; others have damned it. Many are only casually aware of its impact on their lives, even though it has affected everyone in a number of ways and will continue to do so.

In the early 1950s, the potential of the computer could not be measured, even by some of its promoters. One major computer company president predicted that the potential market for the computer in the United States would be less than 100 units. These projections were based primarily on the scientific use of the computer. By the end of the 1950s, the computer had also established itself as a business tool capable of manipulating large amounts of data.

The computer is here to stay and its potential is staggering. It has, among other things, made possible space travel, provided a solution to the information processing explosion, altered industrial processing techniques, improved health care, and been used as an instruction tool in education. Many organizations are now using it, many rely on it, and few can do without it.

The power of the computer has been extended beyond the walls of the computer center through time sharing. This facility is based on the simultaneous use of terminals connected by telephone or telegraph lines to a central computer. Organizations and individuals who cannot afford to own or lease a computer are able to share its cost and its available time and resources. (See also "Time-Sharing Systems" in Chapter 16.)

Terminal systems have become a common sight to most of us. The airlines were among the first to use terminals connected to a computer. They installed them to make seat reservations. Now terminals are used in many retail stores to record sales, reserve tickets for public events, and check customer credit. Computers on a chip are making their appearance in a variety of consumer products, including cars, microwave ovens, electronic games, television sets, and sewing machines.

The widespread use of the computer is due in part to its cost. Consider that today's computer systems are about 40 times cheaper and 10,000 times faster than early computers. Relative to the functions the computer performs, its cost is usually less than any alternative method of performing the same functions.

Our way of life has changed and will continue to change as a result of the computer. No longer can the computer be thought of as just a tool for problem solving; it now predicts, diagnoses, and recommends solutions to problems.

A full discussion of how computers affect society is not within the scope of this text; such a discussion could easily cover several volumes. The purpose of this module is to acquaint the reader with some of the social implications of computer utilization, the control of computer systems in society, and future trends in applications and technology.

INFORMATION PROCESSING

The computer has, of course, been used as a powerful tool for collecting, recording, analyzing, and disseminating large amounts of information. The first nonscientific use of computers on any scale was to perform clerical functions in information processing. Not incidentally, this usage came at a time when our society was on the verge of a paperwork explosion that could have had serious consequences. The flow of information in a highly technological society such as ours is crucial. Many of the institutions in our society continue to require more information. As governmental agencies continue to pass laws that require more recordkeeping and reporting to these agencies, the agencies in turn require more computers to process the additional information. Electronic transfer of data between computers is one method that is used to cut the cost of information processing. The electronic transfer of data between computers can reduce the flow of paper between organizations and provide more efficient information transfer at lower cost.

Without the computer, we could not keep up with our information processing needs. All organizations, whether business, hospital, school, charity, or government, have a need to process data.

DECISION MAKING

The computer has been used successfully in many ways to solve problems confronting organizations and society in general. *Simulation* is one example of the rapidly expanding areas of computer application. It allows a model of a real situation to be acted upon by a computer. Many organizations are finding simulation extremely valuable in improving the decision-making process. By using a computer model of a real situation, an organization can try many alternatives in a short time, yet obtain results that are used to predict the possible consequences of decisions over a long period of time. Simulation has been used in making decisions about such societal concerns as product development and marketing, highway and transportation planning, and urban planning. It is one of many computer applications helping to determine the characteristics and course of society.

AUTOMATION

One of the issues faced by our society as a result of the computer has been that of the replacement of workers by computers. In some instances, the function performed by a person is taken over by a computer; in others, the job itself is eliminated. When human work is replaced by an automatic, computer-directed or machine-directed process, the work is said to be *automated*. The use of machine-directed processes is called *automation*. *Technological unemployment,* or *job displacement,* takes on real meaning to a person whose job is eliminated by an automated system. Automation has also contributed to "silent firing." Under this approach, employees are not fired when an automated system is installed, but jobs are allowed to go unfilled or are eliminated when employees retire or quit.

It is difficult to determine the number of workers who have been replaced by computers. Many studies have been conducted to determine the effects of automation; however, their findings are not consistent. One study estimates that as many as 40,000 worker per week are displaced by the computer. The U.S. Labor Department, in a study of 20 companies using computers for the first time, found that the impact was not as great as expected. Of a total of about 3000 employees, only 16 percent either retired or quit one year after the computer was installed. During the same period, nine employees were fired. It may be some time before the full impact of automation can be determined.

Most of the jobs eliminated by computers to date have been low-level jobs requiring a minimum of education. First to go were the accounting-related jobs where manual bookkeeping was done. Computerized accounting required fewer people to prepare the data for processing. In many cases a redefined job required less skill because the computer performed routines and decision making that the worker had done previously. For example, word-processing computer systems are now making an impact on office jobs. These systems allow the preparation of letters from tape or disk master files, thus eliminating most of the typing associated with letter preparation. Clerical jobs involving routine, repetitive tasks are now performed by computers in many organizations.

In some instances, technological unemployment resulting from the elimination of low-level jobs is offset by new jobs created as a result of the computer. However, if new jobs are created, they tend to require a higher level of education than the eliminated jobs did.

A whole new class of jobs may be created with the introduction of the microcomputer. This low-cost computer can be used in a variety of office machines and factory equipment to perform functions that require a degree of skill and decision making. The microcomputer's low cost will encourage its use for many functions now performed by workers. In manufacturing, most machines will use some type of microprocessor. This will increase the productivity of some workers; it may allow one worker to do what formerly was done by several.

For the person with little education or training, job displacement poses a real problem. Many organizations are providing job retraining and education to minimize the impact of job displacement. Nevertheless, in the immediate future, finding employment opportunities for unskilled and minimally educated people will continue to be a problem. If one conclusion can be drawn from the impact of automation, it is that workers will continually need to update their education and/or retrain. In the long run, it seems that the computer will continue to create new jobs requiring varying levels of education and training.

Another challenge, as a result of automation, is what to do with an ever-expanding amount of leisure time. The work week continues to shrink (some predict that by the year 2000, the average work week will be 15 hours). What will the worker do when the work week is reduced because of automation and the computer? This question is yet to be answered. Even the definition of *leisure* is in dispute at this time. One school of thought supports the ancient Greek definition, which is essentially that leisure is freedom from the necessity of doing anything. Many sociologists define leisure as free time. In either case, the question above poses a real problem that needs to be studied. If one agrees that the computer has contributed to the increase in leisure time, one might also hope that new ways to use leisure time will be found.

Many people insist that automation and computers in general will impose conformity upon the members of society. The Industrial Revolution actually began the trend to conformity by allowing the mass production of uniform products. One expert feels that the computer can be used to reverse this trend because he sees the computer as a means of designing individualized objects at a low cost. By using a computer to design objects, it becomes possible to do a large number of different design processes for many people; anything a computer can be instructed to do (even the creation of unique designs) can be done many times.

INDIVIDUALITY AND THE COMPUTER

The impersonal aspects of computerized systems are emphasized repeatedly by those opposing computers. In one student demonstration, for example, a sign read, "Do not fold, bend or mutilate, I am a human being." This message is one indication of a growing frustration with computerized systems. They are seen by many as a threat to our individuality. Everyone has either experienced some frustrating experience with a computer system or heard of someone else's frustrating experiences.

The latitude and power given to the computer is a problem with which one must deal. The computer is allowed in some instances to take extreme action, such as terminating a person's utility service for nonpayment or canceling credit privileges, without human intervention. Mistakes occur in any computerized system; however, the likelihood of such mistakes can be minimized by careful design.

Design strategies can be altered so that extreme actions such as the automatic termination of utility service or credit are no longer possible. Alternatively, the function can remain but steps can be taken to prevent any occasional mistakes. This may be costly. Many computerized systems are designed with minimum cost in mind, and occasional mistakes may be less costly to deal with than designing the system so that they cannot occur. When mistakes do occur, some computerized systems are designed to ignore them even if detected (again, it may be less expensive to lose a customer than to deal with the mistake).

Another aspect of computerized systems that has been attacked is the computer-analysis of information to predict the behavior of individuals and organizations. On a personal level, an individual who has one accident may lose her car insurance despite 15 to 20 prior years of accident-free driving because a computer statistically points her out as a bad risk. If an organization relies on a computerized system for the selection of employees, it may behoove a prospective employee to build a good computer record to enhance the chances of obtaining employment and of future promotions or advancement. Businesses use predictive techniques to create and promote new consumer products. Politicians use similar techniques to determine which voters are important to their campaigns and what issues are likely to be vital.

It seems that everywhere one turns today, one encounters some type of computerized system, whether it be in school, in a hospital, or as a consumer. Some people question whether humanity can be retained; others claim that the computer has gained control. Today, our society is so complex that it could not function without computers. True, computers are slaves, but society is dependent on them. Because computers are useful in so many ways, those knowing how to use them have a key to knowledge. Their ability to organize and store vast amounts of data is a potential source of power to individuals, governments, and other organizations.

PRIVACY AND THE COMPUTER

Those who fear that the computer will impose conformity upon society are also concerned that the computer will be used to invade individual privacy. The term *privacy* as used here refers to the rights of each individual regarding the collection, processing, storage, release, and use of information concerning the activities and characteristics of the individual.

A vast amount of data concerning most Americans has been or is being centralized in computer data banks from which it can be retrieved at the touch of a button. These data banks are large computer files that contain information about an individual for some purpose. They have been established by all types of private and public organizations. The trend was started by the Federal government, which currently has a variety of data banks. The Social Security Administration, Internal Revenue Service, Secret Service, FBI, Veterans Administration, Pentagon, Department of Transportation, Department of Labor, Department of Justice, and Department of Housing and Urban Development are among groups using them. These federal data banks serve a number of purposes, some of which have been attacked as invading the privacy of the individual.

Many of the data banks used by the Federal government are accessed by means of social security numbers. These numbers could serve as a common key, making it easy to retrieve all of the information concerning an individual if the data banks were tied together in one large data bank. To a certain extent, this step was proposed by a government committee in its recommendation for the creation of a *National Data Center*. Its purpose would be to provide for the storage of statistical information and the access to that information for statistical analysis by government agencies needing statistical data. As proposed, it would not include personnel information or dossiers kept by the FBI and other federal law enforcement agencies. Because of the concern expressed by congressmen and others that the creation of such a data bank would result in an invasion of privacy, it appears that the creation of a National Data Center is unlikely.

State and local governments maintain data banks for a variety of uses also. These include motor vehicle registration, tax collection, welfare programs, police information networks, and criminal justice systems.

Another type of data bank that could have potential consequences for individual privacy is being proposed. Bankers have discussed for some time the prospect of a cashless-checkless society. While it is not likely that cash and checks will be eliminated, steps have been taken in that direction.

The first step was the bank credit card, which became an instant success. With the introduction of point-of-sale terminals, credit cards can be used for instant credit verification, cash advances, transfer of savings account funds to cover credit purchases, and check verification.

It is most likely that the majority of transactions dealing with money will be handled electronically in the future. The electronic transfer of money is referred to as *electronic funds transfer*. Basically, it involves communication between two or more computers transferring funds from one account to another electronically. Electronic funds transfer is now used for check clearing, payments of bills through banks and savings institutions, and federal payments to individuals. Check clearing is handled through automated clearing houses used by some banks. It is anticipated that all banks will eventually use electronic funds transfer.

Illustration D-1 shows how an electronic funds transfer system can be used for customer purchases at a shopping center.

The Federal government is expanding its electronic funds transfer program. It plans to eventually make most social security payments in this manner. The Treasury Department has indicated that its goal is to use electronic funds transfer for the some 43 million payments made each month by the government. Most of the financial transactions for an individual would be recorded in a data bank, keyed on some type of identifying number, in a full-scale electronic funds transfer system. Such a system could reveal much about an individual if the data bank was used improperly.

There is a growing concern that any kind of computer data bank is an invasion of privacy. But is it? The government has always collected data about citizens for one purpose or another. Individuals applying for credit agree to credit checking and to the establishment of a credit rating. Applications for bank loans and insurance policies require individuals to reveal personal information, which becomes part of data banks. The collection of data is not new, but the potential for dissemination of it is. The technology

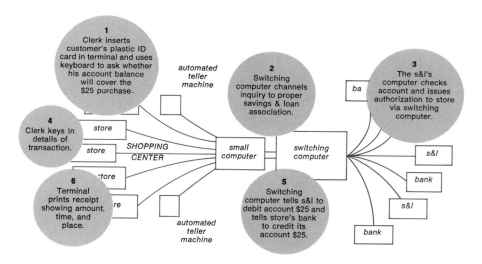

Illustration D-1. An electronic funds transfer system.

for centralization is available. The immediate access to data that was impossible before computer data banks is a reality. Now that terminals can be connected to computers, multiple users can access the same data bank. What kind of safeguards can be built into such a system to prevent unauthorized access? So great is the concern over the invasion of privacy through data banks, that a bill of rights concerning access and challenge of data bank information has been suggested. Already, legislation has been passed to control the collection, use, and dissemination of consumer credit information, most of which is stored in computer data banks.

THE CONTROL OF COMPUTER SYSTEMS

The exercise of control over computerized systems appears to fall into three basic categories: (1) passage of laws, (2) physical safeguards against misuse, and (3) system controls.

Historically, the enactment of legislation has often followed the abuse of a system. For example, it took the stock market crash of 1929 to bring about legislation that established the Securities and Exchange Commission to stop fraudulent stock practices. The first legislation pertaining to a computer-related industry was the *Fair Credit Reporting Act.* This act provides to an individual the right of access to credit information collected about him or her by a credit reporting system and an opportunity to correct errors. Prior to this legislation, an individual had little chance to see or challenge computer-generated credit reports. The *Freedom of Information Act* also provided for access to files concerning an individual that have been collected by federal agencies.

A model code for data banks was developed in 1973 by a special committee of the Department of Health, Education, and Welfare. The code is called the *Code of Fair Information Practices.* It provides guidelines for federal data banks. The code could be used as a model for all governmental and private data banks. Its basic provisions are: (1) no secret data banks containing personal data will be established, (2) the individual must have a method of determining what information is kept about him or her and how it is used, (3) a method for correcting or changing information about an individual must be provided, (4) a method must be provided to keep information collected for one purpose from being used for another purpose, and (5) an organization that creates, maintains, uses, or releases records of individuals containing personal data must insure the accuracy of the data for its defined use and must take steps to prevent its misuse.

The United States Congress enacted the first privacy law, the *Privacy Act of 1974,* with many of the features suggested in the Code of Fair Information Practices. It only applies to data banks maintained by the Federal government. Many state legislatures have similar bills pending, and some states have passed privacy bills.

Unfair information practices are subject to criminal and civil penalties under the Privacy Act of 1974. Fines of up to $5000 can be imposed on any officers or employees who violate the act or who request information under false pretenses. The act specifically exempts law enforcement agencies of the Federal government and intelligence agencies.

A Privacy Protection Study Commission was also established as a part of the Privacy Act of 1974. Its purpose was to study and recommend to the president what information practices should be applied to private groups and other organizations. Many businesses expect that complying with privacy legislation, either state or federal, will be very costly. These costs will include making the computer data banks more physically secure, establishing additional computer files for reporting to data subjects, and additional computer processing time for these activities. How much privacy is the consumer willing to pay for? This question is important because individuals must expect to pay for the costs of implementing privacy legislation in both private and governmental data banks.

The implementation of electronic safeguards can insure that the unauthorized use of data files in a computer system is virtually eliminated. Computer hardware can be designed to provide a high degree of security when combined with appropriate programming. The degree of protection required in a computer system depends on the sensitivity and value of its data files. Elaborate safeguards are needed for data files that have significant financial value or contain confidential information such as medical records if they are to be secure from criminals and from those who would invade one's privacy.

A computerized system that operates without an overall set of system controls is subject to abuse. Limits and constraints must be imposed on the system to insure that it consistently achieves its stated purposes. Overall computerized system controls can be categorized as (1) those which check the accuracy of the computer hardware itself, (2) those which check the correct functioning of the programs used in the system, and (3) those which provide backup in case of system failure.

Adequate controls may not be applied in a system because the stated purposes or goals of the system are vague or imprecise. The goals should be redefined. The collection of data that is not necessary for the achievement of the goals should not be allowed. The data that is collected should not be retained unless it will be needed again. Although precise goals may be difficult to state in some cases, it is still possible to provide constraints on the system to avoid abuse.

THE FUTURE

To most observers, computers appear to be highly complex, sophisticated machines. However, one computer expert has commented that we are still in the horse and buggy era of the computer. Technological advancements continue to be made. What can be expected in the next 20 years?

The major hardware advance of the past decade has been the development of large scale integrated (LSI) circuits. These in turn have led to the development of a computer on a chip, the microcomputer. The microcomputer is expected to have far-reaching effects on all of us. It will have an impact on all of the devices we use, and it will create a whole new group of devices to serve us. Its low cost will assure its use in just about every consumer product that requires any type of control or regulation; likely candidates here are appliances, tools, entertainment equipment, and communication equipment. Microcomputers are already used in television sets, microwave ovens, sewing machines, and cars. They will soon be used in many homes for personal accounting, paying bills, home education, entertainment, and communicating with other computer systems via telephones. Many homes now have electronic games controlled by microcomputers that use television sets for display; it is possible that the same television sets can be used for other purposes under the control of these or other microcomputers. Computers will continue to become faster, smaller, lower in price, and easier to use. At the same time, communication with computers will be simplified as easy-to-learn conversational computer languages are developed.

New areas of computer application will be explored. The extension and refinement of present applications will continue as well. The management of large organizations will depend heavily on the development of management information systems and other decision-making tools.

Computer terminals will be a common sight in most offices as distributed processing continues to develop around microcomputers and minicomputers. Small organizations not currently using computerized processing will avail themselves of its benefits as prices become lower and more time-sharing services are offered.

Automation will continue to displace jobs and create new ones as more industrial processes are automated. Industrial robots will be developed and used in environments that are dangerous to humans and for repetitive tasks.

Time sharing will increase as business firms, known as computer utilities, offer their services to increasing numbers of users. Specialized applications will be developed for a wide range of users—homemakers, executives, doctors, lawyers, educators, and students, to name a few.

Education, medicine, and law will depend more on computers to increase the effectiveness of these professions. Education is already using computer-assisted and computer-managed instruction for teaching. This trend will continue as will the development of the computer as a resource tool much like the library. Doctors will increasingly use the computer as a diagnostic and predictive tool as well as in its current passive role as a monitor of patients' conditions. Lawyers and courts will increase their use of computers for case research and their application of computerized techniques for case investigation and analysis.

The move to a cashless-checkless society will continue as electronic funds transfer expands. The use of point-of-sale terminals will become routine for most retail businesses, thus allowing electronic funds transfer to become a widespread reality.

People will become more aware of abuses in computer usage. Legislation will be passed to protect the rights of individuals as they deal with computer systems.

Because the computer is a general-purpose tool, it is inevitable that the number of applications for which it is used will continue to grow. At the same time, it will pose new problems for our society.

Summary

1. The computer is one of the most significant inventions of this century. It has had an impact on our way of life and will continue to do so at an increasing rate. The invention of the microcomputer will lead to universal usage of computers.

2. The computer solved the information processing explosion. It will be used to meet the increasing demands for recordkeeping and reporting imposed by various organizations. Techniques like simulation will be used more frequently to test alternative actions as a part of decision making.

3. While the computer has served as a boon to society in solving the information-processing explosion, it has also created many problems for society. Many jobs of a routine, repetitive nature have been eliminated, and automation has allowed the replacement of many workers with computer-directed machines. Leisure time has increased and with it the problem of how to use it. Data banks are a potential tool for use in the invasion of privacy as information on most individuals is gathered and stored therein. The loss of individuality in dealing with computerized systems and the pressure to conform has led to frustrating experiences on the part of many individuals.

4. Some progress toward the solution of problems created by the computer is being made. Workers losing their jobs as a result of automation are being retrained or offered educational opportunities in many organizations. The Federal government has passed legislation to curb the current and potential abuses of data banks at the federal level. Many states are considering similar legislation. Computer systems are being made more secure to prevent unauthorized access to confidential information in data banks.

5. The use of computers in our society will continue to accelerate. New computers will be smaller, faster, and less expensive. The microcomputer will make computer power available to almost anyone who wants it. Electronic funds transfer will continue to be developed, reducing the use of cash and checks in our society. Computer-directed products will become commonplace to most consumers and will provide a new level of convenience to their users. Our dependence on computers will increase as our use of them continues to expand into new areas.

CHAPTER 18

The Computer Industry

COMPUTER MANUFACTURERS

INDEPENDENT COMPUTER PERIPHERAL
EQUIPMENT MANUFACTURERS

SOFTWARE COMPANIES

LEASING COMPANIES

DATA PROCESSING SERVICE CENTERS

Although the computer was first built for commercial use only about 25 years ago, the computer industry has grown tremendously since that time. This is reflected in the fact that while in 1955 the value of all installed computer systems totaled between $300 million and $350 million, the value of all installed computer systems in 1980 is expected to total $60 billion. It is expected that the computer industry will continue to grow at an even faster pace during the remainder of the 1970s and early 1980s. As a result of this continued growth, the computer industry will become one of the largest industries in the world.

The numerous mature applications of computers, such as payroll and inventory control, are expected to continue to expand from profit and nonprofit organizations and government into other organizations, especially small ones. More efficient and effective computer systems will be implemented. As computer systems become more efficient and effective, applications that are now in their infancy and new applications will be developed and implemented in an increasing number of organizations. This is especially true for applications that are best accomplished by means of time sharing (such as the providing of accurate and timely information to managers for decision-making purposes).

The computer industry can be divided into five segments. These include: (1) computer manufacturers, (2) independent computer peripheral equipment manufacturers, (3) software companies, (4) leasing companies, and (5) data processing service centers. Each of these computer industry segments is discussed in this chapter.

COMPUTER MANUFACTURERS

There are many computer manufacturers, and they supply many kinds of computer hardware and software to the computer marketplace. As mentioned in Chapter 11, six computer manufacturers supply most of the computer hardware and software installed in the United States.

There are two basic ways in which computer manufacturers supply hardware and software to the computer marketplace. They may sell or lease the hardware and software directly to the organization or governmental agency that is going to use it. Alternatively, they may sell the hardware and software directly to a leasing company (discussed later in this chapter), who in turn leases it to a user. As mentioned in Chapter 17, to retain flexibility with respect to making computer hardware and software changes, most hardware and software are leased. Basically, the leasing of the computer hardware and software implies that the manufacturer or leasing company retains ownership.

INDEPENDENT COMPUTER PERIPHERAL EQUIPMENT MANUFACTURERS

Because of the vast size of the leading manufacturers in the computer marketplace, they tend to overshadow the numerous companies that manufacture and provide computer hardware independently of the computer manufacturers. These companies are called *independent computer peripheral equipment manufacturers (ICPEMs)*. Collectively, ICPEMs comprise a market force in the U.S. computer industry larger than any computer manufacturer except IBM. By 1980, it is estimated that these manufacturers will supply several billion dollars annually in computer hardware. Some of the relatively large ICPEMs are Telex, Memorex, Ampex, Mohawk, Calcomp, and Electronic Memories. Many of these firms place much emphasis on research and development, in addition to production and marketing activities.

The advent of the ICPEM has brought more competition to an industry dominated by a few big companies. As noted for computer manufacturers, computer hardware can be either purchased or leased from an ICPEM. On the average, the cost of the hardware purchased from an ICPEM is 20 to 40 percent lower than the cost charged by the computer manufacturer. The cost of hardware leased from an ICPEM is 10 to 20 percent lower. This cost differential becomes more important as increased CPU capabilities are available at less cost. A larger percentage of the user's hardware expenditure is for peripheral equipment. In 1970, peripheral equipment was approximately 55 to 60 percent of a user's hardware cost. Today, this type of equipment is two-thirds to three-quarters of a user's hardware cost.

Quite often, ICPEM's products have exceeded the performance of the computer manufacturer's products that they are designed to replace. As a result, the user has obtained a product that performs better at a lower price. The ICPEMs are often more flexible than computer manufacturers with respect to supplying different hardware options and "little extras" at no additional cost. Finally, in addition to supplying functionally equivalent hardware that plugs into hardware produced by the computer manufacturers, ICPEMs have introduced their own innovative hardware especially for computer input and output. As mentioned above, there has been a large growth in their share of the computer hardware marketplace in the past several years. The computer manufacturers have been forced to take notice of these companies. They have begun to compete with them by lowering their hardware prices, developing new hardware products, and taking an increased interest in the user's needs. As a result, the most successful ICPEMs are those that can supply hardware with uniquely practical capabilities.

SOFTWARE COMPANIES

Software companies provide software and/or system analysis and programming services to organizations who elect to purchase their software and/or services. Many of the software companies can provide specialized software that is either not available from the computer manufacturer or more efficient than the software provided by the computer manufacturer. They provide systems analysts and/or programmers to an organization that does not employ individuals with the qualifications required to complete a particular task. They also supplement an organization's systems analysts and/or programmers during peak or overload periods created by either conversion to a new computer system or preparation of a new, complex program.

LEASING COMPANIES

Most computer system hardware is leased rather than purchased by users. The basic reason for this is that leasing computer system hardware, in contrast to purchasing it, provides a much more flexible approach to changing the hardware. The ability to change computer system hardware in a short period of time is especially relevant in this field because more efficient and effective hardware is continuously being introduced.

While an organization can lease or purchase computer system hardware from the computer manufacturer, the organization can also lease or purchase the hardware from a computer leasing company. Leasing companies acquire computers by purchasing them from computer manufacturers or from users who bought the computers previously. Generally, leasing companies lease their hardware for 10 to 30 percent less than the lease rate charged by computer manufacturers. Because of the risk of functional obsolescence assumed by leasing companies, the computer manufacturers do not consider them to be strong competitors. Nevertheless, the computer manufacturers have used price incentives, primarily, to encourage users to purchase rather than lease computer system hardware.

Since the leasing of computer hardware is a relatively easy business to enter, there is intense competition among leasing companies. However, the computer leasing industry accounts for only about 5 to 8 percent of the computer hardware market.

Most leasing companies depreciate their computers over a much longer period of time than computer manufacturers do. They make the following assumptions:

1. The computers that they lease have a long operational life.
2. The lease rates that they charge in order to make a reasonable profit can be maintained for several years.

3. The introduction of new computers by manufacturers will not result in a mass user movement from current computer systems to the newly introduced computer systems.

The principal risk involved in making these assumptions is the possibility that the computer hardware will become obsolete before it is fully depreciated. The assumptions proved to be correct about users of second-generation computer system hardware when third-generation computer hardware, such as the IBM System/360 series, was introduced. The same result proved true when more efficient and effective third-generation computers were introduced during the last half of the 1960s. However, during the last year or two of the 1960s (and especially in 1970 when the IBM System/370 series was introduced), the rate of computer system hardware innovation increased. The second and third assumptions above were no longer as valid as they had been up to that time. That is, lease rates for third-generation computer equipment introduced during the 1960s had to be reduced when a large number of System/360 users began to change to System/370 computer systems. Leasing companies have had to give greater consideration to the fact that the purchase of older hardware increases the risk of obsolescence prior to recovery of the purchase price of the computer system and the earning of a reasonable profit.

DATA PROCESSING SERVICE CENTERS

A data processing service center (service bureau) is an organization that provides data processing services to organizations for a fee. Many service centers can provide this service periodically, on a continuous basis, or only when needed. In most service centers, data is periodically batch-processed. An increasing number of service centers are providing time-sharing facilities.

Service centers tend to specialize with respect to the type of service they offer. Some service centers, especially the small ones, specialize in commercial-oriented applications, such as those designed for accounting functions. Other service centers specialize in scientific-oriented applications. A few service centers specialize in services for a particular type of industry. For example, some banks with large data processing departments provide a complete line of data processing services for other banks in surrounding areas.

There is also considerable diversity in the amount of services offered by service centers. Some service centers provide only certain types of services, such as just the processing and storing of data. Other service centers, especially the better established ones, provide a complete line of data processing services; they assist the customer in identifying data processing requirements, write the necessary programs, process the data, and provide the results to the customer.

An organization that considers using a service center is generally one that can benefit from using a computer to process one or more applications, but cannot afford to either purchase or lease the computer. The service(s) that a center provides can be used either in place of manual data processing or to supplement data processing performed by the organization's data processing department. Thus, a service center is a way for an organization to take advantage of the benefits that can be obtained from using a computer without having to assume either the problems of organizing and managing a large data processing department or the entire expense of the computer system. In either situation, an underlying consideration for an organization must be whether or not the center can perform the processing at a lower cost and/or on a more timely basis than can be performed within the organization.

The data processing service center industry is diverse with respect to ownership of the service centers. Most of the major computer manufacturers also operate service centers. A large number of service centers are independently owned. These service centers vary in size. The large ones maintain branch offices in major cities throughout the country. Many businesses, such as banks and universities, do not need to use all of the time available on their computer systems. Thus, they enter into part-time service center arrangements with one or more outside organizations. In some cases, the arrangement involves only the sale of blocks of time; that is, the service center provides only its computer hardware and software for stipulated periods of time. In such situations, the outside organizations provide their own user programs and personnel. This type of arrangement is sometimes called *block time*. In other cases, the arrangement involves the selling of a complete line of data processing services. In this type of arrangement, the organization selling the services is in competition with the manufacturer-owned and independent data processing organizations.

Summary

1. The computer industry can be divided into five segments: the computer manufacturer, the independent computer peripheral equipment manufacturer (ICPEM), the software company, the leasing company, and the service center (service bureau). Each of these segments is tailored to a specific portion of the market once held exclusively by the computer manufacturer.

2. Computer manufacturers hold the major portion of the market for computers and computer services. They provide hardware and software through sale or lease agreements directly to the organization or agency that is going to use it. Alternatively, they sell directly to leasing companies.

3. Facing the computer manufacturer in the computer hardware market are independent computer peripheral equipment manufacturers (ICPEMs). This group represents the second largest in relation to the share of the computer hardware market. These companies provide computers at a lower cost, and in more flexible combinations, than the computer manufacturers do.

4. Software companies provide software and/or system analysis and programming services to organizations who elect to purchase their software and/or services. They handle customers on a client basis and can often provide software services superior to that of the computer manufacturer. Software companies also provide systems analysts and/or programmers to supplement the staff of small companies or to aid companies during peak or overload periods.

5. Leasing companies purchase hardware from computer manufacturers or prior user-owners and then lease the equipment to other organizational users. The equipment is made available at a lower cost than that offered by the computer manufacturer. In this case, the leasing company, rather than the organizational user, assumes the risk of functional obsolescence.

6. A data processing service center, or service bureau, works on a fee basis to provide varying degrees of hardware, software, system analysis and programming, and time-sharing services. These services are usually purchased by users who cannot afford a computer, but need some of the processing that a computer can perform. In this way, the service center specializes in an area to which the computer manufacturer is not fully committed, as do the other segments of the computer industry.

CAREER PROFILE

Judith Duchesne
Territory Marketing Manager

Burroughs Corporation

Background Experience

I graduated from Fresno State with a degree in Business Administration. I worked as a computer operator during the summers. Later, while working as a secretary for a man doing computer feasibility studies for companies, I became interested in computers. I analyzed my strong points and decided on computer sales. I was hired by Burroughs as a marketing trainee—which involved sales and computer programming courses, writing programs in a tech pool, and finally, a computer sales course. I was then given a territory and told to go out and develop it. Having met quota within the first six months, I became a territory manager.

Primary Job Responsibilities

Originally I started with the L Series at Burroughs. Then I learned the disk systems. I decided to specialize in wholesalers and distributors. Each time there is a new product, we go back to school. My current customers are accountants and distributors. I market calculators, the small minicomputers (which use ledger cards and cassettes) and disk systems up to the $150,000 range. My responsibilities include developing these markets, managing the installation, and servicing them, as well. I accomplish this primarily on my own, but I do have the support of staff and product managers at Burroughs. On small systems, I do the entire analysis and program modifications. As a territorial manager I am responsible for three people, including one trainee. I supervise their work to make sure they are doing things correctly. The majority of my time is spent developing new business.

Once interest is evident, the hardest part is to qualify who will buy now; there isn't enough time to waste on people who aren't seriously interested. One tool I use is to set up different equipment in our demonstration room and invite people to come and browse to see what is available. On a typical day, I like to make my calls on new people, first thing. I'm brighter then and more energetic, and it's easier for me to go out and approach new faces. Then I'm in the office catching up with return phone calls and dealing with installation situations. Usually, I have 2 or 3 appointments a day, which I like to schedule for the afternoon.

What Has Made You Successful?

A big part of it is the training I've had with Burroughs. Before that I didn't have the technical knowledge to know what computers were, or what they did. So Burroughs' training is just excellent. But that doesn't really make you successful because everyone has the same training—it's what you do from there that counts. I think that whether or not you are successful in sales has a lot to do with personality. You have to like to work with people. You also have to self-motivate. This is probably one of the hardest things to get used to when you first start. I was planning my own day. If I had nothing to do that day, it was my fault. Another thing is you have to be competitive; you have to want to be the best. I really had to work very hard to get where I am now. Mainly because I didn't have the sales experience and a lot of it was new to me. I have super-high personal standards, and I want to be the best at what I do.

BASIC Programming[*]

This appendix is provided for readers who want to become familiar with the BASIC programming language. Like the English language, BASIC must be used in accordance with certain rules and procedures. The rules and procedures that must be considered when writing a BASIC program are explained and used in examples below. The BASIC program in Illustration A-1 calculates and prints the squares of certain numbers. It shows many features of the BASIC language. Illustration A-2 is a flowchart of the program.

As indicated by the flowchart, this program reads a number (READ statement). The number comes from the DATA statement. It is stored in a location called N. The program then tests to determine if the value of N is greater than 500 (IF statement). If the value of N is greater than 500, the computer will go to statement 90. Program execution will be terminated (STOP statement).

If the value of N is less than or equal to 500, the computer will square the number (first LET statement). It will then print the number (i.e., the value of N) and its square (PRINT statement). The computer will then return to statement 20 (the GO TO statement) and start the process over again.

Statement 10 (REM statement) is a comment explaining what the program does, for the benefit of anyone reading the program statements. Statement 100 (END statement) tells the BASIC compiler that there are no more program statements after statement 100.

---

[*]Though an ANSI Minimal BASIC standard (X360) was formally approved in January 1978, BASIC compilers in common use were designed and implemented prior to this standardization. Most of them also contain additional features not addressed in the standard. Therefore, minor language variations exist among current BASIC implementations. These variations are pointed out by footnotes in this appendix. When these differences are taken into account, the programs shown in this appendix can be executed on any computer system for which a BASIC compiler is available. They can be run, unchanged, under IBM's VS BASIC and other fully compatible compilers.

```
 10 REM THE READING AND SQUARING OF CERTAIN NUMBERS
 20 READ N
 30 DATA 50,100,150,200,250,300,350,400,450,500,550
 40 IF N > 500 THEN 90
 50 LET S = N ↑2
 60 LET A$ = "THE SQUARE OF"
 70 PRINT A$;N;" IS ";S
 80 GO TO 20
 90 STOP
100 END
```

Illustration A-1. A BASIC program.

PROGRAM STATEMENT NUMBERS AND LENGTH

Program Statement Numbers

As shown in Illustration A-1, each statement in a BASIC program must be preceded by a statement number. (A *statement number* is sometimes referred to as a *line number*.) The number can be from 1 through 5 numerical characters in length, and successive statements do not have to be numbered sequentially. (The authors suggest that statement numbers be multiples of 10 so that up to nine additional statements can be inserted between two statements if necessary.) Embedded blanks in a statement number will be ignored by the BASIC compiler.

The magnitude of a statement number, relative to the magnitude of other statement numbers in the program, determines the order in which the program statements will be arranged in storage. The compiler arranges all of the statements into ascending order according to the magnitude of the statement numbers (regardless of the order in which they were entered into the computer). Thus, the statement assigned the smallest statement number will be the first statement in the program executed; the statement assigned the largest statement number will be the last statement in the program executed. (The authors suggest that entering statements in the order in which the computer should execute them is a good programming practice.)

If two statements in a program have the same statement number, the compiler replaces the first statement with the second statement. The advantage of this capability is that statements can be corrected while entering the program. A previously entered statement can be eliminated from the program by typing only the statement number assigned to that statement.

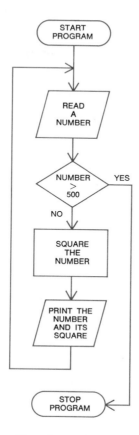

Illustration A-2. Flowchart of the BASIC program
in Illustration A-1.

Program Statement Length

The maximum possible length of a statement is determined by the carriage width of the terminal from which the statement is entered. A statement cannot occupy more than one print line. From the terminals in common use today, the maximum length of a statement varies from 72 to 120 characters.

The use of blanks within a statement is optional. For example, statement 80 in Illustration A-1 could have been written GOTO20. When used, blanks generally help to improve readability.

CONSTANTS AND VARIABLES

Constants

Constants are values that are fixed in a BASIC program; they cannot be changed during execution of the program. There are two types of constants: numbers and character strings.

Numbers. BASIC permits the use of three types of representations for numbers. These are:

1. *Integer* numbers—Numbers that have no decimal point and no fractional part. For example: 1, 437, and 69643.
2. *Real* numbers—Numbers that have a decimal point and may have a fractional part. For example: 1.03, 40., and 0.43992.
3. *Exponential* numbers—Numbers that are expressed in what is sometimes called scientific notation. This type of representation is most often used for very large or very small numbers. For example: 4.639412E + 03, − 8.47693E + 04, and 3.921146E − 04.

Certain rules about the use of numbers must be followed.

1. A positive number can be preceded by a plus sign.
2. If a number is negative, it must be preceded by a minus sign.
3. A number cannot contain embedded commas.
4. A number can be from 1 through 15 digits in length. The maximum number of digits is dependent upon the particular computer used.

The minus or plus sign, if present, is accepted by the BASIC compiler as an allowable additional character. It is not counted in determining the maximum possible length of the number.

The following examples are valid integer numbers:

```
1
150
+ 16777215
0
− 10
− 16777215
```

The following examples are invalid integer numbers:

15.	(contains a decimal point)
4362 −	(minus sign positioned incorrectly)
9,310	(contains an embedded comma)

The following examples are valid real numbers:

+.36
2647.19
0.
−.58
−.1478
−9327.65

The following examples are invalid real numbers:

73446	(no decimal point)
6742.12 −	(minus sign positioned incorrectly)
1,983.17	(contains an embedded comma)

There are instances when a value exceeds the allowable magnitude of a real number. This problem can be handled through the use of the exponential form of representation of a number.

When the exponential form is used, a decimal exponent is attached to the real number. The exponent is composed of the character E followed by a signed or an unsigned 1- or 2-character integer number. If the 1- or 2-character integer number is unsigned, it is assumed to be positive by the BASIC compiler. The decimal exponent causes the computer to multiply the number by 10 raised to the power signified by the signed or unsigned 1- or 2-character integer number. The allowable magnitude of an exponential number varies with the particular computer used.

The following examples are valid exponential numbers:

5.0E0	(equivalent:	$5.0*10^0$)	$= 5.0$
250.34E05	(equivalent:	$250.34*10^5$)	$= 25034000.$
250.34E + 05	(equivalent:	$250.34*10^5$)	$= 25034000.$
250.34E5	(equivalent:	$250.34*10^5$)	$= 25034000.$
−2195.63E15	(equivalent:	$-2195.63*10^{15}$)	$= -2195630000000000000.$
7.1E−3	(equivalent:	$7.1*10^{-3}$)	$= .0071$
890.75E − 08	(equivalent:	$890.75*10^{-8}$)	$= .0000089075$
890.75E − 8	(equivalent:	$890.75*10^{-8}$)	$= .0000089075$
− 6437.19E − 12	(equivalent:	$-6437.19*10^{-12}$)	$= .00000000643719$

The following examples are invalid exponential numbers:

7534.52E	(signed or unsigned 1- or 2-character integer number after the character E is missing)
315.2E1.4	(the 1- or 2-character number following the character E must be an integer)

Character strings.   A character string is any combination of alphabetic characters (A–Z), numeric characters (0–9), and special characters (non-

alphabetic and nonnumeric characters) enclosed in quotation marks.*
The maximum number of characters that a character string can contain
depends upon the computer being used.** There are two character strings
in the program in Illustration A-1. The first is "THE SQUARE OF". The
second is "IS".

Variables

A *numeric variable name* represents a number that is either (1) externally
supplied to the computer prior to or during execution of the program, or
(2) internally calculated by the computer during execution of the program.
A *string variable name* represents a character string that is either (1) externally supplied to the computer prior to or during the execution of the
program, or (2) assigned to a string variable name during execution of the
program. In both instances, the name is called "variable" because the
number or character string represented by the name may be changed one
or more times during execution of the program. However, each numeric
variable name and each string variable name can represent only one
number or one character string at a time. Which numeric variable name
and which string variable name will represent which numbers and strings
is at the discretion of the programmer. (A numeric variable name or a string
variable name is sometimes referred to as a *simple variable*.)

A variable name representing a number is composed of either a single
alphabetic character or a single alphabetic character followed by a single
numeric character. No special characters (e.g., +, *, &) can be used in a
variable name.

The following examples are valid numeric variable names:

A
Q
B1
R7

The following examples are invalid numeric variable names:

AB   (can contain only one alphabetic character)
1A   (must begin with an alphabetic character)
Z50   (can contain a maximum of two characters)
A&   (cannot contain a special character)

_____

*Some BASIC compilers do not require quotation marks around character strings that begin
with alphabetic characters.
**When IBM's VS BASIC is used, the default length for character strings is 18. The maxi-
mum length of a character string is 255 characters.

A variable name representing a character string is composed of a single alphabetic character followed by a dollar sign.†

The following examples are valid string variable names:

A$
C$
Z$

The following examples are invalid string variable names:

A3   (must end with a $)
1A   (must begin with an alphabetic character)

THE ASSIGNMENT STATEMENT

The assignment statement is used to give (assign) a value to a variable. There are two types of assignment statements in BASIC: arithmetic and character string. The arithmetic assignment statement is concerned with arithmetic computation and the assignment of a previously determined value to a numeric variable name. The character-string assignment statement deals with the assignment of a character string to a string variable name.

The LET Statement

The LET statement provides the format for both types of assignment statements. The general form of the LET statement as used for arithmetic assignments is shown in Illustration A-3.

General Considerations of the Arithmetic Assignment Statement

The arithmetic assignment statement is the means by which: (1) computations involving exponentiation, multiplication, division, addition, and subtraction are performed, and (2) the final result is assigned to a variable name. It also provides the means by which the value of a constant or another variable name can be assigned to a variable name.

With respect to both the general appearance and the functioning of the arithmetic operators, the arithmetic assignment statement is similar to an

---

†Some BASIC compilers allow a 0 or a 1 to follow the alphabetic character and precede the dollar sign in a string variable name.

---

sn LET vn = ae

where:

sn represents an unsigned 1 through 5 digit integer statement *n*umber.

LET is a BASIC keyword that distinguishes this statement from the other kinds of statements in the program. (This keyword can be omitted when certain BASIC compilers are used.)

vn represents a *variable name.*

= is a special character used here as required in the BASIC language.

ae represents an *arithmetic expression* that can be composed of one or more numbers, numeric variable names, functions, parentheses, and arithmetic operators.

Illustration A-3. General form of the arithmetic assignment statement.

algebraic equation. However, two distinct factors must be considered when using an arithmetic assignment statement in a BASIC program.

1. There must be one and only one variable name on the left side of the equal sign. Thus, the following statements are incorrect. Statement 10 contains two variable names separated by a plus sign on the left of the equal sign. Statement 20 is similar. Statement 30 contains the number 5 where one variable name is required.

```
10 LET A+B = X↑2+25
20 LET I+6 = A−C+10
30 LET 5 = J+1
```

2. The variable name on the left side of the equal sign is "assigned" the value of the result of the solution of the expression on the right side of the equal sign. In BASIC, the equal sign means that the result of the expression on the right side of the equal sign is assigned to the variable name on the left side of the equal sign. Thus, in the following illustration, the number 15 is assigned to A; the sum of C and 12.5 is assigned to B; and the result of K divided by J is assigned to K. (Note that the same variable name can be used on both sides of the equal sign.)

```
10 LET A = 15
20 LET B = C+12.5
30 LET K = K/J
```

Arithmetic Expressions

An arithmetic expression can be composed of one or more operands. It usually contains one or more arithmetic operators. It may also contain one or more sets of parentheses. An operand may be either a constant or a numeric variable name. Operands must be separated by one or more arithmetic operators. An arithmetic operator is a symbol that tells the computer which arithmetic operation to perform on the two values that it separates. The following symbols are used as arithmetic operators:

Symbol*	Meaning
↑ or **	Exponentiation
*	Multiplication
/	Division
+	Addition
−	Subtraction

The result of an arithmetic expression must always be a number; that is, arithmetic operators cannot be used when dealing with character strings.

An arithmetic expression is constructed according to the following rules.

1. An arithmetic expression can be composed of a single constant or numeric variable name. Thus, the arithmetic expressions in the following arithmetic assignment statements are correct:

```
10 LET M = N
20 LET T = R
30 LET I = 10
40 LET X = 2.5
```

2. An arithmetic expression can be composed of one or more constants, one or more numeric variable names, or a mixture of constants and numeric variable names. If two constants or numeric variable names appear on the right-hand side of the equal sign, arithmetic operators must be used to separate them. Thus, the arithmetic expressions in the following arithmetic assignment statements are correct:

```
10 LET M = I + N * 3
20 LET K = I / 2 + N
30 LET F = T + Y
```

---

*Exponentiation can be represented by the arithmetic operator ↑ and/or the arithmetic operator **. The reader should refer to the BASIC manual for the computer system available to determine which of the arithmetic operators should be used.

3. A variable name cannot be used on the right-hand side of an arithmetic expression until it has been "defined" in the program. That is, a value must be assigned to a variable name prior to its use in an arithmetic expression. Thus, the following series of statements is correct:

```
10 LET P = .25
20 LET T = P*.05
```

If no value had been assigned to the variable name P, then the computer would not have known what number it was to multiply by the constant .05 when it got to statement 20. In the following series of statements, since no value is assigned to the variable name M, the computer will not know what value to add to K when it reaches statement 20. An error will occur.

```
10 LET K = 5
20 LET I = K+M
```

4. Two or more arithmetic operators cannot appear next to each other in an arithmetic expression. One or more sets of parentheses must be used to separate them. Thus, the arrangement of the division symbol and the minus sign in the following statement is incorrect:

```
10 LET J = K/-5
```

Rather, the statement should be written as follows:

```
10 LET J = K/(-5)
```

5. One or more sets of parentheses can be used in arithmetic expressions. The programmer has the option of enclosing in parentheses any combination of operands and operators in an arithmetic expression. When a set of parentheses is used, the operation enclosed in parentheses is performed prior to any operations not enclosed in parentheses. For example:

```
10 LET A = B*2-(Y-T)
```

The operation within the set of parentheses (Y-T) will be performed prior to the multiplication operation (B*2) and the subtraction of the quantity $Y-T$ outside the parentheses.

If more than one set of parentheses is used in an arithmetic expression, the computer will perform from left to right, the operations within each set of parentheses first. It will not perform operations outside the parentheses until after all operations within the parentheses are complete. For example:

```
20 LET T = 5.+(C*2.3)/(T+X)*(E↑2)
```

The operation within the leftmost set of parentheses (C*2.3) will be performed first; the operation within the middle set of parentheses (T+X) will be performed next; and the operation within the rightmost set of parentheses (E↑2) will be performed last. The computer will then perform the rest of the operations according to rule 6 below.

If one or more sets of parentheses are enclosed within another set of parentheses, the computer will perform the operation within each set of parentheses beginning with the innermost set of parentheses and moving to the outermost set of parentheses. For example:

```
30 LET K = ((7+M↑A)-(K*2))↑3
```

The operations within the inner leftmost set of parentheses (7+M↑A) will be performed first. The operation within the inner rightmost set of parentheses (K*2) will be performed next. The result from the inner rightmost set of parentheses will then be subtracted from the result of the inner leftmost set of parentheses (7+M↑A)÷(K*2). Finally, this result will be raised to the third power.

6. The order of performance of the various operations in an arithmetic expression depends upon the types of arithmetic operations involved. The order of evaluation, subject to the order defined by any sets of parentheses, is as follows:

   a. All exponentiations (↑ and/or **) are performed first.
   b. All multiplications (*) and divisions (/) are performed next.
   c. Finally all additions (+) and subtractions (−) are performed.

If we remove all the parentheses from the previous example, we have:

```
30 LET K = 7+M↑A-K*2↑3
```

When this expression is evaluated, it will give a very different result than the original statement did. First M↑A is evaluated; then 2↑3. Then the result of 2↑3 is multiplied by K, and the result of M↑A is added to 7. Finally, the result of K*2↑3 is subtracted from the result of 7+M↑A. The major differences between the sequences of evaluation are: (1) K is multiplied by the result of (2↑3) instead of the result of (K*2) being raised to the third power; and (2) the result of K*2↑3 instead of the result of (K*2)↑3 is subtracted from the result 7+M↑A.

If the operators within the arithmetic expression are of the same level, such as two exponentiation operations, or multiplication and division, or addition and subtraction, execution of the operations is from left to right.
Consider the arithmetic assignment statement:

```
10 LET T = .5*C-P/S+E↑3
```

The operand E↑3 is evaluated first since this is the highest-priority operation. Then .5*C is evaluated. Next, the operand P/S is evaluated. (Note that since * and / are at the same level, these operations are performed left to right.) Next, the result of P/S is subtracted from the result of .5*C. Finally, the result of the subtraction is added to the result of E↑3.

A more complex arithmetic assignment statement is:

```
20 LET Y = ((.4*A)-2.+B)/(A+B-B↑2)
```

The operand within the leftmost set of parentheses (.4*A) is evaluated first. The constant 2 is subtracted from the result, and the value of B is then added to the result of these operations. Next the operations within the rightmost set of parentheses are performed. The operand B↑2 is evaluated first. Then the operand A+B is evaluated. The result of B↑2 is subtracted from the result of A+B. Finally, the overall result of the computations within the leftmost set of parentheses is divided by the overall result of the computations within the rightmost set of parentheses. The result of this division is assigned to Y.

In summary, the computer performs arithmetic operations from left to right, by the level of the operators, subject to the placement of parentheses.

The Multiple Arithmetic Assignment Statement

It is sometimes desirable to assign the same value to several variable names. This can be done by using several arithmetic assignment statements. For example, if it is desired to assign the result of the arithmetic expression B + C + 10 to the numeric variable names A, X, Y, and Z, one method is to write the following statements:

```
10 LET A = B+C+10
20 LET X = A
30 LET Y = A
40 LET Z = A
```

A more efficient programming method, however, is to use the multiple arithmetic assignment statement. Then, one statement to accomplish the above can be written as follows:

```
10 LET X = Y = Z = A = B+C+10
```

The Assignment of a Character String

The LET statement can also be used to assign a character-string value to a string variable name. For example:

```
10 LET A$ = "GROSS PROFIT"
20 LET B$ = Z$
```

The character string GROSS PROFIT will be assigned to the string variable A$. The character string assigned to the string variable Z$ will be assigned to the string variable B$.

Since a character string can only be composed of characters, neither a character string nor a string variable name can be used with arithmetic operators. Thus, the following illustration makes no sense and is illegal.

```
10 LET A = "5"+Z$-B
```

INPUT/OUTPUT STATEMENTS

In BASIC, data may be entered as an integral part of the program or from a terminal during execution of the program. The LET statement, as discussed, is one way in which a value to be processed can be entered as an integral part of the program. The following program is an illustrative example. The program computes the total amount that must be paid back on a $1000.00 loan at 5 percent interest for 10 years.

```
10 REM THE COMPUTATION OF A 10-YEAR INVESTMENT
20 LET P = 1000.00
30 LET I = 5
40 LET N = 10
50 LET A = P*(1+I/100)↑N
60 PRINT A
70 STOP
80 END
```

The first LET statement assigns the number 1000.00 to the variable name P. The second LET statement assigns 5 to the variable name I. The third LET statement assigns 10 to the variable name N. The last LET statement computes the total amount of the principal and interest at the end of N (10) years and assigns the result to A. The PRINT statement prints that result. The STOP statement is then executed; this terminates execution of the program.

The following output is printed:

```
1628.88
```

If a large amount of data must be processed, the use of the LET statement for data entry becomes cumbersome. For example, to find the total payback amount for several amounts at several rates of interest over several periods of time, either a new program must be written for each set of values, or a LET statement must be used for each new value in the program.

One way to overcome this problem is to use READ and DATA statements as described below.

The READ and DATA Statements

The READ statement causes the reading of data entered in one or more DATA statements as part of the program. Illustration A-4 shows the general form of this statement.

The following READ statement could take the place of the first three LET statements (20, 30, and 40) in the example program above.

```
20 READ P,I,N
```

This statement causes values to be assigned to the variable names P, I, and N.

The values to be assigned to the variable names listed in a READ statement are entered into the program via one or more DATA statements. Illustration A-5 shows the general form of the DATA statement.

The following DATA statement could be used to supply data to be

---

sn READ list

where:

    sn represents an unsigned 1 through 5 digit integer *statement number.*

    READ is a BASIC keyword that distinguishes this statement from the other kinds of statements in the program.

    list represents one or more variable names separated by commas and, if desired, one or more spaces.

Illustration A-4. General form of the READ statement.

---

sn DATA list

where:

    sn represents an unsigned 1 through 5 digit integer *statement number.*

    DATA is a BASIC keyword that distinguishes this statement from the other kinds of statements in the program.

    list represents one or more numbers or character strings separated by commas and, if desired, one or more spaces.

Illustration A-5. General form of the DATA statement.

assigned to the numeric variable names listed in the previous READ statement (P, I, and N).

```
30 DATA 1000.00,5,10
```

Each number, from left to right, is assigned to a corresponding variable name in the READ statement. That is, when the READ statement is executed, the number 1000.00 will be assigned to the variable name P; the number 5 will be assigned to the variable name I; and the number 10 will be assigned to the variable name N.

There can be as many READ and DATA statements as needed in a program. The DATA statements can be located anywhere among the other program statements. The placement of the READ statement(s), naturally, is dependent upon the logic of the program. During compilation of the program, the BASIC compiler places all of the values listed in all of the DATA statements into a combined list. The ordering of the values in the combined list is based on two rules: (1) ascending DATA statement numbers, and (2) the order, from left to right, of the values within each DATA statement. That is, the BASIC compiler takes the values in the first DATA statement and places them at the top of the combined list in order from left to right. Then the compiler goes to the second DATA statement and, again moving from left to right, places the values in the second DATA statement in the combined list. The compiler continues this operation until all of the values in all of the DATA statements are in the combined list.

The following sequences of READ statements are equivalent:

```
10 READ P
30 READ I            or     10 READ P,I,N
50 READ N
```

Similarly, the following DATA statements are equivalent:

```
20 DATA 1000.00
40 DATA 5            or     20 DATA 1000.00,5,10
60 DATA 10
```

So that the computer can keep track of which values have been assigned to variables names, and which ones have not, the BASIC compiler uses a "pointer." This pointer is internal to the compiler. It tells the next value to be assigned when the next READ statement is executed. Initially, this pointer is "pointing" to the first value in the first DATA statement (1000.00, in our example). Thus, when statement 10 above is executed, the pointer is pointed at the number 1000.00 in the combined list and that value is assigned to P. The pointer then shifts to point at the number 5 in the combined list. When example statement 30 is executed, the value 5 is assigned to I. The pointer then shifts to point at the number 10 in the combined list. When statement 50 is executed, the value 10 is assigned to N.

If the single statement form shown above is used, the computer performs essentially the same operations in assigning the values to P, I, and N. If there are more variable names in the READ statement(s) than values in the DATA statement(s), an error message is printed on the terminal and program execution is terminated. The following statements, for example, would cause program termination to occur.

```
10 READ P,I,N,K
20 DATA 1000.00,5,10
```

The Reading of a Character String

The READ statement, in conjunction with the DATA statement, can be used to assign a character string to a string variable name. For example:

```
10 READ A$,X,B$,C$
20 DATA "NET PAY", 243.25, "1 JAN.", "1978"
```

The character string NET PAY will be assigned to the string variable name A$; the number 243.25 will be assigned to the numeric variable name X; the character string 1 JAN. will be assigned to the string variable name B$; and the character string consisting of a blank and 1978 will be assigned to the string variable name C$.

As indicated in the illustration, both string variable names and numeric variable names can be listed in a READ statement. Of course, the type of data listed in the DATA statement must match the corresponding variable name in the READ statement.

Two Illustrations of the READ and DATA Statements

The following program illustrates the use of READ and DATA statements in place of LET statements to enter values for investment computation.

```
10 REM THE COMPUTATION OF A 10-YEAR INVESTMENT
20 READ P,I,N
30 DATA 1000.00,5,10
40 LET A = P*(1+I/100)↑N
50 PRINT A
60 STOP
70 END
```

The program below reads the character strings SMITH and 6A74F and the numbers 123 and 64.3. It assigns them to the string variable names J$ and P$ and the numeric variable names F and G, respectively.

```
10 REM THIS PROGRAM READS TWO CHARACTER STRINGS
20 REM AND TWO NUMBERS AND PRINTS THEM OUT
30 READ J$,P$,F,G
40 DATA "SMITH", "6A74F",123,64.3
50 PRINT J$,P$,F,G
60 STOP
70 END
```

The two character strings and the two numbers are printed on the terminal as follows:

```
SMITH          6A74F          123          64.3
```

The RESTORE Statement

In certain instances, it is necessary to re-read data within a program. This can be accomplished via the RESTORE statement. The execution of this statement causes the pointer used by the BASIC compiler to be moved back to the beginning of the combined list of numbers and/or character strings (the first number or character string in the DATA statement with the smallest statement number), regardless of where the pointer is currently located in the combined list. The RESTORE statement is generally used when it is necessary to perform several types of calculations on the same numbers, or to reuse character strings. Illustration A-6 shows the general form of this statement.

The first READ statement below causes the computer to assign the numbers 35.2, 91, and 15 to the numeric variable names A, B, and C, respectively. Execution of the RESTORE statement causes the pointer to be moved back to the beginning of the list of values in the DATA statement. It points to the number 35.2. Thus, when the second READ statement is executed, the numbers 35.2, 91, and 15 are assigned to the numeric variable names D, E, and F, respectively.

```
10 READ A,B,C
20 DATA 35.2,91,15
30 RESTORE
40 READ D,E,F
```

The INPUT Statement

Thus far, two methods of assigning values to variable names have been discussed—the LET statement and the READ and DATA statements. A

```
                        sn RESTORE
where:
        sn represents an unsigned 1 through 5 digit integer statement
        number.
        RESTORE is a BASIC keyword that distinguishes this statement
        from the other kinds of statements in the program.
```

Illustration A-6. General form of the RESTORE statement.

third method of assigning values to variable names is to use the INPUT statement. The distinction between the INPUT statement and the LET and READ statements is that data is entered during the execution of the program, rather than as an integral part of the program itself. Illustration A-7 shows the general form of this statement.

The INPUT statement causes the computer, during execution of the program, to print a question mark on the terminal. The person at the terminal responds by typing (on the same line) the data values to be processed. The values must be separated by commas. After the values have been entered, the person at the terminal presses the RETURN (or ENTER) key. The computer then assigns the values entered to the variable names listed in the INPUT statement and proceeds with the execution of the program.

As an example, consider the following program.

```
10 REM HOW THE INPUT STATEMENT WORKS
20 PRINT "ENTER X,Y,Z TO BE ADDED"
30 INPUT X,Y,Z
40 LET S = X+Y+Z
50 PRINT "THE SUM OF";X;Y;"AND";Z;"IS";S
60 STOP
70 END
```

When this program is executed, the computer first prints ENTER X,Y,Z TO BE ADDED. The computer then executes the INPUT statement, which causes it to print a question mark. The person at the terminal then enters, on the same line, the values to be assigned to X, Y, and Z. Assuming the values are 45.2, 25, and 15, the printing on the terminal appears as follows:

```
ENTER X,Y,Z TO BE ADDED
?   45.2,25,15
```

After the person at the terminal presses the RETURN (or ENTER) key, the number 45.2 is assigned to the numeric variable name X; the number 25 is assigned to the numeric variable name Y; and the number 15 is as-

---

sn INPUT list

where:

    sn represents an unsigned 1 through 5 digit integer statement number.

    INPUT is a BASIC keyword that distinguishes this statement from the other kinds of statements in the program.

    list represents one or more variable names separated by commas and, if desired, one or more spaces.

Illustration A-7. General form of the INPUT statement.

signed to the numeric variable name Z. The computer then adds the three numbers and prints the result as follows:

```
THE SUM OF 45.2 25 AND 15   IS 85.2
```

The following program shows how a previous example could be modified to use the INPUT statement in place of READ and DATA statements.

```
10 REM THE COMPUTATION OF A 10-YEAR INVESTMENT
20 INPUT P,I,N
30 LET A = P*(1+I/100)↑N
40 PRINT A
50 STOP
60 END
```

The following lines are printed on the terminal when the program is run.

```
?   1000.00,5,10
1628.88
```

Like the READ statement, the INPUT statement can be used to assign a character string to a string variable name. The rules that must be observed in the assignment of a character string using a READ statement must also be observed in the assignment of a character string using an INPUT statement. For example, assume the following INPUT statement is included in a program being executed:

```
10 INPUT A$,X,B$,C$
```

Further assume the input to the computer is typed as follows:

```
"NET PAY",243.25,"1 JAN.", "1978"
```

The character string NET PAY will be assigned to the string variable name A$; the number 243.25 will be assigned to the numeric variable name X; the character string 1 JAN. will be assigned to the string variable name B$; and the character string consisting of a blank and 1978 will be assigned to the string variable name C$.

The PRINT Statement

As the examples above have demonstrated, the results of processing can be printed on the terminal by a PRINT statement. This statement also allows the programmer to determine the format (i.e., what is printed where) on a line of output. Illustration A-8 shows the general form of this statement.

The "list" portion of the PRINT statement can take several forms, depending on the format desired for the output. For example, to skip a line on the terminal, a PRINT statement with no "list" should be used.

```
10 PRINT
```

To skip more than one line, the PRINT statement must be re-executed, or another PRINT statement executed, for each additional line. For example, to skip three lines, three PRINT statements should be written as shown below.

```
10 PRINT
20 PRINT
30 PRINT
```

Printing Numbers

Another form of the PRINT statement can be used to print the numbers assigned to one or more numeric variable names. It is also possible to specify arithmetic computations in the "list" portion of a PRINT statement, as shown in the following program. Note that the rules for performing the computations are the same as in the arithmetic assignment statement with regard to the position and use of operators and parentheses.

```
10 READ A,B,C
20 DATA 3,18,50
30 PRINT A
40 PRINT
50 PRINT B,C,6*A+100
```

The number assigned to the variable name A, which is 3, will be printed on the first line. The computer will skip a line. Then the numbers assigned to the variable names B and C, which are 18 and 50 respectively, and the

---

sn PRINT list

where:

      sn represents an unsigned 1 through 5 digit integer *statement number*.

      PRINT is a BASIC keyword that distinguishes this statement from the other kinds of statements in the program.

      list represents one or more variable names, arithmetic expressions, and/or character strings separated by commas or semicolons and, if desired, one or more spaces.

Illustration A-8. General form of the PRINT statement.

result of the arithmetic expression $6*A+100$ will be printed on the next line.

Commas and semicolons are used to control the spacing of the values printed on a line of output.* A terminal line is divided into four standard print fields, each 18 spaces wide. Comma tabs are set by the computer every 18 spaces—at print positions 1, 19, 37, and 55. Each comma tab marks the start of the next print field. After the computer prints a value in a print field, it moves to the next print field to print the next value (even if the first field was not entirely filled).

```
10 READ B,C,D
20 LET Z = 100
30 DATA 43.2,2000.,-17
40 PRINT Z,B,C,D
50 STOP
60 END
```

In the program above, the use of commas to separate the variable names in the PRINT statement causes the number assigned to Z, which is 100, to be printed in print positions 2 through 4; the number assigned to B, which is 43.2, to be printed in print positions 20 through 23; the number assigned to C, which is 2000., to be printed in print positions 38 through 42; and the number assigned to D, which is -17, to be printed in print positions 55 through 57.

In this illustration, the printing of all of the numbers, except the one assigned to the numeric variable name D, begins in the second print posi-

---

*The number and length of the standard print fields vary among computers. Each reader should see the BASIC manual for the available version of BASIC to determine the number and length of the standard print fields.

tion of the field. The first print position of each field is reserved for the number's arithmetic sign (+ or −). If the number is positive, the sign need not be printed, however. So the first print position of the field is blank. (This was the case for the numbers printed in the first, second, and third fields in the illustration.) If the number is negative, the minus sign is printed in the first print position of the field. (This was the case for the number printed in the fourth field of the illustration.)

In many situations it is desirable to print more than four numbers on a line. This can be accomplished by using semicolons rather than commas to separate the variable names in a PRINT statement. The use of a semicolon instead of a comma causes the computer to reduce the size of the print field from the standard print field length to some smaller size. The actual length of each print field depends upon the number of characters composing the number being printed and the particular version of BASIC being used. The following table shows the spacing commonly provided when semicolons are used.

Number of Digits to Be Printed	Width of Print Field in Spaces
1 to 4	6
5 to 7	9
8 to 10	12
11 to 13	15

The computer uses the first print position of each print field for the number's arithmetic sign. If semicolons were used instead of commas to separate the variable names in the PRINT statement of the above program, the output would appear as follows. The computer would print the number assigned to Z, which is 100, in print positions 2 through 4; the number assigned to B, which is 43.2, in positions 8 through 11; the number assigned to C, which is 2000., in positions 13 through 18; and the number assigned to D, which is −17, in positions 22 through 24. If there are more numbers to be printed on a line than there are spaces available within the line, the computer continues printing the numbers on the next line.

Normally, the terminal carriage advances to the beginning of the next line after the execution of a PRINT statement. To continue printing on the same line later in the program, a comma or semicolon should be placed after the last variable name in the PRINT statement. For example:

```
40 PRINT A;B;C;D;
50 PRINT Z
60 PRINT P
```

The values of A, B, C, D, and Z will be printed on the same line, assuming that their overall length does not cause the computer to attempt to go beyond the end of the carriage of the terminal. The value of P will be printed on the next line.

Printing Character Strings

There are two situations in which a character string is printed. The first, and most common situation, is the printing of output headings. For example, the following statement will cause the character strings THE SQUARE OF and IS to be printed.

```
60 PRINT "THE SQUARE OF ";N;" IS ";A
```

Because of the space between the letter F of the word OF and the quotation mark, and the space between the quotation mark and the letter I in the word IS, there will be at least one space prior to the first character and after the last character of the value N. Similarly, because of the space between the letter S of the word IS and the quotation mark, there will be at least one space prior to the first character of the value A.

If there are several headings to be printed, the use of commas to separate these headings causes the computer to use the standard print fields as it does when one or more commas are used to separate several variable names. Thus, in the following illustration, the heading ACCT NO. will be printed in positions 1 through 8; the heading DEPT will be printed in positions 19 through 22; the heading ITEM will be printed in positions 37 through 40; and the heading COST will be printed in positions 55 through 58.

```
10 PRINT "ACCT NO.","DEPT","ITEM","COST"
```

On the other hand, the use of a semicolon between two character strings causes no spacing to occur between the two strings. Thus, the programmer must establish the spacing by placing the desired number of blanks within the quotation marks that enclose each character string. The following illustration shows this point.

```
10 PRINT "THE VALUE OF A";"   THE VALUE OF B";"   THE VALUE OF C"
```

In the last two character strings, there are three spaces between the first quotation mark and the letter T of the word THE. When this statement is executed, the first string will be printed, beginning in column 1. The first word (THE) of the second string will appear in column 18—only three spaces after the ending character of the first string. Semicolon tab positions do not apply.

The second type of character-string printing occurs when the character string to be printed has been assigned to a string variable name. For example:

```
10 LET A$ = "NUMBER"
20 PRINT A$
```

The word NUMBER will be assigned to the string variable name A$. When statement 20 is executed, the word NUMBER will be printed, beginning in column 1.

The TAB Function

One problem may occur when printing output of a BASIC program: The comma and semicolon, due to their predefined field positioning, may not provide a "pretty" printout.

The TAB function is a formatting feature available in many versions of BASIC.* It allows more exact spacing of print fields. For example:

```
10 PRINT A$;TAB(15);"COST"
```

The value assigned to the string variable name A$ will be printed. The terminal will be spaced to the print position specified within the set of parentheses immediately following the keyword TAB (print position 15). Then the word COST will be printed. The number within the parentheses is the number of the column in which the first letter of COST will be printed.

In this illustration, the string variable name A$ is followed by a semicolon. If it had been followed by a comma, the terminal would have spaced to print position 19 before detecting the TAB(15) request. The TAB function is ignored if the terminal has passed the specified print position. Therefore, it is best to use the semicolon rather than the comma in PRINT statements where the TAB function is used.

COMPLETING A BASIC PROGRAM

There are three additional types of statements in the BASIC program at the beginning of this appendix. These three statements control termination of the process of compilation (the END statement), termination of execution (the STOP statement), and the insertion of comments explaining the program (the REM statement).

The REM Statement

The REM statement can be used to identify either an overall BASIC program and/or a specific part of a program. It can also be used to describe the data represented by particular variable names. Illustration A-9 shows the general form of the REM statement.

---

*Each reader should check the BASIC manual for the computer system in use to see if this feature is available.

If, because of its length, a REM statement must be continued on one or more additional lines, the keyword REM must be the first word of each additional line. Blanks can be included in the statement as desired to improve readability.

The REM statement is a nonexecutable statement; that is, it neither is processed by the BASIC compiler (translated into machine language) nor affects the execution of the BASIC program. Rather, it is printed verbatim along with other BASIC statements in the source-program listing.

REM statements are often placed at the beginning of a program as a means of identifying it. If a program is long or contains one or more distinguishable parts, the programmer can insert REM statements as desired throughout the program.

The END Statement

The END statement instructs the compiler to terminate compilation of a program. Illustration A-10 shows the general form of the END statement.

The END statement may be used to cause both program compilation and execution to terminate. The END statement must be the last physical statement in the program. This means the END statement must have the largest statement number.

---

sn REM

where:

    sn represents an unsigned 1 through 5 digit integer *statement number.*

    REM is a BASIC keyword that distinguishes this statement from the other kinds of statements in the program.

Illustration A-9. General form of the REM statement.

---

sn END

where:

    sn represents an unsigned 1 through 5 digit integer *statement number.*

    END is a BASIC keyword that distinguishes this statement from the other kinds of statements in the program.

Illustration A-10. General form of the END statement.

The STOP Statement

The STOP statement instructs the computer to terminate execution of a program. Illustration B-11 shows the general form of this statement.

A STOP statement may be located anywhere in a program prior to the END statement. The basic consideration in deciding specifically where to place a STOP statement in a program is that it must be located at a logical end of the program. If there is more than one logical end to a program, a STOP statement should be located at each logical end. The STOP statement is not necessary if there is only one logical end to the program, but it may be used just prior to the END statement if desired.

CONTROL STATEMENTS

There are three basic groups of program control statements. One group, composed of the STOP and END statements, was just discussed. The second group is concerned with going to, or *branching* to, a specific program statement. It includes the GO TO, IF-THEN, and ON-GO TO statements. The third group of statements is concerned with executing the same program statement(s) a specified number of times, or *looping,* before continuing the normal sequence of instruction execution. The FOR-TO and NEXT statements are in this group.

The GO TO Statement

The GO TO statement is sometimes referred to as an "unconditional" or "simple" GO TO. It causes the computer to branch (go) to an executable program statement other than the statement immediately following the GO TO statement. The statement that the computer branches to may either precede or follow the GO TO statement. Illustration A-12 shows the general form of this statement.

The GO TO statement

    20 GO TO 50

causes the computer to branch to statement 50.

---

                              sn STOP
where:

        sn represents an unsigned 1 through 5 digit integer *statement number.*

        STOP is a BASIC keyword that distinguishes this statement from the other kinds of statements in the program.

Illustration A-11. General form of the STOP statement.

```
                    sn GO TO sn
where:
        sn represents an unsigned 1 through 5 digit integer statement
          number.
        GO TO are BASIC keywords that distinguish this statement
          from the other kinds of statements in the program.
        sn represents the statement number of the statement to which
          a branch will be made.
```

Illustration A-12. General form of the GO TO statement.

The IF-THEN Statement

The IF-THEN statement directs the computer to make a decision regarding the truth or falseness of a relationship between two expressions. The expressions may take the form of variables (either numeric or string), constants, arithmetic expressions that must be evaluated (e.g., $B\uparrow2$ or $(A+B)/C$), or some combination thereof. If the relationship is true, the computer will branch to a specified statement in the program. If the relationship is false, the computer will execute the statement immediately Following the IF-THEN statement. Illustration A-13 shows the general form of this statement.

The way the IF-THEN statement operates is shown in Illustration A-14.

```
                    sn IF e ro e THEN sn
where:
        sn represents an unsigned 1 through 5 digit integer statement
          number.
        IF is a BASIC keyword that distinguishes this statement from
          the other kinds of statements in the program.
        e represents an expression or value.
        ro represents a relational operator.
        e represents an expression or value.
        THEN is a BASIC keyword that distinguishes this statement from
          the other kinds of statements in the program.
        sn represents the statement number of the statement to which
          the computer will branch if the specified relationship between
          the two expressions or values is true.
```

Illustration A-13. General form of the IF-THEN statement.

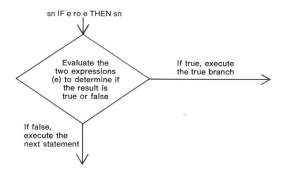

Illustration A-14. Operation of the IF-THEN statement.

The relational operator is a symbol that tells what relationship between two expressions or values is being tested for. There are six relational operators. Each is shown, accompanied by its mathematical meaning, below.

Symbol*	Meaning
$>$	Greater than
$>=$ or $\geq$	Greater than or equal to
$<$	Less than
$<=$ or $\leq$	Less than or equal to
$=$	Equal to
$<>$ or $\neq$	Not equal to

The IF-THEN statement in the following illustration causes the computer to evaluate the expressions A and 50. If the value assigned to A is greater than 50, the computer will branch to statement 40. If the value of A is 50 or less, the computer will execute the statement following the IF-THEN statement (the PRINT statement).

```
20 IF A > 50 THEN 40
30 PRINT A
40 LET C = B/A
```

In the following illustration, if the result of the arithmetic expression B↑2 is less than the result of the arithmetic expression X*Z, the computer will branch to statement 70. If the result of the arithmetic expression B↑2

---

*Where alternatives are shown, which symbol is valid depends on the BASIC compiler used.

is equal to or greater than the result of the arithmetic expression X∗Z, the computer will execute statement 20 (the LET statement).

```
10 IF B↑2 < X∗Z THEN 70
20 LET B = X∗Z
```

An IF-THEN statement can also be used to make a comparison between character strings. If a character-string constant is used, it must be enclosed in quotation marks. The comparison begins with the leftmost character of each string and moves from left to right. In general, one word is "less than" another word if it would appear prior to the other word in a dictionary. That is, BAT is "less than" CAT, and WINDOW is "greater than" HOUSE. If character strings of different lengths compare equally up to the end of the shorter string, that string is "less than" the longer character string. The BASIC compiler adds to the shorter character string the number of blanks necessary to equal the length of the longer character string, and a blank is "less than" any other character.

```
10 IF A$ > X$ THEN 60
20 IF M$ = "FRESHMAN" THEN 70
```

In statement 10, the character string assigned to the string variable name A$ is compared with the character string assigned to the string variable name X$. In statement 20, the character string assigned to the string variable name M$ is compared with the character string FRESHMAN.

The ON-GO TO Statement

The ON-GO TO statement is sometimes referred to as a "computed" GO TO. It causes the computer to branch to a statement on the basis of the value of an arithmetic expression. On some computer systems, the format of this statement is reversed, and it it known as the GO TO-ON statement. Still other systems have neither form of the statement.* The statement branched to may either precede or follow the ON-GO TO statement. Illustration A-15 shows the general form of this statement.

The ON-GO TO statement is used in situations where it is desirable to branch to one of several statements in a program, based on the value of an arithmetic expression or a variable name. For example, assume that it is desired to process certain data of a large number of armed service personnel. The particular branch of service of which a serviceman is a

---

*Each reader should check the BASIC manual for the computer system in use concerning the use of this statement.

---

sn ON ae GO TO sn(s)

where:

> sn represents an unsigned 1 through 5 digit integer *statement number*.
>
> ON is a BASIC keyword that distinguishes this statement from the other kinds of statements in the program.
>
> ae represents an *arithmetic expression*.
>
> GO TO are BASIC keywords.
>
> sn(s) represents one or more *statement numbers*.

Illustration A-15. General form of the ON-GO TO statement.

member determines what character string is to be printed as part of the output. The number 1 indicates the serviceman is a member of the army; the number 2 indicates he is a member of the air force; the number 3 indicates he is a member of the marines; and the number 4 indicates he is a member of the navy. The number 5 is a "dummy"; it serves as a special end-of-file indicator.

```
10 REM  READ CODES AND NAMES AND PRINT
20 REM  NAME, RANK, NUMBER, AND BRANCH OF
30 REM  SERVICE
40 READ A, B$, C, D$
50 ON A GO TO 100,120,160,140,200
60 DATA 4, "JAMES T. KIRK", 49031010, "CAPTAIN"
70 DATA 1, "B. NAPOLEON", 930411, "GENERAL"
80 DATA 2, "S. KING", 332110, "MAJOR"
90 DATA 5
100 PRINT "ARMY"
110 GO TO 170
120 PRINT "AIR FORCE"
130 GO TO 170
140 PRINT "NAVY"
150 GO TO 170
160 PRINT "MARINE"
170 PRINT B$,D$;C
180 PRINT
190 GO TO 40
200 STOP
210 END
```

Statements 10, 20, and 30 explain the purpose of this program. Statement 40 reads data from a DATA statement. The execution of statement 50 is as follows. If the number assigned to the variable name A is 1, the computer will branch to the statement assigned statement number 100; if the number is 2, the computer will branch to statement 120; if the number is 3, the computer will branch to statement 160; if the number is 4, the computer will branch to statement 140; and if the number is 5, the computer will branch to statement 200 and stop execution.

If the value assigned to the variable name or of the arithmetic expression in an ON-GO TO statement is not an integer number, say if it is 4.3, the number will be truncated (not rounded). If its value is negative, zero, or greater than the number of statement numbers listed in the ON-GO TO statement, the ON-GO TO will be ignored.*

The statement numbers can be in any sequence; that is, they do not have to be in either ascending or descending order. A statement number can be specified several times in one ON-GO TO statement.

The FOR-TO and NEXT Statements

The program above contains a GO TO statement that causes the computer to loop back to the beginning of the program to read the next group of data. A "dummy" set of data is included to stop the execution of the program when all the groups of data have been processed.

The FOR-TO and NEXT statements provide a simpler way to perform the loop and to stop program execution at the right time. The FOR-TO statement is considered the most powerful program statement in BASIC because of its looping capability. To tell the computer where the end of a loop is, a NEXT statement is required. The NEXT statement always appears as the last statement in a loop. Illustration A-16 shows the general forms of the FOR-TO and NEXT statements.

The way the FOR-TO and NEXT statements operate is shown in Illustration A-17. Note that this is a trailing-decision loop—the processing steps in the loop are always executed at least once.

A detailed explanation of the following FOR-TO and NEXT statements is given in Table A-1.

With respect to the FOR-TO statement, the following factors should be considered:

1. The numeric variable name, nvn, can be used in statements within the range of the FOR-TO statement. For example, the following use of I is acceptable.

```
10 FOR I = 1 TO 10
20 T = T+I
30 NEXT I
```

*Some BASIC implementations treat these conditions as errors. A message is printed, and program execution is terminated.

sn FOR nvn = in$_1$ TO in$_2$ STEP in$_3$

•

•

•

sn NEXT vn

where:

    sn represents an unsigned 1 through 5 digit integer *statement number.*

    FOR is a BASIC keyword that distinguishes this statement from the other kinds of statements in the program.

    nvn represents a *numeric variable name.* This variable name is sometimes referred to as the index variable of the FOR-TO loop.

    = is a special character used here as required in the BASIC language.

    in$_1$ represents an arithmetic expression, a constant, or a numeric variable name whose value is taken as the initial value of nvn when the FOR-TO statement is encountered by the program during execution.

    TO is a BASIC keyword.

    in$_2$ represents an arithmetic expression, a constant, or a numeric variable name whose value is compared with the current value of nvn after the last statement of the loop has been executed. If the value of nvn *exceeds* the value of in$_2$, the computer goes to the statement immediately following the NEXT statement.

    STEP is a BASIC keyword. It can be omitted if the value of in$_3$ is always 1.

    in$_3$ represents an arithmetic expression, a constant, or a numeric variable name whose value is either added to or subtracted from (if the value of in$_3$ is negative) the current value assigned to nvn after the last statement in the loop has been executed, but *before* the comparison of nvn with in$_2$ is made.

    If STEP and in$_3$ are omitted, the BASIC compiler assumes that nvn is to be incremented by 1 each time the loop is executed.

•

•

•

    sn represents an unsigned 1 through 5 digit integer *statement number.*

    NEXT is a BASIC keyword that distinguishes this statement from the other kinds of statements in the program.

    nvn represents the *numeric variable name* specified in the FOR-TO statement.

Illustration A-16. General forms of the FOR-TO and NEXT statements.

Table A-1. A summary of the FOR-TO and NEXT statements.
10 FOR I = 1 TO 25

STATEMENT NUMBER	10	The statement number assigned to this FOR-TO statement.
STATEMENT KEYWORD	FOR	The keyword FOR indicates that the computer is to execute this statement and all others up to and including the NEXT statement.
NUMERIC VARIABLE NAME	I	Each FOR-TO statement has an associated numeric variable name chosen by the programmer.
INITIAL VALUE	1	The programmer indicates the FOR-TO numeric variable's initial value.
KEYWORD	TO	This is a BASIC keyword.
TEST	25	Upon each execution of the statements in the FOR-TO statement range, the value of the variable name is compared with the test value, which in this case is 25. When the value of the variable name exceeds the test value, the FOR-TO statement is considered satisfied. The variable name is reset to the last value used in the loop. Then control passes outside the range of the FOR-TO statement to the first statement following the NEXT statement containing the variable name in the FOR-TO statement.
INDEXING INCREMENT		The programmer specifies how much the value of the numeric variable name is to increase after each execution of the loop—in this case 1. (If no value is specified, it is understood to be 1.) The incrementation occurs before the comparison of the numeric variable name and the test value.
RANGE	· · ·	The range of the FOR-TO statement is the statements within the loop, which may be executed several times.
LAST STATEMENT OF RANGE	NEXT I	The last statement must be a NEXT statement containing the same numeric variable name as the FOR-TO statement.

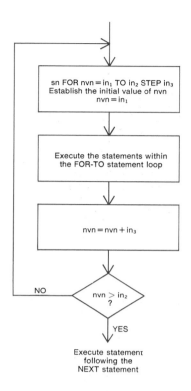

Illustration A-17. Operation of the FOR-TO and NEXT statements.

2. The number assigned to the numeric variable name, nvn, is controlled by the computer during the execution of the statements within the FOR-TO loop. Its value cannot be changed by statements within the loop. For example, the following sequence of statements is not allowed.

```
10 FOR I = 1 TO 10
        •
        •
        •
50 I = J+K
60 NEXT I
```

3. If variable names are used for in_1, in_2, and/or in_3, the number assigned to each of them cannot be changed by statements within the FOR-TO loop. The following sequence of statements is incorrect because in_2 (B, in this case) is changed inside the loop.

```
10 FOR I = 1 TO B STEP C
        •
        •
        •
40 B = N
50 NEXT I
```

4. When the computer goes to the next program statement after the NEXT statement, the value of the numeric variable name, nvn, remains defined. It is the last value used in the loop.* As such, it is available for reference. When the following FOR-TO loop is completed, the numeric variable name I is equal to 10. Therefore, in statement 60, J is assigned the value 13.

```
10 FOR I = 1 TO 10
        •
        •
        •
50 NEXT I
60 J = I+3
```

The program statements within a FOR-TO loop may be located within one or more other FOR-TO loops. If the statements of a FOR-TO loop lie entirely within another FOR-TO loop, the first or "inner" FOR-TO loop is said to be "nested" within the second or "outer" FOR-TO loop.

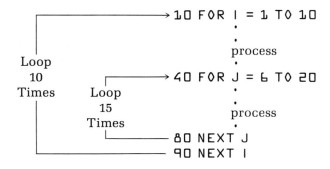

The program statements within an inner or "nested" FOR-TO loop must be entirely within the next outer FOR-TO loop. For example, the following sequence is incorrect.

---

*Some BASIC implementations exit the FOR-TO loop with the variable name set to the first value not used.

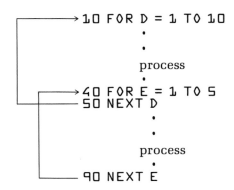

The NEXT statement for an inner FOR-TO loop cannot be the same statement as the NEXT statement for an outer FOR-TO loop. The following sequence will cause an error due to the attempted use of the same NEXT statement for the outer and inner loops.

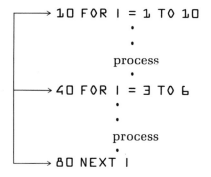

The computer can branch out of a FOR-TO loop at any time during the execution of the statements within the loop. However, a return to a program statement within a FOR-TO loop can be made only under the following circumstances:

1. The values of nvn, in_1, in_2, and in_3 must not have been changed.

2. If a FOR-TO loop is nested within one or more other FOR-TO loops, both the branch and the return must be made from and to the innermost FOR-TO loop.

ARRAYS

In many programs, there is the necessity to process values that are related in some way. For example, assume a program is to do a statistical analysis of daily sales totals for the past year. It is desirable to hold all the daily totals in the computer memory at the same time in a manner which indicates the relationship in time of each total to every other total for the period.

One way to do this would be to assign each value to a unique name. This would require 365 numeric variable names just to represent the data. Since other values used in the computations will require variable names, the total number of variable names required could run easily to over 400.

The BASIC language provides a simple solution to this problem: the use of an *array*. The array is characterized by a single unique variable name and a *subscript*.

In essence, the array is a list of locations in computer memory, and the subscript serves as a pointer to a particular location, or *element*, in the list. When a particular value from the array is needed for processing, the array name tells the computer which array (there can be several arrays in the program); the subscript references the particular location in the array (each location can hold one value).

The Naming of an Array

In most versions of BASIC, an array name can be composed of only a single alphabetic character.* An array and a variable may have the same name in the same program. However, because this can cause confusion, it should not be done. If it is necessary to have an array and a variable with the same name, a digit should be used as the second character of the variable name. For example, if arrays named A and B are used in a program, and it seems necessary to use the names A and B for variables, the variable names A1 and B1 should be used instead.

The DIM Statement

A variable name is declared to be the name of an array by means of the DIM statement. Illustration A-18 shows the general form of this statement.

There can be several DIM statements in a program. They can be located anywhere in the program, provided that the DIM statement defining an array appears before the array name is used in processing. Each DIM statement can contain as many array names as can be accommodated on an input line.

The statement

```
10 DIM E(50)
```

---

*Each reader should check the BASIC manual for the computer system in use to determine how arrays are named.

```
                    sn DIM an₁(in₁, in₂) , . . . , anₙ(in₁, in₂)
where:
         sn represents an unsigned 1 through 5 digit integer statement
            number.
         DIM is a BASIC keyword that distinguishes this statement from
            the other kinds of statements in the program.
         an₁ , . . . , anₙ represent array names.
         ( is a special character used here as required in the BASIC language.
         in₁, in₂, . . . , in₁, in₂ represent sets of one or two unsigned integer
            numbers which specify the number of locations to be reserved
            for the immediately preceding array name. If there are two integer
            numbers, they must be separated by a comma. If one number
            appears inside the parentheses, the array is a one-dimensional
            array. If two numbers appear, separated by a comma, the array is a
            two-dimensional array.
         ) is a special character used here as required in the BASIC language.
```

Illustration A-18. General form of the DIM statement.

causes the computer to reserve 50 locations for a one-dimensional array named E. Once the locations have been reserved for an array name, they cannot be used for anything else. Any unused locations in the array are, in effect, wasted space. The amount of computer memory needed for the program is larger than it would have to be otherwise.

Array Dimensions

An array may be either one-dimensional or two-dimensional. (A one-dimensional array is sometimes called a list or vector. A two-dimensional array is sometimes called a matrix or table.) Whether an array is one- or two-dimensional is determined by whether there are one or two unsigned integer numbers enclosed in parentheses immediately following the array name in a DIM statement. If there is only one number in the parentheses, the array is one-dimensional. The number indicates the number of locations or rows in the array. If there are two numbers in the parentheses, the array is two-dimensional. The first number specifies the number of rows, and the second number specifies the number of columns.

In the following statement, the one-dimensional array named P is reserved 10 rows and the two-dimensional array named T is reserved 2 rows and 3 columns.

```
10 DIM P(10),T(2,3)
```

The following list and matrix show how the arrays P and T are set up. The small numbers are the location subscripts. In the two-dimensional array T, the first number indicates the row and the second number indicates the column of each location. In the one-dimensional array P, the numbers are row numbers.

$$P_1$$
$$P_2$$
$$P_3$$
$$P_4 \qquad T_{1,1} \qquad T_{1,2} \qquad T_{1,3}$$
$$P_5 \qquad T_{2,1} \qquad T_{2,2} \qquad T_{2,3}$$
$$P_6$$
$$P_7$$
$$P_8$$
$$P_9$$
$$P_{10}$$

The total number of locations reserved for an array can be found by multiplying the number of rows by the number of columns. (The number of columns is 1 if the array is one-dimensional.) Thus, in the preceding illustration, the first array is composed of 10 locations. The second array is composed of 6 locations.

Subscripts and Array Elements

A subscript is composed of one or two arithmetic expressions or numerical values (separated by a comma if there are two) enclosed in a set of parentheses. The subscript immediately follows the array name. The array name and its accompanying subscript refer to an array element; that is, they "define" a location. An array element is a particular location in the array. Similar to a variable name, an array element can be assigned a value via a LET, READ, or INPUT statement. The construction and use of a subscript are based on the following rules.

1. A subscript can be composed of numeric variable names, arithmetic expressions, and constants.
2. A subscript can take any form that an arithmetic expression can take.
3. The hierarchy of evaluation of the operands composing a subscript is identical to the hierarchy of evaluation of an arithmetic expression.
4. Depending upon the version of BASIC being used, the subscript must be zero and/or a number greater than zero.
5. If the evaluated result of an arithmetic expression is not an integer, the fractional portion is truncated and the decimal point is ignored in determining the specific array element in an array.

6. An array element can be used in any program statement in which a variable name can be used.

The following statements reserve space for an array named E through the use of the DIM statement and then store a real number in the 10th element of the array.

```
10 DIM E(60)
20 READ E(10)
30 DATA 37.5
```

There is a distinct difference in meaning between mention of an array name and its accompanying subscript in a DIM statement, and mention of an array name and its accompanying subscript in another type of statement, such as a READ, PRINT, or LET statement. If the array name and subscript are used in the DIM statement, the computer is being told the number of locations to reserve for the array. However, if the array name and subscript are used in one of the latter types of statements, reference is being made to a specific location within that array for the processing of data.

The Default Creation of an Array

The computer will automatically reserve storage space in its memory for arrays that have no more than 10 rows, or no more than 10 rows and 10 columns. Thus, it is not necessary to use the DIM statement for one-dimensional arrays which are equal to or smaller than 10 or for two-dimensional arrays which are equal to or smaller than 10 by 10.

To create an array by default, the programmer need only use a variable name as an array, that is, use the variable name followed by a subscript as a part of a program. The following statements cause the default creation of two arrays, A and B. Array A has 10 rows; array B has 10 rows and 5 columns.

```
10 FOR I = 1 TO 10
20 A(I) = I
30 FOR J = 1 TO 5
40 B(I,J) = I+J
50 NEXT J
60 NEXT I
```

The Storage of a Character String in an Array

A character string can be stored in an array. The procedure described above applies to the dimensioning of an array in which character strings are to be stored except that the array name ends with $. For example:

```
10 DIM A$(25),B(15),X$(15),M(5,10)
```

The array A$ is dimensioned to store up to 25 character strings. The array X$ is dimensioned to store up to 15 character strings. As shown in this example, arrays in which character strings are to be stored can be dimensioned in the same DIM statement as arrays in which numbers are to be stored.

In the following example, a two-dimensional character-string array B$ is defined. Since the array has 80 rows and 3 columns, you can think of it as able to hold 240 character strings. For example, the names, numbers, and major suppliers of 80 items from a bill of materials list can be read and stored in this array.

```
20 DIM B$ (80, 3).
```

THE MAT STATEMENTS

The ability to define two-dimensional arrays, or matrices, and to perform operations on these matrices, is a powerful programming tool. While operations on matrices can be programmed using the BASIC statements presented thus far, a set of 13 matrix (MAT) statements is also included in most versions of BASIC as a convenience for programmers. (See Table A-2.) This set allows you to use fewer BASIC statements to specify a matrix operation. It makes setting up calculations a much easier task. As shown in Table A-2, each of the matrix statements begins with the word MAT. (In these examples, X, Y, and Z are matrices.)

Matrix Input/Output

The MAT READ, MAT INPUT, and MAT PRINT statements are used to read data into or print data from a matrix without referencing each element individually. Any number of matrices can be read or printed within the limits of the input line. When using the MAT READ statement, all of the array must be filled; if not, an error will occur.

In the following illustration, the MAT READ statement stores six numbers in a matrix named X. The MAT PRINT statement prints these six numbers in horizontal (*row*) sequence. Row sequence means that the statement operates on all of row 1 first, then all of row 2, and so on.

---

*Most BASIC implementations require an array in which character strings are stored to be one-dimensional. Some, like IBM's VS BASIC compiler, also allow characters to be stored in two-dimensional arrays. The default for a character string is 18. However, a length specification in the range from 1 through 255 can be included following the array name, if necessary. For example:

```
20 DIM B$ 12 (80, 3).
```

Table A-2. BASIC matrix (MAT) statements.

Example	Explanation
MAT READ X,Y,Z	Read data from DATA statement(s) into previously dimensioned matrices in row sequence.
MAT INPUT X,Y	Input data into previously dimensioned matrices in row sequence.
MAT PRINT X	Print the elements of matrix X.
MAT Y = X	Set the elements of matrix Y equivalent to the corresponding elements of matrix X; the elements of matrix X are not altered.
MAT Z = X+Y	Add the corresponding elements of matrices X and Y; store the sum in the corresponding element of matrix Z.
MAT Z = X−Y	Subtract the elements of matrix Y from the corresponding elements of matrix X; store the difference in the corresponding element of matrix Z.
MAT Z = X*Y	Multiply the elements of matrix X by the elements of matrix Y; store the products in matrix Z.
MAT Z = (V)*X	Multiply each element of matrix X by the value V (scalar multiplication) and store the product in the corresponding element of matrix Z; V can be a constant, a variable name, or an arithmetic expression. It must be enclosed in parentheses.
MAT Z = TRN(X)	Transpose matrix X; store the result in matrix Z; X is not altered.
MAT X = ZER	Store the value of zero (0) in all elements of matrix X.
MAT X = CON	Store the value of one (1) in all elements of matrix X. (CON stands for constant.)
MAT X = IDN	Establish matrix X as an "identity" matrix (diagonal elements = one; nondiagonal elements = zero).
MAT Z = INV(X)	Invert matrix X; store the inverse in matrix Z; the elements of matrix X are not altered.

```
10 DIM X(2, 3)
20 MAT READ X
30 MAT PRINT X
40 DATA 37,5,91,−27,−12,−43
50 STOP
60 END
```

The order in which the above program reads the data elements is as follows:

```
X(1,1) =   37
X(1,2) =    5
X(1,3) =   91
X(2,1) = −27
X(2,2) = −12
X(2,3) = −43
```

The output of the above program appears as follows:

```
  37        5      91
 −27      −12     −43
```

The MAT READ and MAT INPUT statements can also be used to change the size of, or re-dimension, a matrix at execution time; that is, to make one or both of the previously stated (or assumed) subscripts of a matrix *smaller*. The forms are:

```
10 DIM A(25,25),B(15,7)
20 INPUT R,C
30 MAT READ A(R,C)
40 MAT INPUT B(R,C)
```

where R is the new number of rows and C is the new number of columns of arrays A and B. Re-dimensioning of arrays is a technique for conserving the amount of space required for an array in a program which requires varying amounts of array space each time it is run.

Matrix Arithmetic

Matrices can be made equivalent, added, subtracted, or multiplied using the five arithmetic MAT statements.

MAT Z = X	Equivalence
MAT Z = X + Y	Addition
MAT Z = X − Y	Subtraction
MAT Z = X*Y	Multiplication
MAT Z = (V)*X	Scalar multiplication

Certain rules must be followed in the use of these MAT statements. They are explained below.

1. For addition and subtraction, the dimensions of all matrices to the right of the equal sign must be identical. Each dimension on the left side of the equal sign must be large enough to permit the result of the operation to be stored.

```
10 DIM X(5,10),Y(5, 10)Z(5,10)
 .
 .
 .
50 MAT Z = X+Y
```

2. For multiplication, the number of *columns* of the first matrix must be the same as the number of *rows* of the second matrix. Each dimension on the left side of the equal sign must be large enough to permit the result of the operation to be stored.

```
10 DIM X(9,7),Y(7,12),Z(9,12)
 .
 .
 .
50 MAT Z = X*Y
```

3. The same matrix can appear on both sides of the equal sign in addition, subtraction, and scalar multiplication. Thus, the following statements are legal, if the matrices X and Y have the same dimensions.

```
10 MAT X = X+Y
20 MAT X = (.05)*X
30 MAT X = X-Y
```

4. Only one arithmetic operation is allowed per MAT statement. Thus, the following statement is illegal.

```
10 MAT X = X+Y-Z
```

This illegal statement can be rewritten as shown below. Two separate MAT statements are needed to accomplish the two arithmetic operations.

```
10 MAT X = X+Y
20 MAT X = X-Z
```

Matrix Transposition

The MAT READ and MAT INPUT statements accept data in row sequence. The MAT TRN statement has the effect of resequencing a matrix into vertical (*column*) order. That is, the rows become columns and the columns become rows. The dimensions of the new matrix must be such that its column-row values equal the row-column values of the old matrix.

```
10 DIM X(5,2),Y(2,5)
.
.
.
50 MAY Y = TRN(X)
```

Most versions of BASIC do not allow transposition into the original matrix. That is, the same matrix cannot appear on both sides of the equal sign when using the MAT TRN statement.

Initializing Matrices

The MAT statements ZER, COM, and IDN allow you to load specific values into the elements of a matrix without having to READ or INPUT them. All three can be used to re-dimension a matrix using the same format as the MAT READ statement.

```
MAT Z = ZER(R,C)
MAT Z = CON(R,C)
MAT Z = IDN(R,C)
```

Initializing to zero. The statement

```
MAT Z = ZER
```

stores a zero in each element of matrix Z.

Initializing to one. The statement

```
MAT W = CON
```

stores a one in each element of matrix W.

The identity matrix   The IDN statement creates an identity matrix. In this matrix, the diagonal elements are equal to one and the nondiagonal elements are equal to zero.

```
10 MAT X = IDN(3,3)
20 MAT PRINT X
30 STOP
40 END
1   0   0
0   1   0
0   0   1
```

Note that statement 10 re-dimensions matrix X. Since there is no DIM statement defining X, it would be assumed to be 10 by 10 if the dimensions (3,3) were not included.

The IDN statement requires that the number of rows equals the number of columns—for example, DIM X(15,15), defines a matrix that can be operated on by the IDN statement.

Matrix Inversion

The statement

MAT Z = INV(Y)

calculates the inverse of matrix Y (1/Y or Y^{-1}). Matrix inversion is the most powerful of the BASIC matrix operations, accomplishing in a single statement what would be a mammoth task using regular BASIC features. Its main use is in solving simultaneous linear equations. (For a full discussion of matrix inversion and its uses, see a matrix algebra text.)

AN ILLUSTRATION

It is often useful to have the computer generate the results of a program in the form of a graph. One of the easiest graphs to produce is a bar chart.

The bar chart indicates—by the relative heights or lengths of bars—the relationships between values.

The following program illustrates one method of printing a horizontal bar chart representing sales figures for 10 years.

The sales data to be processed by the program follows:

Year	Sales (in millions)
1969	19
1970	23
1971	26
1972	31
1973	36
1974	38
1975	40
1976	41
1977	37
1978	35

The following output is to be printed:

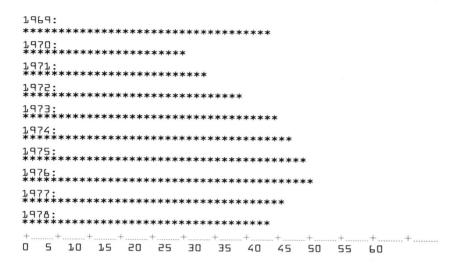

```
1969:
**********************************
1970:
**********************
1971:
***********************
1972:
*****************************
1973:
**********************************
1974:
*************************************
1975:
*****************************************
1976:
*******************************************
1977:
****************************************
1978:
**********************************

  +........+........+........+........+........+........+........+........+........+........+........+........+........+..........
  0    5    10   15   20   25   30   35   40   45   50   55   60
```

The program works by using the sales figures to determine how many asterisks to place in a one-dimensional array for each year. After the array has been printed for a year, it is "blanked out" (that is, filled with blanks). Illustration A-19 is a flowchart of the program; A-20 shows the program.

FUNCTIONS

The BASIC language provides several predefined, specialized functions to solve frequently occurring mathematical problems that are relatively difficult to program. Among them are square root, absolute value, sine, cosine, and logarithm. The functions common to most versions of BASIC are discussed below. (Most versions of BASIC provide several additional functions.)

The BASIC language also provides a facility that the programmer can use to define additional, special functions. He or she does so by means of the DEF statement. This statement is also discussed.

Predefined Functions

BASIC predefined functions can be grouped into four categories: trigonometric, exponential, arithmetic, and utility. The general form of each function is a three-letter name followed by an *argument* enclosed in parentheses. The argument—represented by X in the following illustrations—is a value passed to the function, to be operated on. It is expressed as an appropriate constant, variable name, or arithmetic expression.

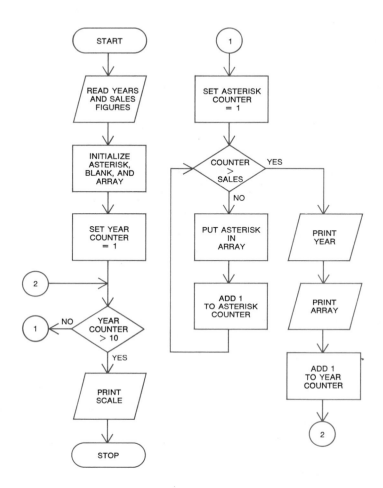

Illustration A-19. Flowchart of a bar-chart graphing program.

The trigonometric functions. There are four BASIC trigonometric functions. Their names and meanings follow:

SIN(X)	The sine of X is calculated.
COS(X)	The cosine of X is calculated.
TAN(X)	The tangent of X is calculated.
ATN(X)	The arctangent (principal value in radians) of X is calculated (angle whose tangent is X).

The BASIC trigonometric functions require the argument X to be measured in radians. (To convert a value expressed in degrees to radians,

```
10 REM A PROGRAM TO PRODUCE A HORIZONTAL BAR CHART
20 DIM P$(70)
30 FOR I = 1 TO 10
40 READ Y$(I)
50 READ A(I)
60 NEXT I
70 REM INITIALIZE THE VARIABLES AND THE GRAPH ARRAY
80 LET S$ = "*"
90 LET B$ = " "
100 FOR I = 1 TO 70
110 LET P$(I) = B$
120 NEXT I
130 FOR K = 1 TO 10
140 FOR I = 1 TO A(K)
150 LET P$(I) = S$
160 NEXT I
170 PRINT
180 PRINT Y$(K)
190 FOR I = 1 TO 70
200 PRINT P$(I);
210 NEXT I
220 PRINT
230 FOR I = 1 TO 70
240 LET P$(I) = B$
250 NEXT I
260 NEXT K
270 FOR I = 1 TO 70
280 LET P$(I) = "-"
290 NEXT I
300 FOR I = 1 TO 70 STEP 5
310 LET P$(I) = "+"
320 NEXT I
330 MAT PRINT P$;
340 PRINT "0   5   10   15   20   25   30   35   40   45   50   55"
350 PRINT
360 PRINT "END OF RUN"
370 DATA "1969:",19
380 DATA "1970:",23
390 DATA "1971:",26
400 DATA "1972:",31
410 DATA "1973:",36
420 DATA "1974:",38
430 DATA "1975:",40
440 DATA "1976:",41
450 DATA "1977:",37
460 DATA "1978:",35
470 STOP
480 END
```

Illustration A-20. Bar-chart graphing program.

you can multiply the number of degrees by .0174533 or divide the number of degrees by 57.2957795.)

In the following illustration, the sine of 20° is calculated and assigned to the variable name Z.

```
10 LET Z = SIN(20*.0174533)
```

The exponential functions. There are three BASIC exponential functions. Their names and a short explanation of each follow:

EXP(X)   The natural exponent e^X is calculated; e = 2.7182818.

LOG(X)   The natural logarithm $\log_e X$ is calculated (X must be greater than 0.)

SQR(X)   The square root of X is calculated (X must have a non-negative number assigned to it).

The result obtained by using the SQR function can also be obtained by raising the argument to the one-half power—that is, .5. However, since the SQR function is incorporated in the BASIC language, execution of the function is faster than execution of a statement such as 10 LET Y = X**.5.

The arithmetic functions. There are three arithmetic functions. Their names and a short explanation of each follow:

ABS(X)   Determines the absolute value of X.

SGN(X)   Determines the sign of X. The result is either −1, 0, or +1, depending upon whether X is negative, zero, or positive, respectively.

INT(X)   Calculates the largest integer which is less than or equal to X. X may be thought of as being located on a number scale that extends from negative infinity to positive infinity. It is used by itself to round or truncate numbers for printing or other purposes and is especially useful in conjunction with the RND function (discussed below).

Three illustrations of the ABS(X) function follow:

1. ABS(X) = 4.3   (where X = 4.3)
2. ABS(X) = 0   (where X = 0)
3. ABS(X) = 4.3   (where X = −4.3)

Three illustrations of the SGN(X) function are:

1. SGN(X) = −1   (where X = − 4.2)
2. SGN(X) = 0   (where X = 0)
3. SGN(X) = 1   (where X = 54.32)

The INT function is used as shown below:

1. INT(12) = 12
2. INT(4.3) = 4
3. INT(0.5) = 0
4. INT(−7) = −7
5. INT(−4.3) = −5

To round a number to the nearest integer, the following statement can be used.

```
10 LET Z = INT(X+.5)
```

Assuming X = 6.1, then X+.5 = 6.6, then INT(X+.5) = 6, which is assigned to Z. If X = 6.7, then X+.5 = 7.2, then INT(X+.5) = 7, which is assigned to Z.

To round a number to the nearest tenth, the following statement can be used.

```
10 LET Z = INT(10*X+.5)/10
```

Assuming X = 5.23, then 10*X+.5 = 52.8, and INT(10*X+.5) = 52; therefore, INT(10*X+.5)/10 = 5.2, which is assigned to Z.

The utility functions. The two utility functions and a short explanation of each follow:

TAB(X)   Used in the PRINT statement to provide an additional formatting option for output.

X specifies a print position. (This function is discussed together with the PRINT statement, earlier in this appendix.)

RND(X)   Randomly generates a six-digit number between 0 (inclusive) and 1 (exclusive).*

Two illustrations of the RND(X) function follow.

1. Assume you want to simulate a coin-tossing experiment. A 0 will represent a tail, and a 1 will represent a head. On any particular toss of the coin, the probability of a 0 or 1 occurring is 0.5. The statement

```
10 LET Z = INT(RND(X)+.5)
```

will result in RND(X) having a value between 0 and 1, and the result of RND+.5 will be a number in the range from 0.5 through 1.5. The result of the evaluation of the expression INT(RND(X)+.5) will be either 0 or 1. Each has a probability of 0.5 of occurring. This result will be assigned to Z. To simulate a biased coin, say in favor of heads occurring, for example, you can add .6, .7, .8, or .9 (rather than .5) to RND(X).

2. Now assume you want to simulate the tossing of a die, where the numbers 1 through 6 can each occur with equal probability on a particular toss of the die. Use the statement

```
10 LET Z = INT(6*RND(X)+1)
```

If RND(X) generates .3, then 6*RND(X) = 1.8+1=2.8; and INT(6*RND(X)+1) = INT(2.8) = 2, which is assigned to Z.

---

*The value which should be assigned to the variable name X before it is used as the RND argument varies among BASIC implementations. Each reader should check the BASIC manual for the computer system in use.

User-Defined Functions

The BASIC language facility that the user can take advantage of to define functions is the DEF statement. There may be up to 26 DEF statements in one program. Illustration A-21 shows the general form of this statement.

When a user-defined function is executed, say, in a LET or PRINT statement, the computer transfers each value assigned to each variable name or constant within the argument to its corresponding variable name in the arithmetic expression of the DEF statement. The expression is then evaluated. The result is transferred through the user-defined function name and its accompanying argument (in the DEF statement) to the original program statement. It replaces the user-defined function name and its accompanying argument in the program statement.

For example, assume it is necessary to compute the area of a circle at several places in a program. Each computation of area uses a different value for the radius. The following illustration shows one way this can be done.

```
10 DEF FNA(X) = 3.1415*X↑2
   .
   .
   .
40 LET A = FNA(7.2)
   .
   .
   .
90 LET B = FNA(A)
   .
   .
   .
120 LET C = FNA(A+B)
```

When LET statement 40, 90, or 100 is executed, the computer will replace X in the arithmetic expression of the DEF statement with 7.2, A, A+B, respectively. The arithmetic expression will then be evaluated. The result will be assigned to A, B, or C, respectively.

A variable name can be used more than once in the arithmetic expression of a DEF statement. For example:

```
10 DEF FNA(X) = (3.1415*X↑2)/X
```

More than one variable name can appear in the arithmetic expression. However, all variable names other than one specified in the argument must have been assigned values before the function is referenced in the program. For example:

```
10 DEF FNB(X) = X**2/Y+5000
   .
   .
   .
100 LET Y = 52
110 LET R = FNB(A)
```

The execution of statements 100 and 110 has the same effect as execution of the following statement:

```
100 LET R = A**2/52+5000
```

Another possible alternative is to include multiple variable names in the argument when defining the function (that is, in the DEF statement).* This permits multiple values to be passed to the function whenever it is used in the program. For example:

```
10 DEF FNC(X,Y) = X**2/Y
  .
  .
  .
300 LET R = FNC(A,B)
  .
  .
  .
420 LET U = FNC(K,L)
```

The first function reference above causes the current value of A to be squared and divided by B. The second reference causes the current value of K to be squared and divided by L.

---

sn DEF FNA(X) = ae

where:

   sn represents an unsigned 1 through 5 digit integer statement number.

   DEF is a BASIC keyword that distinguishes this statement from the other kinds of statements in the program.

   FNA is the name of a user-defined function. The function name must consist of three alphabetic characters, the first two being FN and the third being a letter (A through Z) chosen by the user.

   (X) is an argument composed of one or more variable names. (Some versions of BASIC allow only one variable name.)

   = is a special character used here as required in the BASIC language.

   ae represents an arithmetic expression.

Illustration A-21. General form of the DEF statement.

---

*Some versions of BASIC allow only one variable name to be specified in a user-defined function argument list. Each reader should check the BASIC manual for the system in use concerning the DEF statement.

SUBROUTINES

Some applications require that, at several different points in a program, identical sequences of operations be performed. While it is possible to write the statements describing the operations at each point where they are needed, it is more efficient to write what is called a *subroutine*. The subroutine is composed of the necessary statements. Then, it is possible to refer to the subroutine at each point in the program where the statements would otherwise have to be included. The effect is the same as if the statements were written at each point where the subroutine is referred to in the program.

A subroutine is a group of statements that solves part of an overall problem. As such, it is not used by itself; rather, it is a part of a program. The use of subroutines simplifies the writing of programs in which performance of the same computations at different points is required.

A second reason for writing subroutines is to modularize distinct functions. For example, calculating the mean, sorting numbers, and calculating the median are distinct functions. Each one can be coded within the framework of a subroutine. Each subroutine can be referred to, wherever the function it carries out is needed, in the program.

A subroutine is, either directly or indirectly, connected to a *main program* by a *calling program*. The calling program can be either the main program itself or another subroutine that is either directly or indirectly connected to the main program.

The GOSUB and RETURN Statements

The group of statements within a subroutine should follow the main program. As shown in the following illustration, a GOSUB statement is used to transfer control to a subroutine. The GOSUB statement contains the statement number assigned to the first statement in the subroutine. In this illustration, it is a REM statement. When the computer executes a GOSUB statement, it branches to the statement assigned the statement number in the GOSUB statement. There can be as many GOSUB statements as needed. They can be located anywhere in the main program and/or in subroutines.

```
90 GOSUB 170
 .
 .
160 STOP
170 REM THE STATEMENTS COMPOSING THE SUBROUTINE FOLLOW
 .
 .
200 RETURN
210 STOP
220 END
```

After executing the statements in the subroutine, the computer does not stop. Rather, it returns to the calling program. This is caused by the RETURN statement. Upon encountering the RETURN statement in the subroutine, the computer returns to the statement *immediately following* the GOSUB statement which "called" the subroutine and continues execution from that point.

The general forms of the GOSUB and RETURN statements are shown in Illustration A-22.

Just as there can be as many GOSUB statements as needed, there can be as many subroutines as necessary. A RETURN statement can be located anywhere in a subroutine. The basic consideration in deciding where to place a RETURN statement in a subroutine is that it should be located at a *logical end* of the subroutine. If there is more than one logical end to a subroutine, multiple RETURN statements can be used.

An Illustration of GOSUB and RETURN

The following program illustrates the use of the GOSUB and RETURN statements. The program accepts a maximum of 10 numbers from a terminal. Then it finds the mean and the median of the numbers.

The mean is the sum of all the numbers divided by the number of numbers.

```
              sn   GOSUB   sn
                     •
                     •
                     •
          sn •   •   •
              •   •   •
              •   •   •
          sn   RETURN

where:
      each sn represents an unsigned 1 through 5 digit integer
         statement number.
```

Illustration A-22. General forms of the GOSUB
and RETURN statements.

The median is found by first sorting the numbers into ascending order. The median is the number in the middle of the sorted set of numbers. That is, if the number of numbers is N, and N is odd, then the median is the number in position (N/2) + .5. If N is even, then the median is the average of the numbers in the N/2 and the (N/2) + 1 positions.

Illustration A-23 is a flowchart of the program. A listing of the program is shown in Illustration A-24.

Assume that a control number of 10 (indicating that 10 numbers are to be processed) and the numbers from 1 through 10 are entered as input to this program. The interactions between the terminal user and the program will be printed out on the terminal as follows:

```
THIS PROGRAM FINDS THE MEAN AND MEDIAN FOR A MAXIMUM OF TEN NUMBERS
ENTER THE NUMBER OF NUMBERS
?10
NOW ENTER THE NUMBERS THEMSELVES ONE AT A TIME
?8
?7
?3
?2
?4
?5
?6
?10
?1
?9
THE MEAN IS = 5.5
THE MEDIAN IS = 5.5
```

A SUMMARY OF THE BASIC LANGUAGE

The types of BASIC statements introduced in this appendix are summarized in Table A-3. The BASIC predefined functions introduced in this appendix are listed in Table A-4. BASIC arithmetic and relational operators are listed in Table A-5.

QUESTIONS AND PROBLEMS

The reader should refer to the *Study Guide* for questions and additional illustrations concerning the material in this appendix. Complete programming problems requiring the use of many of the BASIC language constructs presented in this appendix are given in Appendix B.

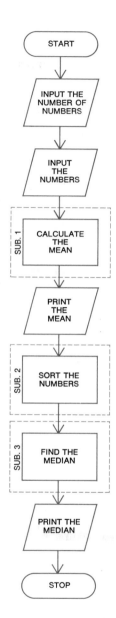

Illustration A-23. Flowchart of a program that calculates the mean
and finds the median.

```
 10 DIM A(10)
 20 PRINT "THIS PROGRAM FINDS THE MEAN AND MEDIAN FOR A MAXIMUM OF TEN NUMBERS"
 30 PRINT
 40 PRINT "ENTER THE NUMBER OF NUMBERS"
 50 INPUT N
 60 IF N  = 10 THEN 90
 70 PRINT "NUMBER MUST BE LESS THAN OR EQUAL TO 10"
 80 GO TO 40
 90 PRINT "NOW ENTER THE NUMBERS THEMSELVES ONE AT A TIME"
100 REM
110 FOR I = 1 TO N
120 INPUT A(I)
130 NEXT I
140 GOSUB 240
150 PRINT "THE MEAN IS =";M
160 GOSUB 330
170 GOSUB 460
180 PRINT "THE MEDIAN IS =";M
190 STOP
200 REM
210 REM    **** THE SUBROUTINES FOLLOW ****
220 REM
230 REM    **** THIS SUBROUTINE FINDS THE MEAN ****
240 T = 0
250 FOR I = 1 TO N
260 T = T+A(I)
270 NEXT I
280 M = T/N
290 RETURN
300 REM
310 REM    **** THIS SUBROUTINE SORTS THE NUMBERS TO ASCENDING ORDER ****
320 REM
330 F = 0
340 FOR I = 1 TO N-1
350 IF A(I)<A(I+1) THEN 400
360 S = A(I)
370 A(I) = A(I+1)
380 A(I+1) = S
390 F = 1
400 NEXT I
410 IF F = 1 THEN 330
420 RETURN
430 REM
440 REM    **** THIS SUBROUTINE FINDS THE MEDIAN ****
450 REM
460 J = INT(N/2)
470 K = N/2
480 IF J <> K THEN 510
490 M = (A(N/2)+A((N/2)+1))/2
500 RETURN
510 M = A(N/2)+.5
520 RETURN
530 END
```

Illustration A-24. A program that calculates the
mean and finds the median.

Table A-3. BASIC statement types

Statement	Explanation	Example	Page
DATA	Provides data	DATA 7,4,3,27	438
DEF	Defines functions	DEF FNA(X) = 3*X	476
DIM	Dimensions arrays	DIM A(50) DIM X(5,3)	461
END	Last statement of a program	END	449
FOR-TO • • • NEXT	Begins a loop Statements with the loop Ends a loop	FOR I = 1 TO 15 • • • NEXT I	455
GOSUB • • • RETURN	Branches to a subroutine Subroutine statements Returns control from a subroutine	GOSUB 50 • • • RETURN	478
GO TO	Unconditional branching	GO TO 120	450
IF-THEN	Conditional branching statement	IF A > 100 THEN 30	451
INPUT	Inputs data from terminal during execution	INPUT X,Y,Z	441
LET	Computes and assigns a value to a variable name	LET A = C+D LET X = Y = D	431
MAT	Simplifies matrix operations	*Note:* See Table A-2.	466
ON-GO TO	Conditional branching statement	ON Z GO TO 200, 300,400	453
PRINT	Prints program output at terminal	PRINT A,B,C PRINT "ACCT NO."	444
READ	Reads data from DATA list	READ A,B,C	438
REM	Allows comments	REM PROBLEM 1	448
RESTORE	Allows DATA list to be re-read	RESTORE	441
STOP	Stops execution of a program	STOP	450

Table A-4. BASIC predefined functions

Statement	Explanation	Page
COS(X)	Calculates the cosine of X.	472
EXP(X)	Calculates the natural exponent of X (e^X, where e = 2.7182818).	474
INT(X)	Calculates the largest integer which is less than or equal to X. X may be thought of as being located on a number scale that extends from negative infinity to positive infinity. It is used by itself to round or truncate numbers for printing or other purposes and is especially useful in conjunction with the RND function.	474
LOG(X)	Calculates the natural logarithm of X ($\log_e X$).	474
RND(X)	Randomly generates a number between 0 (inclusive) and 1 (exclusive).	475
SGN(X)	Determines the sign of X. The result is either -1, 0, or $+1$, depending upon whether X is negative, zero, or positive, respectively.	474
SIN(X)	Calculates the sine of X.	472
SQR(X)	Calculates the square root of X.	474
TAB(X)	Used in the PRINT statement to tabulate output. X specifies a print position.	475
TAN(X)	Calculates the tangent of X.	472

Table A-5. BASIC Arithmetic and Relational Operators

Operator	Explanation
↑ or **	Exponentiation
*	Multiplication
/	Division
+	Addition
−	Subtraction
>	Greater than
>= or ≥	Greater than or equal to
<	Less than
<= or ≤	Less than or equal to
=	Equal to
<> or ≠	Not equal to

BASIC Programming Problems

This appendix contains six programming problems. Their solutions involve the use of many of the BASIC language statements, functions, and operators introduced in Appendix A. They are designed to encourage the use of MAT statements, functions, and subroutines in problem solving.

Representative examples of correct solutions to the problems are also given in this appendix. Each solution shows one way of solving the problem. (But it is not the *only* way.) You should first write a BASIC-language solution, and then compare it with the representative solution provided. If you have questions, you can refer to the applicable BASIC language discussions in Appendix A.

PROGRAMMING PROBLEMS

Problem Set 1.   MAT Statements

1. Write a program, using MAT statements, to multiply matrices A and B. The data values for A and B should be supplied in a DATA statement. These values are shown below:

$$A = \begin{matrix} 3 & 0 & 2 \\ 6 & 3 & 1 \end{matrix}$$

$$B = \begin{matrix} 1 & 0 \\ 8 & 7 \\ 0 & 1 \end{matrix}$$

First, read the number of rows and the number of columns for matrix A and matrix B. Then read the data for each matrix in row order. Print the data for matrix A in row order. Do the same for matrix B. Then print the result of the multiplication of the two matrices.

2. One method of solving simultaneous linear equations of a small size is to multiply the inverse of the coefficient matrix for the equations by the matrix formed by the equivalent values on the other side of the equal signs in the equations. Write a program using this method to solve the following set of simultaneous linear equations:

$$2A + 3B + C = 18$$
$$A + B + C = 2$$
$$4A + 2C = 18$$

Print the coefficient matrix. Then print the solution values for A, B, and C.

Problem Set 2. Functions

1. Write a program using a user-defined function statement to approximate the square root of a number. Compare the approximate square root computed by the function with the result of the BASIC predefined function SQR(X). Continue this processing until an approximation within a $\pm.005$ range of the result provided by SQR(X) is calculated. Print both the user-defined function result and the result provided by SQR(X) as output.

Hints:
(a) A good algorithm to approximate square root is $X = (X^2 + A)/2X$, where $X = \sqrt{A}$.
(b) You may want to use the BASIC predefined function ABS(X) as well as SGR(X) to solve this problem.

Problem Set 3.   Subroutines

1. Write a program that calls a subroutine to approximate a square root. The subroutine should compare the result calculated in the subroutine with the result obtained by using the BASIC predefined function SQR(X) in the main program. The subroutine should return control to the main program when the result it calculates is within a $\pm.005$ range of the result provided by SQR(X). Then both results should be printed out.
Hints: See hints (a) and (b) for Problem 1 of Set 2 above.
2. Write a program to calculate the following production totals:
   (a) The total number of units produced for each of 5 products during a 4-week period.
   (b) The total number of units produced each week. Before printing any

results, cross-check the totals by determining whether or not the sum of the products equals the sum of the weeks. If they do not, print an error message and terminate processing. (Recheck your program logic if it ever provides this message; there's a bug because the situation should never occur.) The data values to be processed should be supplied in DATA statements. These values follow:

PRODUCT	1	2	3	4
132	100	300	600	543
176	763	1105	1732	1800
4173	9744	8813	9542	9000
5411	2154	2000	3701	4213
6124	1780	1700	1650	1600

The output is to be printed in the following format:

	WEEK				
PRODUCT	1	2	3	4	TOTAL
XXX	XXX	XXX	XXX	XXX	XXXX
XXX	XXX	XXXX	XXXX	XXXX	XXXX
XXXX	XXXX	XXXX	XXXX	XXXX	XXXXX
XXXX	XXXX	XXXX	XXXX	XXXX	XXXXX
XXXX	XXXX	XXXX	XXXX	XXXX	XXXXX
	XXXXX	XXXXX	XXXXX	XXXXX	XXXXX

3. Write a program to do the following functions (using data at top of next page):
(a) Read 50 two-digit numbers supplied in DATA statements into an array A.
(b) Find the mean.
(c) Find the standard deviation, using the following formula:

$$SD = \frac{\Sigma X^2 - \dfrac{(\Sigma X)^2}{N}}{N}$$

(d) Find the mode (the number that occurs most frequently in the array). [Use a subroutine.]
(e) Find the median (sort the numbers into ascending order; the median is the number in the $(N/2)+1$ position if N is odd, or the average of the two numbers at the $N/2$ and the $(N/2)+1$ positions in the sorted array if N is even). [Use a function.]
(f) Print out the mean, standard deviation, median, and mode.

The following data should be processed:

43, 21, 75, 33, 21, 49, 83, 87, 66, 77
31, 53, 75, 26, 73, 99, 21, 43, 87, 50
66, 21, 43, 39, 87, 43, 21, 38, 46, 87
11, 71, 39, 23, 36, 51, 26, 87, 49, 83
14, 31, 22, 31, 66, 33, 75, 93, 42, 18

REPRESENTATIVE SOLUTIONS

Problem Set 1. MAT Statements

1.
```
 10 READ R1,C1,R2,C2
 20 DATA 2,3,3,2
 30 MAT READ A(R1,C1),B(R2,C2)
 40 DATA 3,0,2,6,3,1,1,0,8,7,0,1
 50 MAT PRINT A
 60 MAT PRINT B
 70 MAT C = A*B
 80 MAT PRINT C
 90 STOP
100 END
```

2.
```
 10 DIM Y(3,3),I(3,3),M(3),Z(3)
 20 MAT READ Y,Z
 30 DATA 2,3,1,1,1,1,4,0,2
 40 DATA 18,2,18
 50 MAT I = INV(Y)
 60 MAT M = I*Z
 70 PRINT "THE COEFFICIENT MATRIX IS:"
 80 MAT PRINT Y
 90 PRINT "THE UNKNOWN QUANTITIES ARE:"
100 MAT PRINT M
110 STOP
120 END
```

Problem Set 2. Functions

1.
```
10 REM THIS PROGRAM APPROXIMATES THE SQUARE ROOT
15 REM OF A NUMBER
20 DEF FNA(X) = (X↑2+A)/(2*X)
30 READ A
40 DATA 9
50 LET X = 10
60 LET M = SQR(A)
70 FOR Z = 1 TO 50
80 LET Y = FNA(X)
90 IF ABS(X−Y)<.005 THEN 120
100 LET X = Y
110 NEXT Z
120 PRINT "NUMBER","APPROX. SQR ROOT","EXACT"
130 PRINT A,Y,TAB(50),M
140 STOP
150 END
```

Problem Set 3. Subroutines

1.
```
10 REM THIS PROGRAM APPROXIMATES THE SQUARE ROOT
15 REM OF A NUMBER
20 READ A
30 DATA 9
40 LET Y = SQR(A)
50 GOSUB 90
60 PRINT "EXACT","APPROXIMATED"
70 PRINT Y,K
80 STOP
90 REM THIS SUBROUTINE APPROXIMATES THE SQUARE ROOT
100 LET X = 10
110 REM START THE APPROXIMATION WITH X = 10
120 FOR Z = 1 TO 50
130 LET K = (X↑2+A)/(2*X)
140 IF ABS(X−K)<.005 THEN 170
150 LET X = K
160 NEXT Z
170 RETURN
180 END
```

2.
```
 10 REM THIS PROGRAM PRODUCES A REPORT ON PRODUCTION
 20 REM FOR FIVE TYPES OF TOYS
 30 FOR J = 1 TO 5
 40 FOR K = 1 TO 5
 50 READ A(J,K)
 60 DATA 132,100,300,600,543
 70 DATA 176,763,1105,1732,1800
 80 DATA 4173,9744,8813,9542,9000
 90 DATA 5411,2154,2000,3701,4213
100 DATA 6124,1780,1700,1650,1600
110 NEXT K
120 NEXT J
130 REM THE ARRAY P WILL HOLD THE PRODUCT TOTALS
140 REM THE ARRAY W WILL HOLD THE WEEKLY TOTALS
150 GOSUB 440
160 GOSUB 520
170 REM CHECK TO SEE IF THE SUM OF THE PRODUCT TOTALS
180 REM EQUALS THE SUM OF THE WEEKLY TOTALS
190 LET W1 = 0
200 LET P1 = 0
210 REM W1 CONTAINS THE SUM OF THE WEEKLY TOTALS
220 FOR Z = 2 TO 5
230 LET W1 = W1+W(Z)
240 NEXT Z
250 REM P1 CONTAINS THE SUM OF THE PRODUCT TOTALS
260 FOR Z = 1 TO 5
270 LET P1 = P1+P(Z)
280 NEXT Z
290 IF P1 = W1 THEN 340
300 REM AN ERROR HAS OCCURRED
310 PRINT "THE SUM OF THE PRODUCT TOTALS DOES NOT"
320 PRINT "EQUAL THE SUM OF THE WEEKLY TOTALS"
330 STOP
340 PRINT TAB(25),".........WEEK........."
350 PRINT "PRODUCT";TAB(10);"1";TAB(20);"2";
TAB(30);"3";TAB(40):"4";
360 PRINT TAB(50);"TOTAL"
370 FOR K = 1 TO 5
380 PRINT A(K,1);TAB(10);A(K,2);TAB(20);A(K,3);
385 PRINT TAB(30);A(K,4);
390 PRINT TAB(40);A(K,5);TAB(50);P(K)
```

```
400 NEXT K
410 PRINT TAB (10);W(2);TAB(20);W(3);TAB(30);W(4);
415 PRINT TAB(40); W(5);TAB(50);
420 PRINT W(1)
430 STOP
440 REM THIS SUBROUTINE CALCULATES WEEKLY TOTALS
450 FOR K = 2 TO 5
460 LET W(K) = 0
470 FOR J = 1 TO 5
480 LET W(K) = A(J,K)+W(K)
490 NEXT J
500 NEXT K
510 RETURN
520 REM THIS SUBROUTINE CALCULATES PRODUCT TOTALS
530 FOR K = 1 TO 5
540 LET P(K) = 0
550 FOR J = 2 TO 5
560 LET P(K) = A(K,J) + P(K)
570 NEXT J
580 NEXT K
590 RETURN
600 END
```

3.
```
10 REM THE FOLLOWING PROGRAM FINDS THE MEAN,
15 REM MEDIAN, MODE, AND
20 REM STANDARD DEVIATION FOR 50 NUMBERS
30 DIM A(50)
40 FOR I = 1 TO 50
50 READ A(I)
60 NEXT I
70 DATA 43,21,75,33,21,49,83,87,66,77
80 DATA 31,53,75,26,73,99,21,43,87,50
90 DATA 66,21,43,39,87,43,21,38,46,87
100 DATA 11,71,39,23,36,51,26,87,49,83
110 DATA 14,31,22,31,66,33,75,93,42,18
120 REM COMPUTE THE MEAN AND ACCUMULATE THE SUMS
130 REM FOR COMPUTING THE STANDARD DEVIATION
140 LET X = X2 = 0
150 FOR I = 1 TO 50
160 LET X = X+A(I)
```

```
170 LET X2 = X2+A(I)**2
180 NEXT I
190 LET M1 = X/50
200 LET S = SQR (X2-(X**2/50)/50)
210 GOSUB 260
220 REM THIS SECTION SHOWS ONE OF THE MANY WAYS OF
230 REM SORTING VALUES
240 FOR J = 1 TO 49
250 LET K = J+1
260 FOR L = K TO 50
270 IF A(J) < = A(L) THEN 310
280 LET B = A(J)
290 LET A(J) = A(L)
300 LET A(L) = B
310 NEXT L
320 NEXT J
330 REM END OF SORT
340 LET M3 = FNR(M3)
350 PRINT "THE MEAN IS";M1;
360 PRINT "AND THE STANDARD DEVIATION IS";S
370 PRINT "THE MEDIAN IS";M3
380 PRINT "THE MODE IS";M2;"AND OCCURS";F;"TIMES"
390 STOP
400 REM THIS SUBROUTINE FINDS THE MODE
410 DIM Y(100)
420 FOR I = 1 TO 100
430 LET Y(I) = 0
440 NEXT I
450 FOR I = 1 TO 50
460 LET Y(A(I)) = Y(A(I))+1
470 NEXT I
480 LET F = 0
490 FOR I = 1 TO 100
500 IF Y(I) <= F THEN 530
510 LET M2 = I
520 LET F = Y(I)
530 NEXT I
540 RETURN
550 DEF FNR(Z) = A(25)+A(26)/2
560 STOP
570 END
```

Glossary and Index

A

Access cycle, 133, 344–345. A computer cycle during which one access width of data is moved into or from the storage unit.

Access mechanism, 183–184, 186. The portion of a disk drive on which read/write heads are mounted.

Access speed, 133–134, 344. The time it takes for one access cycle.

Access time, 186, 193. The speed with which a magnetic disk drive operates; the speed at which a magnetic drum functions.

Access width, 133, 344. The number of bytes into or.from which data is moved at one time during the execution of a program statement.

Accounting machine, 6, 132, 205. A piece of punched-card equipment capable of taking data in the form of punched cards and converting it, through addition and subtraction if necessary for totals, into printed reports and documents.

Accounts payable application, 26, 36

Accounts receivable application, 26, 30–31
    Direct access system, 186–188
    Distributed system, 380
    Tape system, 168–173

Accounts receivable documents, 30–31
    Aged Trial Balance, 11–12, 31
    Invoice, 28–29, 37, 91–93, 168–173, 186–188
    Ledger card, 30–31
    Statement, 31, 206

Accounts receivable, flowchart for, 44, 169, 187

Accounts receivable objectives, 30

Accuracy, 8, 29, 48–50, 108–109
    Card computer system, 146
    Disk system, 184–185
    Printer, 148–149
    Tape system, 156–157, 160–162, 168

Acronym, 123–124, 316, 319, 320. A word formed from the first letter or letters of the words it represents; for example, FORTRAN is formed from FORmula TRANslator, and COBOL is formed from COmmon Business Oriented Language.

Address, 117–118. The identification assigned to a storage location.
    See also Disk address; Storage address

Aged Trial Balance, 11–12, 31. A management report containing the names of customers owing money and the period for which each amount has been owed.

Alphabetic character, 19–20, 23–24, 117. A letter; a combination of one zone punch and one digit punch in the Hollerith code; a combination of one or more zone punches and one or more digit punches in the 96-column punched-card code.

Alphameric BCD
    See 6-bit BCD

Alphameric characters, 117. Any combination of alphabetic, numeric, and special characters.

American National Standards Institute
    See ANSI

American Standard Code for Information Interchange (ASCII), 124, 130, 157. An 8-bit code promulgated as a standard by the American National Standards Institute.

Analog computer, 112–113. A computer that measures continuous electrical or physical magnitudes rather than operating on digits.

Analytical engine, 102. A machine developed by Charles Babbage to perform mathematical calculations on numbers in a storage unit within it.

Annotation symbol, 262–263. A flowcharting symbol used to clarify the intent of other flowcharting symbols.